ENTERPRISE

AI in the Cloud

ENTERPRISE AI IN THE CLOUD

A Practical Guide to Deploying End-to-End Machine Learning and ChatGPT™ Solutions

Rabi Jay

WILEY

I dedicate this book in memory of my dad, Jayachandar, who is my eternal hero and has always been my inspiration during good and tough times.

I also dedicate this to my mom, Leela Jayachandar, who is the epitome of kindness.

Finally, I dedicate this to you, dear reader, for picking up this book and bringing positive change and innovation into your companies.

ACKNOWLEDGMENTS

THERE HAVE BEEN so many people who helped make this book a reality. Without them you would not be reading this today.

I would like to thank my wife, Suji, my son Rohan, my friends Dominic, Sundi, Karthik, J Siva, Ramkumar, Aravind, Rajesh, Kumaran, Stanley Mammen, for his tips, CM for helping me promote the book, and many others for their ongoing support and for putting up with me through it all.

I had the opportunity to learn from many of the top minds in the enterprise AI space, as well as some brilliant authors, during the development of this book. I hope some of that has been translated into the knowledge I have imparted here in this book.

Special thanks to everyone who helped edit this book. Thanks to Kenyon Brown, acquisition editor, who helped me throughout the writing process and made it a pleasant experience.

Thanks to Kezia Endsley for her tireless editing assistance, for always being quick and positive, and for keeping me on target through it all. She was very supportive of my efforts, and her kind approach helped me when the going was tough. Her feedback and input on every chapter of the book helped make it ten times better than it would have otherwise been. I would also like to thank Evelyn Wellborn for catching many errors as part of the proofreading process that has certainly elevated the quality of this book.

Thanks to Navin Vijayakumar, managing editor, and Pete Gaughan, senior managing editor, for their insight into planning the content and marketing tips. Also many thanks to Magesh Elangovan and Vijayprabhakar Settu for their help with proofreading and images respectively.

A huge thanks to my friend and technical editor, Irwin Castelino, for reading the first drafts and making his technical edits. His critical evaluation and suggestions helped me make this a valuable product from the reader's perspective.

Without these folks and more, this book simply would not have happened.

Thank you,

—Rabi Jay

ACKNOWLEDGMENTS

ABOUT THE AUTHOR

RABI JAY IS a seasoned digital transformation specialist with more than 15 years steering a ship through the uncharted waters of industries such as retail, aerospace, and software technology. Armed with a plethora of certifications, including AWS Machine Learning, Azure, ITIL, and SAP, he's your go-to guy for anything cloud and AI.

In various roles, from digital platform lead to VP of architecture, he's led transformative projects in Martech, AI, and business process optimization. But Rabi Jay isn't just about executing projects; he's about shaping the very landscape of digital transformation. As a global alliance manager for major cloud corporations, he's had a bird's-eye view of tech upheavals across diverse industries.

The author of *SAP NetWeaver Portal Technology*, published by McGraw-Hill, Rabi Jay is also the voice behind the LinkedIn newsletter and podcast *Enterprise AI Transformation*, where he dishes out cutting-edge insights. In his role as VP of digital transformation, he has championed the convergence of human-centric design with state-of-the-art AI platforms and change management methodologies.

Why does all this matter? Because Rabi Jay is not just an expert; he's a visionary. Passionate about guiding companies through the evolving maze of AI and digital transformation, he's got his finger on the pulse of what's next. And he's bundled all this expertise into this latest endeavor: *Enterprise AI in the Cloud: A Practical Guide to Deploying End-to-End Machine Learning and ChatGPT Solutions*.

He is excited about what the future holds for us and looks forward to playing a lead role in shaping this AI-fueled smart world of the future. Connect with him to be part of this revolution.

- ➤ **LinkedIn:** www.linkedin.com/in/rabijay1
- ➤ **Website:** rabiml.com
- ➤ **Twitter:** https://twitter.com/rabijay1
- ➤ **YouTube:** www.youtube.com/@rabijay1
- ➤ **Podcast:** https://open.spotify.com/show/7vCeNI8c02pvIgeYDE8xwS

How to Contact the Author

Connecting and community are vital to the growth of artificial intelligence, which I am passionate about. If you are passionate about AI strategy, machine learning, generative AI, platform operations, and governance, I encourage you to connect with me on LinkedIn at www.linkedin.com/in/rabijay1. You can also continue the discussion about AI with me on Twitter at @rabijay1. I also encourage you to join my Enterprise AI Newsletter at www.linkedin.com/newsletters/7033665977435222016.

I appreciate your input and questions about this book. If you have feedback or questions, please contact me.

ABOUT THE TECHNICAL EDITOR

IRWIN CASTELINO IS an executive with 15+ years of experience in digital transformation and data analytics, leveraging AI and ML to optimize business processes for organizations. His expertise spans the implementation and integration of enterprise applications such as SAP and Oracle. He has delivered predictive solutions to optimize container shipments and improve equipment maintenance to enable better ROI and uptime of resources. The solutions he has delivered have consistently been a mix of internal and external data flows, with very large datasets being an integral part of the delivered solutions. His clients have ranged across the supply chain, beverage, food distribution, pharmaceuticals, personal products, banking, energy, chemicals, manufacturing, automotive, aerospace, and defense industries.

CONTENTS

Introduction

WELCOME TO *Enterprise AI in the Cloud: A Practical Guide to Deploying End-to-End Machine Learning and ChatGPT Solutions*. This book is the definitive guide to equip readers with the methodology and tools necessary to implement artificial intelligence (AI), machine learning (ML), and generative AI technologies. You have in your hands a powerful guide to potentially transform your company and your own career.

In this book, you learn how to

> Develop AI strategy, solve challenges, and drive change

> Identify and prioritize AI use cases, evaluate AI/ML platforms, and launch a pilot project

> Build a dream team, empower people, and manage projects effectively

> Set up an AI infrastructure using the major cloud platforms and scale your operations using MLOps

> Process and engineer data and deploy, operate, and monitor AI models in production

> Use govern models and implement AI ethically and responsibly

> Scale your AI effort by setting up an AI center of excellence (AI COE), an AI operating model, and an enterprise transformation plan

> Evolve your company using generative AI such as ChatGPT, plan for the future, and continuously innovate with AI

From real-world AI implementation, AI/ML use cases, and hands-on labs to nontechnical aspects such as team development and AI-first strategy, this book has it all.

In a nutshell, this book is a comprehensive guide that bridges the gap between theory and real-world AI deployments. It's a blend of strategy and tactics, challenges, and solutions that make it an indispensable resource for those interested in building and operating AI systems for their enterprise.

HOW THIS BOOK IS ORGANIZED

This book is not just a theoretical guide but a practical, hands-on manual to transform your business through AI in the cloud. My aim is to provide you with the tools and knowledge you need to harness the power of AI for your enterprise with a methodology that is comprehensive and deep.

> **Part I: Introduction:** In Part I, I explain how enterprises are undergoing transformation through the adoption of AI using cloud technologies. I cover industry use cases for AI in the cloud and its benefits, as well as the current state of AI transformation. I also discuss various case studies of successful AI implementations, including the U.S. government, Capital One, and Netflix.

> **Part II: Strategizing and Assessing for AI:** In this part, I discuss the nitty-gritty of AI, such as the challenges you may face during the AI journey, along with the ethical concerns, and the four phases that you can adopt to build your AI capabilities. I then discuss using a roadmap to develop an AI strategy, finding the best use cases for your project, and evaluating the AI/ML platforms and services from various cloud providers. It's like a step-by-step guide to your AI adventure.

> **Part III: Planning and Launching a Pilot Project:** This part covers all the challenges and tasks centered on planning and launching a pilot project, including identifying use cases for your project, evaluating appropriate platforms and services, and launching the actual project.

➤ **Part IV: Building and Governing Your Team:** People make magic happen! Part IV explores the organizational changes required to empower your workforce. I guide you through the steps to launching your pilot and assembling your dream team. It's all about nurturing the human side of things.

➤ **Part V: Setting Up Infrastructure and Managing Operations:** In this part, you roll up your sleeves and get technical. Part V is like your DIY guide to building your own AI/ML platform. Here, I discuss the technical requirements and the daily operations of the platform with a focus on automation and scale. This part is a hands-on toolkit for those who are hungry to get geeky.

➤ **Part VI: Processing Data and Modeling:** Data is the lifeblood of AI. Part VI is where you get your hands dirty with data and modeling. I teach you how to process data in the cloud, choose the right AI/ML algorithm based on your use case, and get your models trained, tuned, and evaluated. It is where the science meets the art.

➤ **Part VII: Deploying and Monitoring Models:** Yay! It is launching time. Part VII guides you through the process of deploying the model into production for consumption. I also discuss the nuances of monitoring, securing, and governing models so they are working smoothly, safely, and securely.

➤ **Part VIII: Scaling and Transforming AI:** You have built it, so now you can make it even bigger! In Part VIII, I present a roadmap to scale your AI transformation. I discuss how to take your game to the next level by introducing the AI maturity framework and establishing an AI COE. I also guide you through the process of building an AI operating model and transformation plan. This is where AI transitions from the project level to an enterprise-level powerhouse.

➤ **Part IX: Evolving and Maturing AI:** This is where you peek into a crystal ball. I delve into the exciting world of generative AI, discuss where the AI space is headed, and provide guidance on how to continue your AI journey.

WHO SHOULD READ THIS BOOK?

This book is primarily meant for those serious about implementing AI at the enterprise level. It is for those focused on understanding and implementing AI within the context of enabling and executing upon an enterprise-wide AI strategy. It is a substantive, content-rich resource that requires focused reading and note-taking, with takeaways that you can go back to your company and start implementing. Below are some examples of roles that will benefit.

Data Scientists and AI Teams

This includes data scientists, ML engineers, data engineers, AI architects, and AI/ML project managers interested in learning about the technical and operational aspects of implementing AI in the cloud.

Data scientists and AI teams often struggle with scaling AI/ML models. This book provides comprehensive guidance on processing large volumes of data, choosing the right AI/ML algorithms, and building and deploying models in the cloud.

IT Leaders and Teams

This includes IT managers, cloud architects, IT consultants, system administrators, and solution architects who are responsible for the deployment and operation of AI systems and workloads using the cloud.

This book can help you build a scalable and robust AI infrastructure using cloud components. After reading this book, you can confidently choose the right cloud provider, manage the entire machine learning lifecycle, and integrate with the backend systems.

Students and Academia

This book helps students and people in academia learn about AI and its practical application beyond just theory. It is of particular relevance to those studying business, data science, computer science, and AI-related subjects. If you are looking for a comprehensive and up-to-date treatment of AI implementation, this book is for you.

I encourage you to read the entire book and supplement your reading with additional resources when needed.

Consultants and Advisors

This book will be of great help to consultants and professionals who advise executives, business and technology professionals about implementing AI for their companies. They are looking for best practices and a structured methodology.

Business Strategists and Leaders

These are people who may not be technically savvy but are interested in improving their business processes and strategies using AI.

C-Level Executives

This is a great book for C-level executives who want to learn about the strategic impact, business case, and execution of AI transformation at scale across the enterprise.

One of their major struggles is applying AI practically and profitably into their business processes and strategies. This book provides a detailed list of AI use cases and guides them to develop an AI strategy and business case, thus helping them make intelligent and informed decisions.

WHY YOU SHOULD READ THIS BOOK

We are living in a world where technology is changing rapidly and is impacting both our personal and business lives. In particular, AI and cloud technologies are moving at the speed of light, and businesses are racing to keep up.

For companies, AI and cloud together form the secret weapon to staying competitive, driving cost efficiency, innovating, and delivering outstanding customer experiences.

However, implementing these technologies is not easy. These technologies are constantly evolving with countless tools, platforms, strategies, and the added complexity of ethical considerations. Therefore, you need a comprehensive, practical guide that helps you to adopt these AI and cloud technologies successfully.

You need a guide that is not just theoretical but is also practical so that you can easily understand, access, and implement these technologies successfully. This book will act as your roadmap and as a co-pilot to drive the engine, namely, the cloud and AI technologies.

UNIQUE FEATURES

This book is a toolbox with tools to achieve end-to-end AI transformation. This isn't your regular technical book, and here's why.

Comprehensive Coverage of All Aspects of Enterprise-wide AI Transformation

Most books on AI and ML focus on one or two aspects of AI transformation, such as strategy, architecture, or operations. Most of them are focused on building and deploying machine learning models. However, this book covers the entire end-to-end process, from defining an AI strategy to identifying use cases, initiating projects, scaling your operations, and deploying and operating AI models in production. It elevates pet, PoC ML projects to real-world production-grade deployments.

Case Study Approach

I take a case study approach, using real-world examples to illustrate the concepts I discuss. I include a number of detailed strategies, step-by-step processes, templates, checklists, best practice tips, and hands-on exercises.

Coverage of All Major Cloud Platforms

I cover all the major cloud platforms, meaning AWS, Azure, and Google Cloud Platform. Most books focus on only one cloud provider or a specific aspect of AI and ML. But I cover them all, thus making this book a comprehensive guide to AI transformation.

Discussion of Nontechnical Aspects of AI

In addition to the technical aspects of AI and ML, I cover the nontechnical aspects, such as AI growth potential, team development, and AI-first strategy. I believe that it is important to understand the business implications of AI, as well as the technical aspects.

Best Practices for MLOps and AI Governance

I discuss best practices for MLOps and AI governance. MLOps is the practice of bringing together machine learning and DevOps, and AI governance is the process of ensuring that AI systems are used responsibly and ethically.

Up-to-Date Content

I believe that my book is the most comprehensive and up-to-date guide to AI transformation available. It is a must-read for anyone who wants to use AI to transform their business.

I wish you the best on your enterprise AI transformation journey. You can reach me at www.linkedin.com/in/rabijay1. You can also keep in touch with my latest progress via rabiml.com.

Hands-on Approach

The chapters in this book have been aligned to the various steps in an enterprise AI implementation initiative, starting all the way from Strategy to Execution to Post go-live operations. And each Chapter contains a number of review questions to cement the understanding of the topics covered in the book. In addition to that, I have added a number of hands-on exercises, best practice tips, and downloadable templates with examples to guide you in your enterprise-wide AI implementation.

PART I

Introduction

In this section, we dive into how enterprises are undergoing transformation through the adoption of AI using cloud technologies. I cover industry use cases for AI in the cloud and its benefits, as well as the current state of AI transformation. I also discuss various case studies of successful AI implementations, including the U.S. Government, Capital One, and Netflix.

1

Enterprise Transformation with AI in the Cloud

The future of computing is at the edge, powered by AI and the cloud.

—*Satya Nadella*

Welcome to the exciting journey of enterprise transformation with AI in the cloud! This chapter is designed for anyone eager to understand the power and potential of AI in today's business landscape. You're probably here because you sense that AI isn't just another buzzword, but a game-changer. But how exactly can it transform your business? That's the question explored in this chapter.

UNDERSTANDING ENTERPRISE AI TRANSFORMATION

Enterprise transformation with AI in the cloud is about more than just adopting the latest technology; it's a holistic approach that redefines how your business operates, competes, and delivers value in the modern world. Through the integration of AI and machine learning with cloud computing, your business can revolutionize its processes, creating efficiencies, personalizing customer experiences, and fostering innovation like never before.

This chapter sets the stage for the entire book, explaining why some companies succeed with AI, and others fail, and how you can leverage AI to become a world-class, responsive, and innovative enterprise. It's not just about the technology; it's about reimagining what's possible in your business. Whether you're looking to automate processes, enhance customer experiences, or drive innovation, you'll find insights and practical exercises here to help you embark on this transformation.

If you're planning to follow the approach outlined in this book, the deliverables from the hands-on exercises and the downloadable templates in the accompanying website will become crucial building blocks as you progress through the later stages of implementing AI in your organization. Let's get started on this exciting journey!

> **NOTE** *ML stands for* machine learning *and includes generative AI.*

Why Some Companies Succeed at Implementing AI and ML While Others Fail

Implementing AI and ML solutions has not been easy. A 2022 PWC Research report shows that only about 20 to 25 percent of the companies have been able to implement AI across the enterprise in a widespread manner (see Figure 1.1). The research also shows that the majority of the companies have launched limited AI use cases or pilots but have not been able to scale AI enterprise-wide. Implementing AI comes with several challenges around data preparation, building models, scalability, and ethical concerns. Companies need a systematic methodology to leverage several foundational capabilities across business and technology to implement AI and ML technologies across the enterprise. In this book, you learn how to adopt a step-by-step, practical approach to achieving enterprise-wide AI transformation.

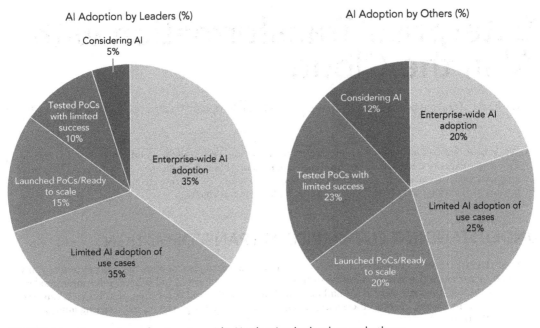

FIGURE 1.1: Comparison of enterprise-wide AI adoption by leaders and others

Source: Adapted from www.pwc.com/us/en/tech-effect/ai-analytics/ai-business-survey.html

Transform Your Company by Integrating AI, ML and Gen AI into Your Business Processes

Companies now have in their hands a fantastic opportunity to change the way they operate. It is now possible to integrate AI, ML, and Generative AI in many of your business processes to attain outstanding results. For example, you can detect quality issues in production, translate documents, and even analyze the sentiments of your clients in a Twitter feed.

> **NOTE** *Enterprise AI transformation involves the implementation of end-to-end AI, ML, and Gen AI systems to drive business outcomes.*

> **HANDS-ON CONCEPTUAL EXERCISE: UNDERSTANDING ENTERPRISE AI TRANSFORMATION**
>
> Define enterprise AI transformation and the importance of adopting AI and ML, including generative AI technologies for enterprises.

Adopt AI-First to Become World-Class

This chapter covers several crucial factors to consider for enterprise AI transformation, what it implies to be an AI-first company, and why cloud computing is a game-changer in implementing robust, scalable, and ethical AI. In the next chapter, I present three case studies and introduce the path these businesses took to become world-class AI-first organizations. The book's focus is to help you leverage these best practices across business, technology, process, and people domains so you, too, can excel as a professional and propel your company to become world-class, no matter what your role is. As you learn in subsequent chapters, everyone has a role to play.

Importance of an AI-First Strategy

The AI-first mindset introduces a new way to do business. When implementing AI transformation across the enterprise, it is essential to adopt this AI-first strategy and an AI-first approach. See Figure 1.2.

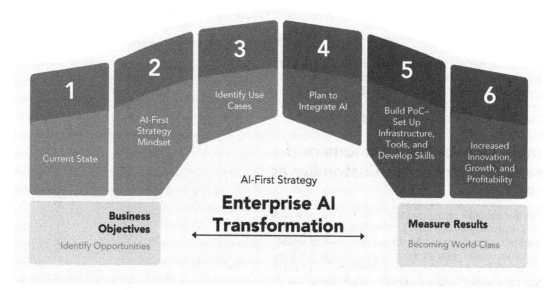

FIGURE 1.2: An AI-first strategy leads to an enterprise transformation.

An AI-first strategy is first a change in mindset that seeks to embrace AI to achieve business objectives. It involves identifying use cases to adopt AI, planning for proof of concepts (*PoCs*), and coming up with a plan to integrate AI into various aspects of an organization, such as customer service, product development, and decision-making. It includes building the necessary infrastructure, tools, and skills; building a commitment to learning; partnering with experts and vendors to be at the forefront of AI; and embracing AI for business opportunities.

Prioritize AI and Data Initiatives

Having this AI-first strategy helps organizations prioritize AI and data initiatives ahead of other projects, embrace AI technologies to stay at the forefront of innovation, and identify new business opportunities with the help of data.

It also promotes greater collaboration between IT and business and gives companies a competitive advantage to drive innovation, growth, and profitability.

If you do not adopt the AI-first strategy, you run the risk of losing your competitive advantage. You may not use the resources effectively, continue to live in silos between the business and IT, and, more importantly, lose out on opportunities to drive innovation, growth, and increased profits.

Adopting an AI-first strategy is the scope of this book. By following the steps outlined in this book, you learn to implement an AI-first strategy in your company.

HANDS-ON EXERCISE: AI-FIRST STRATEGY FROM CONCEPTS TO APPLICATIONS

Explain what AI-first strategy means and mention at least three benefits of an AI-first strategy.

Using Netflix or any other case study, explain how the adoption of cloud and AI technologies led to process transformation.

Explain the role of cloud computing in implementing robust, scalable, and ethical AI.

LEVERAGING ENTERPRISE AI OPPORTUNITIES

The rise of AI and the recent developments in generative AI have been incredible. Let's discuss the reasons behind such a surge.

One of the main reasons it has taken off is the cloud computing factor. The other two pillars of this phenomenal growth in AI are the growth of big data and the power of computer algorithms to build models (see Figure 1.3). However, the common denominator contributing to this growth is cloud computing.

Enable One-to-One, Personalized, Real-Time Service for Customers at Scale

We are currently seeing two trends in the modern world. One is that customers constantly demand immediacy and relevancy in service. Moreover, they want to be able to communicate with their service providers in real time. This, combined with the desire of companies to leverage data to constantly improve their products and services and renovate to build new business models, has been an exciting trend.

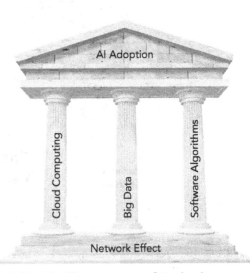

FIGURE 1.3: The triumvirate of AI: cloud computing, big data, and software algorithms
Source: Regormark/Adobe Stock

To provide this level of personalized service that scales in real time with such large amounts of data, it is no longer possible to rely on traditional rule-based programming. This is where the increased, scalable power of cloud computing powers with large amounts of data streaming from sensors to create new possibilities.

ML algorithms can crunch the same datasets in just a few minutes, something that took thousands of hours before. This capability makes it possible to provide one-to-one personalized service to your customers rather than segment-based marketing.

Companies are no longer tethered to their physical data centers. Thanks to Amazon, Google, and Microsoft's cloud services, companies can now set up a lot of computing and networking power in minutes.

The cloud provides machine learning frameworks (such as MXNet, TensorFlow, and PyTorch) and AI services (such as transcription, image recognition, and speech recognition) that anyone can leverage to do intense machine learning computations to predict, classify, and enable quick actions.

Recently, generative AI has caught the attention of many. It was made possible by the underlying computing power that the cloud technologies provide, along with the data infrastructure to process petabytes of data to train these models.

The Network Effect: How AI-Powered Services Create a Virtuous Cycle of Value Generation

Another reason for this explosive growth of AI is the network effect, which comes from the fact that you are quickly providing value to the customers, who, in turn, are generating more data and generating more insights. The generation of new insights allows you to provide better services, generating more data and creating a virtuous cycle (see Figure 1.4).

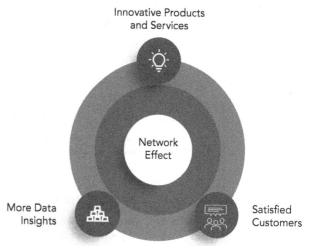

FIGURE 1.4: The network effect

Leverage the Benefits of Machine Learning for Business

Companies have realized that machine learning can help their businesses reduce costs, increase revenue, and drive innovation. It does create demand for large amounts of computing network and storage power that can be provided only through cloud computing. Moreover, 90 percent of their costs come from the inference stage of their machine learning lifecycle.

Cloud Computing Meets Unique ML Hardware Demands

Different machine learning use cases, such as forecasting and image recognition, place different demands on the underlying hardware, which make it challenging to meet the workload demands with just a standard type of underlying infrastructure.

> **NOTE** *The need for different architectures for different use cases has forced companies to rely increasingly on cloud computing, which can meet these unique demands on infrastructure.*

Cloud Computing: An Accelerator for the Growth of AI

Cloud computing is scalable, easily accessible from anywhere, and cost-effective. Cloud infrastructure can be easily integrated with backend systems, allowing models to be hosted in on-prem, cloud, or hybrid mode.

All these factors make cloud computing a significant disruptor and a powerful force that all companies must leverage.

HANDS-ON RESEARCH PRESENTATION EXERCISE: EXPLORING THE CLOUD AND ITS IMPACT ON AI

Objective: Exploring the cloud and its impact on AI.

Step 1: Divide the students into groups and have them research the following:

➤ Relationship between cloud computing and big data on AI

➤ Popular cloud-based machine learning frameworks such as PyTorch, MXNet, TensorFlow

➤ Cloud and AI services

➤ Network effects

➤ Cloud computing and its impact on various use cases

Step 2: Prepare a paper on their findings with real-world examples and future trends. Discuss how it could impact their careers.

Enterprise-wide AI Opportunities

Speaking of AI opportunities, you can categorize AI opportunities as enterprise-wide and industry-specific opportunities. Let's discuss enterprise AI opportunities first.

Automate Processes for Increased Efficiency and Cost Reduction

You can integrate AI into existing processes to increase operational efficiency, reduce costs, and free up human time through optimization and automation.

PROCESS AUTOMATION USE CASE EXAMPLES	
Customer complaint categorization	Some examples of automation include sorting out and categorizing incoming customer complaints using natural language processing to understand the content and classify it as technical issues, shipping issues, or billing issues.
Computer vision systems in quality control	Computer vision systems can be used to analyze videos and images to spot defects in products in a car assembly or computer manufacturing plant.

Optimize Business Processes with AI

AI can also be used to optimize business processes, which is much broader than automation. It includes analyzing current processes to identify improvement opportunities, such as predicting demand, forecasting resource needs, and improving team communication. See Figure 1.5.

AI Applications for Improving Customer Experience

AI can help improve customer experience through the following:

CUSTOMER SERVICE USE CASE EXAMPLES	
Personalization	Using predictive analytics to analyze past customer interactions, AI can better understand customers' needs and behavior and recommend personalized offers and product solutions to problems.

CUSTOMER SERVICE USE CASE EXAMPLES	
Improved customer service via chatbots	Better customer service through chatbots using NLP to answer queries 24/7, route to the right person, and schedule appointments.
Targeted marketing campaigns	Targeted marketing campaigns by analyzing customer data to generate relevant messages and thus increase customer loyalty.
Customer recognition with computer vision and speech recognition	Using computer vision and speech recognition to recognize customers on the website and contact centers and to tailor the experience accordingly.
Sentiment analysis	Conduct sentiment analysis of reviews, complaints, and surveys to recommend solutions to problems.
Speech recognition for call and chat analysis	Use speech recognition to analyze phone calls and chat to identify areas of improvement as well as to train agents.

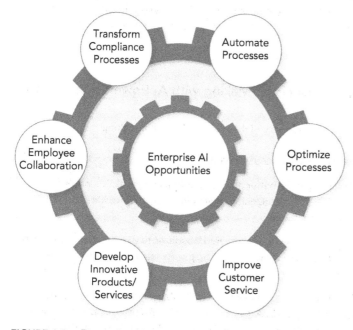

FIGURE 1.5: Enterprise AI opportunities

Identify New Customer Needs and Develop Innovative Products and Services

AI can identify new customer needs to develop new products and services by analyzing social media, purchase history, reviews, complaints, and browsing behavior.

Use Case Example

A financial company may find that customers are paying a third-party service higher fees to move money overseas, in which case the company can create a money transfer service that's cheaper and better quality.

INNOVATION USE CASES	
Cross-selling and bundling products	Companies can use AI algorithms such as recommendation systems to discover that customers who buy certain products also buy other related products. Hence, this gives the company the opportunity to cross-sell or bundle the products for sale.
Competitor analysis	Companies can analyze competitors' products, pricing, and customer reviews to identify customer pain points to meet a need in the marketplace.
Network analysis for business expansion	Companies can use network analysis of internal and external partners and individuals to identify influential clusters in gaining access to more business ideas and new customers and contact them via social media.

Enhance Employee Collaboration and Decision-Making with AI-Powered Tools and Workflows

Consider the following use cases that promote employee collaboration and decision-making:

EMPLOYEE COLLABORATION AND DECISION-MAKING USE CASES	
Enhanced collaboration via chatbots and predictive insights	Using chatbots, better decision-making, and predictive insights, employees can collaborate more effectively to drive better business outcomes.
AI-powered workflows for complex projects	Employees can use AI-powered workflows to collaborate more effectively on complex projects. This can help automate routine tasks so employees can work more strategically.
Analysis of project management and collaboration tools	By analyzing project management tools, collaboration tools, and productivity apps, AI can explain why breakdowns happen along with solutions. AI can recommend which employee is best suited for a job.
Videoconferencing for remote collaboration	Employees can use AI-powered videoconferencing to work remotely and collaborate virtually from anywhere. AI can recommend ideal times to have calls.

Transform Compliance Processes by Streamlining Documentation, Risk Assessment, and Audit

Here are some compliance-related use cases:

COMPLIANCE-RELATED USE CASES	
Automating compliance processes	AI can automate compliance processes such as documentation, audits, and risk assessment to reduce human errors and help employees use time more strategically.
Predictive analytics for proactive issue identification	You can use predictive analytics to identify issues proactively before they happen and deal with individuals and departments accordingly.
Chatbots and virtual assistants for compliance	You can also use chatbots and virtual assistants to answer compliance questions from employees.
Changing compliance requirements	AI can help keep pace with changing compliance requirements by staying up-to-date and proposing improvement areas in compliance programs.

CASE STUDY ANALYSIS: EVALUATING AI OPPORTUNITIES ACROSS INDUSTRIES

Objective: Evaluate the practical AI opportunities across industries.

Materials: HBR case collection, Stanford Graduate School of Business case collection, and so on.

Step 1: Assign a student or group of students to an industry.

Step 2: Choose a real-world company from an industry and assess the following:

➤ Specific AI opportunities, technologies, and applications used by the company and the purpose or problem they solve

➤ AI's impact on people, processes, products, services, and customer experiences

➤ Challenges faced by the company during the implementation

➤ Measurable outcomes or benefits from the AI implementation

Growing Industry Adoption of AI

Different industries are at different stages of adoption of AI depending upon the availability of the data, the complexity of the industry, and the compliance requirements. Table 1.1 shows the leading companies across pure play AI, leading pioneers, visionaries, industry leads, and enterprise majors, as well as leaders in generative AI.

TABLE 1.1: Companies Leading the Way in Adopting AI

AI GIANTS	PIONEERS	VISIONARIES	GENERATIVE AI	ENTERPRISE MAJORS	INDUSTRY
Microsoft	OpenAI	Adept	Rephrase.ai	Salesforce	Medtronic
Amazon	c3.ai	Synthesia	Midjourney	BMC Software	GE Healthcare
AWS	H2O.ai	Cohere	Infinity.ai	HPE	Capital One
Google	DataRobot	Abacus.ai	Podcast.ai	Dell	Carnegie Learning
IBM	Snowflake	Runway	Hugging Face	SAP	Century Tech
Baidu	Dataiku	Anthropic	Stability AI	ServiceNow	Duolingo
Oracle	RapidMiner		Jasper	Broadcom	Crowdstrike
Alibaba	Databricks			SAS	Palo Alto
NVIDIA	Alteryx			Informatica	Shelf Engine
	Cloudera				McDonald's

Fraud Detection, Risk Management, and Customer Service in the Finance and Insurance Industries

Here are some finance and insurance industry–related use cases:

FINANCE AND INSURANCE INDUSTRY–RELATED USE CASES	
Fraud detection, risk management, and customer service	AI is widely adopted in the finance industry for use cases such as fraud detection, risk management, and customer service.
Loan processing by smart robots	Human agents are now being replaced by smart robots that can process loans in just a few seconds.
Robo-advisors for investment decisions	Financial advisors are being replaced by robots that can process large amounts of data to make the right investment decisions for customers. These robots are smart enough to analyze data from social media, emails, and other personal data.
Claims processing and product recommendation in insurance	AI is used in the insurance industry to reduce claims processing time and recommend insurance plans and products based on customer data.

Revolutionizing Healthcare with AI: From Diagnoses to Robotic Surgery

The healthcare industry was an early adopter of AI.

➤ AI is used for medical image analysis, personalized medicine, and drug discovery.

➤ AI is also used for diagnosing diseases and treatment, medication management, and robotic surgeries.

> **NOTE** *Adoption of AI can enable better patient outcomes such as better health due to better diagnosis and treatment, reduced costs due to reduced patient readmissions, and increased operational efficiency.*
>
> | HEALTHCARE USE CASES | |
> | --- | --- |
> | Medical image analysis, personalized medicine, and drug discovery | AI is used for medical image analysis, personalized medicine, and drug discovery. |
> | Disease diagnosis, treatment, and robotic surgeries | AI is also used for diagnosing diseases and treatment, medication management, and robotic surgeries. |
> | Improving patient outcomes | Adoption of AI can enable better patient outcomes such as better health due to better diagnosis and treatment, reduced costs due to reduced patient readmissions, and increased operational efficiency. |

Transforming Manufacturing with Predictive Maintenance, Quality Control, and Collaborative Robots

In the manufacturing industry, AI is quite widely used.

MANUFACTURING USE CASES	
Predictive maintenance, quality control, and supply chain optimization	AI is used for predictive maintenance, quality control, and supply chain optimization.
Improving production operations	It is used to improve production operations ranging from workforce planning to product design to defect management and employee safety.
Collaborative robots (cobots)	This industry is also seeing the advent of *cobots*, which are robots that work collaboratively with humans.

Revolutionizing Retail: AI-Powered Customer Service, Personalized Marketing, and Inventory Control

In the retail industry, AI is used for customer service chatbots, personalized marketing, inventory control, and forecasting demand.

Use Case Example

Amazon is a classic example of how AI can be used to provide product recommendations based on the user's browsing behavior.

Autonomous Vehicles, Predictive Maintenance, and Traffic Management in the Transportation Industry

In the transportation industry, AI is used for autonomous vehicles, predictive maintenance, and traffic route management.

TRANSPORTATION USE CASES	
Self-driving cars	Active research is being carried out by Tesla, Volvo, Uber, and Volkswagen, and though it's used in controlled situations, pretty soon we will be seeing self-driving cars more commonly on the road.
Navigational and driver assistance systems	Some of the practical applications of AI are navigating obstacles and roads, driver assistance systems such as adaptive cruise control, automatic emergency braking, lane departure warning, radars, and cameras to enable safer driving.
Warehouse automation and shipment optimization	AI-powered robots are sorting out products in warehouses for delivery, moving cases within warehouses, delivering for pallet building, and so on. AI algorithms are used for shipment route determination and optimization for cost minimization.
Public transport management	Even in public transport, AI is used for traffic light management, transportation scheduling, and routing.

From Pizza Quality to Smart Farming in Food and Agriculture

AI is also used in food tech in the following ways:

FOOD AND AGRICULTURE USE CASES	
Taking orders and serving food	AI is used to take orders and serve food.
Quality control in food preparation	It is even used to ensure the quality of pizzas.
Crop management in agriculture	In agriculture, it is used to raise crops by analyzing salinity, heat, UV light, and water.
Smart machinery in farming	Smart tractors and plucking machines are also being used in the farming sector.

Predicting Prices, Automating Processes, and Enhancing Customer Experience in Real Estate

Here are some AI examples in real estate:

REAL ESTATE USE CASES	
Price prediction, buyer-seller matching, and market analysis	Predict prices and rental income, match buyers with sellers, analyze market conditions and trends, process real estate documents automatically, and use chatbots to answer customer queries

REAL ESTATE USE CASES	
Automated document processing and customer support	Smart home technology for increased security and energy efficiency in the home
Smart home technology	Voice assistants like Alexa, Google Assistant, and Siri; smart appliances like refrigerators, washing machines, thermostats, smart lighting, home security systems

AI-Powered Personalization in Entertainment: Netflix, Amazon, and the Gaming Industry

Here are some use cases in the entertainment industry:

ENTERTAINMENT AND GAMING INDUSTRY	
Recommendation systems in streaming platforms	Netflix and Amazon use AI to recommend movies and songs to users based on their preferences and viewing behavior.
Storyboarding and music composition in movies	In the movie industry, AI is used to build a script for storyboarding and is even used to compose music.
Storyline advancement in gaming	AI is used in the gaming industry to advance the storyline in a specific direction to keep the player engaged.

Improving Efficiency, Reducing Costs, and Advancing Sustainability in the Energy Industry

Examples in the energy industry follow. The adoption of AI is contributing to lower costs and improved environmental sustainability.

ENERGY USE CASES	
Predictive maintenance and energy management	Predictive maintenance of equipment such as transmission lines and power plants, managing the supply and consumption of energy, and integrating with renewable energy to reduce costs.
Energy efficiency in buildings	Improve energy efficiency in consumption in office spaces and homes by adjusting cooling and heating systems and lighting
Fraud prevention	Prevent fraud such as billing errors and meter tampering

WORKBOOK TEMPLATE - *ENTERPRISE AI TRANSFORMATION CHECKLIST*

Download the "Enterprise AI transformation checklist" template from the download section of the book (www.wiley.com/go/EnterpriseAIintheCloud). Please use this as an initial starting point to assess where your company is on its journey to implement AI across the enterprise. In areas where you answered "no," it indicates that more work is needed. Continue working on each section as you progress through this book. Use this as a healthy reminder for your team to track their progress throughout the AI transformation journey and celebrate minor and significant milestones.

SUMMARY

The key takeaways from this chapter underscore the necessity for organizations to take AI seriously to gain a competitive edge. This means elevating machine learning projects from mere PoC pet projects into large-scale, enterprise-wide transformative efforts. To achieve this, you need to adopt a more systematic AI-first strategy and methodology, the primary focus of this book.

This chapter also delved into the transformative power of cloud computing, enabling many use cases previously unattainable and providing a pathway to thrilling consumer experiences. You reviewed some of the use cases that AI and ML enabled and realized their broad adoption and impact across various industries.

The next chapter showcases three case studies of companies that successfully implemented AI on an enterprise-wide level.

REVIEW QUESTIONS

These review questions are included at the end of each chapter to help you test your understanding of the information. You'll find the answers in the following section.

1. AI and ML can be incorporated into business processes to
   A. Detect quality issues in production
   B. Analyze the user sentiment in a Twitter feed
   C. Translate documents
   D. All the above

2. An AI-first strategy
   A. Prioritizes customer service over AI and ML technologies
   B. Focuses on product management over AI technology
   C. Focuses on embracing AI to achieve business objectives
   D. Focuses on building a solid technology platform for AI

3. Prioritizing data and AI initiatives helps
   A. Companies to focus on customer service
   B. Companies to identify new business opportunities
   C. Companies to enable greater collaboration between IT and business
   D. Companies to build stronger business cases

4. Neglecting an AI-first strategy will lead to
   A. Losing the competitive edge
   B. Not using resources effectively
   C. Living in silos between AI and the business
   D. Innovation, growth, and increased profits

5. What is the main advantage that digital natives have when it comes to adopting AI?
   A. They have a risk-taking culture and view failure as a steppingstone for success.
   B. They have a lot more money to invest in AI.
   C. They have a better brand image than traditional companies.

6. What are the factors to consider for an organization's AI journey?
   A. Its AI readiness
   B. Its risk-taking culture
   C. Data and resources availability
   D. All the above

7. Which of the following is NOT one of the three pillars of AI growth?
   A. Cloud computing
   B. Big data
   C. Computer algorithms
   D. Robotics

8. _____is NOT one of the benefits of cloud computing for businesses using machine learning.
   A. Scalability
   B. Accessibility
   C. Increased costs
   D. Cost effectiveness

9. Explain the network effect in the context of AI-powered services.
   A. Companies can now set up computing power in minutes.
   B. Machine learning helps businesses reduce costs, increase revenue, or drive innovation.
   C. Companies can provide better services to customers, generating more data and insights in a virtuous cycle.
   D. Different machine learning use cases place different demands on the underlying hardware.

10. Choose an example of how AI can improve customer experience.
    A. By analyzing project management tools to recommend solutions
    B. By identifying clusters that are influential to gain access to more business ideas
    C. By using chatbots to answer queries 24/7
    D. By automating compliance processes such as documentation and risk assessment

11. Choose an example of how AI can be used to identify new customer needs.
    A. By using computer vision to recognize customers on websites and contact centers
    B. By analyzing social media, purchase history, and reviews
    C. By using network analysis to gain access to more business ideas
    D. By automating compliance processes such as audits and risk assessment

12. Cobots are used in the manufacturing industry for which purpose?
    A. Workforce planning
    B. Product design
    C. Collaborating with humans
    D. Defect management

13. AI is used in the entertainment industry for which purposes?
    A. Building a script for storyboarding
    B. Composing music
    C. Advancing the storyline in a certain direction
    D. All the above

ANSWER KEY

1.	D	**6.**	D	**11.**	B
2.	C	**7.**	D	**12.**	C
3.	B	**8.**	C	**13.**	D
4.	A	**9.**	C		
5.	A	**10.**	C		

2

Case Studies of Enterprise AI in the Cloud

Every company is a software company. You have to start thinking and operating like a digital company. It's no longer just about procuring one solution and deploying one. It's not about one simple software solution. It's really you yourself thinking of your own future as a digital company.

—Satya Nadella, CEO, Microsoft

Now that you have learned about some of the possibilities of AI in the previous chapter, this chapter dives deeper into the fascinating world of enterprise transformation with AI in the cloud through three real-world case studies. If you are interested in knowing how AI transforms industries, this chapter is tailor-made for you.

You not only learn how giants like the U.S. government, Capital One, and Netflix have leveraged AI and cloud technologies, but their stories also serve as practical examples that inform the methodology that I present in this book.

The key takeaway is how these organizations built resilient systems by embracing cloud-native principles and AI technologies to become AI-first companies, which is essential for any enterprise aspiring to thrive in the digital age.

CASE STUDY 1: THE U.S. GOVERNMENT AND THE POWER OF HUMANS AND MACHINES WORKING TOGETHER TO SOLVE PROBLEMS AT SCALE

This is an excellent example of an augmented AI case study. The U.S. government spends nearly $2.5 trillion trying to serve millions of customers with social and safety net programs such as Social Security, Medicaid, Medicare, and the Supplemental Nutritional Assistance Program (SNAP).

Figure 2.1 shows a high-level view of the challenges, benefits, and solutions for this case study.

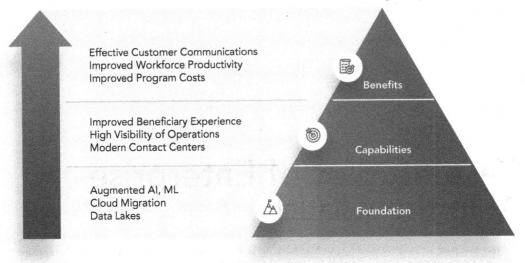

FIGURE 2.1: Challenges, benefits, and solutions adopted by the U.S. government

The following table lists the challenges faced by the U.S. government:

CHALLENGES	DETAILS
Enrollment process complexity	Given the large volume of applications, one can only imagine how complex this process can be and how long it can take. Millions of customers depend on this for their healthcare, unemployment needs, and to stay out of poverty. The challenge with the enrollment process includes complex application processes, huge backlogs in processing the claims, and lengthy adjudication, evaluation, and eligibility processes.
Long customer response time	Customers had to wait several weeks to get a response even though a large workforce was trying to serve them.
Inadequacies of legacy systems	Legacy systems provided poor customer experience and inability to scale during times of surge in demand. They also lacked self-service capabilities and did not have a mobile application submission option. Text communications for case status and the ability to schedule appointments online needed to be included.
Multisource application processing	The applications came from multiple sources, such as the web, mail-in, and contact centers, and in multiple formats, such as PDFs and images. Reviewing these applications in such large quantities took a lot of time and effort, was error-prone, needed domain expertise, and was not an efficient process. Setting up human review systems to process this many applications not only was costly but also took a long time. It involved custom software for review tasks, complex workflows, and many reviewers.

CHALLENGES	DETAILS
Security concerns	Another challenge was the need to maintain data security as millions of documents amounting to terabytes of data needed to be stored and sensitive data needed to be protected and encrypted.
High volume of customer service calls	Another major challenge was the number of customer service calls, amounting to more than 50 million calls just for the Social Security Administration team. These calls were related to pending application status disputes and other benefits-related questions.
Lack of management insight	Moreover, management lacked insight into the program operations, enrollment issues, backlogs, budgeting, waste, fraud, and abuse.

Revolutionizing Operations Management with AI/ML

The solution to these problems involved simplifying the application process by automating some of the workflows behind the approvals using AI/ML technology, enabling self-service capabilities, streamlining the interview and appeal process, and adding insights around the operations to help management solve issues and propose improvement opportunities.

Enabling Solutions for Improved Operations

To resolve these challenges, the solution capabilities outlined in this table were enabled:

SOLUTION CAPABILITY	BENEFITS
Chatbots	Improved customer experience
AI and A2I technologies	Automated some of the workflow steps such as adjudication and approvals
Data-driven insights	Provided leadership with the required information to take remedial actions
Contact center	Served customers efficiently with their queries
Cloud migration	Leveraged some of the operational efficiencies that come with the cloud such as scalability, efficiency, and performance

CASE STUDY 2: CAPITAL ONE AND HOW IT BECAME A LEADING TECHNOLOGY ORGANIZATION IN A HIGHLY REGULATED ENVIRONMENT

Capital One wanted to be a technology organization, irrespective of the fact that they were in the finance industry. They achieved this through a specific growth and innovation template that many organizations must adopt to become a leading technology organization, regardless of which industry they belong to.

Capital One had to solve a number of challenges, some of which are listed here:

CHALLENGES	DETAILS
Data management	To begin with, they had the data challenge. They had data spread across multiple parts of the organization, such as customer relationship management (CRM), enterprise resource planning (ERP), and streaming data from social media. They had to bring all that into one place, which they did with Amazon S3.
Infrastructure challenges	They wanted to solve their infrastructure problems. They wanted to become an agile company and reduce their development time from months to days or even minutes.
Cloud migration challenge	They wanted to migrate their 11 data centers to the AWS cloud and leverage the cloud-native development capabilities to develop a resilient system.

Building Amazing Experiences Due to Data Consolidation

To solve their data challenge, they built a data lake. It allowed them to use data as fuel for their present and future AI models, and they were able to train their models continuously. This helped them to understand human behavior across multiple channels and time zones in real time and helped them to design amazing human experiences. See Figure 2.2.

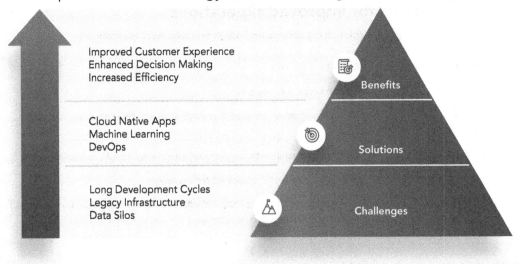

FIGURE 2.2:   Challenges, benefits, and solutions adopted by Capital One

Becoming Agile and Scalable by Moving Data Centers Into the Cloud

How did they do it?

➤ They moved their eight data centers to the cloud.

➤ They built an 11,000-member technology team over eight years.

➤ They instituted training plans and programs for the AWS cloud.

In the process, they were able to reap the following benefits:

➤ They reduced the environment build time from three months to three minutes.

➤ They had a high-performing agile and scalable infrastructure, which helped them go to market with their products much earlier, from months to days.

➤ They were even able to release applications that took months and weeks to more than once a day.

Moving to the cloud was one of the secrets that many organizations took on this journey to become an AI-first company.

Building a Resilient System by Embracing Cloud-Native Principles

So far, this section has discussed Capital One's cloud adoption journey, where they overcame data challenges and migrated their apps to the cloud across the data centers. However, this transition was a lot of work. Throughout this process, though, the cloud offered them new capabilities and hence new possibilities.

Adopting cloud-native principles enabled Capital One to build a resilient system by adopting microservices architecture, CI/CD pipelines for automated workflow deployments, blue-green switching, A/B testing, and failover techniques that resulted in minimal impact to the end-user experience. We will cover these topics in this book.

Impact of Cloud-First Thinking on DevOps, Agile Development, and Machine Learning

However, what is even more significant is the mindset shift that the cloud adoption created, making DevOps and the Agile development methodology possible. The ability to release features quickly allowed product owners to become more customer-centric, creating more engaging user experiences not only from a functional perspective but also even a technical perspective through good performance, high availability, and resiliency. As a result, the teams also became more product-centric, breaking down organizational silos due to the adoption of DevOps.

> **NOTE** *Cloud-first thinking lays the foundation for a machine learning platform by adopting cloud principles when developing applications, deploying them, and serving your customers.*

Becoming an AI-First Company: From Cloud Adoption to Thrilling Customer Experiences

By becoming a cloud-first company, it became easier for Capital One to become an AI-first company. With a data lake and an agile and scalable infrastructure, it became possible to process large amounts of data in real-time from multiple sources and then feed them into AI/ML models, which in turn could process them using ample computing resources and generate insights in real time. This ability to generate insights in real time opened several opportunities for Capital One.

Moreover, by combining AWS's high-level AI services and machine learning services like natural language processing (NLP), Capital One could provide thrilling customer experiences through their Eno chatbot and detect and prevent fraud in real time. They also leveraged machine learning for speech recognition technology in their call centers to automate training and validation systems. Other applications included credit risk modeling, investment portfolio analysis, risk management, and image recognition to open bank accounts; they even used ML to ensure image recognition to open bank accounts. As shown in Figure 2.3, Capital One transformed itself into a pioneering AI-first company and unleashed the power of its 50,000 associates.

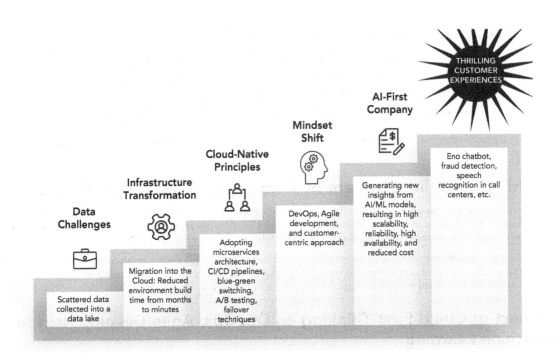

FIGURE 2.3: Capital One's transformation journey to AI-first status

CASE STUDY 3: NETFLIX AND THE PATH COMPANIES TAKE TO BECOME WORLD-CLASS

This section discusses the path organizations take (Netflix, particularly) to become world-class companies (see Figure 2.4). It can be the path your company may take to become world-class.

Knowing this will help you understand the foundational capabilities you need to adopt and improve as part of the enterprise AI transformation effort. This section explains what Netflix did to become world-class and the foundational capabilities they leveraged, which is the core subject of this book—to help companies leverage their foundational capabilities to become world-class.

> **NOTE** *You will find that most companies follow this path—adopting technology results in process improvement. Process improvement leads to organizational change, which results in product transformation, which leads to innovation in developing new products and services, thus generating new business outcomes.*

Netflix's story can easily be applied to any digital-native company such as Uber, Amazon, and Airbnb. They have all followed this path to become world-class, AI-first companies.

Cloud and AI Technology: A Game-Changer for Netflix's Business Model and Success

By adopting cloud and AI technologies, Netflix has been able to drive process transformation. Here are some of the benefits:

Technology Adoption
Cloud Computing
Big Data
Machine Learning

Organizational Excellence
Customer-Centric
Collaboration
Product-Centric

Process Improvement
DevOps
Agile
Product Management

Product Transformation
Product Innovation
Intelligent Products
New Business Models

FIGURE 2.4: The path to becoming world-class

ADOPTION OF CLOUD AND AI TECHNOLOGIES	IMPACTS AND OUTCOMES
Transition to streaming service	By adopting the cloud, Netflix could switch from DVDs to a streaming service. It helped Netflix not only disrupt its competitors but also become a global company almost overnight, as it could reach people worldwide.
Implementation of machine learning algorithms	Cloud technology also allowed Netflix to use complex, sophisticated machine learning algorithms to provide personalized recommendations to customers and improve their experiences.
Adoption of a content delivery network	Similarly, by adopting a content delivery network, it became possible for Netflix to deliver high-quality video services to its customers and enhance their experiences.
Utilization of data analytics	Netflix used customer behavior and profile data from a data analytics platform to generate new insights and drive their content production, acquisition, and marketing to focus on their customer's needs.

Cloud Infrastructure and AI Adoption Drives Process Transformation

From a pure infrastructure perspective, by adopting cloud computing, Netflix has been able to reduce its infrastructure costs, store and stream data continuously, and scale its computing resources up and down based on the fluctuating demand on its systems.

Netflix was able to leverage cloud and AI technology to drive process change. Netflix transformed its business and technology operations by reducing its infrastructure costs, increasing the speed at which it delivers content to its customers, and enhancing the customer experience through personalized recommendations and marketing insights through data.

Process Transformation Drives Organizational Change

The next question is how this process transformation caused organizational transformation at Netflix. It is essential to note that technology adoption led to process transformation, making specific organizational transformation opportunities possible; this table shows the organizational transformation stages at Netflix:

ORGANIZATIONAL TRANSFORMATION STAGES	DESCRIPTION
Technology adoption	By adopting technology, Netflix reduced costs while improving its operational efficiency and customer experience.
Driving process change	It also allowed them to drive process change by changing their operating model around products and services.
	This ability to quickly develop new software helped Netflix focus more on products and reorganize their business model around the products and services.
Breaking down of functional silos and organizational transformation	It has also helped them break down their functional silos. In the process, they became an agile, product-centric, and customer-focused organization.
	Thus, the process transformation led them to drive organizational change as a product-centric, customer-centric, agile organization.
Product innovation driven by organizational transformation	Netflix leveraged its new organizational transformation to drive product innovation.
	By being customer-centric, Netflix has been able to come up with ideas such as new products and services, for instance, streaming original content. Their customer centricity has also helped them prioritize their recommendation algorithms as part of their streaming service.
Continuous innovation and customer centricity	Being agile helped Netflix identify the requirement for new customer experiences on a regular basis. They created local material to fulfill regional demands, which has helped them increase globally.
	Their customer centricity is also helping them determine the need for new programs, such as helping customers pick their journey in their hit program called *Bandersnatch*.

> **NOTE** *The cloud made becoming agile easy. By adopting the cloud, Netflix could develop software iteratively and quickly. In other words, it helped them adopt an agile development approach rather than a waterfall methodology. Agile, in turn, helped them become more product-centric and customer-focused.*

By adopting cloud/AI innovation, you can see that companies find it simpler to transform their processes, causing organizational transformation. Consequently, they become more product-centric and customer-centric.

In turn, this creates the right conditions for innovation, breaking down silos and encouraging experimentation that eventually results in new products, services, and business models like you just saw in the Netflix example.

AI helps you respond quickly to business events in an agile manner. Agility is one of the few competitive advantages companies have today.

Today's customers want to be treated with unique offers based on their specific needs, and in real time. That means the business must crunch mass amounts of data to generate new insights and act in minutes rather than what used to be days and weeks. Machine learning has now made this possible. You too can achieve these feats by adopting the best practices and the comprehensive methodology in this book.

HANDS-ON EXERCISE 1: ANALYZE THE NETFLIX AI TRANSFORMATION

Explain how Netflix enabled process transformation, organizational change, and product innovation. Research other companies that have achieved similar transformation.

WORKBOOK TEMPLATE - AI CASE STUDY

Download the "AI Case Study" template from the download section of the book (www.wiley.com/go/ EnterpriseAIintheCloud). Capture the case studies from other organizations that you plan to explore and drive your AI implementation with the benefit of a comprehensive view of the AI implementation process, from inception to results. Adopt their best practices and avoid their mistakes.

SUMMARY

This chapter delved into case studies of how three organizations transformed into world-class organizations by adopting technology that spurred process improvement and organizational change. This transformative journey eventually helped them become customer-centric, leading to product innovation and even pioneering new business models.

The next chapter unravels some of the challenges of implementing a machine learning deployment that might prevent organizations from deploying one into production.

REVIEW QUESTIONS

These review questions are included at the end of each chapter to help you test your understanding of the information. You'll find the answers in the following section.

1. The U.S. government solved its challenges processing multisource applications by
   A. Setting up human review systems
   B. Using custom software to manage review tasks
   C. Automating some of the workflows using AI/ML technology
   D. All the above
2. What is the common theme among companies that have become world-class?
   A. They focus on reducing business risks.
   B. They prioritize enhancing their performance in terms of the environment, society, and governance.

     C.   They leverage technology to achieve business outcomes.

     D.   They aim to decrease their revenue.

3.   Netflix's process transformation led to which of the following?

     A.   Organizational change

     B.   Decrease in customer experience

     C.   Increase in infrastructure costs

     D.   Decrease in operational costs

4.   ____ helped Netflix become agile and adopt a product-centric approach.

     A.   Blockchain

     B.   Augmented reality

     C.   Cloud computing

     D.   Machine learning

5.   The path to becoming world-class is

     A.   Technology ⇨ Process ⇨ Organization ⇨ Product transformation

     B.   Organization ⇨ Technology ⇨ Process ⇨ Product transformation

     C.   Process ⇨ Organization ⇨ Product transformation ⇨ Technology

     D.   Product transformation ⇨ Organization ⇨ Process ⇨ Technology

ANSWER KEY

1.	D	**3.**	A	**5.**	A
2.	C	**4.**	C		

PART II
Strategizing and Assessing for AI

In this part, we discuss the nitty-gritty of AI, such as the challenges you may face during the AI journey along with the ethical concerns, and the four phases that you can adopt to build your AI capabilities. I then discuss the roadmap to develop AI strategy, finding the best use cases for your project, and evaluating the AI/ML platforms and services from various cloud providers. It's like a step-by-step guide to your AI adventure.

3

Addressing the Challenges with Enterprise AI

Our greatest weakness lies in giving up. The most certain way to succeed is always to try just one more time.

—*Thomas A. Edison*

This chapter might just be your ally on your path to AI transformation. As someone keen on implementing AI, whether you are a business strategist, technology leader, data scientist, or curious innovator, you must be aware that deploying AI, ML, and generative AI solutions is exciting, but it can also be like navigating a minefield. That's because AI isn't just about algorithms and models; it's also intrinsically connected to data, infrastructure, change management, regulations, and strategic decision-making. You will soon realize that an AI transformation is markedly different from a digital transformation.

This chapter is designed to help you understand the technical challenges, ethical dilemmas, and strategic hurdles. Recognizing these challenges is the first step toward preparing your organization for them. In later chapters, I guide you with a practical, systematic methodology to address these challenges with clearly defined steps, best practices, case studies, hands-on exercises, and templates. Each chapter in this book maps to the tasks in the phases shown in Figure 3.1.

Note that these challenges by no means represent a complete list. Although the challenges are many, they are not insurmountable. You can convert these challenges into opportunities for innovation and growth based on the insights and best practices I share throughout this book.

CHALLENGES FACED BY COMPANIES IMPLEMENTING ENTERPRISE-WIDE AI

Let's take a quick peek into various kinds of challenges. This list is not exhaustive but should give you an idea.

Enterprise AI Journey Map

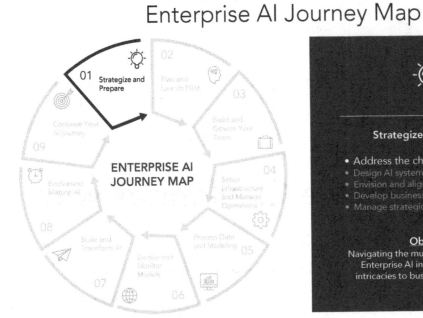
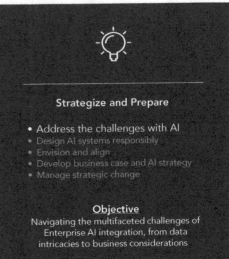

FIGURE 3.1: STRATEGIZE AND PREPARE: Address the challenges with AI

Business-Related Challenges

Here is a sample of business-related challenges:

BUSINESS-RELATED CHALLENGES	
Cost of running ML workloads	The cost of running intensive machine learning workloads may come in the way of deploying models into production.
Keeping up with change	AI and machine learning are constantly evolving, and it is challenging for AI/ML practitioners and cloud engineers to keep up with those changes.
Selecting the right use cases	Choosing the right use cases can be challenging, as you need to understand the business problem, ensure data availability for the use cases, choose the right ML model, integrate with backend systems, factor in the ethical and legal issues, and measure ROI for the use cases.
Alignment with business strategy	Alignment between AI/ML and business strategies can be challenging if not handled properly with business prioritization of requirements, understanding AI impact, and stakeholder communication.
Skills and talent shortages	Challenges include having the right skills and talent due to the shortage of qualified professionals, needing cross-functional expertise, and trying to keep up with new developments.

Data- and Model-Related Challenges

Here is a sample of data- and model-related challenges:

DATA- AND MODEL-RELATED CHALLENGES	
Collecting high-quality data	Collecting high-quality data can be challenging and time-consuming. Models require data in the right format, so data cleaning and labeling data for model training is required, which can be time-consuming and costly.
Complexity of machine learning	Machine learning can be complex, with statistics, mathematical concepts, and machine learning programming skills that make navigating challenging.
Measuring model performance	Measuring the performance of models, coming up with the proper performance metrics, and validating them during changing business conditions and data can be challenging.
Monitoring model performance	Monitoring the model performance can be challenging because of changing business conditions, the ability to measure model drift, and the need to ensure the model performs well over time and aligns with the business needs.
Choosing the right model	Choosing the right model is a challenge as simpler models do not capture all the underlying data patterns; complex models can capture complex patterns, but they can remain black boxes and are difficult to interpret.

NOTE *Poor data quality can impact model performance and sometimes prevent models from being deployed in production.*

Platform-Related Challenges

Here is a sample of platform-related challenges:

PLATFORM-RELATED CHALLENGES	
Integrating with backend systems	Integrating with backend systems and infrastructure can be challenging due to technical, data, security, scalability, human-in-the-loop integration, and regulatory challenges.
Managing the entire machine learning lifecycle	Managing the entire machine learning lifecycle is challenging due to the complexity around data preparation, feature engineering, model selection, and tuning, evaluation, deployment, monitoring, model interpretation, and scaling for large datasets.
Scaling machine learning workloads	Scaling machine learning workloads for large amounts of data in real-time can be challenging, as doing so can require significant computational resources.
Selecting the right cloud provider	Selecting the right cloud provider to ensure proper performance, scalability, reliability, and security, choosing from a wide range of available complex options, and ensuring alignment with the business goals and culture.

Table 3.1 summarizes all the challenges related to AI transformation covered so far.

TABLE 3.1:   AI Transformation Challenges

DOMAIN	CHALLENGES
Business	The cost of running intensive machine learning workloads.
	AI and machine learning are constantly evolving fields.
	Choosing the right use cases is tricky.
Data	Collecting high-quality data.
	Alignment between AI and ML strategy with the business strategy.
	Ability to process large amounts of data.
Model	Machine learning can be complex.
	Measuring the performance of models is tricky.
	Monitoring the model performance is a challenge.
Platform	Integrating with backend systems.
	Managing the entire ML lifecycle.
	Scaling ML workloads.
	Selecting the right cloud provider.
Operations	Model should be monitored for bias, data, and model drift.
Security	Managing end-to-end security.
	Ensuring compliance with legal regulations.
Governance	Having the right skills and talent.
	Ensuring responsible and ethical AI.

Here is a sample of security-related challenges:

SECURITY-RELATED CHALLENGES	
Managing end-to-end security	Managing end-to-end security across the entire machine learning lifecycle can be challenging, as security needs to be implemented across the data layer, models, infrastructure, network, and cloud components.
Ensuring compliance and avoiding bias	Ensuring compliance, maintaining data privacy, implementing security, and avoiding bias and ethical discrimination in models can be challenging.

HANDS-ON BRAINSTORMING EXERCISE: DEVELOP IMPLEMENTATION PLAN TO OVERCOME AI CHALLENGES

Brainstorm with your team the different ways AI, ML, and Generative AI can integrate with your company or a company of your choice.

HOW DIGITAL NATIVES TACKLE AI ADOPTION

Digital natives, which are companies born in the digital age, are technology savvy and have embraced technology as a primary driver for achieving business results, such as cost reduction, efficiency, and innovation. They are agile, adaptable, and innovative and are quick to adopt new technologies, such as machine learning, artificial intelligence, and now generative AI. They are better able to implement AI transformation across the enterprise when compared to other traditional companies. Let's see why.

They Are Willing to Take Risks

When it comes to adopting new technology, such as AI, digital natives tend to be more willing to take risks and experiment with new technology. Unlike traditional companies, they have a culture that encourages risk-taking and views failure as a stepping stone to success.

They Have an Advantage in Data Collection and Curation Capabilities

When it comes to data, digital-native companies have been adept at gathering large amounts of data from multiple sources and curating them for business purposes. This is something that traditional companies are not able to do because of the technical debt they have been accumulating as more and more systems have been developed over several years. It is a challenge to get the data consolidated into one place to enable consumption.

They Attract Top Talent Through Competitive Compensation and Perks

Digital-native companies have been able to hire the best talent in the industry by giving them good pay, attractive career opportunities, and work amenities that attract good talent.

For this reason, I recommend that traditional organizations spend more time and effort on change management. They should plan for internal employee training and partner with other AI experts to provide guidance and support during the AI transformation journey.

BEST PRACTICE TIPS TO TACKLING AI ADOPTION

➤ Start AI projects with small scope and gradually scale.

➤ Partner with other AI experts and companies.

➤ Invest in training programs for employees on AI technologies.

GET READY: AI TRANSFORMATION IS MORE CHALLENGING THAN DIGITAL TRANSFORMATION

AI transformation is more challenging than digital transformation. Understanding these challenges will help you to plan, execute, and manage your AI implementation. Let's look at those reasons.

Complexities of Skill Sets, Technology, and Infrastructure Integration

One of the main reasons is that AI transformation is much more complex given the many skills (such as machine learning, data science, cloud engineering) required, the complexity of the underlying technology, and the need for business domain knowledge. Bringing the data, the technology, the skill sets, and the infrastructure together takes a lot of work. A strong mix of technology and business domain knowledge is the foundation for success in this journey. Figure 3.2 shows the different skills you need. It shows how these skills are a combination of domain, mathematics, and computer science knowledge areas.

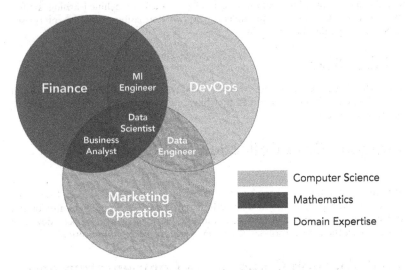

FIGURE 3.2: Skill sets required in a typical AI/ML project

The Importance of Data Infrastructure and Governance

Deploying high-performing models in production requires high-quality data in large quantities. A robust data infrastructure pipeline, from collection to consumption, is vital (see Figure 3.3). Collecting, ingesting, cleaning, storing, and consuming data is a challenging task. Companies that do not have this in place already are at a disadvantage in getting started.

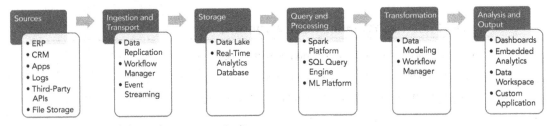

FIGURE 3.3: A typical data infrastructure pipeline

Change Management to Redefine Work Processes and Employee Mindsets

AI transformation, unlike digital transformation, demands shifts in work processes and mindsets. Successfully managing this change is a significant task.

> **BEST PRACTICE TIP** *Enterprise-wide AI transformation is complex, so change management is required to train employees and guide them through the process.*

Regulatory Concerns: Addressing Bias, Ethical, Privacy, and Accountability Risks

AI introduces regulatory concerns such as bias, ethics, and privacy that must be tackled before deploying models.

HANDS-ON ROLE-PLAY EXERCISE: DECIDING TO PROCEED WITH AN AI-FIRST STRATEGY

Imagine a scenario where a company is contemplating adopting an AI-first strategy. Form groups and have each group or an individual take on roles such as CEO, CFO, data scientist, machine learning engineer, business analyst, product manager, and so on.

Have each person defend their role and brainstorm reasons for and against adopting an AI-first strategy.

Come up with a presentation capturing your decision in favor or against an AI-first strategy with justifications.

CHOOSING BETWEEN SMALLER PoC POINT SOLUTIONS AND LARGE-SCALE AI INITIATIVES

Let's discuss the pros and cons of choosing between single point and large-scale AI initiatives. This will help you to manage your resources better, balance risks versus benefits, and, more importantly, ensure alignment of your AI initiatives with your organizational goals.

The Challenges of Implementing a Large-Scale AI Initiative

Large-scale AI initiatives are much more complex than smaller point-based PoC solutions. Choosing a large-scale AI initiative or a smaller-point PoC solution depends on your organization's needs, goals, strategic objectives, and readiness.

Navigate the Moving Parts, Stakeholders, and Technical Infrastructure

Large-scale AI initiatives are complex simply because of the many moving parts, such as the data pipeline, the underlying systems and processes, the models, the business requirements, and the many stakeholders you need to work with. Getting to know the processes, the data, and the technical infrastructure takes time and effort.

Resource Allocation Challenges in Large-Scale AI Initiatives

Large-scale AI initiatives require a lot of technological, financial, and human resources. It naturally involves coordinating with lots of stakeholders within the organization. Getting buy-in and consensus takes work.

Overcome Resistance to Change

Implementing a large-scale AI initiative across an enterprise requires a change in employee processes, systems, practices, org structure, and culture. Getting the stakeholder's trust in the value of AI systems to enable this change takes work.

Data Security, Privacy, Ethics, Compliance, and Reputation

Because the scope of a large-scale AI initiative is large, the risks associated with the initiative are also large in terms of costs, data security, privacy, ethics, compliance, and reputation.

Build a Business Case for Large-Scale AI Initiatives

It is more challenging to build a business case for large-scale AI initiatives as compared to a smaller point solution. However, the benefits of a large-scale AI initiative are also much larger.

Factors to Consider

In a nutshell, given all these considerations, whether an organization should proceed with a small-scale PoC solution or a more significant AI transformational effort will depend on where they are in their AI journey.

➤ If your company is just beginning to test AI and has not identified a particular use case, then a point PoC solution may be a good fit.

➤ However, if your company has already gained some experience through a previous point-based PoC solution and has identified several use cases, as well as the right resources, skill sets, infrastructure, and data available for a large-scale initiative, then a large-scale initiative may be the way to go, given the vast benefits it can have for the organization.

It is recommended that you kick-start the AI transformation effort with a PoC and then follow it up with a larger-scale AI transformation initiative.

> **NOTE** *Deciding between a smaller PoC and large-scale AI transformation depends on the risk-taking culture and org change capability of the organization as well as the maturity of their AI processes, practices, data, and org structure.*

HANDS-ON CASE STUDY EXERCISE: ENTERPRISE AI TRANSFORMATION DECISION: PoC VS. LARGE SCALE AI

Objective: Evaluate the challenges of embarking on an enterprise AI transformation effort, evaluate the cost benefits, and make strategic decisions about the implementation of AI projects.

Materials needed: Online research, pen, and paper for note-taking, PPT, or Google Slides.

Step 1: Divide the students into groups and share the case study.

Positives: You're with a midsize retail company with some PoC experience, a risk-taking culture, and potential transformative initiatives. Yet, you face backend integration challenges, large dataset management, and employee resistance.

Negatives: The company also has several challenges such as integration with backend systems, managing large datasets, and having employee resistance to change.

Step 2: The groups should assess the situation and factor in aspects such as skill sets, technology, infrastructure integration, data management, governance, security, change management, regulations, resource needs, and so on.

Step 3: The teams need to decide the next course of action, whether to go forward into a large-scale AI initiative or continue with their PoCs. The teams must give a short presentation capturing the situation, their decision, and their reasons.

Step 4: Once all the teams have presented, discuss as a class regarding common viewpoints and differences in the approach. The individual can capture their own notes and decide how they would want to apply it in a real-world setting.

WORKBOOK TEMPLATE: *AI CHALLENGES ASSESSMENT*

Download the "AI challenges assessment" template from the download section of the book (www.wiley.com/go/EnterpriseAIintheCloud). Gain a good understanding of the potential challenges you may face when implementing AI enterprise wide. Use it as a proactive tool for planning and to prioritize areas that need special attention.

SUMMARY

While embarking on the AI transformative journey can be quite exhilarating, the landscape ahead can also be pretty daunting. Without a doubt, the promises are alluring, but it is essential to approach them with both enthusiasm and preparation. This chapter is your first step in the journey ahead.

This chapter considered some challenges in implementing a machine learning deployment that prevents organizations from deploying them into production. Given the immense power behind an AI solution, it is also vital for the implementation team to factor in some of the social, ethical, and humanitarian considerations when deploying an AI solution. The next chapter discusses the requirements to implement responsible AI.

REVIEW QUESTIONS

These review questions are included at the end of each chapter to help you test your understanding of the information. You'll find the answers in the following section.

1. What is the main advantage that digital natives have when it comes to adopting AI?
    A. They have a risk-taking culture and view failure as a steppingstone for success.
    B. They have a lot more money to invest in AI.
    C. They have a better brand image than traditional companies.

2. What are the challenges when deploying AI/ML solutions in a business environment? Choose all that apply.
    A. AI and ML technologies are complex to deliver value.
    B. The cost of running machine learning workloads can be a barrier to deployment.
    C. All business problems are easily solvable using AI/ML.
    D. There is a surplus of qualified AI/ML professionals in the market.

3. What is a common data-related challenge in machine learning?
    A. There's usually an excess of high-quality data available.
    B. Models don't need data in a specific format, making the process easier.
    C. Measuring the performance of models is straightforward and easy.
    D. Collecting high-quality data and preparing it for machine learning can be time-consuming and costly.

4. What is a significant challenge when managing the entire machine learning lifecycle?

    A.   It is easier to conduct feature engineering and select models.

    B.   It is easy because data preparation does not require any significant effort.

    C.   The complexity around data preparation and feature engineering makes it challenging.

    D.   None of the machine learning tasks presents any significant challenge.

5. What makes AI transformation more complex than digital transformation?

    A.   AI transformation requires basic IT skills and infrastructure.

    B.   AI transformation involves changes in how work is done and the interaction of employees with technology.

    C.   AI transformation does not require a substantial amount of high-quality data.

    D.   AI transformation does not present any challenges related to bias, ethics, privacy, and accountability.

ANSWER KEY

1. A
2. A, B
3. D
4. C
5. B

4

Designing AI Systems Responsibly

The real problem is not whether machines think but whether men do.

—B.F. Skinner

This chapter grapples with one of the most pressing issues of our time: designing AI systems responsibly. It is even more critical if you are a data scientist, project manager, AI developer, or executive involved in implementing AI. It is not just about developing code or training models but about ensuring that what you develop is aligned with human values, ethics, and safety.

This chapter explores the key pillars of Responsible AI, from robustness and collaboration to trustworthiness and scalability. This chapter also shares the essential pillars of a Responsible AI framework, the four key principles of Responsible AI, and some of the nuances of AI design, development, and deployment. As shown in Figure 4.1, this chapter sets the stage for subsequent chapters for the practical deployment and scaling of AI. Whether you have just started or are trying to refine an existing implementation, this chapter will guide you.

THE PILLARS OF RESPONSIBLE AI

Organizations have a social and humanitarian responsibility to ensure that pre-existing prejudices and biases do not continue to operate in the post AI-deployment world.

Responsible AI is a framework created to protect human principles such as dignity, fairness, and privacy (see Figure 4.2). It is used to design and build AI systems that are ethical, transparent, fair, and socially responsible. Responsible AI basically recognizes the impact that AI systems can have on humanity, including individuals, communities, and society overall. Its goal is to minimize the negative impacts of AI while trying to maximize the positive impacts on those involved. The implications to the design of AI systems are that they must not only be built for robustness and reliability but also should focus on minimizing bias and discrimination and protecting privacy.

This section covers some of those things you need to consider when building a real-life AI system. A real-life AI system needs to be robust, collaborative, responsible, trustworthy, scalable, and human-centric.

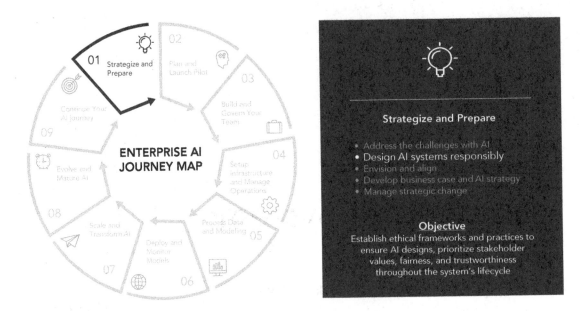

FIGURE 4.1: STRATEGIZE AND PREPARE: Design AI systems responsibly

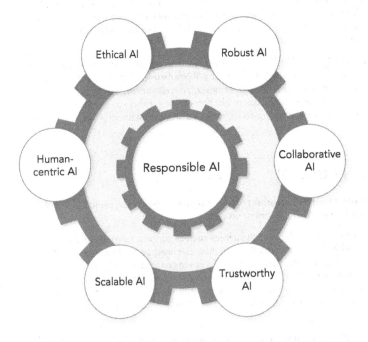

FIGURE 4.2: Key pillars of Responsible AI

Without these Responsible AI attributes, it will be challenging to deploy it in production because users will not have the required trust and confidence to use the system. The following sections look at each one of those attributes and explain what they mean.

Robust AI

You need to design AI systems to be robust, meaning they should be able to perform well even in situations in which they have not been previously trained. It is especially critical for use cases such as defense, autonomous vehicles, and robotics, where the consequences could be catastrophic if the system misbehaves.

> **BEST PRACTICE TIP** *A robust AI system should perform consistently even when the data constantly changes, especially in an enterprise setting, where many data sources are feeding the model. If the system produces unreliable insights, users will lose trust and confidence when using the system. You need to test the system for any surprising attacks or situations.*

Collaborative AI

The idea behind collaborative AI is to leverage the strengths of both AI and humans. While humans have creative thinking, leadership, judgment, and emotional and social skills, robots can crunch large amounts of data and help humans with physical labor, information gathering, speed, and routine tasks such as customer service. By combining the strengths of both humans and AI, you can build better systems to improve business processes. Figure 4.3 shows examples of this collaboration, such as chatbots, cobots, virtual assistants, and other intelligent machines. These intelligent machines work alongside humans to make decisions and carry out tasks collaboratively.

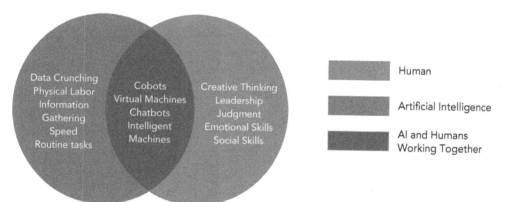

FIGURE 4.3: Collaborative AI: Enhancing human capacity with AI

The critical takeaway from collaborative AI systems is that AI will not replace humans but will complement and enhance human decision-making capacity. While taking care of mundane, repetitive tasks, they help humans focus on unique, high-value tasks and increase their capacity to deliver on more tasks.

Collaborative AI has created the need for humans to train AI systems so that they behave correctly, as well as explain why AI systems behave in a certain way. For example, in the case of car accidents, you need to explain why an accident happened or why the car failed to prevent one. It has also created the need for human supervision to ensure that AI systems work responsibly.

It's been shown that companies that replace humans can realize only short-term gains. In contrast, companies that use AI to improve human capacity to make decisions and carry out mundane tasks faster at scale can redesign business processes and reap greater long-term benefits.

Use Case Example

Some examples of collaborative AI are HSBC and Danske Bank using AI to improve the speed and accuracy of fraud detection. Another example is that of Mercedes Benz, which has replaced robots with AI-enabled cobots, which are robots working with humans to achieve flexibility in the process. This redesigned their human-machine collaborations.

Trustworthy AI

You need to build trustworthy systems, meaning they should behave consistently, reliably, and safely. They should also protect the user's well-being, safety, and privacy. The goal is to build trust between the user and the system. You should also be able to explain to the user how the system took its actions and be accountable to the user regarding how it concluded or made a prediction. Figure 4.4 shows the key elements of a trustworthy system.

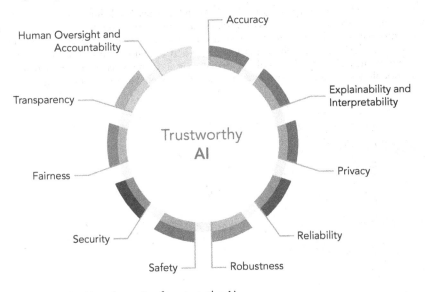

FIGURE 4.4: Key elements of trustworthy AI

Use Case Example

The Google search engine is an excellent example of a trustworthy system. It has algorithms to ensure that results are shown based on the relevance of those websites to the search query. It also ranks the results and filters all the spam and malicious websites when presenting the results. It provides transparent and explainable results to the user regarding how it came up with those results. Google has also developed a set of ethical guidelines and principles and has explained to the users how they collect the data, protect, and use it by being transparent to the users. Google has built a reputation among users as a trustworthy search engine AI system.

Scalable AI

You must build AI systems that can handle large amounts of data without compromising performance during operation. For a system to be scalable, you need to ensure not just the scalable management of data and models but also scalability during development and deployment, as well as scalable algorithms and infrastructure (see Figure 4.5). This section also discusses how to solve data scarcity and collection, data reusability to scale data in the subsequent chapters on cloud platform architecture, automating operations, and data and model processing. To address the development and deployment scalability, the book discusses using production pipelines and scalable architectures, including distributed cloud computing and edge devices.

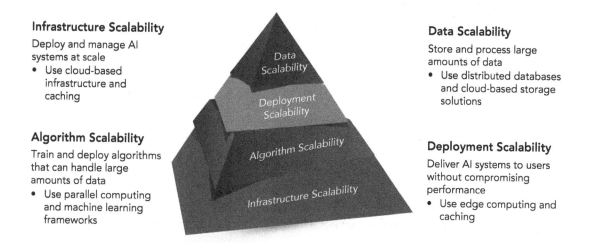

Infrastructure Scalability

Deploy and manage AI systems at scale
- Use cloud-based infrastructure and caching

Algorithm Scalability

Train and deploy algorithms that can handle large amounts of data
- Use parallel computing and machine learning frameworks

Data Scalability

Store and process large amounts of data
- Use distributed databases and cloud-based storage solutions

Deployment Scalability

Deliver AI systems to users without compromising performance
- Use edge computing and caching

FIGURE 4.5: Scalable AI: Key considerations and case study

SCALABILITY CASE STUDY: GOOGLE

Scalability is essential when building natural language processing–based AI solutions. These systems must handle large amounts of data without decreasing performance. Google Cloud's natural language processing system is an excellent example of a system that has handled this. It uses natural language processing algorithms to analyze and extract insights from large amounts of data. It can integrate with other Google services that businesses use for their operations. One good use case for this is social media platforms. They can use Google Cloud natural language to process millions of user comments in multiple languages to understand user sentiments and use it to tailor their end-user experiences and engagement and increase customer satisfaction without losing performance.

Human-centric AI

You need to build AI systems that are human-centric. Human-centric means that they should respect humans' values and enable them to make decisions. For this to happen, a conscious effort needs to be made to incorporate human values and needs in the design. You should factor in social, ethical, and human behavioral impact. These systems must be built to be transparent, explainable, and accountable to the users. They should understand how these systems work and be able to make informed decisions based on the system's recommendations. Figure 4.6 shows some of the key considerations when building a human-centric AI system.

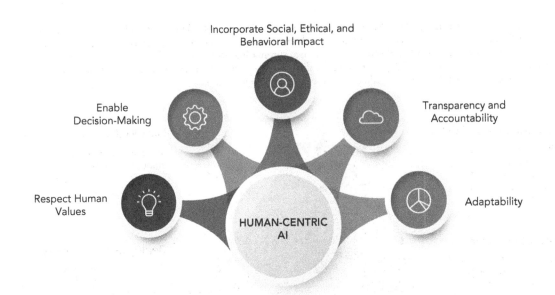

FIGURE 4.6: Building human-centric AI systems with human values at the forefront

---

Use Case Example

A healthcare system that provides personalized treatment recommendations to patients based on their historical medical data, genetics, and lifestyle is an excellent example of a human-centric AI system because it ensures that the treatment is not based on a one-size-fits-all approach but is personalized based on the patient's unique needs and circumstances. The developers must also consider the data privacy of the user. They should also be careful about the potential impact of making wrong recommendations. That is why it would be necessary for the system to explain how a decision was made. This is critical because it will help the doctors trust this system more, allowing them to make recommendations to patients much more confidently. Moreover, you should continuously monitor the system to ensure it operates as expected. It should also adapt to the changing patient and healthcare system requirements.

HANDS-ON ROLE-PLAYING EXERCISE: IMPLEMENTING RESPONSIBLE AI

Identify potential social, humanitarian, and ethical issues when implementing AI and proposing ethically sound solutions. Use this understanding to explore the key design elements to ensure the AI system is robust, collaborative, trustworthy, scalable, safe, and human-centric.

TASK DESCRIPTION	TASK OWNER	DELIVERABLES
Context setting: Briefly describe your AI system's purpose, users, and current/desired potential societal impact.	Project manager	Project details document

TASK DESCRIPTION	TASK OWNER	DELIVERABLES
List potential ethical challenges: List possible prejudices, biases, privacy, security, safety, transparency, or other ethical considerations relevant to the scenario.	Ethics analyst and team	List of identified ethical challenges
Develop solution for prejudices and bias: Propose methods to address biases in data collection, model training, and deployment.	Data scientist	Strategies for minimizing biases
Develop solutions for privacy and security: Design controls to ensure data privacy and compliance with relevant regulations.	Security expert	Data privacy and security plan
Develop solutions for accountability and transparency: Outline ways to keep AI models transparent and accountable.	Compliance officer	Accountability and transparency plan
Develop solutions for safety and security: Develop strategies for robust testing and risk mitigation.	QA engineer	Safety and security plan
Consider stakeholder needs and wellness: Explain how the AI system considers the needs and values of stakeholders, including users, employees, and the wider community.	Stakeholder manager	Stakeholder consideration document
Divide into groups: Each group represents a different stakeholder. Debate the proposed solutions and make adjustments based on different perspectives.	Facilitator (team lead)	Adjusted solutions based on role-play
Summarize the key principles and specific actions: Include reflections on what was learned and how it could be applied to future AI projects.	Business analyst	Comprehensive document detailing the approach
Discuss challenges and successes: As a group or individually, write about the challenges and successes experienced during the exercise, and how these insights might influence future AI projects.	All participants	Reflection document

HANDS-ON EXERCISE FOR STUDENTS

Step 1: Assign a student or a group of students to a topic related to Responsible AI, such as potential ethical issues, biases, privacy concerns, or other challenges.

Step 2: Have them present a short presentation with their scenario, challenges, and proposed solutions. Identify the common themes and unique insights and document them for applying it to their future projects.

WORKBOOK TEMPLATE: *RESPONSIBLE AI DESIGN TEMPLATE*

Download the "Responsible AI Design" template from the download section of the book (www.wiley.com/go/EnterpriseAIintheCloud). Use this template to come up with a comprehensive plan to address the ethical and responsible design of your AI system. Treat this as a working document that keeps evolving with the project.

SUMMARY

This chapter explained the importance of Responsible AI to ensure AI systems are designed and deployed with ethical, social, and human-centric principles in mind. Users should be able to understand AI decisions, and the systems should eliminate bias and prioritize human values. These systems must behave consistently and reliably and should be scalable to large amounts of data. That means you must ensure adherence to data privacy regulations, implement robust security and testing, and involve stakeholders during design.

In the next chapter, we will discuss developing the AI strategy, the roadmap, and getting alignment from various stakeholders.

REVIEW QUESTIONS

These review questions are included at the end of each chapter to help you test your understanding of the information ere. You'll find the answers in the following section.

1. Transparency in AI design means
   A. The models used in AI systems should not introduce bias when they are adapted to changing conditions.
   B. The data used as input to a model should be biased.
   C. The users and organizations understand how an AI system operates and makes its predictions so that they can use it appropriately.
   D. It should not be possible for either humans or the programs to change the predefined model development process.

2. Which of the following is NOT a best practice tip for Responsible AI?
   A. The data used as input to a model should not be biased.
   B. The organization implementing AI should focus only on the positive impacts of AI.
   C. Humans or programs should not be able to change the predefined model development process.
   D. The models used in an AI system should not introduce bias when they are adapted to changing conditions.

3. What is one of the elements of trustworthy AI?
   A. The system should make predictions without any explanation.
   B. The system should behave consistently, reliably, and safely and protect the user's well-being, safety, and privacy.
   C. The system should always agree with the user's decision.
   D. The system should operate independently of any data.

4. What is NOT a characteristic of a human-centric AI system?
   A. Transparent and explainable to users
   B. Able to operate without any human intervention
   C. Accountable to users
   D. Understands how the systems work and able to make informed decisions based on the system's recommendations

5. What does it mean for an AI system to be robust?
   A. It should perform well even in situations in which they have not been previously trained.
   B. It should be able to replace human workforce completely.
   C. It should be able to operate without human intervention.
   D. It should be cheaper than human workforce.

ANSWER KEY

1.	C	3.	B	5.	A
2.	B	4.	B		

5

Envisioning and Aligning Your AI Strategy

By failing to prepare, you are preparing to fail.

—*Benjamin Franklin*

This chapter not only sets the tone for your AI transformation but also ensures that every step you take from now on resonates with your company's broader objectives.

Targeting business strategists struggling to find their AI direction, technology leaders grappling with business and technology alignment, and AI enthusiasts eager to embed AI meaningfully into their business, this chapter is focused on charting a clear vision for your AI initiatives and aligning it with your business objectives. Without a clearly defined vision and business case, even the most robust AI implementation can fail when not aligned with the business goals.

This chapter presents a methodology that clearly lays down the tasks and deliverables you can follow across various stages of your AI implementation journey. It serves as a bridge between the groundwork laid in Chapters 1–4 for idea generation and later chapters, teeing it up for developing the business cases in Chapter 6 to managing strategic changes in Chapter 7 (see Figure 5.1).

By the end of this chapter, you will have a toolkit of strategies, a clear roadmap of tasks, a business case, and a checklist of tasks vital for your AI journey.

STEP-BY-STEP METHODOLOGY FOR ENTERPRISE-WIDE AI

As you can see in Figure 5.2, you need to manage everything, from strategy to portfolio management to architecture, infrastructure, operations, governance, trust, ethics, and security. You need to manage the business, technical, and change management challenges in a systematic, programmatic manner.

> **NOTE** *To successfully deploy AI enterprise-wide, you need to address challenges ranging from people to data issues to security to trust.*

I know that implementing enterprise-wide AI is not an easy thing to do. However, to drive business transformation with AI rather than solve one or two AI use cases, enterprise-wide AI is the answer, and this book is your end-to-end guide. As shown in Figure 5.2, the chapters in the book are arranged in a manner that should help you manage all these challenges and implement enterprise-wide AI using a systematic methodology.

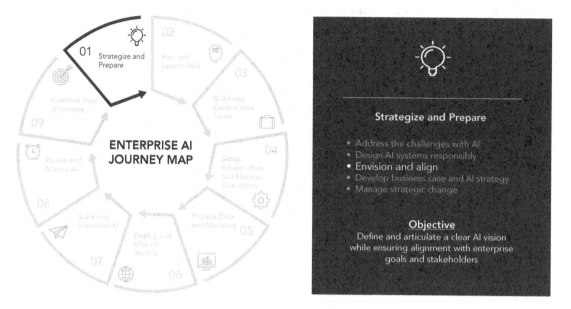

FIGURE 5.1: STRATEGIZE AND PREPARE: Envision and align

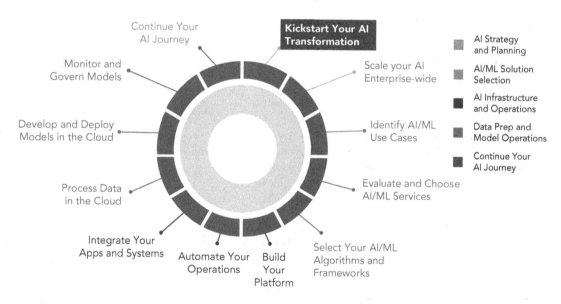

FIGURE 5.2: Steps to implement enterprise AI

The Envision Phase

Your AI journey starts with the Envision phase, which is where you start seriously thinking about how to deploy AI within the organization.

Primary Objective: Define Your AI Strategy

The primary objectives of the Envision phase are to define the AI strategy, ensure it aligns with the business goals, identify different AI initiatives, and prioritize them. I break this down into simple steps, as shown in Figure 5.3.

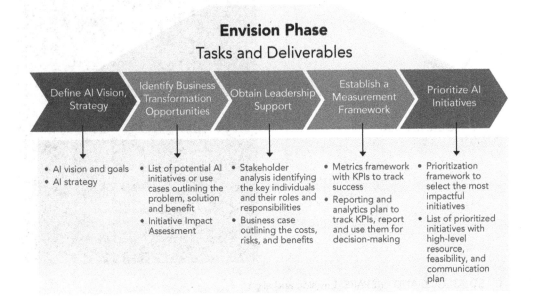

FIGURE 5.3: Envision phase: tasks and deliverables

Steps of the Envision Phase

These steps are part of the Envision phase:

TASK	DESCRIPTION	TASK OWNER	DELIVERABLES
Identify opportunities: Identify your business transformation opportunities	Brainstorm ways AI can transform your business across different domains, such as technology, process, organization, and product.	Innovation team, product managers	List of potential AI transformation opportunities across domains
Align leadership: Obtain your leadership's support	Once potential AI initiatives or use cases have been identified, run them by the leadership team to get their buy-in and align them with measurable business outcomes. The leadership team should include those who can influence and drive change within their respective capability areas.	Senior leadership, department heads	Approved AI initiatives, alignment document with business outcomes

TASK	DESCRIPTION	TASK OWNER	DELIVERABLES
Create a measurement framework: Establish your measurement framework	Have clearly defined business outcome goals to demonstrate the value that AI and cloud technology can bring to your company. A measurement framework helps ensure your company's business goals are in line with the overall business strategy.	Business analysts, data scientists	Measurement framework, business outcome goals aligned with strategy
Prioritize Initiatives: Prioritize your AI initiatives across multiple areas	Identify the different areas that AI can impact and prioritize their value.	Project managers, strategy team	Prioritized list of AI initiatives, impact assessment across areas

---

CASE STUDY EXAMPLE: IDENTIFYING AI INITIATIVES DURING THE ENVISION PHASE

Say you are working for a retail company to improve its supply chain. As part of the Envision phase, you have identified the AI strategy, brainstormed several AI initiatives, obtained leadership buy-in, established a measurement framework, and prioritized your AI initiatives. For example:

➤ **Business strategy:** Leverage AI to improve supply chain operations.

➤ **AI strategy:** Use appropriate algorithms to analyze supply chain data and generate insights to optimize operations. This includes processing data, building models, and leveraging appropriate AI tools.

➤ **Business goals:** Reduce lead times by 20 percent, increase on-time delivery to 98 percent, and reduce transportation costs by 10 percent.

➤ **Measurement framework:** This is a set of metrics used to track progress. In this case, it includes lead times, on-time delivery, transportation costs, inventory turnover, and order cycle time.

➤ **AI initiatives:** These include demand forecasting for better inventory management, route optimization to minimize transportation costs, and warehouse automation to reduce labor costs.

The Align Phase

Now that you have identified the list of potential AI initiatives during the Envision phase, it is time to move on to the Align phase.

Primary Objective: Build Your Business Case

During the Align phase, the primary objective is to build a business case for AI so that you can get alignment from the stakeholders to marshal and align the resources to proceed with your AI initiative, which you identified during the Envision phase. Figure 5.4 illustrates this process.

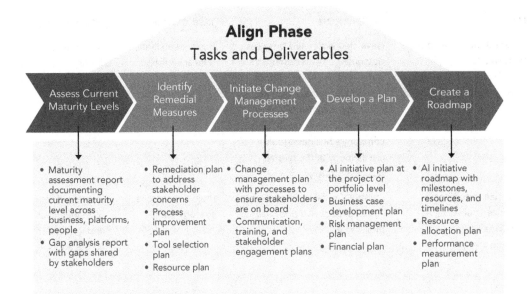

FIGURE 5.4: Align phase: tasks and deliverables

Steps of the Align Phase

Here are the steps of the Align phase:

TASK	TASK OWNERS	DELIVERABLES
Assess your current maturity levels: You focus on identifying the current maturity level in your organization, across business, technology, people, process, security, and governance. Document the concerns, limitations, or gaps shared by your stakeholders.	Business analysts, technology leaders	Maturity assessment report, list of concerns and limitations
Identify remedial measures: By understanding the current gaps and limitations, you can put in place remedial measures to address stakeholders' concerns, such as new processes, procedures, or tools. You may even identify any cross-organizational dependencies and plan to bring in untapped resources for this initiative.	Process managers, cross-functional teams	Remedial action plan, resource allocation plan
Initiate your change management processes: You can then put in place organizational change management processes to adequately address any hurdles. You also talk to different stakeholders for their support; for example, you may have to speak with IT partners to procure the right resources or the training curriculum lead for putting together the right set of courses. Your goal is to ensure that all the stakeholders are fully on board and incredibly supportive of this AI initiative.	Change managers, IT partners, training leads	Change management plan, stakeholder support documentation

TASK	TASK OWNERS	DELIVERABLES
Develop your plan: During this phase, you capture these gaps in the form of a plan so that you can work toward launching the AI initiative in the next phase. There are two types of plans. One is at the project level to implement the identified AI POC as part of the Launch phase, and the other enables enterprise AI from a transformation perspective. The latter is known as the AI transformation plan.	Project managers, strategy team	Project plan, AI transformation plan
Create your roadmap: Create a roadmap with clearly defined milestones with your idea of the resources and timelines.	Strategic planners, project managers	AI initiative roadmap, milestone chart

---

CASE STUDY EXAMPLE: BUILDING A BUSINESS CASE AND PLANNING DURING THE ALIGN PHASE

Continuing with the retail example, you may perform the following tasks during the Align phase:

➤ **Change communication plan:** You find out during your gap analysis that some stakeholders are concerned about AI's impact on their jobs. So you put together a change management process that involves periodic communication about the value of the AI initiative along with reassurances about how it benefits their jobs.

➤ **Skills gap:** You identify remedial action items to address technical skills gaps. One of those measures is hiring new employees with AI and ML skills and working with the training curriculum team to develop AI courses for your employees to bring them up to speed with the technologies.

➤ **Data issue:** During the gap analysis you also realized that your company does not have all the data required to build and train the models. You assess different options to generate or acquire necessary data from various marketplaces. While discussing this with your IT leads, you also learn that you need to build certain aspects of the AI platform.

➤ **Roadmap:** You consolidate all the action items into a plan and define a roadmap with clear timelines and milestones.

➤ **Business case:** At the end of this phase, you build a strong business case to launch the project and ensure all the impacted stakeholders are supportive and committed to the success of this AI initiative.

WORKBOOK TEMPLATE: *VISION ALIGNMENT WORKSHEET*

Download the "Vision Alignment Worksheet" template from the download section of the book (www.wiley.com/go/EnterpriseAIintheCloud). Use this template to ensure alignment between the AI goals, organizational vision, and mission.

SUMMARY

In this chapter, you took a tour of the Envision and Align phases for implementing enterprise AI across the organization. By now, you must be aware of the challenges in implementing enterprise AI and why a detailed step-by-step methodology is not just helpful but also essential.

In Chapter 10, you will learn about the Launch phase and in subsequent chapters, I will dive into how to scale your AI adoption across the enterprise. If you have ever wondered how to make AI work for your company, these four phases—Envision, Align, Launch, and Scale—must be your allies and guide on this journey. Think of these as the signposts that guide you on your path to becoming an AI-first organization.

In particular, the essence of strategically implementing AI and aligning your AI initiatives with your business goals cannot be underplayed. Your journey has just begun. A clear roadmap, coupled with strategic alignment, is a must for success.

REVIEW QUESTIONS

These review questions are included at the end of each chapter to help you test your understanding of the information. You'll find the answers in the following section.

1. Which one of the following is not a fundamental building block in an enterprise AI initiative?
   A. Data
   B. People
   C. Business
   D. Marketing

2. What is the primary objective of the Envision phase?
   A. To launch a pilot to evaluate the idea
   B. To define the AI strategy and prioritize AI initiatives
   C. To take an iterative approach to learn from the pilot and scale it
   D. To align the stakeholders for AI readiness

3. Which of the following is not a primary objective of the Align phase?
   A. To assess current maturity levels
   B. To identify remedial measures
   C. To implement AI initiatives identified in the Envision phase
   D. To initiate change management initiatives

4. What is the primary objective of the Launch phase?
   A. To identify pilot projects
   B. To implement pilot projects
   C. To deploy a full-scale AI initiative

5. Which of the following is not part of the Scale phase?
   A. To implement a robust AI/ML platform
   B. To implement strong security controls
   C. To establish an automated operations process to track and remedy issues
   D. To implement a pilot project

ANSWER KEY

1.	D	3.	C	5.	D
2.	B	4.	B		

6

Developing an AI Strategy and Portfolio

All men can see these tactics whereby I conquer, but what none can see is the strategy out of which victory is evolved.

—Sun Tzu, The Art of War

This chapter transitions from mere ideation and vision, as laid out in Chapters 3 to 5, to translate that vision into a compelling business case. Even the most exciting AI ideas will not gain traction, the necessary resources, or the support in your organization unless you have a robust, strategically aligned business case.

In addition to the business case, this chapter crafts the AI strategy that guides the direction, scope, and approach for your AI initiatives, thus setting the stage for planning the pilot and building the team (see Figure 6.1). By the end of this chapter, you will have a well-defined business case and a comprehensive AI strategy aligned with your organizational goals.

LEVERAGING YOUR ORGANIZATIONAL CAPABILITIES FOR COMPETITIVE ADVANTAGE

This section discusses how you can leverage nontechnical aspects such as business, governance, and people to execute your AI transformation effort. Note that you do not have to address all these capabilities at once. You can identify which ones you want to focus on based on your needs. You can decide based on what you discovered during the maturity levels assessment of those areas during the Align phase. Chapter 21 covers conducting an AI maturity assessment.

You can classify your company's capabilities into business and technical categories. This chapter reviews the business activities, such as developing an AI strategy in line with your business goals, managing an AI portfolio to deploy various use cases, and marshaling the people to get involved in your AI implementation. In Chapter 23, I help you build an AI operating model that serves as a framework to bring your strategy, portfolio, people, platforms, and operations together to achieve your AI goals.

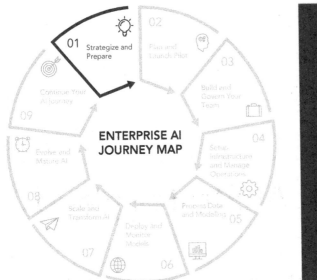

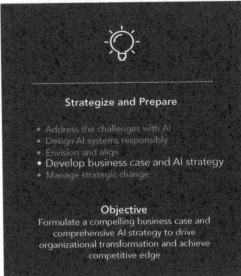

FIGURE 6.1: STRATEGIZE AND PREPARE: Develop business case and AI strategy

CASE STUDY: HOW NETFLIX LEVERAGED THEIR CAPABILITIES FOR COMPETITIVE ADVANTAGE

In Chapter 2, I talked about how a company like Netflix transformed their business by leveraging cloud and AI technology. I discussed how technology drove process transformation, enabling them to become more efficient and scale globally. Process transformation, in turn, created new opportunities for organizational transformation, enabling them to become product-centric, customer-focused, and agile. And this organizational transformation resulted in their ability to identify new products, services, and, eventually, new business models.

To achieve business transformation and build its *competitive advantage*, Netflix had to leverage processes to deploy various resources, tangible and nontangible, from within and outside the enterprise. Typically, these resources can be a mix of people, processes, and technology. The ability to bring together all those resources to achieve a favorable business outcome is known as *capability*.

In the case of your AI effort, you would do the same to build your AI capability to achieve a competitive advantage. You will leverage a team of skilled data scientists, cloud and data engineers, software engineers, and business teams using the Agile methodology to develop machine learning models on a complex, scalable cloud infrastructure employing leading-edge best practices.

Focus Areas to Build Your Competitive Advantage

To build your competitive advantage, you need to bring together your organization's capabilities in these eight major areas of focus, as shown in Figure 6.2:

- ➤ Strategy and planning
- ➤ People
- ➤ Data

➤ Platforms

➤ Machine learning

➤ Operations

➤ Security

➤ Governance

Different organizations have different strengths and weaknesses in these categories, which determines the success rate and the path they take toward achieving their business goals. For example, a few companies may be good at product design, which may help them design new products and drive innovation. In contrast, other companies may be good at supply chain management, helping them deliver products quickly and cheaply. These capabilities have been developed over time through investments in people, processes, and technology and have become a competitive advantage for an organization.

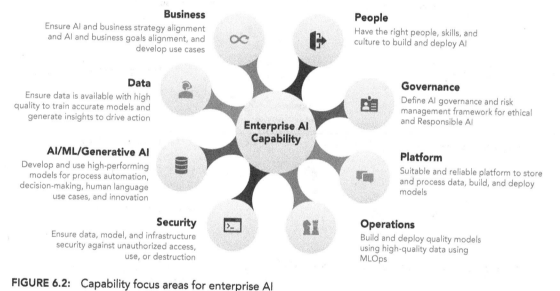

FIGURE 6.2: Capability focus areas for enterprise AI

Driving Competitive Advantage Through AI

In the case of an AI initiative, this competitive advantage would come from how good the company is at having its employees learn and excel at adopting AI technologies; how scalable, robust, and secure their cloud infrastructure is; how mature their DevOps and ML operations are; and how quickly they can act on these insights in real time to drive customer experience, reduce cost, and manage risks.

From an AI transformation journey standpoint, your focus is to leverage these capabilities to build your competitive advantage and achieve your business goals. How well you succeed depends on how well you engage with the stakeholders who own these capabilities and navigate the AI transformation effort. Follow the best practices in this book to increase your probability of success.

INITIATING YOUR STRATEGY AND PLAN TO KICKSTART ENTERPRISE AI

The following sections review the business and people aspects. In subsequent chapters, I discuss building the capabilities within the platform, operations, and security dimensions. See Figure 6.3.

In the context of an enterprise-wide AI initiative, below are the focus areas for you to manage effectively:

- ➤ Define your AI strategy
- ➤ Manage your portfolio
- ➤ Encourage innovation
- ➤ Manage your product lifecycle
- ➤ Develop strategic partnerships
- ➤ Monetize data
- ➤ Draw business insights
- ➤ Maximize machine learning capability

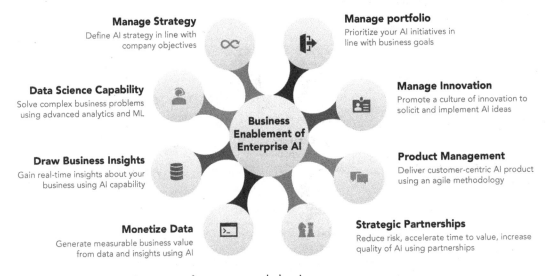

Manage Strategy
Define AI strategy in line with company objectives

Manage portfolio
Prioritize your AI initiatives in line with business goals

Data Science Capability
Solve complex business problems using advanced analytics and ML

Manage Innovation
Promote a culture of innovation to solicit and implement AI ideas

Business Enablement of Enterprise AI

Draw Business Insights
Gain real-time insights about your business using AI capability

Product Management
Deliver customer-centric AI product using an agile methodology

Monetize Data
Generate measurable business value from data and insights using AI

Strategic Partnerships
Reduce risk, accelerate time to value, increase quality of AI using partnerships

FIGURE 6.3: Business focus areas for strategy and planning

Leveraging the eight business aspects shown in Figure 6.3 effectively will increase the probability of success of your AI transformation effort, enterprise-wide.

Manage Your AI Strategy, Portfolio, Innovation, Product Lifecycle, and Partnerships

Table 6.1 shows a list of deliverables that you need as part of the Envision and Align phases.

Define Your AI Strategy to Achieve Business Outcomes

The following case study discusses an example of a company that managed its AI strategy to achieve its business goals.

TABLE 6.1: AI Strategy and Portfolio Deliverables

CAPABILITIES	DELIVERABLES	DESCRIPTION
Define your AI strategy	AI strategy document	A comprehensive document that captures the strengths, weaknesses, opportunities, and threats, and the AI vision and business goals • For example, evaluating the growth of technology platforms, customer expectations, regulatory requirements
	Current state assessment	Assessment of the company's current capabilities and resources related to AI
	AI technology strategy	To achieve the company's business goals • For example, using machine learning to personalize customer experiences
	Technology plan to implement AI	Plan to implement technology strategy. For example: • Adopting an agile methodology and organizing teams around products • Setting up an AI COE
	AI initiatives	A prioritized list of high-level AI initiatives, use cases, and products
	Metrics	To measure the success of the AI initiatives
Manage your AI portfolio	Portfolio analysis	Analyze your portfolio based on short- and long-term goals • For example, categorize your list of AI initiatives into high value, low value, low risk, high risk, high complexity, and low complexity in terms of delivery capability
	AI portfolio roadmap	Sequence your initiatives based on the portfolio analysis in the previous step
Encourage innovation	An innovation management charter	Define the goals of the innovation program, including how the AI solutions will be aligned with organization's goals
	Innovation roadmap	List of innovative ideas, both innovative and incremental. These could be innovative ideas, prototypes, proof of concepts, or even finished products and services
	Metrics	They measure the success of innovative ideas
	Senior leadership support	Critical to ensuring employee motivation levels

continues

TABLE 6.1: *(continued)*

CAPABILITIES	DELIVERABLES	DESCRIPTION
Manage your AI product lifecycle	AI product strategy and roadmap	Develop the product strategy from a customer-centric point of view to solve a problem identified through customers and data
	Product backlog and product requirements document	Manage product requirements
	Product development and delivery plan	Helps to have a clear roadmap so all parties are clear about their role; helps to manage plans, resources, milestones, and risks effectively
Develop your strategic partnerships	List of potential partners	Helpful to identify companies with machine learning, data analytics, and AI skills
	Partnership agreements	Includes a list of the roles and responsibilities of all the parties involved
	Metrics	Evaluate partners in terms of reducing risk, accelerating time to value product quality, and increasing the probability of success

---

CASE STUDY: HOW A SUPPLY CHAIN MANAGEMENT COMPANY MANAGED THEIR AI STRATEGY TO ACHIEVE THEIR BUSINESS OUTCOMES

The company wanted to optimize its supply chain operations using AI. During the Envision and Align phases, the company evaluated the competitor landscape, technology developments, regulatory changes, and customer expectations to understand the business impact.

By looking at its business goals and the impact assessment, it decided to leverage predictive analytics to optimize its operations and meet its long-term goals.

The company developed its *technology strategy* to deploy AI technology to improve its supply chain operations and meet its business goals. As part of its strategy, it reorganized its teams around products and value streams to become more customer-centric. To ensure a successful implementation, it solicited feedback from many stakeholders, such as customers, employees, leadership teams, and third-party vendors.

In the end, the company achieved its business goals using AI technology.

Figure 6.4 shows examples of business strategy, AI strategy, business goals, and AI initiatives.

Prioritize Your Portfolio

Managing the portfolio you identified for AI helps you have a holistic view of your products and services and ensure that your AI strategy and plan meet your customers' needs. When prioritizing your products, you should focus on improving the customers' end-to-end experience across all channels and business operations.

CASE STUDY: NETFLIX AND PORTFOLIO MANAGEMENT

Consider the example of Netflix. They employed portfolio management to prioritize their products to deliver an engaging customer experience and maintain their competitive edge.

Netflix used data about their customers' behavior to personalize their viewing experience. They also prioritized the products that optimized their content delivery network to allow faster streaming and reduce buffer times. They also ensured they had the necessary technical skills, resources, and infrastructure to deliver the customer experience without compromising on performance, security, and reliability. Using portfolio management to prioritize their AI products based on their need to achieve strategic goals to personalize the customer experience, operational efficiency would have helped them ensure superior performance and their ability to deliver.

Business Strategy	AI Strategy	Business Goals	AI Initiatives			
			Q1	Q2	Q3	Q4
Increase customer loyalty and revenue	Improving Customer Retention	• Increase customer retention rate by 20% in the next 12 months. • Increase revenue by 15% in the next 12 months. • Improve customer satisfaction by 10% in the next 12 months.	Develop personalized recommendation engine			
			Implement a chatbot			
			Analyze customer behavior data to identify patterns and offer promotions			
Increase efficiency and reduce operational costs	Automating Manual Processes	• Reduce production time by 20% in the next 12 months. • Decrease production costs by 10% in the next 12 months. • Improve product quality by 15% in the next 12 months.	Develop predictive maintenance models to reduce machine downtime.			
			Implement computer vision systems to automate quality control and defect detection.			
			Use machine learning algorithms to optimize production schedules and reduce waste.			

FIGURE 6.4: Examples of business strategy, AI strategy, business goals, and AI initiatives

Strategy and Execution Across Phases

Figures 6.5 and 6.6 are representations of how you might phase your deliverables for strategy, portfolio, data, modeling tasks, and managing innovation. Feel free to customize this based on your organization's needs and best practices. Note that this can be waterfall or agile, although an agile approach is recommended.

HANDS-ON STRATEGIC PLANNING AND PROJECT MANAGEMENT EXERCISE TO LEVERAGE ORGANIZATIONAL CAPABILITIES

Scenario: Assume you are part of an AI team trying to improve supply chain operations using AI.

Goal: Leveraging your company's organizational nontechnical capabilities in strategy, portfolio, data, modeling, and innovation.

Step 1: Define your AI strategy.

Step 2: Manage your AI portfolio.

Step 3: Encourage innovation.

Step 4: Manage your AI product lifecycle.

Step 5: Develop your strategic partnerships.

Deliverables:

Develop the following:

➤ AI strategy document with the business goals

➤ Portfolio analysis and AI portfolio roadmap

➤ Innovation management charter and roadmap with success metrics

➤ AI product strategy and roadmap along with product backlog

➤ List of potential AI partners and partner agreements

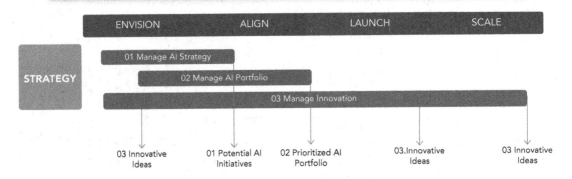

FIGURE 6.5: AI strategy: phases and capabilities

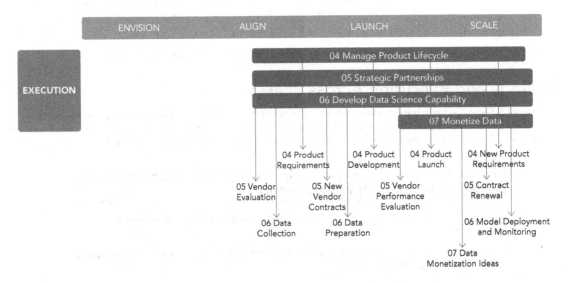

FIGURE 6.6: AI execution: phases and capabilities

WORKBOOK TEMPLATE: *BUSINESS CASE AND AI STRATEGY*

Download the "Business Case and AI Strategy" template from the download section of the book (www.wiley .com/go/EnterpriseAIintheCloud). Use this template to develop an AI strategy for your company. This template offers a business-centric view of planning an AI initiative, focusing on financial forecasts, stakeholder engagement, and alignment with strategic business objectives. Feel free to adapt it to your organization's specific needs.

SUMMARY

This chapter delved into the task of translating AI ideas into actionable and impactful AI strategies. This chapter was a step-by-step guide to craft a compelling AI strategy and a prioritized portfolio.

You also learned how to chart out a comprehensive AI strategy that provides direction and focus for your future AI endeavors. This chapter serves as the bridge between your overarching AI strategy and execution. In the next chapter, let's discuss the critical components to accelerate AI adoption in your company.

REVIEW QUESTIONS

These review questions are included at the end of each chapter to help you test your understanding of the information. You'll find the answers in the following section.

1. The ability to bring together resources to achieve a business outcome is called what?
   A. Innovation
   B. Achievement
   C. Capability
   D. Transformation
2. What is the first step in developing an AI strategy?
   A. Identify your business goals.
   B. Assess your current AI capabilities.
   C. Develop a roadmap for AI adoption.
   D. Identify potential use cases.
3. What is the purpose of managing your portfolio in the context of an AI strategy?
   A. To ensure all projects have the same priority
   B. To get a holistic picture of all the products and services to meet customer needs
   C. To prioritize products and services based on their cost
   D. To focus primarily on customer experience
4. What is the key to leveraging organizational capabilities for competitive advantage in AI projects?
   A. Choosing the latest machine learning models and algorithms
   B. Increasing the technical skills of your team
   C. Focusing on nontechnical aspects such as business, governance, and people
   D. Investing in the most expensive AI technologies

ANSWER KEY

1.	C		3.	B
2.	A		4.	C

7

Managing Strategic Change

Change is the only constant in life, but with strategic management, we navigate its tides.
—Inspired by Heraclitus

If you are an executive, team leader, change leader, or someone driving strategic change in your organization, this chapter is for you. The world of AI, in particular generative AI, is fast-moving, and being able to manage change is not merely a nice thing to have but a must. While earlier chapters focused on understanding the promise of AI, this chapter delves into how to strategically manage and accelerate that change (see Figure 7.1).

FIGURE 7.1: STRATEGIZE AND PREPARE: Manage strategic change

This chapter guides you through a three-phase approach to accelerate AI adoption, from developing an AI acceleration charter to ensuring leadership alignment and creating a change acceleration strategy. I also tie these steps to tangible deliverables that will serve as evidence of your progress. And also note that the steps outlined here apply to both traditional AI and generative AI implementations.

Whether you are trying to reposition a team or redefine an entire company, this chapter provides you with the tools needed to drive strategic change. Remember that though every organization's AI journey is unique, the change management principles are universal.

ACCELERATING YOUR AI ADOPTION WITH STRATEGIC CHANGE MANAGEMENT

Change acceleration is about accelerating the adoption of innovative technology by addressing concerns that help you stay ahead of the competition and establish yourself as an industry leader. The fact is, despite implementing all the measures outlined here, you may still find that the employees are not willing to adopt AI at the speed at which you want them to. That's why you need the change acceleration program discussed here.

The next section reviews the change acceleration toolkit shown in Figure 7.2. It brings all the previous people's capabilities together into a cohesive plan.

FIGURE 7.2: AI change acceleration strategy: phases and capabilities

Phase 1: Develop an AI Acceleration Charter and Governance Mechanisms for Your AI Initiative

The AI acceleration toolkit consists of assembling the team, aligning the leaders, and envisioning the future. The AI acceleration charter is a vital tool that helps you assemble the team. It documents the goals, objectives, and metrics for your AI initiative (see Figure 7.3). Let's dive into the details.

FIGURE 7.3: Develop AI acceleration charter and governance mechanisms

Develop an AI Acceleration Charter

Your organization needs an AI acceleration charter that identifies the dependencies and stakeholders involved in the AI initiative. It focuses on increasing speed, maximizing adoption, and reducing risks. Your stakeholders can be the IT team, the business team, the data science team, and the legal team. The charter includes a review process, stakeholder responsibilities, and metrics to measure AI activities. You can use it to gather input from various stakeholders and establish initial relationships to achieve business outcomes.

Analyze Value Drivers: For Strategic Planning and Performance Measurement

Value driver analysis helps you identify those factors that drive value, such as operational efficiency, cost reduction, and revenue generation. You can use these drivers to assess the strategic importance of the initiatives for planning and enable your managers to focus their activities on what is important.

Establish Governance for the AI Initiative

You should establish a governance mechanism for your AI initiative to set up the right processes for decision-making, escalations, issue management, assigning ownership, and accountability. This provides clarity and ensures alignment between the workstreams and the overall organizational governance. It ensures alignment between the leadership, stakeholders, working teams, and change management teams. You must ensure alignment between parties and governance by establishing a cadence of meetings and scrum ceremonies that synchronize with the program-level cadence and reporting mechanisms.

> **BEST PRACTICE TIP** *Develop an AI charter, analyze value drivers, establish governance, build an AI team, and then define the goals, vision, metrics, and budget to implement AI successfully.*

Build an Enterprise AI Acceleration Team for Enterprise AI

You should set up an AI change acceleration team in addition to a center of excellence team who together are responsible for handling change management issues, organizational changes, role changes, communication strategies, training requirements, and securing executive sponsorship. They help mitigate the risks of AI implementation from concerns such as poor communication, lack of cross-functional collaboration, and AI implementation-related challenges such as data handling and model building, trust, and ethics.

Establish AI Initiative Goals

You need to collaborate with various stakeholders to establish clearly defined goals so that you can monitor the progress of this initiative and align your activities accordingly. You can use these goals to align the people, process, and technology to achieve outcomes such as improving customer experience and driving sales.

Define Your Future-State AI Vision

You should define your future-state vision that can be achieved through AI technology and ensure it aligns with your organization's goals, structure, processes, culture, and technology. It will help guide your change acceleration program to transform your company's processes, people, and technology. Leverage analysis techniques such as decision analysis, process analysis, and business capability analysis. Remember that the future-state model will evolve as new developments happen in the AI space.

Define Change Acceleration Metrics to Measure the Success of AI Adoption

You can then define change acceleration metrics to measure the success of how people are adapting to the recent changes in the organization resulting from the introduction of AI initiatives. You should define these early in the project lifecycle and track them throughout the course of the initiative. You can use this to track where the organization is struggling to cope with the changes and make the necessary changes to the plan. Examples of change acceleration metrics are user adoption rate, employee satisfaction, time to proficiency, productivity, and ROI.

Estimate the Budget for AI Activities

Develop a realistic and achievable budget for change management activities. You should include costs for the team resources, material development, development of skills and knowledge, travel, events, software licensing costs, hardware costs, and physical costs.

Phase 2: Ensure Leadership Alignment

Leaders play a vital role in the success of any AI initiative. It is therefore important to get their alignment at the onset of the initiative. Leaders set the vision, motivate employees, manage stakeholders, and guide the organization.

Ensure Leadership Alignment to Lead by Example, Take Risks, and Motivate Employees

You must secure leadership alignment at the beginning of the AI initiative. It is a particularly crucial factor to the success of the AI transformation effort and impacts the ability to transition to the future state. It involves stakeholder management, leadership support, and ensuring participation in stakeholder updates.

Your leadership needs to communicate your company's AI vision and strategy to the employees and motivate them about this AI initiative. Figures 7.4 and 7.5 show the objectives, steps, and tasks mapped to the phases. Feel free to customize these to your company's needs.

Assess Stakeholders to Transform Your Workplace with Career Development and Performance Alignment

Stakeholder assessment is the first step in the process of managing stakeholders, and it involves understanding their needs, their concerns, and their predisposition to the AI initiative. Understanding these concerns helps you manage their reactions as you proceed throughout the initiative. You should conduct this assessment in the initial stages of the initiative and continuously review this throughout the AI initiative.

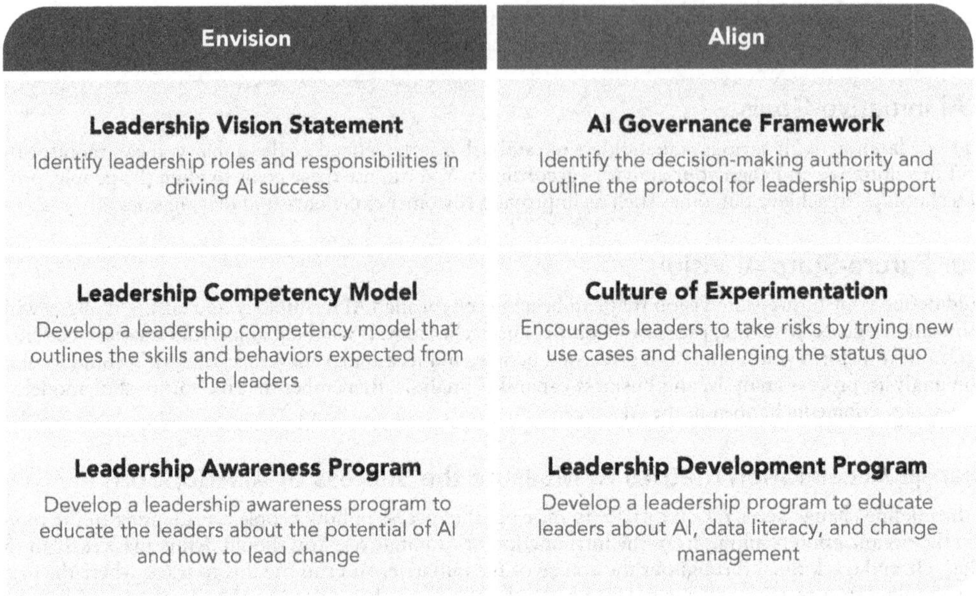

Envision	Align
Leadership Vision Statement Identify leadership roles and responsibilities in driving AI success	**AI Governance Framework** Identify the decision-making authority and outline the protocol for leadership support
Leadership Competency Model Develop a leadership competency model that outlines the skills and behaviors expected from the leaders	**Culture of Experimentation** Encourages leaders to take risks by trying new use cases and challenging the status quo
Leadership Awareness Program Develop a leadership awareness program to educate the leaders about the potential of AI and how to lead change	**Leadership Development Program** Develop a leadership program to educate leaders about AI, data literacy, and change management

FIGURE 7.4: Transform your leadership: Envision and Align phases

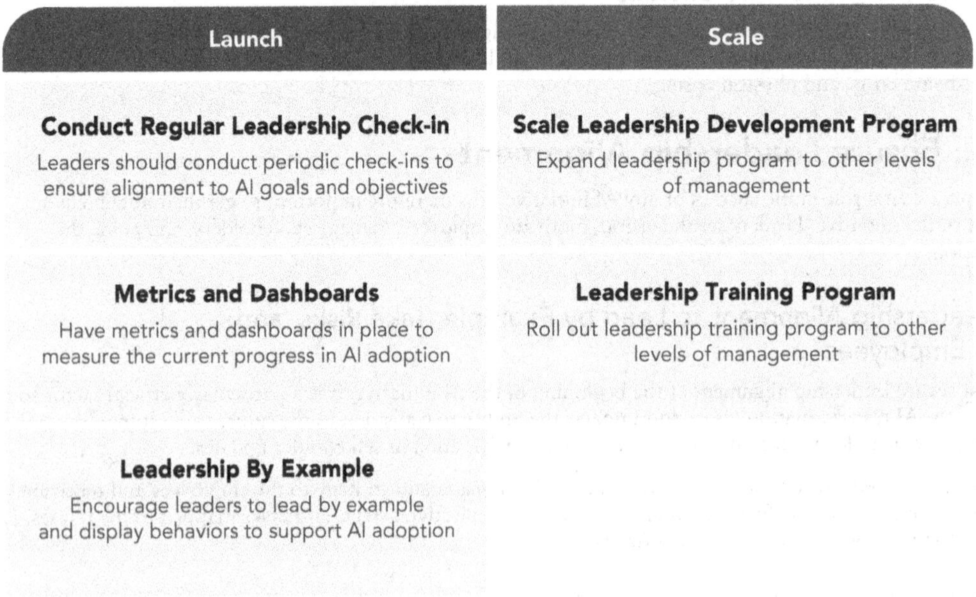

Launch	Scale
Conduct Regular Leadership Check-in Leaders should conduct periodic check-ins to ensure alignment to AI goals and objectives	**Scale Leadership Development Program** Expand leadership program to other levels of management
Metrics and Dashboards Have metrics and dashboards in place to measure the current progress in AI adoption	**Leadership Training Program** Roll out leadership training program to other levels of management
Leadership By Example Encourage leaders to lead by example and display behaviors to support AI adoption	

FIGURE 7.5: Transform your leadership: Launch and Scale phases

Transforming your workplace involves assessing your current capabilities in your workforce and producing strategies to fill the gaps. Figure 7.6 shows the steps and deliverables.

Envision	Align	Launch	Scale
CAREER DEVELOPMENT PLAN Create a career development path for employees involved in AI roles to facilitate their career progression	**ROLE TRANSITION PLAN** Develop a change management plan that outlines how employees will transition into the new role comfortably **PERFORMANCE MANAGEMENT SYSTEM** Develop a performance management system that aligns with the new roles that arise in an AI implementation **SKILLS GAP ASSESSMENT** Conduct a skills gap analysis that outlines the gaps in skill sets and areas where upskilling is required	**IMPLEMENT CAREER DEVELOPMENT PLAN** In the launch phase, you should implement the change management plan and performance management system that was decided in the align phase **TALENT PROGRAM** Develop a talent program that includes hiring third-party consultant, vendors, as well as in-house training program	**REVIEW CHANGE MANAGEMENT AND PERFORMANCE MANAGEMENT PLAN** During the scale phase, you will refine the change management plan and the performance management system as new developments happen in AI **BRAND COMMUNICATION STRATEGY** Develop brand communication strategy and promote your brand

ACTIVITIES

FIGURE 7.6: Transform your workspace: tasks and deliverables

IBM CASE STUDY: IBM'S NEW COLLAR JOB INITIATIVE: A MODEL FOR WORKFORCE TRANSFORMATION

IBM's new collar job initiative is a notable example of workforce transformation. IBM, with this program, is trying to fill the skills and experience gap in the technology space by helping those who cannot get a traditional four-year degree to get into these high-tech jobs. With the advent of modern technologies such as AI, ML, and advanced analytics, there is a need for people who can maintain and operate these systems. This does not require a four-year degree; a nontraditional vocational program suffices. IBM created a variety of training and education initiatives, such as online courses, apprenticeships, and internship programs.

Since its launch in 2017, this has found tremendous success. According to IBM, in 2018, about 50 percent of their new employees came from those who had nontraditional education, and most of them came from this new collar initiative. More importantly, it has helped IBM diversify its workforce by including people from all kinds of educational backgrounds.

Overall, this has been a new trend in the industry, and this is something that you need to consider as you look for ways to augment your workforce.

Conduct a Change Impact Assessment

Conduct a change impact assessment to assess how the AI initiative will impact various stakeholders and produce a training, communication, and change management plan. This helps identify the stakeholders impacted and decide on the channels of communication your team should use, along with the necessary governance structures, decision points, and policy reviews. It helps you decide how and when the stakeholders will be involved and produce specific plans to address those impacts.

Figure 7.7 sums up your journey to get buy-in from the leadership and stakeholders to create a case for change.

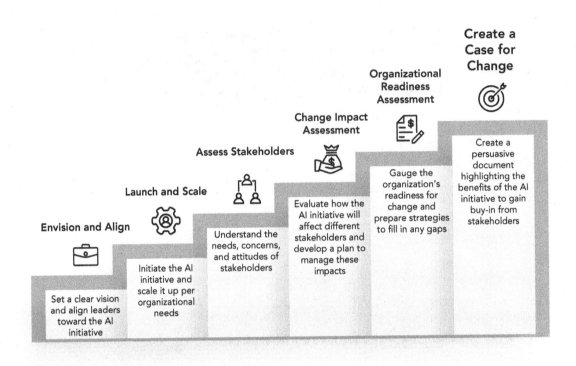

FIGURE 7.7: Ensuring leadership alignment for AI, including generative AI initiatives

Conduct Organizational Readiness Assessment

Conducting an organizational readiness assessment will help you understand the organization's willingness, desire, and ability to cope with change and put measures in place to address any gaps, such as skills training, communication, sponsorship, and changes to the change acceleration.

Create a Case for Change

The case for change is a document that outlines the benefits that the organization will gain through this AI initiative. You should create it after the stakeholder assessment and use it in various communications to get buy-in from the employees. It should be clear, concise, and persuasive to the audience and be documented with data.

Phase 3: Create a Change Acceleration Strategy

The change acceleration strategy is a plan that includes the different steps the organization must take to manage changes resulting from the AI initiative. There should be a built-in collaboration with different stakeholders from HR, business functions, third-party vendors, leadership, sponsors, and employees. You should create this at the beginning of the initiative and update it continuously. You should ensure minimum disruption and maximum adoption. This helps ensure stakeholder alignment, cultural transformation, and business continuity.

Create a Communication Strategy and a Plan

A communication strategy and plan is a document that outlines different stakeholders to be communicated, the channels to communicate, and the frequency with which to communicate. It should include a communication, training, and risk management plan.

> **BEST PRACTICE TIP** *Create a comprehensive change acceleration strategy, communication plan, and training plan to ensure successful AI implementation by keeping stakeholders informed.*

Create an Engagement Strategy and a Plan

You should create this engagement strategy and plan after creating the change acceleration strategy and the communication strategy. It helps engage with the stakeholders throughout this initiative when the situation demands. It helps you manage the pace at which the different stakeholder groups must go through.

Create a Training Strategy and a Plan to Develop AI Skills

The training strategy and plan outline different training programs the employees will have to take as part of the AI initiative. It should include a learning needs assessment, a training curriculum, and a training delivery plan.

The success of your AI program directly depends on the skills and capabilities of your employees in these leading-edge technologies. Figure 7.8 shows the steps you can take to build the skills of your employees.

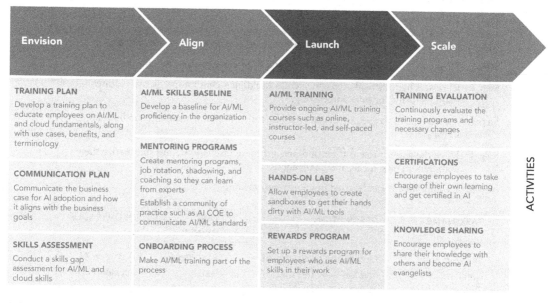

FIGURE 7.8: AI strategy: phases and capabilities

When you implement these recommendations effectively, you will see a significant increase in the number of employees using AI/ML and generative AI in their work, leading to increased efficiency, improved customer satisfaction, and revenue. You will notice that your culture has become innovative and agile, with employees taking ownership of their learning and adopting AI in their workplace. All this will eventually help you become competitive in a highly competitive landscape and even position you as an industry leader.

Create a Risk Management Strategy and a Plan

This communication strategy and plan are essential to ensure that the risks associated with your initiative are carefully identified, evaluated, and mitigated. The plan helps you identify the action items to mitigate the risks and to assign ownership to tasks to ensure they complete the deliverables on time, with quality and within the planned cost.

Create a Sponsor Roadmap

A sponsor roadmap is a document that outlines how to engage and support the sponsors throughout the AI initiative. It holds sponsors accountable to provide leadership support and helps them maintain consistency in their messaging to achieve business outcomes.

Create an AI Sustainability Plan

You should create a sustainability plan to ensure that everyone is adopting AI continuously, even after you have completed the initial AI initiative. The plan will continue to evolve as the organizational structure and recent technology developments in the AI space evolve. You will typically create it once the team has gained sufficient experience with AI transformation.

HANDS-ON CHANGE ACCELERATION WORKSHOP

This is a type of hands-on workshop focused on promoting discussions and collaboration. It enables critical thinking and promotes the sharing of different real-world perspectives among the participants.

Goal: In this exercise, you explore different change acceleration strategies such as leadership alignment, workforce transformation, and risk management. The goal is to develop a concrete AI acceleration charter, align leadership, and create a change acceleration strategy.

Step 1: Divide the team into groups representing different functions in your company.

Step 2: Choose a hypothetical scenario such as building a chatbot, predictive maintenance in manufacturing, or sales forecasting.

Step 3: Ask the teams to execute the steps in the following table using the methodology in the book.

Step 4: Have the teams present their findings, promote discussions, and summarize the common themes, ideas, and challenges.

Step 5: Explore how it can be used in your organization.

TASK NAME	DESCRIPTION	TASK OWNER	DELIVERABLE
Develop an AI acceleration charter	Outline the goals, principles, and key activities that will define your AI initiative.	AI strategy lead	A written AI acceleration charter
Ensure leadership alignment	Create a presentation or document that clearly conveys the importance of AI to your organization and how it aligns with current business objectives.	Executive sponsor	A presentation or document and feedback

continues

continued

TASK NAME	DESCRIPTION	TASK OWNER	DELIVERABLE
Create a change acceleration strategy	Develop a detailed strategy that outlines how your organization will accelerate the adoption of AI, including key milestones, potential challenges, solutions, and a timeline.	Change management team	A change acceleration strategy document
Implement role-playing	Engage in a role-playing exercise where participants take on different organizational roles and work through implementing the AI acceleration strategy.	Training and development	Insights and lessons learned

WORKBOOK TEMPLATE: *STRATEGIC CHANGE MANAGEMENT PLAN*

Download the "Strategic Change Management Plan" template from the download section of the book (www
.wiley.com/go/EnterpriseAIintheCloud). The strategic change management plan guides your organization through the important phases of implementing an AI initiative, with an emphasis on managing change.

SUMMARY

This chapter discussed the critical components of accelerating AI adoption in your company. By building the AI
acceleration charter, achieving leadership alignment, and developing a systematic AI acceleration strategy, you can
galvanize your employees around AI to achieve business outcomes.

You learned that you could achieve organizational transformation by adopting a systematic, programmatic
approach to business transformation and people empowerment.

In the next chapter, let's discuss finding the right AI/ML use cases for your company.

REVIEW QUESTIONS

These review questions are included at the end of each chapter to help you test your understanding of the information. You'll find the answers in the following section.

1. Which of the following is not included in Phase 1 of the change acceleration program?
   A. Analyze value drivers
   B. Establish governance for the AI initiative
   C. Develop an AI acceleration charter
   D. Ensure leadership alignment

2. What is a crucial step in securing leadership alignment at the beginning of an AI initiative?
   A. Conducting a change impact assessment immediately
   B. Ignoring stakeholder concerns
   C. Communicating the company's AI vision and strategy to the employees
   D. Excluding leadership from stakeholder updates

3. Which of the following is not a step in creating a change acceleration strategy for an AI initiative?
   A. Conducting a change impact assessment
   B. Creating a communication strategy and plan
   C. Creating an engagement strategy and plan
   D. Developing AI skills for employees

4. Which of the following components is not involved in ensuring proper organizational alignment for AI adoption?
   A. Aligning business strategies with technology strategies
   B. Aligning business strategy with organizational structure
   C. Implementing an AI system without considering cultural alignment
   D. Prioritizing AI projects appropriately

ANSWER KEY

1. D
2. C
3. D
4. C

PART III
Planning and Launching a Pilot Project

This part covers all the challenges and tasks centered on planning and launching a pilot project, including identifying use cases for your project, evaluating appropriate platforms and services, and launching the actual project.

8

Identifying Use Cases for Your AI/ML Project

The only way to do great work is to love what you do.

—*Steve Jobs*

In the next few chapters, let's discuss planning and launching a pilot (see Figure 8.1). This chapter focuses on identifying the right use cases. Having addressed challenges, approached design responsibly, and charted the AI strategy and vision, it is time to identify the right use case for your AI/ML project.

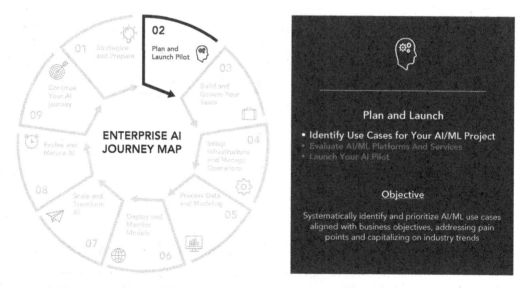

FIGURE 8.1: PLAN AND LAUNCH: Identify Use Cases for Your AI/ML & Gen AI Project

Whether you are a business executive looking to solve business problems or a developer trying to develop state-of-the-art applications, this chapter is for you. Selecting the right use case is more than just a decision—it's the compass that sets your AI journey in the right direction. It will not only help your team solve the business problem by choosing the suitable set of technologies, but it will also lead to increased operational efficiency, reduced costs, and even new business opportunities for a competitive edge.

You also learn to prioritize your use cases, which will help you focus all your energies on the most pressing problems and maximize business impact. It's your path to positive stakeholder results and a higher probability of success. Let's get started.

> **TIP** *Prioritize your use cases that have the highest business impact to reduce costs, increase efficiency, and gain a competitive advantage.*

THE USE CASE IDENTIFICATION PROCESS FLOW

Figure 8.2 shows a process flow you can use to identify use cases for your company. It starts with identifying the business problems and pain points that you want to solve.

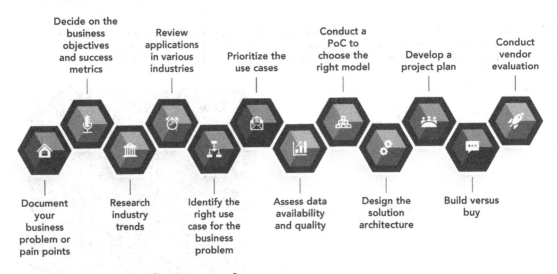

FIGURE 8.2: Use case identification process flow

Educate Everyone as to How AI/ML Can Solve Business Problems

Defining the business problem is one of the first steps in your use case identification process. To do that, the implementation team should understand the various business problems that need to be solved. A significant part of this chapter is all about that, and I cover that in greater detail in the following few sections.

Consider the business problems your company is facing as it relates to customer service, fraud detection, risk assessments and predictions, supply chain optimization, predictive maintenance, quality control, marketing, and product development. All of these are candidates for AI/ML.

Remember that machine learning helps you identify patterns in your dataset to predict outcomes. This feature/capability can be used to improve existing processes while also enabling new opportunities. Processes that are well suited to AI/ML are those

➤ Where decisions are based on data

➤ Where decisions happen repeatedly, either thousands or millions of times

➤ That use software to automate

➤ That are slow

Define Your Business Objectives

As shown in Figure 8.3, you should start by identifying the business objectives you want to aim for based on the business problem you are trying to solve. Examples of business objectives are increasing customer satisfaction, revenue, efficiency, reducing costs, and enhancing productivity. Examples of pain points include customer churn, high number of claims/returns, equipment failures, managing inventory, and so on.

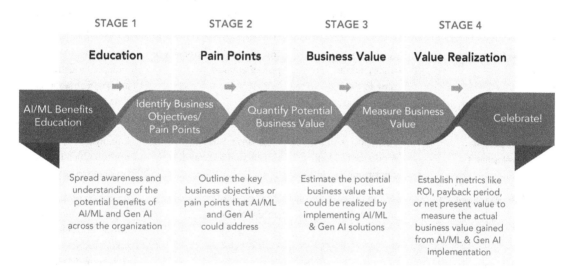

STAGE 1	STAGE 2	STAGE 3	STAGE 4
Education	**Pain Points**	**Business Value**	**Value Realization**
AI/ML Benefits Education	Identify Business Objectives/ Pain Points	Quantify Potential Business Value	Measure Business Value	Celebrate!
Spread awareness and understanding of the potential benefits of AI/ML and Gen AI across the organization	Outline the key business objectives or pain points that AI/ML and Gen AI could address	Estimate the potential business value that could be realized by implementing AI/ML & Gen AI solutions	Establish metrics like ROI, payback period, or net present value to measure the actual business value gained from AI/ML & Gen AI implementation	

FIGURE 8.3: Defining business objectives for your AI initiative

> **TIP** *Start by educating everyone about the benefits of AI/ML and Gen AI. Define the business objectives and quantify the potential business value to measure success.*

Based on these business objectives/pain points, you can quantify the business value that can be realized upon completion of your use case. Some examples of business value are cost savings, revenue growth, improved accuracy, automation, better customer experience, and faster decision-making. You should be able to measure the business value using ROI, payback period, or net present value.

Identify the Pain Points

The next step is identifying the pain points that prevent you from achieving your business objectives. Here are some examples:

PAIN POINT CATEGORY	DESCRIPTION	BENEFIT OF ADDRESSING WITH AI	EXAMPLE
Inefficient or slow processes	You can automate and optimize specific processes in the company.	Improves efficiency by reducing the overall time and effort to complete tasks.	A logistics company optimizing its supply chain routes and delivery schedules.
Customer experience improvement	Using customer data to personalize recommendations.	Helps increase customer engagement, satisfaction, and loyalty.	It's a common use case to personalize marketing campaigns and targeting ads.
Complex data analysis	Automating analysis of large data datasets.	Provides insights to support decision-making.	A financial services company that analyzes market data to make investment decisions.
Fraud detection	Analyzing transactional data to detect unusual patterns.	You can notify customers of potential fraud.	Many companies across multiple industries analyze transactional data to detect fraudulent activity.
New product development	Analyzing customer feedback to identify opportunities.	Increases customer satisfaction and sales.	Identifying opportunities for new product features.
Risk assessment	AI can assess risks in various areas.	Proactively manage potential risks.	Assessing risks proactively such as customer default on a loan, product recall risks, or natural disaster risks.

Pain points can be manual processes, redundant processes, complex processes, data quality issues, and other inefficiencies in your process.

Start with Root-Cause Analysis

Once you have a good idea of your pain points, you can start the root-cause analysis (RCA) to get to the origin of the problem. Knowing the root cause will help you shortlist the proper use case. For example, suppose you find out that customer satisfaction could be better. In that case, your root-cause analysis might point you to poor website design, lack of personalization, slow speed (response times), customer support issues, and so on.

> **TIP** *Identify the pain points that hinder your business, and conduct root-cause analysis to shortlist your use cases.*

Identify the Success Metrics

Once you have identified the root cause, you can choose the proper success criteria. For example, in the previous scenario, your success criteria could be increasing the speed/response time of your website, adding personalization, or improving your website design. You then define your success metrics around customer satisfaction, increased revenue, or reduction in manual effort.

Success metrics help you measure your AI solution's effectiveness and ensure it aligns with your business objective. See Figure 8.4 for some examples of success metrics, such as the following:

➤ **Cost savings:** Cost savings is the apparent metric you will choose when automating business processes, eliminating errors, or improving process efficiency. For example, a company trying to optimize its supply chain operations could reduce inventory costs and shipping times.

➤ **Revenue growth:** This is used when you are improving the customer experience, which results in increased sales and revenue.

➤ **Risk reduction:** This metric is used for use cases such as fraud detection, cybersecurity, and compliance.

➤ **Customer satisfaction:** This metric can be used in use cases where you can provide better customer service, resolve customer issues quicker, and provide personalized customer experiences. For example, a retail company can use AI to provide chatbots that can answer questions 24/7.

➤ **Employee productivity:** AI can automate repetitive employee tasks, reduce errors, and provide real-time insights. For example, AI can be used to generate leads, thus allowing employees to focus on closing deals.

FIGURE 8.4: Define success metrics for your AI initiative

> **TIP** *Define success metrics that align with your business objectives and use cases to measure the effectiveness of your AI solution.*

Explore the Latest Industry Trends

You also need to assess market trends as part of your use case identification process. I'll talk about the latest AI developments in later sections of this chapter. Consider attending other conferences and discussing with other industry experts to learn more about the latest developments in AI, which is a very fast-moving space. Knowing the latest trends in the AI space will help you understand the status of the industry and assess where it is going and therefore decide your use cases accordingly. For example, suppose you're working in the manufacturing industry. In that case, you find out that supply chain optimization is prevalent. Therefore, you can also adopt supply chain optimization use cases, such as using predictive analysis to optimize your inventory management.

It can also give you awareness of the latest potential roadblocks that other companies face so you can also be prepared. For example, you may find that companies are facing issues with data privacy and regulations. It can help you be proactive and manage your own risks accordingly.

Review AI Applications in Various Industries

You should also review the applications of AI in other industries. By reviewing these applications, you can learn from the latest AI industry trends, other industry applications, and other best practices.

ACTION	PURPOSE	EXAMPLE	RESOURCES
Review AI applications	Understanding the breadth of AI applications across industries to gain insights on how AI is used	Understand how AI is applied in healthcare, finance, retail, etc.	Industry reports, case studies
Research best practices	Gaining insights on other successful AI strategies and methodologies by investigating other best practices	Understand why certain strategies are adopted in specific industries	Industry forums, online communities, Kaggle.com, AI/ML forums
Learn from pitfalls	Preempting and preparing for potential challenges by understanding pitfalls faced by others	Learn about risk factors from healthcare industry applications	Case studies, industry reports

> **TIP** *Look to AI industry trends and other AI applications across other industries to learn from best practices and avoid potential pitfalls.*

HAND-ON EXERCISE 1: STRATEGIC AI/ML USE CASE IDENTIFICATION

This is a strategic planning exercise that involves a combination of research, brainstorming, analysis, and strategic decision-making thus making it a valuable strategic planning exercise.

Goal: The goal of this exercise is to understand your company's business objectives, pain points, and suitable use cases to develop an AI/ML application to address those pain points.

TASK	INSTRUCTIONS	DELIVERABLES	EXAMPLES
Form Groups Break into teams to collaborate.	Get into groups of three to four people.	Groups formed	Team 1, Team 2, Team 3.
Educate Everyone The team understands the potential of AI/ML in solving business problems.	Discuss different business problems related to customer service, risk assessment, supply chain optimization, etc.	A list of potential business problems that can be addressed by AI/ML	Predicting customer churn, automating responses to common customer queries, detecting fraudulent transactions, etc.
Define Business Objectives Identify the business objectives that your AI/ML project should aim for.	Spend 10 to 15 minutes to identify clear, quantifiable business objectives to aim for.	Clearly defined and quantifiable business objectives	Increase customer satisfaction score by 20 percent Reduce operating costs by 15 percent Increase revenue by 30 percent, etc.
Identify Pain Points Identify issues that are hindering you from achieving your business objectives.	Take 5 to 10 minutes to analyze your business processes and identify two to three pain points such as inefficient processes, poor customer experience, complex data analysis issues, etc.	A list of identified pain points in your business processes	Pain points like high customer churn rate, slow response times to customer queries, high error rate in transaction processing, etc.
Conduct Root-cause analysis Determine the root cause of your identified business problems.	Conduct a thorough analysis to understand the underlying issues causing the identified business problems.	Detailed report on the root causes of the identified business problems	If customer churn rate is high, the root cause could be poor customer service, lack of personalized customer experience, etc.

continues

continued

TASK	INSTRUCTIONS	DELIVERABLES	EXAMPLES
Identify Success Metrics Define metrics that can measure the success of your AI/ML project.	Identify three to five success metrics that align with your business objectives and the chosen use case, like cost savings, revenue growth, risk reduction, customer satisfaction, etc.	Clearly defined success metrics for your AI/ML project	Success metrics could be "Reduce customer churn rate by 10 percent" "Increase customer satisfaction score by 20 percent" "Increase revenue by 30 percent," etc.
Explore Latest Industry Trends Stay updated with the latest trends in the AI industry.	Attend conferences, engage in discussions with industry experts, and read up on the latest developments in AI.	Knowledge of the latest trends in the AI industry	Attending AI/ML conferences like NeurIPS, ICML, ACL, etc., and reading AI/ML research papers and articles.
Review AI Applications in Various Industries Learn from the AI implementations in other industries.	Review how other industries are leveraging AI and learn from their best practices and pitfalls.	Insights documented from AI applications in other industries	Reviewing how healthcare industry is using AI for disease diagnosis, how finance industry is using AI for fraud detection, etc.
Ideate Use Cases Come up with AI/ML and Gen AI solutions.	Spend five minutes ideating use cases per pain point.	List of use cases	Predictive maintenance, personalized recommendations.
Choose One Use Case Select one use case to focus on.	As a team, choose one use case to move forward with.	One use case selected	Predictive maintenance.
Map Use Case to Business Problem Choose a suitable use case that can address your business problem.	Refer to the "Use Cases to Choose From" section and select a use case that aligns with your business problem.	Chosen use case that aligns with your business problem	Choosing a use case like "Predictive Maintenance" if your business problem is high equipment downtime.

continued

TASK	INSTRUCTIONS	DELIVERABLES	EXAMPLES
Prepare Presentation Summarize use case findings.	Prepare a five-minute presentation on use case.	Presentation slides	
Present Use Cases Share use cases with other teams.	Take turns presenting use cases.	Use case presentations	Team 1 presents predictive maintenance use case, Team 2 presents personalized recommendations, and so on.

Map the Use Case to the Business Problem

Refer to the later section "Use Cases to Choose From" to choose your list of use cases.

PRIORITIZING YOUR USE CASES

The next step is to prioritize your list of use cases. For this, you must develop a set of impact and feasibility criteria. The following sections outline these steps.

Define the Impact Criteria

Clearly define the criteria for impact by discussing with your stakeholders. Some of these could be as follows:

➤ Revenue impact

➤ Cost impact

➤ Efficiency impact

➤ Customer satisfaction

Define the Feasibility Criteria

To evaluate your feasibility, consider factors such as these:

➤ Complexity of required technology

➤ Cost

➤ Availability of skill sets

➤ Availability of data

➤ Platform readiness

➤ Time to implement

➤ Risks, if any

As part of your feasibility analysis, you need to consult various stakeholders across your organization from business and technology, to identify their concerns and address them appropriately, as well as get buy-in.

Assess the Impact

Using the impact criteria, you can do a cost-benefit analysis or estimate the potential ROI.

Assess the Feasibility

Using the feasibility criteria, you can then evaluate the feasibility of the use cases.

Prioritize the Use Cases

Once you have assessed the impact and the feasibility, you can then create a matrix using these two criteria to prioritize the use cases, as shown in Figure 8.5.

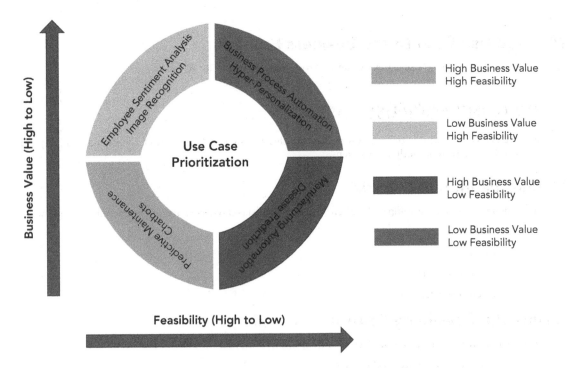

FIGURE 8.5: Business value and feasibility analysis to prioritize use cases

As shown in Figure 8.5, you can classify the use cases based on the business value and feasibility. Your business value criteria can include factors such as cost reduction, revenue growth, and customer satisfaction, and feasibility criteria can include factors such as technical feasibility and organizational readiness.

➤ **High business value and high feasibility use cases:** Your priority use cases will be those that deliver high business value and are easier to implement. Predictive maintenance in manufacturing can prevent equipment downtime and extend the life of machinery. The business value is very high, and with the necessary sensor data and appropriate ML models, it is often easier to implement. Similarly, chatbots are easier to implement and can have a significant impact on customer service and efficiency.

➤ **High business value and low feasibility use cases:** Under this category fall use cases such as predicting diseases and full automation of manufacturing processes. While these use cases can save millions of lives and save costs, they can be challenging to implement due to technology limitations.

➤ **Low business value and high feasibility use cases:** Use cases such as employee sentiment analysis to analyze employee feedback may be easier to implement but may have little impact on the business. Similarly, employing AI to tag images automatically may be easy to implement but have a low business impact.

➤ **Low business value and low feasibility use cases:** Hyper-personalization of advertisements may appear very attractive, but the cost of implementing it may make it highly prohibitive due to data privacy and technical requirements. Similarly, complete automation of all business processes may appear very attractive but may be of limited value for a small business and technically and financially prohibitive.

Review and Refine the Criteria

You can then review the criteria used for assessing your impact and feasibility and continue to refine it along with the ranking criteria, working with your stakeholders to finalize your priority of use cases.

> **TIP** *Prioritize your use cases based on their potential impact and feasibility.*

Choose the Right Model

Once you have prioritized your use cases, the next step is to identify the right model for your use case. You have to continue this process iteratively until you reach a point where you've finalized your success criteria, feasibility prioritization, and so on.

To do this, you must consult with many organizational stakeholders to define your use case concept. An essential part of choosing a use case is being able to justify the value of implementing it.

HANDS-ON USE CASE: PRIORITIZATION WORKSHOP

This is a use case prioritization workshop that involves collaborating with various stakeholders to compare different use cases and arrive at a decision.

DESCRIPTION	HANDS-ON TASK	DELIVERABLES	EXAMPLE
Form Groups if Needed Break into teams to collaborate.	Get into groups of three to four people	Groups formed	Team 1, Team 2, Team 3

continues

continued

DESCRIPTION	HANDS-ON TASK	DELIVERABLES	EXAMPLE
Brainstorm use cases. Generate potential use case ideas.	In groups, come up with two to three use case ideas	List of two to three use case ideas	
Define impact criteria. Brainstorm the potential impacts of implementing the use case.	Discuss with stakeholders and define metrics like revenue impact, cost impact, efficiency impact, customer satisfaction, etc.	Clearly defined impact criteria	Improve customer satisfaction by 30 percent Reduce operating costs by 20 percent, etc.
Define Feasibility Criteria Identify the feasibility factors of implementing the use case.	Discuss with stakeholders and define feasibility factors like complexity of technology, cost, availability of skill sets, data availability, platform readiness, etc.	Clearly defined feasibility criteria	Implementation cost should not exceed $100,000 Should be able to be implemented within 6 months, etc.
Assess the Impact Evaluate the potential impact of the use case. Brainstorm factors like revenue, costs, efficiency.	Based on the defined impact criteria, carry out a cost-benefit analysis or estimate the potential ROI.	Detailed analysis of the potential impact	Potential revenue increase of $500,000 Estimated cost savings of $200,000, etc.
Assess the Feasibility Evaluate the feasibility of the use case. Brainstorm factors like technology, skills, data.	Based on the defined feasibility criteria, assess the feasibility of implementing the use case.	Detailed assessment of the feasibility	Implementation cost will be $80,000 Can be implemented within four months, etc.
Prioritize Use Cases Based on the impact and feasibility assessments, prioritize the use cases.	Create a matrix using the impact and feasibility criteria to rank the use cases.	Ranked list of use cases	Use case A: High impact, high feasibility Use case B: High impact, low feasibility, etc.

DESCRIPTION	HANDS-ON TASK	DELIVERABLES	EXAMPLE
Review and Refine Criteria Review the criteria used for assessing impact and feasibility and refine as necessary.	Consult with stakeholders to refine the ranking criteria and adjust the ranking of use cases as necessary.	Refined criteria and adjusted ranking of use cases	Updated impact criteria to include customer retention rate Updated ranking of use cases based on refined criteria, etc.
Choose the Right Model Identify the appropriate model for the use case.	Consult with data scientists or ML experts to choose the right model for the use case.	Chosen ML model for the use case	Chose a decision tree model for use case A Chose a convolutional neural network for use case B, etc.
Iterate Till Finalization Repeat the process until the use case, success criteria, feasibility, and prioritization are finalized.	Conduct multiple iterations of discussions with stakeholders, refining criteria and rankings, choosing models, etc.	Finalized use case, success criteria, feasibility assessment, prioritization, and chosen model	Finalized use case A with success criteria of increasing customer satisfaction by 30 percent, feasibility assessment showing implementation within four months, high-priority ranking, and decision tree model chosen, etc.
Present Priorities Share and discuss prioritized list.	Justify your prioritization.	Presentation of priorities	

USE CASES TO CHOOSE FROM

Listed in this section are close to 80 use cases to choose from across multiple industries and business processes. You can expect more use cases as the technology evolves.

AI Use Cases for DevOps

AI for DevOps leverages ML to innovate your DevOps process by solving security, defects management, resource allocation, and concurrency issues. Some examples include predictive analytics, defects management, continuous delivery, and resource management.

Success Stories: Microsoft implemented ML in DevOps to detect bugs, and Google used it for Chrome testing.

Tools: Amazon CodeGuru Reviewer for code quality, Amazon DevOps Guru for application performance and scalability, Azure DevOps, Azure Pipelines for CI/CD, Google Cloud Build for CI/CD.

> **TIP** *Use AI for DevOps to automate, optimize, and improve the DevOps process.*

AI for Healthcare and Life Sciences

Healthcare and life science organizations face physician burnout, complex health data, and rising healthcare costs. The benefits of AI in healthcare include personalized treatments, better disease diagnosis, and higher efficiency.

Some use cases include medical imaging, drug discovery, personalized treatments, forecast diseases, and clinical trials.

Success Stories: The University of San Francisco California used data analysis to identify sepsis early; IBM Watson Health identified cancers through medical image analysis; and startup Atomwise developed an AI tool to treat Ebola.

Tools: Amazon HealthLake, Amazon Transcribe Medical, Amazon Comprehend Medical, IBM Watson Health, Google Cloud Healthcare API, Microsoft Healthcare Bot.

> **TIP** *Ensure data privacy and compliance with regulations like HIPAA to build trust and safeguard patient information.*

AI Enabled Contact Center Use Cases

Traditional contact centers are helping automate and streamline processes as well as improve overall customer satisfaction. Some examples include virtual agents, speech analytics, predictive analytics, call routing, and customer churn.

Success Stories: HR Block and Capital One optimized costs with chatbots; Intuit's analytics enhanced support for 11,000 agents; and Wix's sentiment analytics boosted visibility from 12 to 100 percent.

Tools: Amazon Connect can be used for NLP, automated speech recognition, and machine learning, Google DialogFlow, IBM Watson Assistant.

> **BEST PRACTICE TIP** *AI should enhance customer experience, streamline processes, and complement rather than replace human agents to maintain a personal touch.*

Business Metrics Analysis

Machine learning can be used to analyze large amounts of business data to track business metrics to learn from the past, current, and planned data. Benefits include being able to analyze large volumes of data, more easily identify trends and patterns, forecast future performance, detect anomalies, determine root causes, and adapt to changing conditions.

Sales, marketing, and CX insights can help identify growth and strategy opportunities; IT monitoring can help manage disruptions; inventory and workforce planning can optimize resources; and AI for Data Analytics (AIDA) enhances existing analytics with ML.

Success Stories: Foxconn boosted forecast accuracy by 8 percent with AWS Forecast, saving approximately $500,000. Digitata used Amazon Lookout for Metrics and saved 7.5 percent in sales revenue in hours instead of a day.

Tools: Amazon's Business Metrics Analysis ML solution helps analyze business metrics dynamically to changing business conditions, Azure ML, and Google BigQuery.

> **TIP** *Use AI to analyze business metrics, adapt to changing business conditions, and identify new growth opportunities.*

Content Moderation

To create high-quality content in large quantities, you need scalable platforms and extensive resources, which the cloud provides. AI has been facilitating personalized content creation at scales beyond human capacity, with machine learning that produced varied content. AI-enabled content creation allows for the following:

➤ Personalized content

➤ Automated generation

➤ Machine learning models

➤ Massive scale

Success Stories: News media companies such as the Associated Press, the *Washington Post*, and Forbes have used content generation tools.

Tools: GANs, neural language processing and computer vision tools, ChatGPT, Claude, WriteSonic, Perplexity, BARD, and Copy.ai.

> **TIP** *Use AI to generate more personalized and engaging content at scale.*

AI for Financial Services

AI can be used in financial services to improve core business processes such as fraud detection and claims processing and to improve customer experiences by sending personalized offers. They can be used in small startups as well as large enterprises. Some use cases include risk management, customer service, investment management, personalized finance, loan underwriting, trading, and insurance claims.

Success Stories: JP Morgan uses the COIN platform for document validation; BlackRock uses Aladdin to recommend tailored investment decisions; and PayPal's system detects real-time transaction frauds to minimize losses.

Tools: IBM Watson Financial Services, Alteryx, and Darktrace.

> **TIP** *Financial services companies can use AI for applications such as risk management, personalized finance, and trading.*

Cybersecurity

Cybersecurity is the practice of protecting systems, networks, and data from external hacking, unauthorized access, disclosure, modification, use, or destruction of systems. It involves the use of systems, processes, and policies to protect assets from cyber-threats such as viruses, malware, hacking, phishing, and ransomware attacks.

Cybersecurity ensures business continuity to prevent downtime and aids in compliance with regulations such as GDPR. It uses tools like IBM's Qradar for network security and Symantec's software for AI-driven endpoint protection.

Success Stories: FICO uses AI for fraud detection; Splunk uses SOAR to address security incidents; Firefly's Helix detects malicious activity; and Dell uses Cylance for cybersecurity.

Tools: You can use natural language processing to detect malware, filter emails, and identify fraudulent transactions, while deep learning can detect malicious images, analyze videos for unauthorized access, and recognize scams.

> **TIP** *Use AI to improve the security of systems, networks, and data by proactively identifying and preventing cyber-attacks.*

Digital Twinning

The digital twin is a virtual replica of a physical system or object. As shown in Figure 8.6, you can use that replica to simulate system behavior and identify any potential issues or improve the performance of those systems. They are created by gathering the data from multiple sources or sensors and then using that data to create a virtual model of that system.

FIGURE 8.6: Digital twin of jet airplane engine
Source: chesky/Adobe Stock

Success Stories: Rolls Royce, GE Healthcare, Johnson Controls, Siemens, and ENGIE utilized digital twins to optimize performance, reduce equipment failures, and improve energy efficiency in their respective industries.

Tools: AWS IOT twin maker, Google Cloud IOT, Core and Microsoft's Azure IOT hub can be used to create digital twins. Combined with these twins, you can use machine learning models to detect patterns for further action.

> **TIP** *Use digital twins to improve the efficiency, safety, and performance of physical systems by creating a virtual replica and simulating behavior to identify issues and optimize operations.*

Identity Verification

Identity verification is essential for customers creating new accounts or accessing different accounts, systems, and information. Identity verification is used in the healthcare industry to access patient records, in the financial services industry to access or open new accounts, and in the government sector to access services based on authentication. You can verify identities through document and biometric authentication methods like passports or facial recognition or by using personal information for authentication.

Success Stories: Goldman Sachs uses Google Cloud Vision for verifying transactions; Gamestatix uses Azure's facial recognition for user access; and HealthTab utilizes Amazon Rekognition to authenticate medical professionals to access patient records.

Tools: You can use Azure cognitive services and Active Directory for identity verifications, Amazon Rekognition for facial and text recognition. Google provides Google Cloud Identity Platform and Google Firebase Authentication.

> **TIP** *Use identity verification to protect individuals and organizations from fraud and identity theft.*

Intelligent Document Processing

Intelligent document processing (IDP) can automate manual processes to extract valuable information from various documents, such as claims, invoices, receipts, contracts, forms, and so on. IDP uses machine learning algorithms to automatically extract this data using natural language processing to classify the data and then verify, validate, and integrate it with various backend systems for further processing.

Benefits include accelerated document processing, reduced manual work, improved data quality, and faster insights and decisions.

Success Stories: KPMG utilizes Amazon Textract for cost-effective document processing; HSBC and Johnson & Johnson use Google's Document AI for tasks like invoice automation using OCR and NLP. Swiss Re and Chevron use Microsoft's Azure Form Recognizer to minimize manual data entry.

Tools: Google Cloud Vision API analyzes images for data extraction, while Amazon Textract processes documents and Azure Cognitive Services offers various APIs for IDP tasks.

> **TIP** *Use IDP to automate manual processes and extract valuable information from documents; this frees employees' valuable time.*

Intelligent Search

Intelligent search is a type of search that uses AI to understand the meaning of the search term and the context behind that search and to rank the search results based on relevance. Figure 8.7 shows how by understanding the context and the meaning of the search queries, intelligent search improves the search accuracy, efficiency, and user engagement. It's used in ecommerce, customer service, and knowledge management.

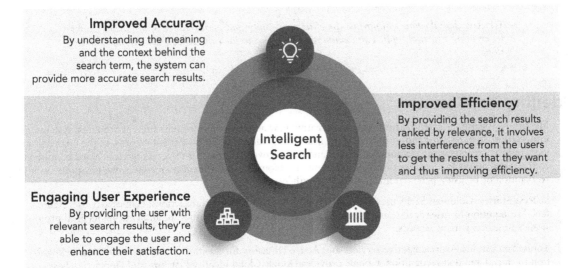

Improved Accuracy
By understanding the meaning and the context behind the search term, the system can provide more accurate search results.

Improved Efficiency
By providing the search results ranked by relevance, it involves less interference from the users to get the results that they want and thus improving efficiency.

Intelligent Search

Engaging User Experience
By providing the user with relevant search results, they're able to engage the user and enhance their satisfaction.

FIGURE 8.7: The benefits of intelligent search

Success Stories: Coursera uses Amazon machine learning to provide the right recommendations to their students on their platform.

Tools: You can use Amazon Kendra for intelligent search; Microsoft Graph for relational data; and IBM Watson Health to analyze medical data for doctor recommendations. AWS Comprehend can help with text analysis using NLP, and you can use unsupervised machine learning and NLP techniques for relevant result retrieval and contextual understanding of search terms.

> **TIP** *Use intelligent search to provide more relevant and accurate search results, save users' time, and avoid frustration.*

Machine Translation

Machine translation involves translating from one language to another using AI and ML technologies.

Success Stories: It is used in education, government, and healthcare to communicate between people speaking different languages. It helps with enhanced learning, collaboration, government services, travel, safety, and better healthcare through better communication.

Tools: Machine translation uses AI for text or speech conversion, while AWS Translate, Microsoft Azure Translator, and Google Cloud Translate all provide translation services.

> **TIP** *Use machine translation to translate text or speech from one language to another, leading to greater collaboration, learning, and safety.*

Media Intelligence

The demand for media in the form of images, video, and audio is increasing at an unprecedented rate in industries across education, entertainment, and advertisement. Companies must engage with their customers through content, and a lot of manual work is required to label, tag, review, and come up with headlines, summaries, and so on. By adding machine learning to content workflows, you can increase these assets' lifetime value, reduce costs, and increase speed in delivering content.

Some of the use cases include audience analysis, market research, public relations, and social media monitoring. Benefits include faster content processing, reduced costs, increased lifetime value, and higher quality experiences.

Success Stories: Netflix employs machine learning for personalized content streaming, while the *New York Times* uses media intelligence to curate engaging topics for its readers.

Tools: AWS Elemental Media Insight, Amazon Rekognition, Google Cloud Language, Microsoft Cognitive Services, and Azure HDInsight enable sentiment analysis, data extraction, and content pattern analysis from media content such as video, audio, and text.

> **TIP** *Use media intelligence to analyze media content and gain insights into audience demographics, trends, and brand perception.*

ML Modernization

ML modernization involves updating existing machine learning models and pipelines to adopt new technologies and tools and make them better by improving their efficiency accuracy and performance (see Figure 8.8).

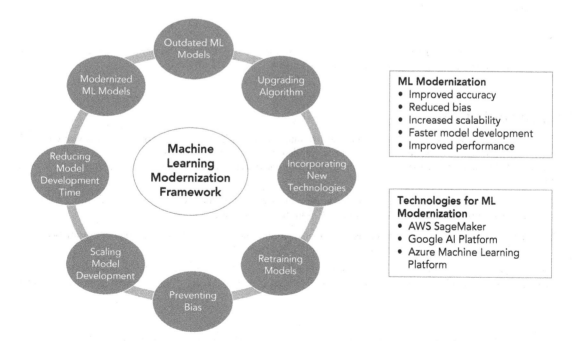

FIGURE 8.8: Machine learning modernization framework, benefits, and technologies

Some of the focus areas of ML modernization are upgrading the algorithm, incorporating new technologies, retraining, preventing bias, scaling model development, and reducing model development time.

Success Stories: Intuit uses AWS SageMaker for accurate fraud detection in financial transactions. Airbus utilizes the Google AI platform to enhance airplane wing design, achieving cost savings and better fuel efficiency.

Tools: AWS offers AWS SageMaker, which is a comprehensive ML platform with prebuilt models and AWS integrations. Google Cloud Auto ML is useful for those with limited ML knowledge, whereas Google AI Platform is for custom model development with Google Cloud integrations. Microsoft's Azure Machine Learning Platform is an all-encompassing platform integrated with Azure storage and serverless computing functions.

> **TIP** *Use ML modernization to keep your machine learning models and pipelines up-to-date with the latest technologies and tools, improving their accuracy, performance, and efficiency.*

ML-Powered Personalization

ML-powered personalization involves analyzing user demographic and behavioral data to predict their interests and provide them with personalized product services and content. It is used in recommendation engines, search engine results, social media posts, and ecommerce products.

Success Stories: Yamaha Corporation boosted sales by 30 percent using Amazon Personalize. YouTube enhanced user engagement by 60 percent with Google Cloud Recommendations API, and Air France raised sales by 13 percent by adopting Azure Machine Learning and Azure Personalizer.

Tools: Using machine learning, natural language processing, and computer vision, services like Amazon Personalize, Amazon Forecast, Google Cloud Auto ML, and Microsoft Azure Learning offer personalized content and user experiences.

> **TIP** *Use ML algorithms to predict user interests and provide personalized product services and content, such as recommendation engines, search engines, and social media.*

Computer Vision

Computer vision involves the ability of computers to interpret and understand visual data from the world around them such as images, videos, and other visual data to identify objects, track movements, and analyze scenes. Figure 8.9 illustrates the various applications of computer vision, use cases, and the technologies that can be used to implement it.

Computer vision can be used to detect objects, understand scenes, recognize actions in videos, identify diabetic retinopathy for proactive screening, and spot defects in manufacturing.

Success Stories: Amazon uses computer vision in its Go store to monitor customer behavior and automatically adds products to carts.

Tools: Amazon uses Rekognition to analyze images and videos and SageMaker for building models. Google provides Google Cloud Vision and GAN and CNNs for image analysis. Azure Cognitive Services provides similar capabilities.

> **TIP** *Use computer vision in applications for object detection, scene understanding, facial recognition, action recognition, and more.*

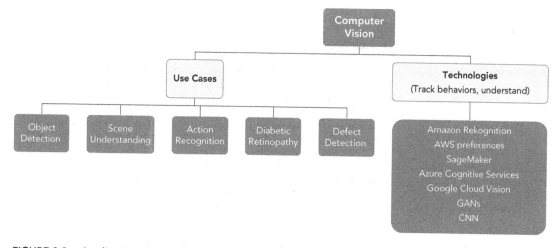

FIGURE 8.9: Applications and technologies behind computer vision

Personal Protective Equipment

Personal protective equipment involves using machine learning algorithms to detect if a person is wearing protective equipment such as masks, helmets, and gloves. It became especially important during COVID-19.

Computer vision is used in the healthcare, manufacturing, and construction industries to ensure workers are wearing protective equipment such as goggles, masks, and gloves.

Success Stories: Honeywell used computer vision to enforce PPE compliance during COVID-19.

Tools: Google Cloud Vision API can be used for image analysis. Similarly, Azure Cognitive Services is useful for computer vision use cases.

> **TIP** *Use machine learning for personal protective equipment detection to ensure workers are wearing the proper safety gear in manufacturing, healthcare, and construction industries.*

Generative AI

Generative AI refers to a type of machine learning where it can generate new types of data like the data it was trained on. It can be used to generate new content such as images, speech, natural language, and data augmentation. This feature makes generating new product descriptions, news articles, and other types of content possible. You can also use it to generate new types of videos and images, which is helpful in marketing.

Generative AI can keep users engaged through marketing campaigns and by creating new fashion designs in the fashion industry. It has been making waves ever since ChatGPT, discussed in more detail in Chapter 24, was released in November 2022. I include a few use cases to employ generative AI, but note that this is a very fast-moving space, and new use cases are continuously emerging. Figure 8.10 shows the different types of data supported currently by generative AI.

Here are text-related generative AI use cases:

USE CASE	DESCRIPTION	EXAMPLE
Content creation	You can create content such as blogs, articles, and reports based on keywords or questions.	News agencies create news articles or sports reports.
Drafting emails	AI suggests full sentences or even paragraphs to draft an email.	Gmail Smart Compose feature
Advertising content	Creating engaging promotional content for products and services.	Product descriptions on ecommerce websites
Creative writing	Writing stories, scripts, or poetry based on user prompts.	Scripts for movies or commercials
Personalized recommendations	Personalized recommendations based on user history or preferences.	Recommend news articles based on reader browsing behavior
Language translation	Translating between languages.	Google Translate
Sentiment analysis	Identifying sentiments in a text.	Analyzing customer comments or reviews on websites
Screening résumés	Assessing résumés based on certain criteria.	Screening job applications for companies
Text summarization	Create summaries for large pieces of content.	Summarizing large articles and reports
Chatbots	Generate human-like responses in a conversation.	Chatbots used for customer service, sales, HR, etc.

Here are code-related use cases:

USE CASE	DESCRIPTION	EXAMPLE
Generate code	Generate code based on keywords or requirements	Microsoft's CoPilot and AWS Code Whisperer.
Detect bugs	Identify bugs	DeepCode can detect bugs in static code.
Refactoring	Suggest improvement in code	Codota now known as Tabnine suggests code improvements.
Review code	Assist in code review process by suggesting improvements or identifying issues	Code Climate provides automated code review for test coverage and maintainability.
Code documentation	Generate documentation for code	DeepAffects Code Summarizer generates summaries for code blocks.
Unit testing	Generate unit test cases	Diffblue Cover generates unit tests using AI.

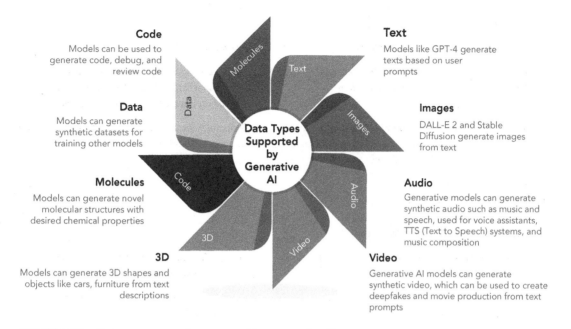

Code
Models can be used to generate code, debug, and review code

Data
Models can generate synthetic datasets for training other models

Molecules
Models can generate novel molecular structures with desired chemical properties

3D
Models can generate 3D shapes and objects like cars, furniture from text descriptions

Text
Models like GPT-4 generate texts based on user prompts

Images
DALL-E 2 and Stable Diffusion generate images from text

Audio
Generative models can generate synthetic audio such as music and speech, used for voice assistants, TTS (Text to Speech) systems, and music composition

Video
Generative AI models can generate synthetic video, which can be used to create deepfakes and movie production from text prompts

Data Types Supported by Generative AI

FIGURE 8.10: Data types currently supported by generative AI

Here are some image-related generative AI use cases:

USE CASE	DESCRIPTION	EXAMPLE
Image synthesis	Generates new images resembling the original images	DALL-E by OpenAI can create images from text descriptions.
Style transfer	Applies the style of one image to another	DeepArt can recreate photos in the artistic style of any painting.
Image enhancement	Improves the image quality by increasing resolution, removing noise, etc.	Let's Enhance can increase the image resolution without losing quality.
Image segmentation	Identifies individual objects within an image	Google's DeepLab uses AI for semantic image segmentation.
Image colorization	Adds color to black-and-white images or videos	DeOldify colorizes black and white images and videos.
Image captioning	Generates a textual description of an image	Google's Cloud Vision API provides a text description for an image.
Facial recognition	Identifies or verifies a person in a digital image or a video frame	Face++ can do facial recognition in security systems, payment gateways, etc.
Object detection	Detects instances of objects in images	Amazon Rekognition can identify objects, people, text, scenes, and activities in images.

continues

(continued)

USE CASE	DESCRIPTION	EXAMPLE
Image super-resolution	Converts low-resolution images to high-resolution	Enhanced Super-Resolution Generative Adversarial Networks (ESRGAN) used for enhancing the quality of low-res images.
Augmented reality	Integrates digital information with the user's environment in real time	Snapchat's lenses can overlay digital content onto the physical world.

Here are some audio-related use cases:

USE CASE	DESCRIPTION	EXAMPLE
Speech synthesis	Generates human-like speech	Google Text-to-Speech and Amazon Polly convert text into lifelike speech.
Music composition	Generates new music compositions	OpenAI's MuseNet composes new music in various styles.
Voice cloning	Replicates a person's voice after learning from a small sample	ElevenLabs and Resemble AI's voice cloning technology can create unique voices for virtual assistants or voiceover.
Speech enhancement	Enhances the quality of speech signals by reducing noise	Krisp, an AI-based app, can mute background noise in any communication app.
Sound classification	Recognizes and categorizes audio events	Google's AudioSet, a dataset of sound events, can be used to train models for sound classification.
Speech-to-text	Converts spoken language into written text	Google's Cloud Speech-to-Text converts audio to text for transcription services.
Audio fingerprinting	Identifies unique components of a sound for recognition	Shazam uses AI to recognize music tracks by their sound.

Here are some video-related use cases:

USE CASE	DESCRIPTION	EXAMPLE
Deepfake generation	Synthesizes human-like videos from images and other videos	DeepFaceLab is an open-source software that creates deepfakes.
Video synthesis	Generates new video content based on specific instructions or data	Nvidia's GANs can create videos of virtual environments, such as cityscapes.

USE CASE	DESCRIPTION	EXAMPLE
Video colorization	Adds color to black-and-white videos	DeOldify is an AI model for colorizing and restoring old images and videos.
Super resolution	Increases the resolution of video content	Video Enhance AI by Topaz Labs improves video quality using AI.
Motion transfer	Transfers the motion of one person in a video to another person in a different video	First Order Motion Model for Image Animation enables animating new faces in images.
Video compression	Compresses videos without losing quality	H.266/VVC is a video codec standard enabling high-quality video compression.
Predictive video generation	Predicts the next frames in a video sequence	PredRNN is a recurrent network for predictive video generation.
Video inpainting	Fills in missing or removed parts of a video	Free-Form Video Inpainting with 3D Gated Convolution and Temporal PatchGAN restores missing video parts.

Finally, here are some 3D use cases:

USE CASE	DESCRIPTION	EXAMPLE
3D object generation	Creates 3D models from descriptions or data	NVIDIA's GANs can generate 3D models of objects from 2D images.
Virtual reality content creation	Generates immersive VR environments	Artomatix can generate texture maps for virtual reality.
3D animation	Automates 3D animation	DeepMotion does procedural character animation in games.
Predictive 3D modeling	Predicts the 3D shape of a protein or a molecule	AlphaFold, a system from DeepMind, predicts the 3D structure of proteins.
3D reconstruction	Creates 3D models from 2D images	Pix3D, a dataset and method by researchers at MIT and ETH Zurich, generates 3D models from 2D images.
3D printing	Predicts the results of 3D printing	Autodesk's Project Dreamcatcher uses generative design for optimized 3D printing.
Generative design	Suggests design alternatives for designers	Autodesk's Generative Design tool provides design alternatives for maximum efficiency.

WORKBOOK TEMPLATE: USE CASE IDENTIFICATION SHEET

Download the "Use Case Identification Sheet" template from the download section of the book (www.wiley .com/go/EnterpriseAIintheCloud). Use this template to help your team brainstorm, evaluate, and prioritize potential AI use-cases. Use this to make informed decisions considering factors such as business impact, cost, and technical complexity.

SUMMARY

This chapter provided a detailed review of how to find the right AI and ML use cases for your company. It began by exploring the process flow for identifying use cases, starting from educating people about the potential of AI/ML and Gen AI, and how it can solve business problems. It covered defining business objectives, identifying pain points, conducting a root-cause analysis, identifying the success criteria, and exploring the latest AI industry trends.

Armed with this information, you can identify your use cases, prioritize them, choose the suitable model, and finalize them through an iterative process.

In the next chapter, let's discuss cloud-based AI/ML services offered by different cloud providers to bring your AI/ML use cases to life.

REVIEW QUESTIONS

These review questions are included at the end of each chapter to help you test your understanding of the information. You'll find the answers in the following section.

1. Identify the type of processes that are ready for AI/ML.
   A. Automated processes
   B. Processes that depend on data and happen repeatedly
   C. Processes that are easier to automate by software and are fast
   D. All the above
2. The purpose behind conducting a root-cause analysis is
   A. To identify the pain points that are hindering your business
   B. To quantify the business value upon completion of the use case
   C. To measure the success of your use case using ROI, payback period, or NPV technique
   D. To understand the root cause to identify the proper use case
3. Choose the success metric that would result in cost savings.
   A. Improved customer satisfaction
   B. Reduced errors
   C. Increased revenue growth
4. What is the primary purpose of mapping the use case to a business problem?
   A. To assess the potential impact of an AI solution
   B. To ensure the use case aligns with the business objectives
   C. To identify potential pitfalls in the solution
   D. All the above
5. Why is it important to iterate until you finalize the use case?
   A. To get a solid understanding of the problem being solved
   B. To get feedback from the stakeholders

C. To proactively identify risks and challenges

D. All the above

6. Which of the following can be used to improve code quality by automating code reviews during application development

A. Amazon CodeGuru Reviewer

B. Amazon HealthLake

C. Amazon DevOps Guru

D. Amazon Transcribe Medical

7. What benefit can AI provide in log analysis for DevOps?

A. Identify patterns that could turn into issues proactively

B. Increase the speed and reliability of software deployment

C. Automate testing for bug identification

D. Optimize resource allocation based on usage

8. What is document verification?

A. Using personal information such as driver licenses to verify identity

B. Using documents such as passports, driver licenses, ID cards, biometric verification using finger-prints, facial recognition, or voice recognition to verify identity

C. Using facial recognition, emotional analysis, and text recognition for verification

D. Using image and video analysis that uses computer vision technology for verification

9. What is intelligent document processing (IDP)?

A. The process of extracting valuable information from various documents using machine learning algorithms

B. The process of creating new documents using artificial intelligence and machine learning

C. The process of verifying personal information using documents such as passports, driver licenses

D. The process of automating manual tasks using artificial intelligence and machine learning

10. Which of the following is a use case for media intelligence?

A. Upgrading media intelligence models

B. Analyzing financial intelligence

C. Tracking mentions on social media

D. Predicting user interests

ANSWER KEY

1.	B	5.	D	9.	A
2.	D	6.	A	10.	C
3.	B	7.	A		
4.	B	8.	B		

9

Evaluating AI/ML Platforms and Services

Information is the oil of the 21st Century, and analytics is the combustion engine.

—*Peter Sondergaard*

Welcome to the exciting world of evaluating AI/ML platforms and services. Whether you are a data scientist, business analyst, developer, or decision-maker for AI/ML implementation, this chapter will help you choose the right platform and services.

Choosing the right platform and services is pivotal to the success of your AI/ML as well as Gen AI implementation. This chapter covers the various AI and ML services that the cloud service providers such as AWS, Microsoft, and Google provide. The idea is to leverage what's available to get your project kickstarted. Now is an excellent time to look at the different portfolios of AI/ML services and map them to the business problems you are trying to solve. This includes evaluating specialized services for healthcare and industry solutions so that you can embark on a path that resonates with your business goals and regulatory landscape.

It isn't just about choosing the right tool; it is about aligning with the fastest time to market, handling high-intensity workloads, maintaining cost-effectiveness, and staying at the cutting edge of technology. Once you have identified the right use cases, you need the right set of tools, setting the stage to launch your pilot, the focus of the next chapter (see Figure 9.1).

Given the plethora of AI/ML platforms and services, each with its own features and offerings, it can be quite overwhelming. This chapter guides you through a comprehensive evaluation process and presents the choices from the three major cloud providers to help you choose the right platform and services.

This chapter can help you to turn your possibilities into reality. Let's get started.

9 StepsThin Arrows Power Point Diagram

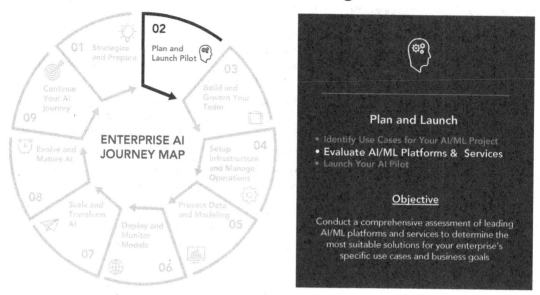

FIGURE 9.1: PLAN AND LAUNCH: Evaluate AI/ML Platforms & Services

BENEFITS AND FACTORS TO CONSIDER WHEN CHOOSING AN AI/ML SERVICE

This section covers the various factors you need to consider when choosing an AI/ML service.

Benefits of Using Cloud AI/ML Services

Cloud service providers provide several AI/ML services that offer a wide range of capabilities and functionalities that you need to build your AI solutions, especially at scale in production. They provide access to several sophisticated algorithms along with pretrained models that can save you a lot of time and money during the model-building process. They also offer several development and deployment tools that accelerate the development process. See the following table for more details:

BENEFIT	DESCRIPTION
Faster time to market	You can speed up your implementation time by leveraging these services because you do not have to build these algorithms from scratch. Instead, you can focus on solving the specifics of your complex business problems. These services come as part of preconfigured environments, which allows for faster prototyping and experimentation, faster time to market, and more cost-effective implementation. **Tip:** Focus on solving complex business problems instead of building algorithms from scratch.

continues

(continued)

BENEFIT	DESCRIPTION
Intensive workloads	These AI services are designed to handle high computational demands and data processing workloads that are typical of enterprise AI. They provide a scalable infrastructure along with high-performance capabilities for these AI services to be developed, trained, and deployed efficiently.
	By leveraging the scalability, reliability, security, and performance offered by these AI services, you can address the common challenges faced by typical machine learning projects easily. The providers offer large GPUs and TPUs that are optimized for large ML workloads and reduce training and inference times.
	Tip: Use these services to handle large data volumes and spikes in processing demands by dynamically allocating cloud computing resources based on need.
Cost-effective solutions	By leveraging these services that are hosted in the cloud, you do not have to invest up front or build in-house expertise. Thus, you save time and money.
	By leveraging the cloud provider's economy of scale, the pay-as-you-go pricing model, you can avoid up-front infrastructure costs, reduce operating costs, and implement cost-effective AI solutions.
	Tip: Monitor the usage of cloud resources to effectively manage costs.
Collaboration and integration	These services allow sharing of models, code repositories, and version control systems. Additionally, since they can easily be integrated with other cloud services, databases, and APIs, it is possible to leverage additional capabilities and data sources to meet the needs of the use cases.
Better security compliance	These AI services can also be compliant with industry standards and regulatory requirements and data privacy laws. You can implement security measures such as data encryption and access control.
Rich capabilities	These services come with capabilities such as natural language processing, computer vision, speech recognition, and recommendation engines in the form of pretrained models and APIs.
	Tip: Integrate these capabilities into business applications, thus empowering your company to deliver personalized experiences, automate processes, and leverage valuable business insights that drive customer-centric actions.
Better tool support	AI services include popular frameworks such as TensorFlow, PyTorch, and AutoML platforms that simplify and speed up the model development process.
Up-to-date with innovation	Cloud providers also invest a lot in innovation and keep releasing new services and updates to existing services, which will help you stay up-to-date and benefit from the latest research and development.

Factors to Consider When Choosing an AI/ML Service

This section covers some of the factors to consider when choosing an AI/ML as well as Gen AI services.

KEY FACTORS WHEN CHOOSING AN AI/ML SERVICE	DESCRIPTION
Identify your business problem	Before choosing an AI service, you need to first identify the business problem you are trying to solve, including the business objectives, the desired outcomes, and the impact expected on your business operations, customer experience, and decisions.
Explore AI/ML service capabilities	Explore the various capabilities offered by these AI services, such as natural language processing, computer vision, and speech recognition, and ensure that they meet your use case.
Evaluate performance and scalability needs	Evaluate the performance and scalability needs of your ML solution and ensure that your service can handle them. Factor in training and inference times, processing speeds, and dataset processing needs. **Tip:** Consider training and inference times, processing speeds, and dataset processing needs.
Assess development and integration needs	Assess the availability of software development kits and the ability to integrate with your company's backend systems, applications, databases, and processes.
Assess model development tools	Assess the tools available for model development, such as SageMaker, PyTorch, AutoML, TensorFlow, and scikit-learn.
Evaluate service's security capabilities	Evaluate your security needs and ensure that the provider can meet your needs.
Evaluate service pricing	Evaluate the pricing models and ensure that they meet your budget expectations. **Tip:** Factor in costs for training, data storage, and API calls to avoid future surprises.
Evaluate vendor support	Evaluate vendor support factors such as their support SLAs, their responsiveness, their uptime guarantees, and their track record with you.
Identify industry regulations	If your company has any industry-specific regulatory requirements, factor them in as well.
Keep up with innovations	Make necessary allowances for the growth of your use case, such as increasing data volumes, innovation, and changing business conditions.

HANDS-ON AI/ML SERVICE EVALUATION EXERCISE

This is a hands-on exercise that needs the team to participate, collaborate, research, and arrive at a solution.

The goal is helping the team identify a business problem, evaluate various AI/ML services available from different cloud providers to address that problem, and then develop an implementation plan for the chosen solution.

At the end of this exercise, the team should be aware of the process involved when selecting an AI/ML service and consider various business and technical factors.

STEPS	TASK OWNERS	DELIVERABLES	RESOURCES	TIPS/EXAMPLES
Identify a business problem	Project manager	Develop a document outlining the business problem, objectives, planned outcomes, and impacts	Company data, business objectives from company strategy, and other company sources including leadership	Include both short-term and long-term objectives
Assess AI/ML service capabilities	Data scientists	Understand and develop a report with the details of the capabilities of each service	List of AI/ML services, online research	Factor in the specific problem requirements
Evaluate performance and scalability needs	Data engineers	Estimate and prepare a document with performance and scalability requirements	Project requirements, data volume estimates	Plan for future growth
Assess development and integration needs	Software developers	Document capturing the development and integration needs	SDKs, backend system documentation	Ensure the selected AI/ML service can be integrated with existing systems

STEPS	TASK OWNERS	DELIVERABLES	RESOURCES	TIPS/EXAMPLES
Assess model development tools	Data scientists	Document comparing different model development tools	Documentation of tools like SageMaker, PyTorch, AutoML, TensorFlow, Google Cloud Platforms, Azure, and scikit-learn	Factor in the team's expertise and comfort with different tools
Evaluate service's security capabilities	Security analyst	Document capturing security needs, security architecture, and service's capabilities	Government and company security standards and protocols	Factor in industry-specific security requirements
Evaluate service pricing	Financial analyst	Document outlining costs	Pricing models of the services	Factor in hidden costs like data storage, API calls
Evaluate vendor support	Project manager	Document comparing different vendor support	Vendor's SLAs, track record	Consider factors like uptime guarantees, responsiveness, and skillsets
Identify industry regulations	Compliance officer	Compliance document	Industry regulations	Ensure regulatory compliance to avoid fines and legal issues
Keep up with innovations	Project manager	Document discussing growth potential of AI/ML	Trends in the AI/ML space	Consider both immediate and long-term needs

AWS AI AND ML SERVICES

AWS provides these ML services in three categories based on the user's expertise—high-level AI Services, Sage-Maker, and AI frameworks—as shown in Figure 9.2.

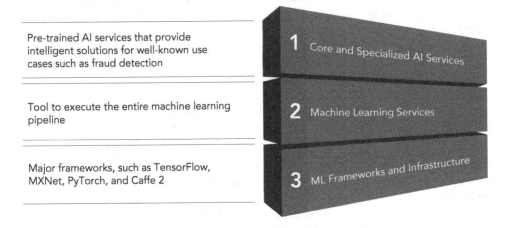

Pre-trained AI services that provide intelligent solutions for well-known use cases such as fraud detection

1 Core and Specialized AI Services

Tool to execute the entire machine learning pipeline

2 Machine Learning Services

Major frameworks, such as TensorFlow, MXNet, PyTorch, and Caffe 2

3 ML Frameworks and Infrastructure

FIGURE 9.2: AWS AI/ML stack

AI Services

AWS provides high-level AI services, which are pretrained AI services that provide intelligent solutions for well-known use cases such as fraud detection, personalized recommendations, contact center intelligence, document processing, intelligent search, business metrics analysis, forecasting, quality control, cybersecurity, and so on.

These AI services can be incorporated into the applications and workflows and used to build end-to-end solutions in AWS.

> **NOTE** *AWS also provides prebuilt, industry-specific AI services, such as the industrial and healthcare industries.*

Amazon SageMaker

In the middle layer, AWS provides SageMaker. This tool is geared toward experts, such as data scientists and ML engineers, who can use it to execute the entire machine learning pipeline, all the way from data ingestion, labeling, data preparation, feature engineering, model building, model training, model tuning, model monitoring, and monitoring deployment. It can also be used for bias detection, AutoML, hosting, explainability, and workflows. These topics are discussed in greater detail in later chapters.

AI Frameworks

At the bottom of the stack are the AI frameworks that can be used by expert practitioners. This provides all the major frameworks, such as TensorFlow, MXNet, PyTorch, and Caffe 2. AWS also provides high-performance instances for annual training, such as P4D instances powered by NVIDIAs, TensorFlow, and core GPUs. For inferences that typically constitute 90 percent of the ML cost, AWS provides EC2 Inf1 instances powered by inferential chips. Please note that this a fast moving space and you should watch out for the latest developments.

Differences Between Machine Learning Algorithms, Models, and Services

It's important to understand the differences between machine learning algorithms, models, and services. These are listed in detail in Table 9.1.

TABLE 9.1: Differences Between Machine Learning Algorithms, Models, and Services

ASPECT	ML ALGORITHMS	ML MODELS	ML SERVICES
Definition	Set of mathematical instructions to analyze data for learning	An algorithm trained with data	Cloud-based platform that provides models and algorithms as APIs
Purpose	To analyze data and learn from it to solve a business problem	To make predictions and decisions	To provide tools and infrastructure for building ML apps
Development	Developed by an expert, such as a data scientist	Created based on algorithms trained on data	Developed by a cloud service company, such as AWS, Google
Training	Trained on labeled or historical data	Generated through a training process	Platform used to train models or perform ML operations
Customization	Parameters can be customized to fit specific requirements	Models can be customized per needs	ML services can be configured for specific needs
Complexity	Can be simple or complex	Depends on the chosen algorithm	A varied range of complexity based on capabilities and use cases
Deployment	Integrated into an application	Deployed to make predictions	Accessed through APIs or cloud platforms

Examples of algorithms are linear regression, logistic regression, decision trees, and support vector machines. Examples of models are deep neural networks, and examples of AI services are AWS SageMaker, Azure Machine Learning, and Google Cloud ML Engine.

The next sections review the AI services. For the sake of easy understanding, they are categorized into core and specialized AI services.

CORE AI SERVICES

This section discusses the core AI services offered by AWS, as shown in Figure 9.3.

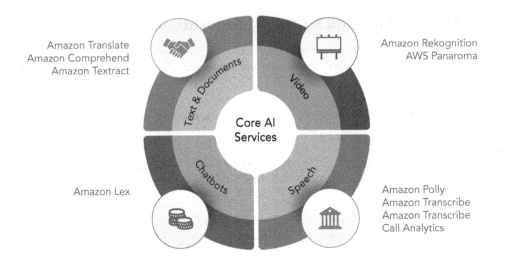

FIGURE 9.3: AWS core AI services

Text and Document Services

This section explains some of the text and document services, including AWS Comprehend, AWS Textract, and AWS Translate.

Amazon Comprehend

Amazon Comprehend is a natural language processing service. It uses machine learning models to classify words and phrases into categories. It can be used to solve business problems such as the following:

FUNCTIONALITY	DESCRIPTION
Key phrase extraction	Extract critical phrases and entities such as people, organizations, and products from text.
Accuracy	Increase the accuracy of your search results, product recommendations, and security.
Sentiment analysis	Identify the sentiment in a text document, whether it is neutral, positive, or negative.
Text classification	Classify text such as product reviews, customer feedback, customer service tickets, news articles, etc.
Language detection	Detect abusive language, phishing attacks in text, and fake news.
Compliance risks	Understand customer feedback better and identify compliance risks.

To get started, you need to create an AWS account, enable the Amazon Comprehend service, upload your text data to Amazon S3, and use Amazon Comprehend to extract insights from it.

AWS Translate

AWS Translate is a fully managed service that can translate content and be integrated into applications. It can translate various text formats such as HTML, JSON, XML, plain text, and speech. It can be used in the following domains:

MARKET	APPLICATION
Ecommerce	Translate website content to increase sales.
Customer support	Translate tickets for better customer support.
Marketing	Translate marketing materials to reach a wider audience.
Online sales	Translate product documentation.
Training	Translate employee training materials for better training.
Healthcare	Translate to local languages for patients.

Amazon Textract

Amazon Textract is a machine learning service that uses optical character recognition to extract information such as text and tables from documents. The document types can be either PDF, image, or image-based documents. It can be used for the following:

FUNCTIONALITY	DESCRIPTION
Document analysis	Identify different types of content such as text, tables, and images.
Form extraction	Extract information from forms such as names, addresses, phone numbers, etc.
Data extraction	Extract information from documents such as invoice numbers, dates, amounts, and recipients.
Text recognition	Recognize text such as authors, document titles, and date created.
Image recognition	Recognize images such as company logos and signatures.

Amazon Textract can save time and money extracting data from various documents. These use cases are shown in Figure 9.4.

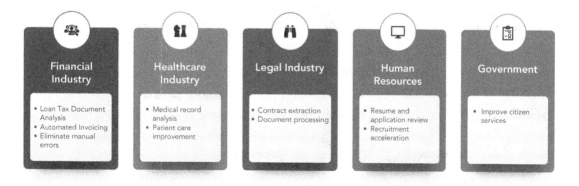

FIGURE 9.4: Amazon Textract use cases

Amazon Textract can help many industries, including the following:

INDUSTRY	APPLICATION
Finance	Extract data from loan tax documents and other documents to speed up the loan approval process and eliminate errors due to manual data entry.
Healthcare	Review medical treatment plans, patient medical records, etc., to provide better patient care.
Legal	Extract data from legal documents such as contracts and court filings to reduce the time required to process this information manually.
Human resources	Use it to review resumes and applications and speed up the recruitment process to recruit the top candidates.
Government	Use it to speed up their services provided to their citizens.

> **TIP** *Be sure that you thoroughly analyze and understand your specific use cases and requirements before choosing AWS Text and Document services such as Amazon Comprehend, AWS Translate, and AWS Textract.*

Chatbots: Amazon Lex

Amazon Lex is used in Alexa, which we are all so used to. Amazon Lex helps build conversational interfaces to applications using voice and text. It uses the same power as Alexa to build those interfaces. As shown in Figure 9.5, it can be used for the following:

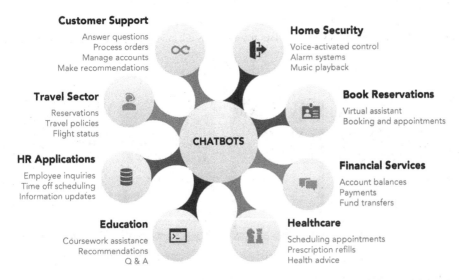

Customer Support
Answer questions
Process orders
Manage accounts
Make recommendations

Home Security
Voice-activated control
Alarm systems
Music playback

Travel Sector
Reservations
Travel policies
Flight status

Book Reservations
Virtual assistant
Booking and appointments

CHATBOTS

HR Applications
Employee inquiries
Time off scheduling
Information updates

Financial Services
Account balances
Payments
Fund transfers

Education
Coursework assistance
Recommendations
Q & A

Healthcare
Scheduling appointments
Prescription refills
Health advice

FIGURE 9.5: Amazon Lex: Conversational interfaces using voice and text

USE CASE	DESCRIPTION
Chatbots	Can create chatbots that can handle customer questions, process orders, check shipping status, manage accounts, and make product recommendations.
Voice activated systems	To control home security systems, alarms, clocks, and play music.
Virtual assistants	Can take orders and book reservations and appointments.

Here are some industry use cases for Amazon Lex:

SECTOR	APPLICATION
Financial	Use chatbots to check account balances, make payments, and transfer funds.
Healthcare	Schedule appointments for patients, refill prescriptions, and make generic recommendations related to health.
Education	Help students find coursework, make course recommendations, and answer course-related questions.
Human resources	Answer employees' questions about benefits and policies, schedule time off, and update personal information.
Travel	Make reservations, learn about travel policies, and check flight status.

Speech

Amazon provides Amazon Polly and Amazon Transcribe for speech related services.

> **TIP** *You should ensure accurate and high-quality speech-to-text and text-to-speech conversions for optimal performance and best user experience.*

Amazon Polly

Amazon Polly is a cloud-based text-to-speech service that uses deep learning to create authentic lifelike voices. These voices can be added to applications to create innovative speech-enabled products. Amazon Polly can be used for the following:

USE CASE	APPLICATION
IVR systems	Develop IVR systems to interact with customers to answer their queries using NLP.
Enterprise applications	Help make applications more accessible by allowing users with visual impairments and reading difficulties.

continues

(continued)

USE CASE	APPLICATION
E-learning and training platforms	Add audio to courses to make the learning experience pleasant for users who prefer to listen rather than read.
Voice-enabled IoT devices	Integrate Amazon Poly with a thermostat to control that device and make the experience much more pleasant.

Amazon Transcribe

Amazon Transcribe is a speech-to-text cloud service capability from AWS that businesses can use to convert large volumes of audio into text for subsequent processing.

INDUSTRY	APPLICATION
Call centers	Convert call center call recordings into text and analyze them to understand customer needs, preferences, and problems.
Media	Convert audio and video content into text to be easily searchable by users and can be analyzed to understand user engagement and preferences.
Legal	Transcribe large volumes of court hearings and proceedings to help law firms and legal departments.
Healthcare	Transcribe notes and records to provide better healthcare.

Vision Services

This section discusses some of the available vision services, such as Amazon Rekognition and AWS Panorama.

Amazon Rekognition

Amazon Rekognition helps businesses add video and image analysis capabilities to their applications. It can detect objects and analyze people and scenes in videos and images. It is used in the following situations:

SECTOR	APPLICATION
Security and surveillance	Identify people in real-time who are trespassing on the premises.
Content moderation	Remove inappropriate content in online communities and other online marketplaces.
Marketing and advertising	Personalize marketing campaigns by analyzing videos and images to understand customer demographics, behavior, and preferences.

SECTOR	APPLICATION
Retail	Categorize products based on images to create catalogs, saving much time.
Manufacturing	Detect product deficiencies during manufacturing.
Healthcare	Detect diseases proactively by looking at medical images.

> **TIP** *You can leverage vision services like Amazon Rekognition and AWS Panorama for enhanced security, personalized marketing, and optimized operations.*

AWS Panorama

AWS Panorama allows you to add computer vision to your applications. It enables you to detect objects, people, and scenes in videos and images and create 3D models of objects and scenes. It has uses in the following industries:

INDUSTRY	APPLICATION
Retail	Track customers and based on their behavior, recommend products they are likely to buy. Use Panorama to determine where customers spend more time in the store by tracking their movements. Use this information to redesign the store layout so that customers can quickly find their products.
Manufacturing	Identify defects in the products. Also, track the movement of products within the manufacturing assembly and improve the manufacturing process.
Supply chain management	Identify the movement of goods through the supply chain, identify potential areas where delays are happening, and identify opportunities to improve.
Warehouse management	Identify the movement of people and vehicles within a warehouse and identify potential opportunities to improve the logistics process.

HANDS-ON PRACTICAL EXERCISE: APPLYING AWS CORE AI SERVICES

This is a hands-on exercise focused on project-based learning experience to leverage AWS AI core services for practical use.

The goal is to use AWS AI/ML tools to solve real-world problems using services such as text and document analysis, speech services, vision services, and chatbots.

STEPS	TOOLS	TASK OWNERS	DELIVERABLES	RESOURCES	EXAMPLES/TIPS
Task 1: Text and document analysis	AWS Comprehend, Translate, Textract	Data scientist	Develop a document detailing results and potential use cases.	AWS Comprehend AWS Translate AWS Textract Sample data	Use AWS Comprehend for sentiment analysis on customer reviews. Use AWS Translate to translate content such as customer support tickets Use AWS Textract to extract data from a set of invoices.
Task 2: Speech services implementation	AWS Polly and Transcribe	ML engineer	Develop a document detailing results and potential use cases.	AWS Polly AWS Transcribe Sample text and audio data	Use AWS Polly to develop IVR systems and add audio to e-learning courses. Use AWS Transcribe to convert call center recordings into text for analysis.
Task 3: Vision services implementation	AWS Rekognition and Panorama	Data scientist	Develop a document detailing results and potential use cases.	AWS Rekognition AWS Panorama Sample images and video data	Use AWS Rekognition for security surveillance to identify trespassers. Use AWS Panorama to track customer behavior in retail stores.
Task 4: Chatbots	Amazon Lex	AI engineer	Develop a working chatbot and document its functionalities.	Amazon Lex Sample prompts for testing	Use Amazon Lex to build a chatbot that handles customer questions, processes orders, and checks shipping status.
Task 5: Evaluation and report writing		Project manager	Develop a comprehensive report on the implementation, evaluation, and potential business use cases of AWS AI Services.	Use the feedback from task owners, objectives, and key results (OKRs)	Collect feedback and results from all task owners. Evaluate the results against the objectives and key results (OKRs). Prepare a comprehensive report detailing the implementation, results, potential business use cases, and future improvements.

SPECIALIZED AI SERVICES

This section covers the specialized AI services from AWS, as illustrated in Figure 9.6.

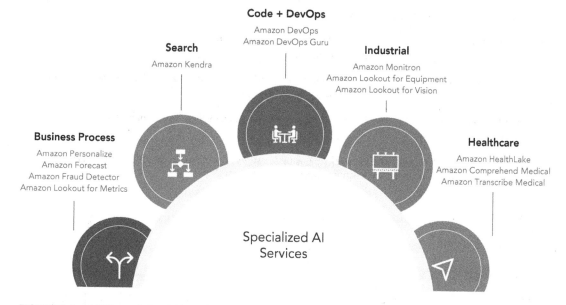

FIGURE 9.6: AWS specialized AI services

Business Processing Services

This section covers the various business processing related services that AWS provides, including Amazon Personalize, Amazon Forecast, Fraud Detector, and Amazon Lookout for Metrics.

Amazon Personalize

Amazon Personalize is a fully managed service that can personalize customer experiences at scale. It can be used to make recommendations for websites to improve search results and in marketing campaigns by recommending the products to customers.

It uses collaborative filtering, content-based filtering, and rule-based filtering. User, behavioral, and product data are used to make these recommendations.

RECOMMENDATION METHOD	DESCRIPTION
Collaborative filtering	Uses data from users interested in these products to recommend them to other users
Content-based filtering	Uses data from the products that the user has already interacted with to recommend other related products
Rules-based filtering	Is based on the rules that you specify to recommend the products

Amazon Forecast

Amazon Forecast is a fully managed service that uses machine learning to generate accurate time-series forecasts. Here are some places where it can be leveraged and a view into some of its features and workings:

RECOMMENDATION METHOD	DESCRIPTION
Collaborative filtering	Uses data from other users interested in these products to recommend them to other users
Content-based filtering	Uses data from the products that the user has already interacted with to recommend other related products
Rules-based filtering	Is based on the rules that you specify to recommend the products

Figure 9.7 shows how Amazon Forecast works by using latest algorithms to predict future time-series data using historical data and needs no machine learning experience on the user's part.

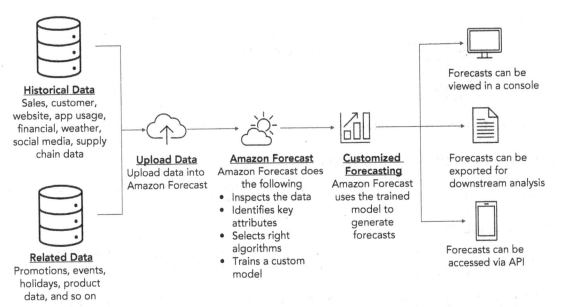

Historical Data
Sales, customer, website, app usage, financial, weather, social media, supply chain data

Related Data
Promotions, events, holidays, product data, and so on

Upload Data
Upload data into Amazon Forecast

Amazon Forecast
Amazon Forecast does the following
- Inspects the data
- Identifies key attributes
- Selects right algorithms
- Trains a custom model

Customized Forecasting
Amazon Forecast uses the trained model to generate forecasts

Forecasts can be viewed in a console

Forecasts can be exported for downstream analysis

Forecasts can be accessed via API

FIGURE 9.7: How Amazon Forecast works

ARIMA

ARIMA stands for Auto-Regressive Integrated Moving Average and is a statistical model that uses past data to forecast future values. It is used for the following:

USE CASE	DESCRIPTION
Forecast financial data	Can be used to forecast financial data such as stock prices and exchange rates
Predict sales or demand	Capable of predicting sales or demand during different times of the year such as holidays or seasons, due to its ability to capture trends and seasonality in data

EDS Prophet

EDS (Extended Kalman Filter Dynamic Linear Model) Prophet is a time-series forecasting tool developed by Facebook. Some of its features include the following:

FEATURE	DESCRIPTION
Additive models	Uses additive models to capture seasonality trends and other data that affect time-series data when making predictions
Use cases	Useful when you have multiple sources of data such as IoT and sensor data, for example, to predict when a machine may require maintenance

DeepAR

DeepAR is a deep learning based supervised learning technique. Some of its features include the following:

FEATURE	DESCRIPTION
Recurrent Neural Networks (RNNs)	RNNs are used to model complex time-series data and can handle multiple time-series data with different levels of granularity.
Use cases	RNNs are used where there are multiple factors that can influence the outcome.
Customer behavior	Often used to forecast customer behavior such as website traffic and sales.
Stock prices	Can be used to predict stock prices based on past data, current events, and other factors.

ETS

ETS (Exponential Smoothing State Space Model) is a time-series forecasting method. Some of its features include the following:

FEATURE	DESCRIPTION
Smoothing approach	ETS uses a smoothing approach by generating a weighted average of past data to predict future values.
Seasonality and trends	ETS works well with seasonal data and trends and is particularly useful for fast-changing situations.
Short-term trends	ETS is useful to predict short-term trends such as forecasting demand for perishable goods, or the demand for different types of medications based on historical and other data.

Note that no forecasting model is perfect. All these models have some degree of error, and you'll get the best results by combining predictions from multiple models. Table 9.2 compares and contrasts these forecast models.

TABLE 9.2: Comparison of Amazon Forecast Models for Various Use Cases

MODEL	TYPE	USE CASES	PROS	CONS
ARIMA	Statistical	Sales data, website traffic, and customer behavior data	Simple and easy to interpret. Handles seasonality and trends well.	Assumes linear relationships. Can be sensitive to outliers.
EDS Prophet	Statistical	Forecasts demand for products and services	Handles seasonality and trends well. Handles missing data well.	Requires manual feature engineering.
DeepAR	Deep learning	Forecast customer behavior, such as website traffic and sales	Handles complex patterns well and automatically learns features.	Takes longer to train and needs more data.
ETS	Exponential smoothing	Demand forecasting, inventory management, and workforce planning	Handles seasonality and trends well. Flexible parameterization is possible and simple to use.	Assumes linear relationships. Can be sensitive to outliers.
NPTS	Neural point forecasting	Demand forecasting, time-series analysis, and anomaly detection	Handles complex patterns well and supports multiple related times series. Powerful and accurate.	Takes longer to train and needs more data.

Amazon Fraud Detector

Amazon Fraud Detector is a fully managed service that can detect frauds like account takeover, payment fraud, return fraud, and other suspicious activities such as large orders and unusual login patterns. Some of its features include the following:

FEATURE	DESCRIPTION
Prebuilt and custom models	You can either use prebuilt models or create your own custom models.
AWS console	You can use the AWS console to create a detector, feed in the labeled data to train the detector, test it, and, when satisfied, deploy it into production.

Amazon Lookout for Metrics

Amazon's Lookout for Metrics is a fully managed service that can be used to monitor metrics or a set of metrics and detect any anomalies and generate alerts. You can then quickly investigate and diagnose issues. Some of its features include the following:

FEATURE	DESCRIPTION
Detect anomalies	Used to detect anomalies in websites, traffic, machine downtime, sales data inventory levels, customer satisfaction, and operational data.
Automatic detection	Automatically detects and labels anomalous data points and even identifies the root cause behind those anomalies.
Integration	Designed to be fully integrated with other AWS data storage solutions such as Redshift, S3, RDS, and other third-party databases.

Kendra for Search

Amazon provides Kendra for the Search capability. Amazon Kendra is a fully managed service that can automatically index your documents using machine learning algorithms and thus provide more relevant search results. Kendra makes it easy to find documents quickly.

Figure 9.8 shows some of the inner workings of Amazon Kendra.

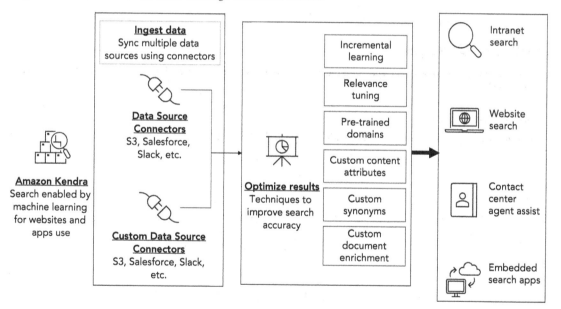

FIGURE 9.8: How Amazon Kendra works

Some of Kendra's features include the following:

USE CASE	DESCRIPTION
Employee knowledge base	Set up an enterprise search solution that includes content from databases, websites, and other internal documentation such as FAQs, employee handbooks, and product documentation.
Customer support knowledge management system	For customer support teams that include FAQs, troubleshooting guides, product documentation, and customer support tickets.

continues

(continued)

USE CASE	DESCRIPTION
Partner management	Index partner agreements, FAQs, and sales content.
Customer satisfaction	Improve employee productivity, customer satisfaction, and partner satisfaction.
Ecommerce	Create a custom search engine where customers can find their products quickly, thus increasing customer service satisfaction and sales.
Healthcare	Create a medical search engine that enables doctors and professionals to find their information quickly; this can help doctors make better decisions and improve patient outcomes.
Legal	Create a legal search engine for lawyers to find their information quickly, which can improve their service to customers by building more robust legal cases and providing better legal advice.

Code and DevOps

This section covers some of the code and DevOps-related AWS services, including Amazon CodeGuru and Amazon DevOps Guru.

Amazon Code Guru

Amazon CodeGuru leverages AI and ML algorithms to do the following (see Figure 9.9):

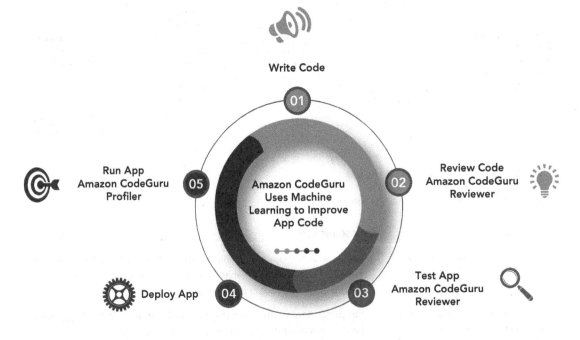

FIGURE 9.9: Amazon CodeGuru uses machine learning to improve app code.

BENEFIT	DESCRIPTION
Improve code quality	Conduct code reviews, automated suggestions, and remediations to enhance the quality of the code.
Find and fix bugs	Reduce development time by providing suggestions to improve the code.
Improve security	Find security bugs and help comply with regulations by providing suggestions to improve the code.
Improve performance	Provide suggestions to code so that you can leverage the appropriate infrastructure to improve performance.

> **TIP** *Use Amazon CodeGuru to enhance code quality, security, and performance, and use DevOps Guru to proactively monitor DevOps processes and detect issues.*

Amazon DevOps Guru

Amazon DevOps Guru uses machine learning to identify potential operational issues before they impact the customers. Some of its capabilities include the following:

FEATURE	DESCRIPTION
Anomaly detection	Leverages operational data from AWS CloudWatch, CloudTrail, and other AWS services, continuously analyzes them, and detects anomalies that are then used to generate alerts for subsequent reactive or proactive action
Real-time alerts	Generates alerts through integration with AWS Systems Manager, Amazon EventBridge, Amazon SNS, and other third-party incident management systems
Performance, security, and availability	Helps improve performance, provides security, and ensures high availability by preventing downtime

> **TIP** *The integration capability of DevOps comes in handy, especially for AI and ML applications, because they are often complex, require considerable computer resources, and are challenging to monitor in real time.*

HANDS-ON PROJECT-BASED LEARNING EXERCISE

This is a type of learning exercise that is focused on applying the skills and knowledge gained about AWS services to a series of tasks in the real world.

continues

continued

OBJECTIVE	DELIVERABLES	RESOURCES	EXAMPLE
Get access to AWS Services.	AWS Account	Internet connection Email ID	Create an AWS account.
Learn to create solutions and campaigns, import, or create datasets, and generate personalized recommendations for customers.	Understand Amazon Personalize	Amazon Personalize AWS Console	Use Amazon Personalize to make recommendations based on user behavior.
Learn to import time-series data, select the appropriate predictor algorithm (e.g., ARIMA, Prophet, DeepAR, ETS), and visualize forecasts.	Forecast model using Amazon Forecast	Amazon Forecast Time-series dataset	Use ARIMA, Prophet, DeepAR, ETS to generate forecasts for sample dataset.
Learn to use historical event data and known fraud labels to train a model, create rules, and make decisions using Amazon Fraud Detector. Test the model with sample transactions to identify potential fraud.	Fraud detection model	Amazon Fraud Detector Fraud labeled dataset	Use Amazon Fraud Detector to identify potential fraudulent transactions in sample data.
Monitor a sample dataset for anomalies. Learn how to set up anomaly detectors, add datasets, and interpret anomaly detection results.	Anomaly detection model	Amazon Lookout for Metrics Dataset	Set up an anomaly detector and identify anomalies in the sample data.
Create an intelligent search service using sample documents. Learn to create an index, add data sources, and test the search functionality.	Intelligent search service using Kendra	Amazon Kendra Document dataset	Create an intelligent search service for a set of sample documents.

OBJECTIVE	DELIVERABLES	RESOURCES	EXAMPLE
Stop or delete all services to prevent any additional charges.	Cleaned up AWS services	AWS Console	Ensure to stop or delete services to avoid any additional charges.
Learn how to apply these learnings to your project for the benefit of your company.	Reflection on learning	N/A	Reflect on what you learned in this hands-on exercise and how you can apply these services in your business or project.

Industrial Solutions

Amazon provides a few industrial solutions, including Amazon Monitron, Amazon Lookout for Equipment, and Amazon Lookout for Vision (see Figure 9.10). These solutions apply artificial intelligence (AI) and machine learning (MI) to vast amounts of industrial data generated by sensors and systems to generate insights so they can optimize industrial processes and improve quality and safety.

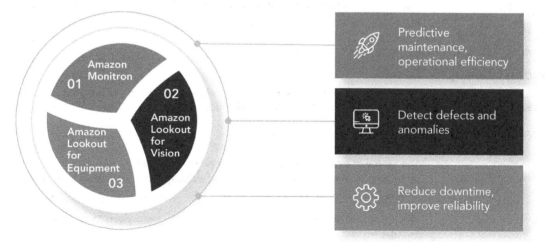

FIGURE 9.10: Amazon industrial AI solutions

Amazon Monitron

Amazon Monitron is an industrial solution that can detect anomalies in industrial equipment. Some of its features include the following:

FEATURE	DESCRIPTION
Monitoring	Monitron monitors temperature, vibration, and sound.
Predictive maintenance	Combines sensors, gateways, and machine learning to reduce unplanned downtimes and improve predictive maintenance.
Operational efficiency	Leverages industrial IT and edge-creating technologies to integrate with industrial equipment and systems to provide real-time insights, improving operational efficiency.

Amazon Lookout for Equipment

Amazon's Lookout for Equipment is another service focused on preventing downtime and improving the operational efficiencies of equipment for industrial companies. Some of its features include the following:

FEATURE	DESCRIPTION
Issue detection	Detects vibration, flow, temperature, sound, and pressure to identify potential issues.
Equipment care	Improves equipment reliability, reduces maintenance costs, and improves safety.
Industry adoption	Can be used in several industries, such as manufacturing, transportation, and energy automotive, to monitor equipment such as pumps, motors, bearings, valves, and more.
Use cases	Industrial use cases include quality control, energy optimization, predictive maintenance, and asset management.

Amazon Lookout for Vision

Amazon's Lookout for Vision is used to detect defects in industrial images. This includes defects such as cracks, scratches, and missing parts. Some of its features include the following:

FEATURE	DESCRIPTION
Detect visual damages	This service or tool can identify visual damages including dents and water damage and safety hazards due to oil spills, leaks, blocked walkways, and product quality issues such as color and texture anomalies.
Use cases	This tool is particularly useful in industries such as manufacturing, packaging, and logistics.

Healthcare Solutions

AWS provides several healthcare-related services, including Amazon HealthLake, Amazon Comprehend Medical, and Amazon Transcribe Medical, each of which is discussed in the following sections.

Amazon HealthLake

HealthLake is a managed service that stores, transforms, and analyzes healthcare data to improve healthcare quality, reduce costs, and improve the efficiency of healthcare organizations. Here are some of its features:

FEATURE	DESCRIPTION
Proactive care	HealthLake can look into patients' data and try to identify those with the risk of developing complications and then proactively treat or educate them.
Cost reduction	Hospitals can use HealthLake to understand where they are spending money, such as on prescription drugs, and then negotiate that with the drug companies for better pricing.
Appointment scheduling	Hospitals can automate scheduling appointments using HealthLake, which will not only impart efficiency to the hospital's operations but also result in better patient satisfaction.
Clinical trials	HealthLake can analyze large datasets to identify anomalies, which can help medical researchers identify potential participants for clinical trials and lead to new therapies and treatments.
Clinical support system	HealthLake can also act like a clinical support system by providing physicians with the latest clinical research and insights to help them change their treatment plans or identify other potential treatment options.
Population health	Healthcare organizations can also track the trends in population health over time and then proactively produce means to prevent diseases or improve overall health.

> **TIP** *You can leverage Amazon healthcare services for proactive treatment, cost optimization, automation, clinical support, and secure medical transcription.*

Amazon Comprehend Medical

Amazon Comprehend Medical is like Amazon HealthLink in that it also helps reduce costs, improve patient care, and improve hospital operations. Here are some of its features:

FEATURE	DESCRIPTION
Population health	Helps with population health management by better understanding the patient's health and developing personalized treatments.
Medical coding	You can also use Amazon Comprehend Medical to automatically code medical diseases and procedures for billing purposes, thus saving the time and effort required for medical coding.

Amazon Transcribe Medical

Amazon Transcribe Medical is a HIPAA-eligible service that uses Automatic Speech Recognition to allow physicians, vendors, and payers to securely transcribe medical speech, such as physician-patient conversations, medical dictations, and clinical notes. Here are some of its features:

FEATURE	DESCRIPTION
Compliance	HIPAA-eligible
Technology	Uses automatic speech recognition
Users	Physicians, vendors, and payers
Use case	Securely transcribes medical speech, such as physician-patient conversations, medical dictations, and clinical notes
Clinical notes	Includes progress notes, discharge summaries, and consultation notes

HANDS-ON EXERCISE: APPLYING AMAZON INDUSTRIAL AI SOLUTIONS USING AMAZON MONITRON, LOOKOUT FOR EQUIPMENT, AND LOOKOUT FOR VISION

The focus of this exercise is to provide a practical experience to using these Amazon Industrial solutions to improve operational efficiency, predictive maintenance, and quality control in an industry setting.

OBJECTIVE	STEPS AND DELIVERABLES	RESOURCES	EXAMPLE
Assume that you are working with an industrial manufacturing company experiencing equipment downtime. The goal is to monitor the equipment to identify the underlying causes.	Step 1: Configure Amazon Monitron service and connect it to the company's equipment. Step 2: Monitor temperature, pressure, vibration, sound data. Step 3: Analyze this data using Amazon Monitron to identify potential issues.	➤ AWS account ➤ Amazon Monitron ➤ Documentation	Set up Amazon Monitron to monitor a hypothetical conveyor belt system in a warehouse.

OBJECTIVE	STEPS AND DELIVERABLES	RESOURCES	EXAMPLE
The goal is to move away from manual inspections to developing their predictive maintenance capability.	➤ Configure Amazon Lookout for Equipment and connect it to their data sources. ➤ Ingest historical data and detect anomalies. ➤ Evaluate the effectiveness of the new system by comparing it with the accuracy of the predictions during manual approach.	➤ AWS account ➤ Amazon Lookout for Equipment ➤ Documentation ➤ Sample industrial dataset	Use Amazon Lookout for Equipment to analyze the historical data of a hypothetical motor to detect any anomalies.
The goal is to improve the quality control process.	➤ Configure Amazon Lookout for Vision service. ➤ Connect it to the company's production line cameras. ➤ Analyze images for defects. ➤ Monitor the service performance and optimize the parameters to improve accuracy.	➤ AWS account ➤ Amazon Lookout for Vision ➤ Documentation ➤ Sample industrial images	Use Amazon Lookout for Vision to analyze images of a production line to detect any defects in products.
Apply it in the real world.	Develop a detailed report evaluating the results obtained from Amazon Monitron, Amazon Lookout for Equipment, and Amazon Lookout for Vision.	➤ Results from the previous steps ➤ Evaluation metrics relevant to the use case	➤ Evaluate the number of true positives, false positives, true negatives, and false negatives detected. ➤ Compare the benefits and challenges while using these AWS services.

MACHINE LEARNING SERVICES

This section covers the ML services. Within the AWS ML services section, there are the SageMaker Canvas, SageMaker itself, and the SageMaker Studio Lab, as shown in Figure 9.11.

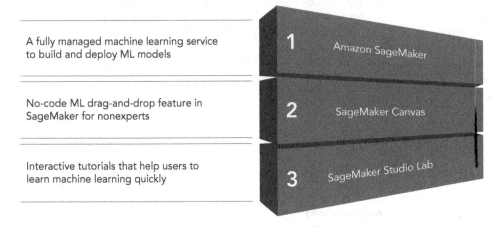

A fully managed machine learning service to build and deploy ML models

1 Amazon SageMaker

No-code ML drag-and-drop feature in SageMaker for nonexperts

2 SageMaker Canvas

Interactive tutorials that help users to learn machine learning quickly

3 SageMaker Studio Lab

FIGURE 9.11:   AWS ML services

Amazon SageMaker

Amazon SageMaker is a fully managed machine learning service provided by AWS to build, train, and deploy machine learning models. It provides end-to-end support for the entire machine learning lifecycle, as shown in Figure 9.12. It allows developers and data scientists to deploy models at scale in production.

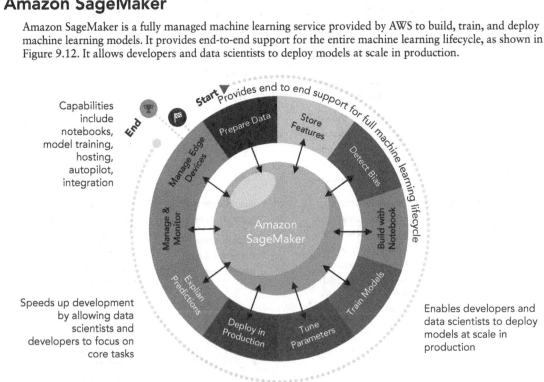

Capabilities include notebooks, model training, hosting, autopilot, integration

Speeds up development by allowing data scientists and developers to focus on core tasks

Enables developers and data scientists to deploy models at scale in production

Start ▶ Provides end to end support for full machine learning lifecycle

End

Prepare Data
Store Features
Detect Bias
Build with Notebook
Train Models
Tune Parameters
Deploy in Production
Explian Predictions
Manage & Monitor
Manage Edge Devices

Amazon SageMaker

FIGURE 9.12:   SageMaker's capabilities

Some of its features include the following:

CATEGORY	FEATURES
Capabilities	➤ Uses Jupyter notebooks to develop and train machine learning models
	➤ Provides training environments that can be local cloud or on edge
	➤ Offers deployment options such as real-time or batch inference
	➤ Provides monitoring options such as metrics, logs, and traces
Benefits	Helps companies to reduce costs, improve efficiency, and make better business decisions

Amazon SageMaker Canvas

SageMaker Canvas is a new drag-and-drop feature in SageMaker that helps democratize the use of SageMaker for non-experts. Here are some of its features:

FEATURE	DESCRIPTION
Collaboration	Enables more collaboration between developers, data scientists, and business analysts.
Speed	Helps organizations speed up the machine learning workflow and deploy models quickly.
Democratization	Business analysts can use SageMaker with limited machine learning knowledge.
Use Cases	Includes fraud detection, product recommendations, and customer churn prediction.

SageMaker Studio Lab

Amazon SageMaker Labs are interactive tutorials that help users learn machine learning quickly. They offer an opportunity to learn with a hands-on approach. Here are some of its features:

FEATURE	DESCRIPTION
Upskill	An essential tool for organizations to upskill their employees
Hands-on experience	Helps employees to learn machine learning development through guided, hands-on experiences
Experimentation	Allows users to learn and experiment with different models without worrying about the underlying hardware and infrastructure
Collaboration	Allows users to collaborate and share their work

> **TIP** *Use Amazon SageMaker's end-to-end support for ML lifecycle, democratize ML with SageMaker Canvas, and upskill employees with SageMaker Studio Lab.*

THE GOOGLE AI/ML SERVICES STACK

AI/ML services can be categorized into three major use cases—for the data scientist, for the developers, and for the infrastructure specialists. These first two use cases are covered in this chapter, and the infrastructure-level services are covered when I talk about the cloud platform in Chapter 13.

For Data Scientists

The following AI/ML services are available for data scientists, as shown in Figure 9.13.

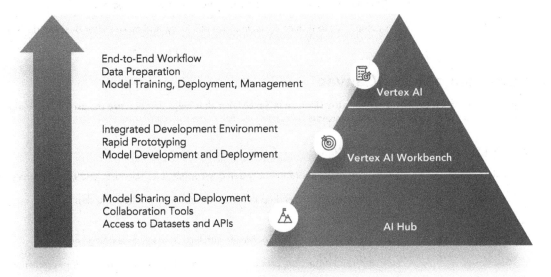

FIGURE 9.13:   Google AI/ML stack for data scientists

Vertex AI

Vertex AI is a cloud-based machine learning platform that helps companies build, train, and deploy models in production. It helps with the end-to-end machine learning workflow, including data preparation, model training, deployment, and management.

Vertex AI Workbench

A Vertex AI Workbench is a single development environment for data scientists who can develop and then deploy models. Here are some of its features:

FEATURE	DESCRIPTION
Easy transition from development to production	Integrated with Vertex AI and other tools, which helps minimize the transition from development to production
Rapid prototyping	Facilitates rapid prototyping and model development

AI Hub

Google's AI Hub is a centralized platform where data scientists, machine learning engineers, developers, and other AI practitioners discover, share, and deploy models from within the hub. Here are some of its features:

FEATURE	DESCRIPTION
Share assets	Gain access to other assets such as datasets and APIs.
Collaboration tools	Access other tools for collaboration, such as version control, code reviews, and issue tracking.

GOOGLE'S AI/ML EXERCISE FOR MACHINE LEARNING

This hands-on exercise is focused on helping data scientists and AI practitioners to use Google's AI/ML services such as Vertex AI, Vertex AI Workbench, and AI Hub. It will help the team members to create and deploy models and prototype solutions.

Task 1: Assume you are working for a retail company to improve the sales using a predictive model.

TOOLS	STEPS
Vertex AI	Gather and prepare necessary data such as historical sales data and data related to external factors that could impact the sales.
	Train a model for sales predictions using Vertex AI.
	Deploy the trained model and create a mechanism for new data input.
	Monitor and adjust the model's performance as needed.

Task 2: Experimenting with different recommendation systems to personalize the customer's shopping experience using rapid prototyping.

TOOLS	STEPS
Vertex AI Workbench	Use Vertex AI Workbench to prototype various recommendation system models.
	Select a model to integrate with the company's e-commerce platform for a pilot test.
	Monitor the effectiveness of the recommendation system and adjust as necessary.

Task 3: Streamlining asset sharing and collaboration across various teams.

continues

continued

TOOL	STEPS
AI Hub	Set up a workspace on AI Hub for sharing assets such as datasets, models, and APIs.
	Establish workflow for version control, code reviews, and issue tracking.
	Monitor and adjust team collaboration and asset utilization.

For Developers

The AI/ML services listed in Table 9.3 are available to developers.

TABLE 9.3: Google AI/ML Services for Developers

AUTOML	CLOUD NATURAL LANGUAGE	DIALOGFLOW	IMAGE AND VIDEO SERVICES	MEDIA TRANSLATION
Automated model development ➤ AutoML Vision ➤ AutoML Natural Language ➤ AutoML Tables	**Sentiment analysis** ➤ Entity recognition ➤ Syntax analysis ➤ Content classification ➤ Text classification	**Conversational Interfaces** ➤ Chatbots/voice assistants ➤ Natural language understanding ➤ Media Translation ➤ Multi-device support	**Video AI** ➤ Video tagging recommendations ➤ Transcription and translation ➤ Content moderation ➤ Label detection **Vision AI** ➤ Object and face detection ➤ Text recognition ➤ Image search ➤ Landmark detection	**Speech-to-text** ➤ Audio to text conversion ➤ Real-time or prerecorded audio **Text-to-speech** ➤ Text-to-speech conversion ➤ Personalized communications **Translation AI** ➤ Cloud translation API ➤ Google Translate ➤ Neural machine translation

AutoML

AutoML is a set of tools and techniques that facilitates the development of models accessible by automating many tasks. Some of its features include the following:

FEATURE	DESCRIPTION
Easier model development	Intended to make model development easier for those with limited knowledge of machine learning
Development tools	Provides several tools, such as AutoML Vision, AutoML Natural Language, and AutoML Tables, to solve specific ML problems

Cloud Natural Language

Cloud Natural Language is a cloud-based natural language processing service offered by Google Cloud for developers to analyze and understand human language in text format. Some of its features include the following:

FEATURE	DESCRIPTION
Natural language tasks	Helps with sentiment analysis, entity recognition, syntax analysis, content classification, and more.
Application integration	Developers can apply natural language processing to applications using this API.
Sentiment analysis	Developers can train machine learning models to classify, extract, and detect sentiments.

Dialogflow

The Google Dialogflow platform enables developers to create conversational interfaces for applications such as chatbots, voice assistants, and other conversational agents. Some of its features include the following:

FEATURE	DESCRIPTION
Device support	Works across multiple devices and platforms.
User requests	Leverages machine learning and natural language understanding techniques to understand user requests and provide responses.
Human-like interactions	Facilitates natural interaction and human-like capabilities and offers enterprise-wide scalability.
Application development	Helps developers develop such applications very quickly.

> **TIP** *Use Vertex AI for data scientists, AutoML and Dialogflow to streamline development, and Cloud Natural Language and Vision AI to enhance applications.*

Media Translation

Media translation enables real-time translation of audio or video content into text in the language of your choice. Currently, it supports 12 languages. The following sections discuss the services that AWS offers under the media translation umbrella.

> **TIP** *Media translation can be used to make your content more accessible to a global audience.*

Speech-To-Text

FEATURE	DESCRIPTION
Applications	Applications such as dictation, podcast, voice commands, and more.
Google Contact Center AI	Speech to Text plays a vital role in the Google Contact Center AI by converting spoken words into written text, which helps real-time transcription, sentiment analysis, call analytics, and interactive voice response (IVR).
Text-to-speech conversion	Provides real-time text conversion into speech and can be used for video captioning, voice-enabled chatbots, transcribing meetings and calls, and so on.
Supports multiple languages	This includes English, French, Spanish, and Japanese. It can understand multiple dialects and accents.
Personalized communications	Can be used to personalize communications and engage with customers via voice-based user interfaces in devices and applications.

Translation AI

Google offers this translation service, which can be used to translate text and speech between different languages. Some of its features include the following:

FEATURE	DESCRIPTION
Global reach	Helps reach customers globally and provides compelling experiences by engaging with them in their local languages.
Translation options	Google provides three translation options: Cloud Translation API, Google Translate, and Neural Machine Translation.
Language support	Google Translate is free and can be used for nearly 100 languages. It translates text, images, speech, and web pages.
Google Translate API	A paid service that can be used to integrate translation into your applications and services.
Neural machine translation	A much more accurate translation service that uses neural networks for translation.

Image and Video Services

This section covers some of the AI/ML image and video services offered by Google.

Video AI

Google Video AI is used in many applications such as Google Photos, YouTube, and Google Cloud. It provides automatic video tagging, video recommendations, video transcription and translation, and content moderation.

Vision AI

Google Vision AI is a cloud-based image analysis service that detects and analyzes objects, faces, text, and other visual entities from videos and images. It is helpful for label detection, face detection, text recognition, optical character recognition (extracting text for scanned documents), image search (finding similar images), and landmark detection.

PROJECT-BASED EXPLORING GOOGLE AI/ML SERVICES FOR DEVELOPERS

In this exercise, the project team will build an application using Google AI/ML services using image recognition, natural language processing, translation, and chatbot functionality.

STEP NO.	GOOGLE AI/ML SERVICES	HANDS-ON TASK	EXPECTED OUTCOME
1	Automated Machine Learning (AutoML)	Use Google's AutoML to develop a machine learning model for a simple problem such as image classification or text analysis.	A functional machine learning model developed with minimal coding effort
2	Cloud Natural Language	Develop a simple application that uses the Google Cloud Natural Language API to analyze sentiments in user-provided text.	An application capable of analyzing sentiments from text
3	Dialogflow	Create a simple chatbot using Dialogflow that understands user intents and responds accordingly.	A chatbot capable of conversational interactions with users
4	Media Translation	Integrate Google's Media Translation into the application and test it with different input languages.	An application capable of real-time translation across various languages

continues

continued

STEP NO.	GOOGLE AI/ML SERVICES	HANDS-ON TASK	EXPECTED OUTCOME
5	Speech-to-Text	Implement a feature in the application that converts spoken words into written text for transcribing meetings or voice commands.	An application feature capable of converting voice inputs to text
6	Translation AI	Use Google's Translation AI to translate text from one language to another, preferably by auto-translating user-generated content.	An application feature capable of translating text into a specified language
7	Vision AI	Implement Google's Vision AI in the application to analyze images or videos, such as identifying objects within an uploaded image.	An application feature capable of analyzing and identifying objects or components in an image or video
Bonus challenge	Integration of Services	Integrate these functionalities into a cohesive user journey within the application.	A seamless user journey across various AI/ML services in a single application

THE MICROSOFT AI/ ML SERVICES STACK

The Microsoft AI/ML services stack can be broadly categorized into four areas that enable more advanced AI/ML practitioners and the novice. The Azure Applied AI services are geared toward data scientists and machine learning engineers, while Azure machine learning is a platform for developers.

Azure Applied AI Services

Azure Applied AI services are capabilities that developers, data scientists, and other AI practitioners can use in their applications without needing expertise in machine learning. Figure 9.14 shows an overview of the various Azure-applied AI services and their capabilities.

Azure Cognitive Services

Azure Cognitive Services is a suite of cloud-based APIs and services that helps developers integrate AI and ML capabilities into their applications, websites, and devices.

Extract entities from audio and videos

Extract entities such as key value pairs, tables, and text from forms

Use AI and NLP to search for data such as images and text

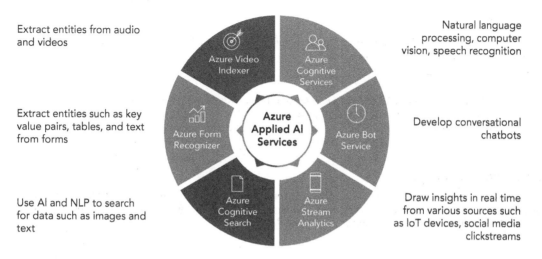

Natural language processing, computer vision, speech recognition

Develop conversational chatbots

Draw insights in real time from various sources such as IoT devices, social media clickstreams

FIGURE 9.14: Azure-applied AI services

FEATURE	DESCRIPTION
Purpose	Helps developers integrate AI and ML capabilities into their applications, websites, and devices
Capabilities	Includes natural language processing, computer vision, speech recognition, and more
Use cases	Can improve customer service, fraud detection, product recommendations, image classification, and natural language processing
Method	Just make an API call to embed the ability to speak, hear, see, search, understand, and thus include decision-making into the apps
Specific services	Can be used for speech-to-text, text-to-speech, speech translation, and speaker recognition

Cognitive Services for Language

Cognitive Services for Language offers capabilities such as entity recognition, language translation, sentiment analysis question answering, conversational language understanding, and translation.

Cognitive Services for Vision

Cognitive Services for Vision analyzes content within images and videos and provides custom image recognition. It has the following features:

FEATURE	DESCRIPTION
Cognitive service for decisions	Provides content moderation and personalization of experiences for the users, and addresses device problems earlier, all contributing to better decision-making
Open API service	Provides an open API service for advanced language models and coding

Azure Bot Service

Azure Bot Service is a cloud-based platform for developing conversational chatbots that interact with users across websites, messaging apps, and voice assistants.

> **TIP** *Use Azure Applied AI services to integrate AI capabilities into your applications and unlock the power of natural language processing, computer vision, real-time analytics, and intelligent search.*

Azure Stream Analytics

Azure Stream Analytics is a cloud-based analytics platform that draws insights in real-time from various sources, including IoT devices, social media clickstreams, and more. It can integrate with Azure events hubs, Azure IoT hub, and Azure functions to create complex streaming data pipelines.

> **TIP** *Azure Stream Analytics can be used to monitor and analyze streaming data in real time, which can help you make better decisions and take action more quickly.*

Azure Cognitive Search

Azure Cognitive Search allows developers to integrate enterprise-grade search into their applications. Some of its features include the following:

FEATURE	DESCRIPTION
AI and NLP	Uses AI and Natural Language Processing to search for data such as images and text
Search features	Provides semantic search, faceted navigation, fuzzy matching, and geospatial search features
Unstructured data	Can extract insights from unstructured data such as sentiment analysis, key phrase extraction, and entity recognition

Azure Form Recognizer

Azure Form Recognizer helps to extract entities such as key-value pairs, tables, and text from forms. It enables data entry to be faster and error-free as compared to manual data entry. It can be used on documents such as invoices, receipts, and custom documents.

Azure Video Indexer

Azure Video Indexer is a cloud-based platform that extracts entities from audio and videos. Once you upload the content to a portal, it extracts information using speech-to-text, facial recognition, sentiment analysis, scene detection, and so on. Users can then search through this information, either through a portal or through an API.

Using Azure Video Indexer is easy; just go to videoindexer.ai and upload a video after signing up. Figure 9.15 shows the results for a video that I uploaded. It came up with a list of relevant topics, transcripts, keywords, named entities, and emotions.

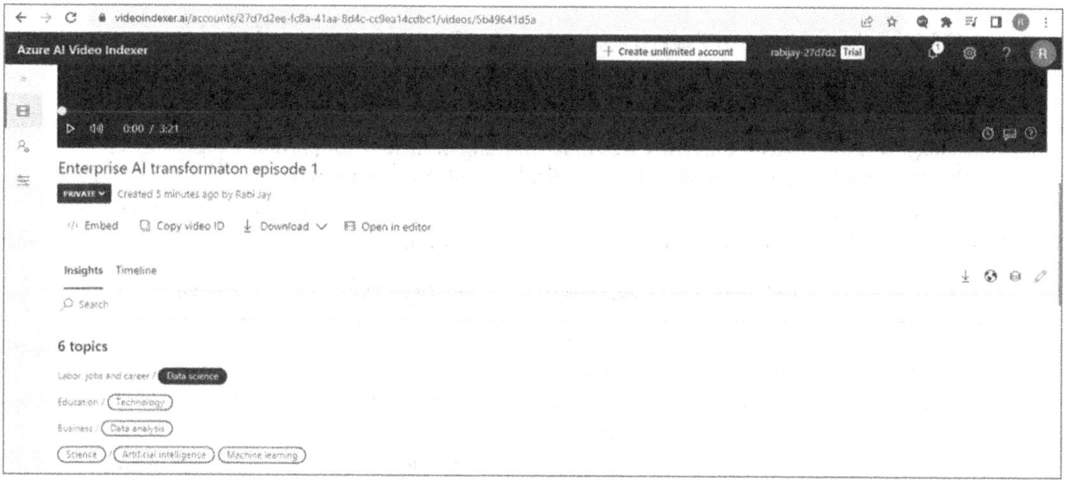

FIGURE 9.15: Using Azure Video Indexer tool

Azure Machine Learning

Azure Machine Learning is a cloud-based machine learning platform. Developers can use it to build, train, and deploy machine learning models into production. It allows developers to prepare data, build and train models, validate, deploy, manage, and monitor the results.

PHASE	FEATURE
Data preparation	During data preparation, developers can label training data, manage label projects, use analytics to explore data, and access and share datasets.
Build and train models	Provides notebooks, automated machine learning capability, the ability to run experiments, accelerate training using a scalable compute engine, access to a secure compute instance, and access to open-source libraries such as Scikit-learn, PyTorch, TensorFlow, Keras, and more.
Validate and deploy models	Provides the ability to deploy model endpoints for real-time and batch inference, pipelines and CI/CD workflows, prebuilt instances for inference, model repository, and hybrid and multi-cloud deployment options.
Manage and monitor models	Provides the ability to track logs, analyze data and models, detect drift, maintain model accuracy, debug models, trace machine learning artifacts for compliance, and ensure continuous monitoring of security and cost control features, including quota management and automatic shutdown.

EXERCISE: BUILDING, DEPLOYING, AND MONITORING AN AI MODEL WITH AZURE SERVICES

This exercise is to give your team practical experience with building, training, and deploying a machine learning model using Azure Machine Learning. It includes important aspects such as data preparation, model training, validation, deployment, and monitoring.

Remember to clean up resources at the end of the exercise to avoid unnecessary charges. Also note that the roles in the exercise can vary in your organization.

STEP NAME	TASK OWNER	OBJECTIVE	INSTRUCTION	DELIVERABLE
Data preparation	Data engineer	Prepare data for model training	Import a dataset and use Azure's data preparation tools to preprocess the data.	A cleaned and preprocessed dataset ready for model training
Model building and training	Data scientist/ML engineer	Build and train a machine learning model	Choose a suitable ML algorithm and use it to train a model on the prepared dataset. Monitor the training process using Azure's tracking tools.	A trained machine learning model
Model validation	Data scientist/ML engineer	Evaluate the model's performance	Evaluate the model's performance using a holdout validation set and appropriate evaluation metrics.	Evaluation metrics and analysis
Model deployment	MLOps engineer/ ML Engineer	Deploy the model for use	Deploy the model using Azure's deployment options for real-time or batch inference.	A deployed machine learning model
Monitoring	MLOps engineer	Monitor the model's performance over time	Use Azure's monitoring tools to track model usage, data drift, and retrain the model as necessary.	Regular performance reports and updated models as necessary

OTHER ENTERPRISE CLOUD AI PLATFORMS

This section covers several other enterprise cloud AI platforms that are worth knowing about and considering.

Dataiku

Dataiku is an enterprise-class data science platform that allows data preparation, machine learning, and collaboration all in one place. It enables use cases such as customer segmentation, fraud detection, product recommendation, inventory management, and supply chain optimization.

Dataiku has key capabilities for explainable AI. It includes interactive reports for feature importance, partial dependence plots, subpopulation analysis, and individual prediction explanations.

DataRobot

DataRobot's specific capabilities include AutoML, which automates the machine learning development and deployment lifecycle, and explainability, which explains how the models work and helps businesses build trust around their models. It facilitates collaboration by allowing users to share their work, including code, models, and workflows, in a collaboration platform. Its governance platform provides the tools to manage risks with machine learning models to comply with regulations and protect data.

KNIME

KNIME is a powerful open-source data analytics tool that helps with data preparation and machine learning modeling. In addition to typical data preparation feature extraction and machine learning modeling tools, it provides a web extraction tool that extracts data from websites.

IBM Watson

IBM Watson is a robust set of AI/ML tools that businesses can leverage to carry out several use cases around natural language processing, speech recognition, machine vision, and so on. It provides capabilities such as natural language processing, machine learning to make predictions, deep learning for highly accurate speech recognition and image recognition, speech-to-text, text-to-speech, visual recognition, and virtual agents.

> **TIP** *When choosing an enterprise cloud AI platform, it is important to thoroughly assess the features, scalability, security, and integration capabilities of the platform.*

Salesforce Einstein AI

Salesforce Einstein AI is a robust set of AI and machine learning tools developed by Salesforce to enhance the CRM experience for businesses. Some of its key capabilities include predictive analytics, NLP, image recognition, automated insights, and intelligent automation for workflows.

Oracle Cloud AI

Developed by Oracle, this product helps developers and businesses to integrate AI into their applications and workflows. It provides capabilities such as machine learning, an autonomous database to manage the data automatically, chatbots that can integrate with messaging platforms and websites, intelligent apps that provide recommendations and automate tasks, and data analytics.

HANDS-ON EXERCISE: EVALUATE PLATFORMS

This hands-on exercise is focused on researching the capabilities of the platforms to implement the use cases under consideration. The team will be evaluating the platforms against the following: features such as AutoML, explainability, collaboration, security, scalability, integration, and deployment options.

STEP	OBJECTIVE	INSTRUCTIONS	DELIVERABLE
Research platforms	Learn about assigned platforms	Research key capabilities and use cases.	Summary of platform capabilities
Define evaluation criteria	Determine metrics to assess platforms	Identify criteria such as features, scalability, security, integration, ease of use, and pricing.	List of six evaluation criteria
Evaluate platforms	Analyze platforms based on criteria	Evaluate platforms based on each criteria.	Completed evaluation table
Present findings	Share evaluation with team	Present assessment within the allotted time.	Presentation summarizing platform assessment
Discuss and finalize	Decide on top platform(s) as a team	Discuss platforms, identify gaps, and determine next steps.	List of top one to two platforms, plan for piloting

WORKBOOK TEMPLATE: *AI/ML PLATFORM EVALUATION SHEET*

Download the "AI/ML Platform Evaluation Sheet" template from the download section of the book (`www.wiley.com/go/EnterpriseAIintheCloud`). Use this template to help your team evaluate various AI/ML platforms for your company's needs. It will help you to evaluate various platforms based on various criteria.

SUMMARY

This chapter reviewed the benefits and factors to consider when choosing a cloud-based AI/ML service. This chapter explained the criteria to consider when choosing an AI/ML service from one of the major cloud service providers—AWS, Google, and Azure.

It began by discussing the benefits of using cloud AI/ML services, including faster time to market, handling intensive machine learning workloads, cost effectiveness, collaboration, integration capabilities, security compliance, rich AI capabilities, tool support, and keeping up with innovations.

To assist you with the evaluation process, the chapter reviewed several factors, including identifying the business problem, exploring service capabilities, reviewing performance and scalability needs, and considering development and integration needs, security capabilities, price points, vendor support, and regulations.

It also examined various AI/ML services offered by the three major cloud providers and obtained a glimpse into the capabilities and tools available for various use cases and industries.

In the following chapters, you continue your journey toward deploying enterprise AI in the cloud. You explore data processing, building AI platforms, modeling pipelines, ML operations, and governance practices, and delve into AI/ML algorithms to train models.

REVIEW QUESTIONS

These review questions are included at the end of each chapter to help you test your understanding of the information. You'll find the answers in the following section.

1. Choose the correct answer regarding AI/ML services.
   A. The ML technology was limited to a few companies in the past but is now spreading to more companies due to the advent of AI/ML services.
   B. The ML technology is still in the periphery and has not reached the core of business applications.
   C. AI and ML are only popular with data scientists and not so much with other team members.
   D. Cloud service providers are still working on providing the right set of AI and ML services for projects.

2. Which of the following is a high-level AI service?
   A. SageMaker
   B. MXNet
   C. Fraud detection
   D. TensorFlow

3. Choose the correct machine learning algorithm.
   A. SageMaker
   B. Azure ML
   C. Decision trees
   D. Google Cloud ML Engine

4. Choose the AWS service that helps developers identify the phrases and entities in a document.
   A. AWS Comprehend
   B. AWS Rekognition
   C. Amazon Textract
   D. SageMaker

5. How can Amazon Polly be used in enterprise applications?
   A. To develop IVR systems
   B. To make applications more accessible to the visually impaired
   C. To create lifelike voices in apps
   D. To add audio to e-learning courses

6. What can AWS Panorama be used for in retail industries?
   A. To personalize marketing campaigns
   B. To track customer behavior and recommend products

     C. To detect diseases proactively

     D. To improve warehouse management

7. What type of filtering does Amazon Personalize *not* use?

     A. Content-based filtering

     B. Collaborative filtering

     C. Role-based filtering

     D. Community-based filtering

8. Which forecasting model in Amazon Forecast is suited for fast-changing situations and short-term trends?

     A. ARIMA

     B. ETS

     C. DeepAR

     D. EDS Prophet

9. How can data scientists use Vertex AI?

     A. Data visualization and exploration

     B. Model development and deployment

     C. Data preparation and cleaning

     D. Code version control

10. What is the purpose of the AI Workbench?

     A. Model development and deployment

     B. Data preparation and cleaning

     C. Rapid prototyping and model development

     D. Collaborative model sharing and deployment

11. How can developers use Cloud Natural language?

     A. Real-time translation of audio or video content

     B. Conversion of speech into text

     C. Analysis and understanding of human language in text format

     D. Detection and analysis of objects, faces, and text in images

12. Which service automates the development of models and is meant for those with limited knowledge of machine learning?

     A. Cloud Natural Language

     B. Dialogflow

     C. AutoML

     D. Translation AI

13. Models can be deployed in the cloud with scalable and distributed machine learning workflows using which of the following?

     A. Deep Learning Containers

     B. Deep Learning VM Image

     C. GPUs

     D. TensorFlow Enterprise

14. What capabilities are offered by Azure Cognitive Services for Language?

     A. Real-time analytics and intelligent search

     B. Entity recognition and sentiment analysis

C. Speech-to-text and text-to-speech

D. Semantic search and faceted navigation

15. Which open-source data analytics tool includes a web extraction tool for extracting data from websites?

A. Dataiku

B. DataRobot

C. KNIME

D. IBM Watson

ANSWER KEY

1.	A	**6.**	B	**11.**	C
2.	C	**7.**	D	**12.**	C
3.	C	**8.**	B	**13.**	A
4.	A	**9.**	B	**14.**	B
5.	B	**10.**	C	**15.**	C

10

Launching Your Pilot Project

The people who are crazy enough to think they can change the world are the ones who do.
—Steve Jobs

This chapter is a pivotal moment in your AI journey, where you transition from strategy to execution. You are on the cusp of introducing AI/ML into your company operations.

Launching a pilot is no small feat, fraught with many challenges and requiring precise coordination, and that's where the methodology comes into play. This chapter assists you in navigating the essential stages of launching, from initial planning to the nitty gritty details of a machine learning process.

This chapter brings all the strategy and vision discussed in the previous chapters to reality through a pilot launch, starting from business objectives to model development, deployment, and monitoring. I make this real through a hands-on project implementation exercise that bridges theory with practice. Ultimately, the goal is to launch a successful pilot that makes your strategic vision a reality. See Figure 10.1.

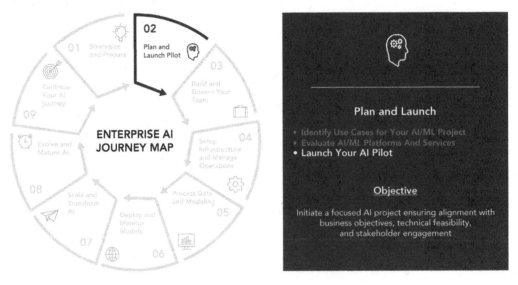

FIGURE 10.1: PLAN AND LAUNCH: Launch your AI pilot

> **NOTE** *Understanding your company's vision and goals while conducting a maturity assessment helps identify gaps and enables you to create an AI transformation plan. This in turn helps you move from pilot to production and make AI a core part of your business strategy.*

LAUNCHING YOUR PILOT

During the Align phase in Chapter 5, you learned that you need to conduct a maturity assessment of AI in the company, which will help address the current state of AI across dimensions such as business, people, data/models, platforms, governance, and security.

Trying to understand your company's vision, business strategy, and goals and reviewing that against the current state is important. This will help you identify gaps that need to be addressed when implementing a proof of concept during the Launch phase.

Once you have completed the current state assessment as part of the Align phase, you should have a clear understanding of the current state of AI adoption. Your capabilities across AI strategy, talent capabilities, data management, platforms, machine learning, operations, governance framework, data/infrastructure, and network security should be clear.

Armed with this knowledge, you can create a roadmap with the list of initiatives, resource allocations, and funding to move forward from the Align phase into the Launch phase, and you can focus on launching a pilot.

Planning for Launch

Your focus is now on putting together a project plan to launch the pilot to implement a particular use case that has been shortlisted through the prioritization of your AI initiatives. It will boil down to putting together a plan to implement a machine learning project.

As a part of the maturity assessment exercise, you now have a list of action items across the business, people, platform, operations, governance, machine learning, and security. Part of these action items are short-term and focused on initiating the launch. In contrast, others are long-term focused on increasing the adoption of AI across your entire organization. The long-term action items go into your AI transformation plan, while the short-term items need to bake into your project plan focused on executing your pilot. I discuss the AI transformation plan in greater detail in Chapter 23. Figure 10.2 shows some of the tasks needed to transition from envision to launching a pilot.

Recap of the Envision Phase

At this point, you have a list of projects for initiatives that you have identified working with various stakeholders that constitutes your AI portfolio. You have also prioritized those initiatives and shortlisted one or two use cases to implement as part of your pilot. In addition, you have defined a few KPIs that you will use to measure the success of your launch when it is completed. Here are some additional activities that you can initiate during this phase:

Change management activities	You have initiated some change-management activities to get leadership alignment and communicated the AI vision to the key stakeholders to get their support. You have also established a smaller version of COE, a group of A-class players from various departments working on the pilot as a core team.
Talent management	You also have to assist with any gaps in the talent required to implement the pilot, such as data scientists, machine learning engineers, or cloud engineers who will be required to establish the platform.

ML platform	From an ML platform perspective, you have identified the steps required to set up the AI platform and any gaps that need to be addressed during the launch.
Data capability	You have assessed the current state of the data, identified any data gaps, and the data infrastructure required to collect, ingest, clean, and process the data to feed the models.
Governance	Lastly, from a governance perspective, you have procured funding for this launch by working with a sponsor, ideally an executive who understands the value of the technology, is behind this launch, and is looking forward to ensuring its success.
Ethical considerations	You should consider the principles to be factored in during the design of the models to ensure trustworthy, ethical, and socially responsible implementation of your AI model.

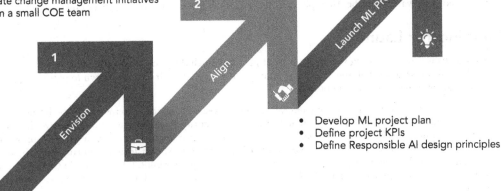

- Complete maturity model assessment
- Shortlist a use case for launch
- Identify short- and long-term action items

- Identify initiatives
- Initiate change management initiatives
- Form a small COE team

1 Envision

2 Align

3 Launch ML Project

- Develop ML project plan
- Define project KPIs
- Define Responsible AI design principles

FIGURE 10.2: Activities to move from Envision to Align to launching a pilot

> **NOTE** *After completing the AI maturity model assessment, use the insights to develop a roadmap and project plan for your AI launch.*

Planning for the Machine Learning Project

Now that you have completed the Align phase, you have a clear set of action items to follow, and ideally, you have a project plan to execute the launch of your pilot. With that in mind, the next section discusses the machine learning lifecycle, some of the important considerations when taking up a machine learning project, and how to develop the business goals, define the KPIs, and identify if machine learning is indeed the right solution for the problem.

FOLLOWING THE MACHINE LEARNING LIFECYCLE

When implementing a machine learning project, you follow a certain lifecycle, which is an iterative process with some defined steps that you should follow to make it a successful implementation.

You can break that cycle down into the following phases:

➤ Defining the business goal

➤ Framing the problem as a machine-learning problem

➤ Processing the data (collection, preprocessing, and feature engineering)

➤ Building the model (testing, tuning, and evaluation)

➤ Deploying the model (inference and prediction)

➤ Monitoring the model

Note that these phases are not necessarily sequential and that there are feedback loops between some phases, such as problem definition and monitoring, data preparation and model building, and model development and model monitoring.

The next sections briefly examine each of these phases shown in Figure 10.3, discuss in greater detail the business goal, and frame the machine learning problem.

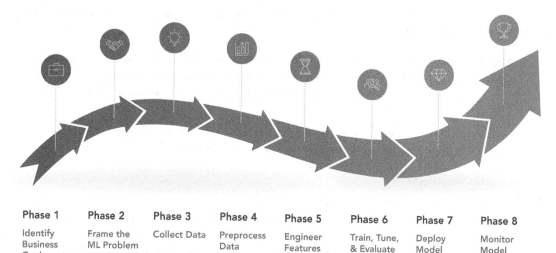

Phase 1	Phase 2	Phase 3	Phase 4	Phase 5	Phase 6	Phase 7	Phase 8
Identify Business Goals	Frame the ML Problem	Collect Data	Preprocess Data	Engineer Features	Train, Tune, & Evaluate	Deploy Model	Monitor Model

FIGURE 10.3: Machine learning phases

Business Goal Identification

Business goal identification is covered in detail in Chapters 5 and 6. During this phase, you do the following:

Identify the business problem	First, you should have a clear idea of the problem you're trying to solve and the business value you get by solving that problem.
Measure the business value	You should be able to measure the business value against specific business objectives and success criteria. The business objective is what you want to achieve, while the business value is what you expect to achieve at the end of this implementation.

Machine Learning Problem Framing

During this phase, you do the following:

Identify the machine learning problem type	Your primary focus is to translate your business problem into a machine learning problem. You try to identify the type of ML problem, such as whether it is a classification problem, regression problem, anomaly detection problem, and so on.
Identify the label	Given a dataset, you will identify one of the attributes as a label, which is the attribute that needs to be predicted.
Define the performance and error metrics	Focus on optimizing the performance and error metrics.

Follow a defined machine learning lifecycle that includes defining business goals, framing the problem as a machine learning problem, data processing, model building, model deployment, and model monitoring, with iterative feedback loops between some of the phases.

Data Processing

Data processing is covered in greater detail in Chapter 15. Data must be input into a model during the build process in the correct format.

Data collection and preparation	This involves identifying the different sources for the data—internal and external—as well as collecting data from multiple sources. You must also preprocess the data, such as addressing the missing data problem, formatting data types, and addressing any anomalies or outliers.
Feature engineering	Feature engineering involves creating new data, transforming data, extracting, and selecting a subset of the data from the existing set.

Model Development

Model development is covered in greater detail in Chapter 17. Model development involves the following:

Model building, tuning, and evaluation	Building, testing, tuning, and evaluating the model before it can be deployed into staging and production.
Setting up CI/CD pipelines for automatic deployment	It also involves setting up a CI/CD pipeline for automatic deployment into staging and production environments based on a set of criteria.

> **NOTE** *A CI/CD pipeline is a set of tools that automate the process of software deployment from source code control to production deployment.*

Model Deployment

Once the model has been tested, tuned, evaluated, and validated, it is ready to be deployed into production to make inferences and predictions. Chapter 18 covers this.

Model Monitoring

Model monitoring involves continuously monitoring the model's performance so that it performs well against a particular set of desired parameters and proactively detects and mitigates performance degradation. Chapter 19 covers this.

> **TIP** *When a model performance tends to degrade, it is important to retrain the model on new data that is representative of the current data distribution.*

HANDS-ON PROJECT IMPLEMENTATION EXERCISE: PLANNING AND LAUNCHING YOUR AI PILOT

Your ultimate goal is to implement AI effectively and scale it across the enterprise. However, you need to start somewhere, and that's the goal of this exercise—to help you plan and launch your pilot project.

TASK DESCRIPTION	TASK OWNERS	DELIVERABLES
Identify Business Problem Select and define a business problem that can be addressed with machine learning. Refer to Chapters 6 and 7 regarding business goal identification.	Business analyst, project manager	Business problem statement, objective
Change Management Develop a strategy to align leadership and stakeholders with the AI vision.	Project manager, leadership team	Change management plan
Assess Capabilities and Identify Gaps Evaluate current AI maturity and identify areas of improvement.	AI team, data scientists	AI maturity assessment, gap analysis
Create Project Plan Develop a project plan including action items, resource allocations, and roadmap.	Project manager	Project plan, roadmap

TASK DESCRIPTION	TASK OWNERS	DELIVERABLES
Ethical Considerations Outline ethical principles for the model's design and implementation. Refer to Chapter 4 for more details regarding ethics.	AI team, ethical oversight committee	Ethical guidelines
Define Machine Learning Problem Translate the business problem into a machine learning problem.	Data scientists	ML problem definition, metrics
Data Processing Collect, preprocess, and prepare data for model building.	Data engineers, data scientists	Processed data set
Model Building and Tuning Train, test, tune, and evaluate the chosen machine learning model.	Machine learning engineers	Trained model, evaluation report
Set Up CI/CD Pipeline (Optional) Create or simulate a CI/CD pipeline for automatic deployment.	DevOps team	CI/CD pipeline setup
Deploy Model into Production Deploy the validated model into staging or production environment.	DevOps team, machine learning engineers	Deployed model
Implement Model Monitoring Outline and implement a strategy for ongoing monitoring of the model's performance.	Data scientists, operations team	Monitoring plan, monitoring tools/setup
Reflect and Document Reflect on lessons learned, successes, and challenges, and document the process.	Entire project team	Reflection report, complete project documentation

WORKBOOK TEMPLATE: AI/ML PILOT LAUNCH CHECKLIST

Download the "AI/ML Pilot Launch Checklist" template from the download section of the book (www.wiley.com/go/EnterpriseAIintheCloud). Use this template to ensure that you have taken care of all the key activities and milestones for your AI/ML project to ensure a successful pilot launch. It will help you to tackle various challenges and tasks when launching an AI/ML project.

SUMMARY

This chapter covered the various steps you take as you move from the Align phase to the Launch phase. The chapter discussed how to prepare for the launch of your machine learning project. It discussed the different phases of a typical machine learning project: business goals, problem framing, data processing, model development, deployment, and monitoring. The chapter also included a hands-on exercise to plan and launch an AI pilot.

In the next chapter, let's discuss putting into motion some organizational change management steps to ensure your people wholeheartedly embrace your AI plans.

REVIEW QUESTIONS

These review questions are included at the end of each chapter to help you test your understanding of the information. You'll find the answers in the following section.

1. The focus of the core team implementing the AI pilot is
   A. To establish the platform
   B. To implement AI initiatives
   C. To conduct a maturity model assessment
   D. To establish a COE

2. Why do you need a label in machine learning problem framing?
   A. To make predictions.
   B. To evaluate the model.
   C. It identifies the type of machine learning problem.
   D. It is a feature created during feature engineering.

3. What is the primary focus of the machine learning problem framing phase in the machine learning lifecycle?
   A. Data processing
   B. Model definition
   C. Defining the business goal
   D. Identifying the type of machine learning problem

4. Feature engineering is used
   A. To evaluate the model's features
   B. To collect and preprocess features
   C. To create new data and transform existing data
   D. To identify the business data

5. Which phase involves translating a business problem into a machine learning problem?
   A. Data processing
   B. Model deployment
   C. Machine learning problem framing
   D. Business goal identification

ANSWER KEY

1.	A	3.	D	5.	C
2.	A	4.	D		

PART IV
Building and Governing Your Team

People make magic happen! Part IV explores the organizational changes required to empower your workforce. I guide you through the steps to launching your pilot and assembling your dream team. It's all about nurturing the human side of things.

11

Empowering Your People Through Org Change Management

Culture eats strategy for breakfast.

—Peter Drucker

This chapter is a pivotal step in the AI implementation methodology. By now, you have a good grip on the AI cloud ecosystem, use cases, and AI strategy. But here comes the crucial part: ensuring your AI plans are wholeheartedly embraced by your people (see Figure 11.1).

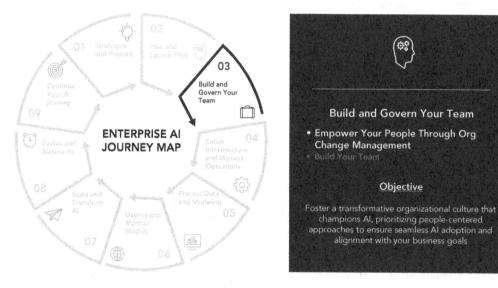

FIGURE 11.1: BUILD AND GOVERN YOUR TEAM: Empower Your People Through Org Change Management

The chapter starts by exploring how to evolve your company culture to foster AI adoption, bring innovation, and enable meaningful change. Knowing that technology alone won't cut it, the methodology delves into strategies to redesign your organization to enable agility and renewed thinking around adopting AI at the core. It is built on three strategies.

➤ Evolving the culture

➤ Redesigning the organization

➤ Aligning the organization

This is where the key deliverables—such as the cultural evolution program and organizational redesign plan discussed in this chapter—come in.

You need to get your entire organization aligned, starting from top executives to frontline staff, around AI adoption. In a world where change is constant, mastering org change management is a must. This chapter helps you with the insights and tools needed to lead change confidently so that your AI initiatives not only survive but thrive. Let's get started.

SUCCEEDING THROUGH A PEOPLE-CENTRIC APPROACH

It is the people who are going to decide whether the initiative is going to be a success. Getting them on board with the initiative helps accelerate your AI journey by making them receptive to change while promoting a culture of continuous learning and growth. The eight people-oriented aspects discussed here focus on enabling the right culture, setting up suitable organizational structures, garnering leadership support, and transforming the workforce.

Figure 11.2 shows the key issues you need to focus on from a people perspective.

➤ Evolving you culture

➤ Transforming your leadership

➤ Developing your cloud fluency

➤ Developing AI skills

➤ Transforming your workforce

➤ Accelerating your change

➤ Redesigning your organization

➤ Aligning your organization

> ### Case Study: How a Company Transformed Itself with AI Using a People-centric Approach
>
> A retail company wanted to leverage cloud and AI technologies to improve its retail operations and gain a competitive edge. Their gap assessment during the Align phase revealed that they needed to address the needs and aspirations of the people to ensure a successful implementation.
>
> #### They Evolved Their Culture
>
> Their gap assessment revealed that their organizational structure was very hierarchical and siloed. This was an impediment to their adoption of cloud and AI technologies. To resolve this, they decided to build a culture of collaboration and innovation. They achieved collaboration by promoting cross-functional teams and encouraging innovation through a culture of experimentation and learning.

They Transformed Their Leadership

They also realized they had to change their leadership to keep pace with the changing times and adopt innovative technologies such as the cloud and AI. They brought in new leadership that was well-versed with cloud and AI technologies. They could lead by example, inspire their teams, and bring about innovation.

They Developed Their Cloud and AI Fluency

They realized that they needed to educate their workforce to leverage the latest developments in cloud and AI technology. They offered training courses, reward programs, certifications, and on-the-job training opportunities for their employees to learn new skills.

They Transformed Their Workforce

They realized that to implement and operationalize new AI projects, they had to transform their workforce. They achieved this by assessing their current skillsets and competencies and filling the gaps by reskilling their employees through training programs and career development opportunities.

They Accelerated the Change Process

They noticed that the change process was terribly slow and that they had to speed up things. They achieved this by creating a change acceleration framework. This involved implementing a change management plan, communicating the change vision to the employees, soliciting employee feedback, addressing their concerns, and communicating the progress periodically. We discussed in great detail in Chapter 7 titled "Manage Strategic Change."

They Redesigned Their Organization

They noticed that communication and decision-making could have been more efficient. They addressed this by redesigning their organizational structure by creating cross-functional matrix teams, changing the lines of reporting, and enabling decentralized decision-making.

They Aligned the Organization for Business Success

They brought their strategy, processes, systems, org structure, and culture together to increase the probability of success. They aligned the projects with the business vision and strategy. They allocated resources accordingly so that the organization was invested in the most important priorities.

BEST PRACTICE TIP *To successfully implement AI at the enterprise level, prioritize a people-centric approach by evolving your culture, transforming leadership, developing cloud and AI fluency, transforming your workforce, accelerating the change process, and redesigning your organization.*

As you can see, you need to take care of the people when implementing the cloud and AI at the enterprise level. In the following two sections, you see how to systematically address people aspects using a comprehensive change management methodology. As part of this methodology, I address the objectives, tasks, and deliverables for these capabilities, such as cultural evolution, org redesign, org alignment, change acceleration, leadership transformation, workforce transformation, and cloud/AI upskilling.

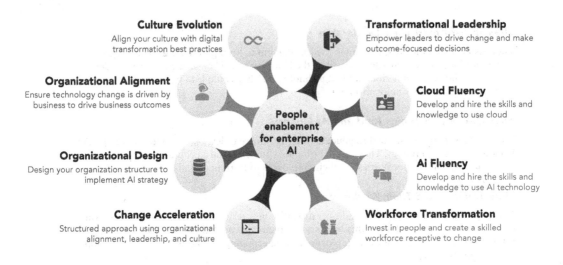

FIGURE 11.2: Change management focus areas for enterprise AI

Note that you would also need to implement change management techniques when choosing the AI/ML platforms and services. AI platforms come with their own training modules, may impact daily workflows, and can act as catalysts for collaboration. AI may also require additional security controls. It is therefore important to get the stakeholders' buy-in when adopting a new AI/ML platform or service and adopt these change management practices enabling growth and development.

Evolve Your Culture for AI Adoption, Innovation, and Change

As shown in Figure 11.3, Gartner reports in their research that transformations bring cultural tensions that fall under these seven broad categories.[1] They even found that many employees face more than one tension.

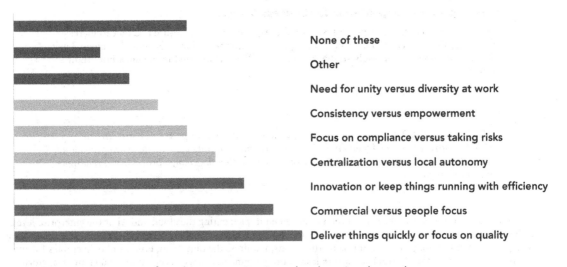

FIGURE 11.3: Percentage of employees experiencing cultural tension due to change

Regardless of the type of stress, the fact is it is going to impact their performance. It is, therefore, important to assess the organization's current culture and how the people react to change. Based on this assessment, you must take a certain number of steps, as shown in Figures 11.4 and 11.5. The focus of these steps is to bring in a change that enables innovation, get them aligned on transformational values, and build an open culture to encourage taking risks. You should also provide resources to build their capability, and foster collaboration between teams.

> **TIP** *If you manage your company culture well, you will see greater employee participation, higher motivation levels, and increased productivity, which translate into innovation and customer satisfaction.*

CURRENT STATE CULTURE ASSESSMENT

Conduct a current state assessment of the culture and identify areas to improve for AI adoption

DEVELOP CULTURE COMMUNICATION PLAN

Develop a cultural evolution communication plan to get employee buy-in

MONITOR AND MEASURE

Monitor the effectiveness of the culture evolution plan and make necessary improvements to increase its effectiveness

IMPLEMENT CULTURE EVOLUTION PLAN

Implement a cultural evolution plan to target employee groups through training programs, workshops, and mentoring

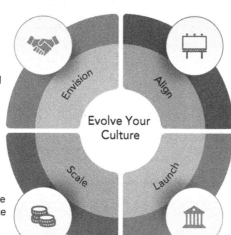

FIGURE 11.4: Evolve your culture: phases and tasks

Envision	Align	Launch	Scale
CURRENT STATE ASSESSMENT: A company found during their assessment that employees were afraid of innovative technologies such as AI due to potential job displacement and lack of skills. **RESULT** To address that, the company developed a cultural evolution program that focused on increasing the awareness of AI and training programs to build their skills in AI/ML technology.	**COMMUNICATION** The company developed a communication plan to socialize culture evolution plan to employees through town halls workshops and training programs. They also created an internal AI community to promote collaboration and learning. **RESULT** The company got the employees to buy into the communication plan.	**TRAINING** The company imparted training to both leadership and frontline workers about AI. **MENTORING** The company paid employees with experienced professionals to provide mentoring and on-the-job training. **REWARDS** They used rewards to encourage risk-taking and innovation.	**MEASUREMENT** The company evaluated the success of its culture evolution program through employee feedback and surveys. It made the necessary adjustments to improve the program by improving training and mentoring. **RESULT** The company was able to sustain its culture evolution efforts and sustain for the long-term resulting in improvement in AI adoption across the company.

ACTIVITIES

FIGURE 11.5: Evolve your culture: phases and deliverables

Redesign Your Organization for Agility and Innovation with AI

The organizational design aims to develop the appropriate structure for your organization to promote agility and innovation and ensure the successful completion of your AI initiatives with appropriate roles, structures, and responsibilities. Figure 11.6 captures the various steps and deliverables you can focus on for this track.

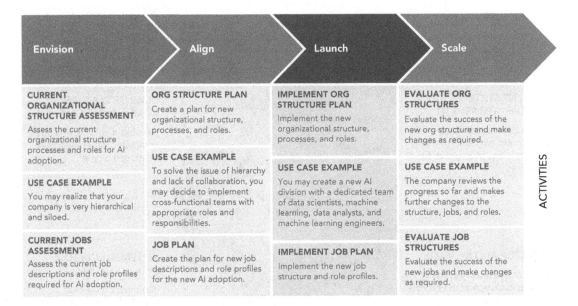

FIGURE 11.6: Redesign your organization: tasks and deliverables

ALIGNING YOUR ORGANIZATION AROUND AI ADOPTION TO ACHIEVE BUSINESS OUTCOMES

The focus of organizational alignment is to ensure that the business and technology teams are aligned toward adopting AI to achieve business outcomes. It involves aligning strategy, processes, systems, culture, team structures, and talent. Achieving proper organizational alignment involves alignment between business strategies and technology strategies, business strategy with organizational structure, and properly structured processes and systems. You should also ensure project prioritization, cultural alignment, and the proper execution of the change accelerated framework discussed in Chapter 7 titled "Managing Strategic Change."

> **NOTE** *Chapter 5 titled "Envisioning and Aligning Your AI Strategy" discussed aligning the organization around the AI vision and strategy. That theme continues to play throughout the book. For example, the people-centric alignment plays an even more vital role at the ground level when it comes to choosing an AI/ML platform or service. It only continues to increase in importance as you scale your AI capabilities. You learn about this more in Part VIII of this book.*

Figure 11.7 shows different components that need to be aligned as part of ensuring organizational alignment.

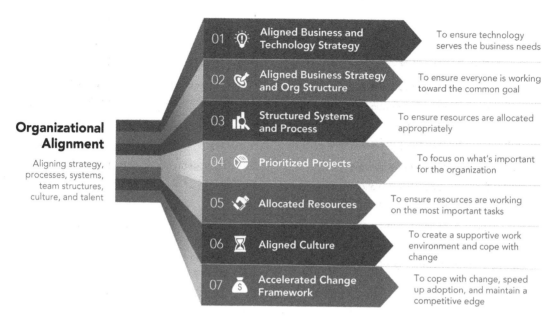

FIGURE 11.7: Organizational alignment

HANDS-ON EXERCISE FOR CULTURAL EVOLUTION AND ORG REDESIGN TO ADOPT AI

This exercise gives you tangible experience in dealing with org change management practices in the context of AI adoption.

TASK DESCRIPTION	TASK OWNERS	DELIVERABLES
Assess Cultural Tensions Identify cultural tensions using surveys, interviews, etc. You can use Figure 11.3 to identify different categories of tension.	HR department, organizational design team	Cultural report
Develop a Cultural Evolution Program Create a strategy to evolve culture focusing on innovation, alignment, risk-taking, resource-building, collaboration. Refer to Figures 11.4 and 11.5 for the steps, phases, and tasks.	Senior management, HR department	Cultural evolution program and strategy document

continues

continued

TASK DESCRIPTION	TASK OWNERS	DELIVERABLES
Create an Organizational Redesign Plan Assess current organizational structure for agility and innovation. Develop redesign plan for implementing AI.	Senior management, operations team	Organizational redesign plan
Develop Alignment Strategies Create a comprehensive alignment plan aligning all parts of the organization with AI.	Senior management, strategic planning team	Organizational alignment plan
Implement and Monitor Implement the strategies. Continuously monitor progress, making adjustments as necessary.	Senior management, operations team, organizational development team	Status reports

HANDS-ON ROLE PLAY EXERCISE TO INCORPORATE PEOPLE-CENTRIC APPROACH TO AI (FOR STUDENTS)

Objective: Including people-centric elements to an AI implementation such as evolving the culture, transforming the leadership, developing the workforce, and aligning the organization around AI.

Instructions:

Step 1: Divide your team into groups of three to five with each group representing a particular business unit, such as HR, marketing, strategy, operations, and so on.

Step 2: Assign each group a specific role such as evolving culture, transforming leadership, cloud/AI fluency, workforce transformation, change acceleration, organizational redesign, and alignment.

Step 3: Each group should discuss challenges, opportunities, gaps, and strategies for each area and present their findings and recommendations.

Step 4: Engage in collective discussions with all the groups to drive overall organizational alignment.

WORKBOOK TEMPLATE: ORG CHANGE MANAGEMENT PLAN

Download the "Org Change Management Plan" template from the download section of the book (www.wiley .com/go/EnterpriseAIintheCloud). Use this template to manage changes in your company's processes, systems, and people roles. It will help you to tackle the changes effectively and ensure successful adoption of AI.

SUMMARY

This chapter explained how companies can empower their people through organizational change management to build a competitive advantage. The key takeaway from this chapter is that technology won't be enough to bring change and innovation at the enterprise scale.

The chapter started by understanding the different cultural tensions that might arise during major transformational efforts and devised strategies to address them. This chapter provided step-by-step instructions to foster innovation, risk-taking, collaboration, and alignment with transformational values.

Remember that it's important to align your organization at all levels to ensure that strategy, processes, systems, culture, and teams work together to achieve the organizational goals. Prioritizing people and culture to drive organizational change, continuous learning, growth, and innovation will translate to business success and customer satisfaction.

In the next chapter, let's discuss building a high performing team that can kickstart your AI transformation effort.

REVIEW QUESTIONS

These review questions are included at the end of each chapter to help you test your understanding of the information. You'll find the answers in the following section.

1. Which of the following is not the only factor in the success of an AI project?
   A. Leadership support
   B. Employee training and development
   C. Adequate resources
   D. Change management plan

2. What are the challenges of evolving your culture evolution for AI adoption, innovation, and change?
   A. Employees are afraid of adopting modern technologies.
   B. Employees lack the necessary skills.
   C. Employees are resistant to change.
   D. It is difficult to measure the ROI of AI projects.

3. Which of the following is NOT one of the eight major areas of focus to build your competitive advantage in an AI initiative?
   A. Strategy and planning
   B. People
   C. Data
   D. Location
   E. Platforms
   F. Operations
   G. Security
   H. Governance

4. What did the case study company identify as an obstacle to the adoption of cloud and AI technologies?
   A. Lack of funding
   B. Hierarchical and siloed organizational structure
   C. Lack of market demand
   D. Technological incompatibility

5. What does organizational alignment focus on in terms of AI adoption?

    A. Ignoring the need for change management

    B. Ensuring that the business and technology teams are aligned toward adopting AI to achieve business outcomes

    C. Focusing only on the technology strategy without considering business strategy

    D. Replacing all business processes with AI technologies

ANSWER KEY

1.	D	3.	D	5.	B
2.	A, B, C	4.	B		

NOTE

1. www.gartner.com/en/corporate-communications/trends/diagnosing-cultural-tensions#:
    ~:text=During%20times%20of%20significant%20change,and%20helping%20employees%20build%20
    judgment.

Building Your Team

Coming together is a beginning, staying together is progress, and working together is success.

—Henry Ford

In this chapter, you embark on the fundamental task of building a collaborative team essential to kick-starting your AI project. The importance of assembling a synergistic team cannot be understated. This chapter delves into the various AI/ML roles and responsibilities involved in an AI implementation, be it the core roles such as data scientists and machine learning engineers or the equally crucial supporting roles such as security engineers.

Given that AI is taking center stage and evolving so rapidly, even noncore roles are quickly becoming core. What is essential, though, is to tailor these roles according to your specific business, project, and company requirements, and that's where this chapter comes in. You should also get good at transforming traditional roles, such as system administrators and business analysts, to harness your company's existing knowledge base and expertise. This, coupled with judiciously tapping into external skill sets, can bridge any looming skills gap.

Building a team is almost an art; the goal is to assemble a diverse, cross-functional team with clear roles and responsibilities to drive effective AI transformation tailored to business objectives. See Figure 12.1.

This dream team will go on to steward your AI operations, starting from data processing in Chapter 15, model monitoring in Chapter 19, and managing the ethics of AI in Chapter 20.

UNDERSTANDING THE ROLES AND RESPONSIBILITIES IN AN ML PROJECT

This section reviews the roles and responsibilities that you need in an ML project. As part of this selection process, the following sections outline some important points to consider.

Build a Cross-Functional Team for AI Transformation

As part of an AI transformation initiative, one of the essential things that you must do, regardless of what role you play, is identify a team that can help you with not only the overall transformation but also deploying the AI prototype as part of the Launch phase.

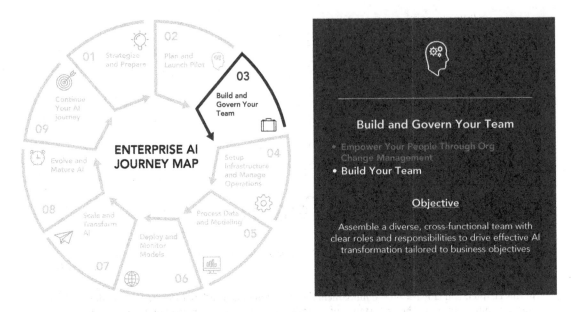

FIGURE 12.1: BUILD AND GOVERN YOUR TEAM: Building your team

When implementing your first enterprise-grade AI/ML project, you will face some challenges in identifying the right resources. This is because the ML platform has many components, and you need to bring together skill sets from multiple organizational units in your company. It includes data science, data management, model building, governance, cloud engineering, functional, and security engineering skills.

Adopt Cloud and AI to Transform Current Roles

You need to assess how the cloud can potentially free current staff to focus on innovation. This, in turn, will drive how their job roles will change when you migrate the ML platform and AI applications to the cloud.

Because the cloud brings with it the benefits of speed, scale, productivity, and innovation, the team can focus on larger, more impactful, innovative, and transformational efforts, now and in the future.

Speed comes from the ability to experiment with multiple models, and scale leads to the ability to serve a broader set of customer segments, geographies, and channels. Adopting infrastructure as code, code deployment pipelines, and security as code enables better compliance and results in higher productivity from automation.

Some current on-prem roles include IT solutions architect, systems administrator, network administrator, and desktop administrator. The applications administrator and database administrator will likely have to be reskilled/redesigned. For example, the system administrator previously responsible for managing the onsite hardware and infrastructure has to be relieved of some of these responsibilities, as the cloud provider (such as AWS, GCP, or Azure) now manages them.

> **TIP** *Create a cross-functional team with the appropriate skill sets, while also adapting existing job roles as needed to align with your company and project goals.*

Customize Roles to Suit Your Business Goals and Needs

Note that the actual job roles and responsibilities vary based on the company, the project goals, and other factors appropriate for a given initiative. You're going to realize that these roles and responsibilities are not very clearly defined, and there is often overlap between these roles. I recommend you use this as a guideline but then customize it so you align your specific needs based on the skill sets that you have in your organization and the hiring plan that you may have to initiate to fill the gaps.

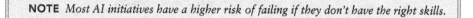

> **NOTE** *Most AI initiatives have a higher risk of failing if they don't have the right skills.*

The following sections review the new roles in the cloud-based AI scenario. Let's first look at the core team and then the extended teams they need to work with. Figure 12.2 summarizes the roles involved in a typical machine learning project.

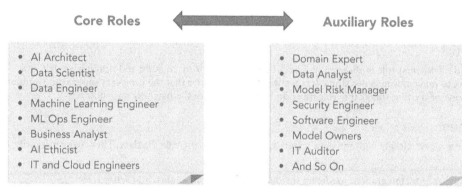

The actual composition of your team and the definition of core versus auxiliary depends on your specific use case and project needs.

FIGURE 12.2: Core and auxiliary roles in a machine learning project

Core AI Roles

Several roles are required on an AI project. Depending on the type of AI project, some roles may be critical for a project's success and in other cases may not. In general, the following roles can be considered core roles. Use this for guidance only, as the actual roles may vary based on your specific needs.

➤ AI architect

➤ Data scientist

➤ Data engineer

➤ Machine learning engineer

➤ MLOps engineer

AI Architect

The AI architect is an emerging role primarily focused on defining the transformational architecture that AI introduces. You can think of AI architects as the glue between the business stakeholders, the data engineers, the data scientists, the machine learning engineers, DevOps, DataOps, MLOps, and others involved in an AI initiative. They are responsible for the following:

TASK	DESCRIPTION
Designing the overall AI strategy	Identifying the AI application opportunities and use cases, as well as the underlying business and technical requirements to enable those use cases. Includes developing the AI roadmap.
Designing the AI architecture	Selecting the right AI technologies and ensuring the right data quality and security.
Defining the overall framework for building and deploying AI applications	Ensuring that the new AI technology is integrated with the existing business processes and applications.

Data Scientist

At its core, the data scientist role is about taking in data and refining it by creating and running models and drawing insights to make business decisions. It is a critical role to ensure that the project is successful. Defining the problem is one of the first things this role must do by working with the business stakeholders.

Data Engineer

The data engineer works closely with the data scientist, to whom they provide the data. They focus primarily on the following:

➤ Data acquisition, integration, modeling the data, optimization, quality, and self-service

➤ Ensuring that the data pipeline is appropriately implemented and is working satisfactorily so that the models get the correct data in the proper format and quality

Machine Learning Engineer

The machine learning engineer role is another crucial role for an AI project, and there is some overlap between a data scientist role, but there are also some subtle differences.

While data scientists focus more on drawing insights from the models, the machine learning engineer focuses on deploying models into production based on clean data from the data engineers.

MLOps Engineer

The MLOps engineer builds and manages automation pipelines to operationalize the ML platform and ML pipelines for fully/partially automated CI/CD pipelines. These pipelines automate building Docker images, model training, and model deployment. MLOps engineers also have a role in overall platform governance, such as data/model lineage, infrastructure, and model monitoring.

Cloud Engineer

Cloud engineers aim to ensure the cloud infrastructure is secure, reliable, and cost-effective. They are responsible for the following:

RESPONSIBILITY	DESCRIPTION
Setting up the cloud infrastructure	This includes configuring virtual machines, setting up databases, and storage. It may also include configuring cloud-based services such as Amazon SageMaker, Azure Machine Learning Studio, and Google Cloud platform.

RESPONSIBILITY	DESCRIPTION
Setting up the accounts and working with security	This includes creating and managing user accounts, setting up access controls, and working with security teams to ensure the infrastructure is secure.
Managing the security and access controls	This includes monitoring and enforcing security policies, managing user permissions, and responding to security incidents.
Monitoring the performance of the system	This includes monitoring resource usage, identifying bottlenecks, and implementing cost-saving strategies.

Business Analyst

Business analysts engage early in the ML lifecycle and translate business requirements into actionable tasks. Their primary role is to bridge the gap between business stakeholders and the technical team.

DATA SCIENTISTS VS. BUSINESS ANALYSTS

Data scientists are responsible for collecting, cleaning, and analyzing data. They use their knowledge of statistics and machine learning to develop models that can be used to make predictions or decisions. Business analysts are responsible for understanding the business needs and requirements for an AI/ML project. They work with data scientists to ensure the project meets the business' goals.

Data scientists typically have a strong mathematics, statistics, and computer science backgrounds. Business analysts typically have a strong background in business, economics, and communication.

Data scientists are typically more focused on the technical aspects of AI/ML, while business analysts are typically more focused on the business aspects. However, both roles are essential for the success of an AI/ML project.

Business analysts need to understand the business requirements and translate them into technical specifications that the developers and data scientists can use to build the AI/ML system. They also need to analyze the data and provide insights to the stakeholders on how the system is performing and how it can be improved.

Use Case Example

Let's say you are working as a business analyst on an AI/ML project for a telecom company. One of the company's fundamental business problems is customer churn when customers cancel their subscriptions and switch to a competitor's service. The company wants to use AI/ML to predict which customers will likely churn so they can take measures to retain them.

As a business analyst, your first step is to gather the requirements from the stakeholders. You need to understand what data sources are available, what business rules need to be applied, and what the system's output should look like. You then work with the data scientists and technical team to design the system architecture and define the data processing pipeline.

Once the system is built, you must work with the data scientists to analyze the data and provide insights to the stakeholders. You need to monitor the system's performance and recommend improvements. For example, specific customers are more likely to churn if they experience network issues, so you should recommend that the company invest in improving its network infrastructure in those areas.

Overall, as a business analyst in an AI/ML project, your role is crucial in ensuring that the AI/ML system is aligned with the business objectives and that the stakeholders are informed about the system's performance and potential improvements.

Noncore or Support Roles

In addition to the core roles, several roles are not critical for the success of an AI project but can facilitate the process. Please note that as the adoption of AI matures in organizations, some of the support roles are turning into core roles.

Domain Expert

Domain experts have valuable functional knowledge and understanding of the environment where you implement the ML solution. They do the following:

RESPONSIBILITIES	DESCRIPTION
Requirements gathering	Help ML engineers and data scientists develop and validate assumptions and hypotheses.
Design involvement	Engage early in the ML lifecycle and stay in close contact with the engineering owners throughout the Evaluation phase.
Industry compliance	Provide valuable insights and help ensure the project adheres to industry standards and best practices.

Domain experts have a deep understanding of their respective fields and are essential to any project involving specialized knowledge. With their expertise, projects can succeed, significantly saving time and money and minimizing reputation losses. Therefore, a domain expert is critical for any project requiring specialized knowledge.

Domain experts are especially important for healthcare, finance and banking, retail and e-commerce, manufacturing, energy, agriculture, real estate, and so on.

> **NOTE** *Not having a domain expert can result in models being created in a vacuum, thus missing critical industry requirements and resulting in poor model performance.*

Data Analyst

A data analyst is a professional who does the following:

RESPONSIBILITIES	DESCRIPTION
Data collection and analysis	Collects, cleans, analyzes, and draws insights from the data.
Business interpretation	Helps interpret that data for the business stakeholders to make business decisions.
Exploratory data analysis	Conducts exploratory data analysis to identify patterns and trends and uses data visualization tools to help interpret the data for the business stakeholders.

RESPONSIBILITIES	DESCRIPTION
Collaboration with data scientists	In the context of enterprise AI, may also work with data scientists to select and preprocess data.
Model testing and validation	Tests and validates the models to ensure they are reliable and accurate.

> **NOTE** *Data scientists have a broader scope and dive deep into advanced computations and predictive analytics, while data analysts are focused on deriving insights from data to guide business decisions. In small organizations, the roles can be played by the same person.*

Model Risk Manager

The primary responsibility of a model risk manager is to ensure that the risks associated with the model are identified and mitigated. They must ensure that the model is reliable, accurate, and meets regulatory requirements.

Model risk managers ensure the following:

RESPONSIBILITIES	DESCRIPTION
Responsible deployment	Ensures the model is deployed responsibly and ethically, protecting the company's brand image, and preventing reputational risk.
Data management	Ensures the data used to train the model is free from bias, is accurate, and is complete.
Model testing and validation	Ensures the model is adequately tested and validated before deploying in production by testing it against several scenarios so that it is robust and can perform well even in unexpected situations.
Compliance and transparency	Ensures the model is transparent, explainable, and complies with legal requirements by working with legal and compliance teams.

Security Engineer

The role of the security engineer is to ensure the security of the AI systems end to end, starting from managing the data, the models, the network, and the infrastructure. They need to do the following:

RESPONSIBILITIES	DESCRIPTION
Implement security controls	Do so at all layers of the AI system, starting from data preparation, model training, testing, and deployment stages.
Risk management	Identify and assess the security risks, implement controls to mitigate risks, and assess the effectiveness of those controls.
Incident response	Respond to security incidents such as ransomware attacks, address data breaches in real-time, identify the root cause, and implement steps to remediate those risks.

RESPONSIBILITIES	DESCRIPTION
Legal compliance	Ensure that the AI infrastructure is legally compliant concerning data privacy and security by working with legal and risk teams.
Model security	Manage the security of machine learning models by ensuring no tampering with training data and no bias introduced into the data.

Software Engineer

The role of a software engineer is to do the following:

RESPONSIBILITIES	DESCRIPTION
Integration and interface development	Integrate the AI algorithms/their output into other back-end applications and develop front-end user interfaces for users to interact with the models.
Deployment	Deploy AI solutions to production and manage different software versions.
Performance and security	Ensure these solutions are performant, reliable, scalable, and secure.
Maintenance	Continue monitoring the AI solution in production, identify bugs, solve them when required, and add new features.

Model Owners

The model owner is a new role primarily responsible for the model's development, maintenance, governance, and performance. The model owner is typically a technical person who works with the business stakeholders. They need to do the following:

RESPONSIBILITIES	DESCRIPTION
Safety and responsibility	Ensure that the model can perform safely and responsibly.
Business problem understanding	Understand the business problem the model is supposed to solve.
Performance metrics definition	Define the performance metrics by which the model will be evaluated.
Data selection and bias checking	Select the correct data to train the model upon and ensure there is no bias in the data.
Algorithm selection and deployment	Work with the data scientists to choose a suitable algorithm, configure it, and deploy it in production.
Model monitoring	Monitor the model's performance to ensure it's working accurately with fairness and transparency.
Model maintenance	Maintain the model by considering new data, retraining it, and addressing any issues.

Model Validators

Model validators are responsible for the following:

RESPONSIBILITIES	DESCRIPTION
Model testing and validation	Test and validate the models to ensure they work accurately and responsibly while meeting the business' objectives and requirements.
Error and bias check	Ensure that the models are working without any errors and bias and with fairness, which may include designing tests for various scenarios and conducting statistical analysis to check for biases or limitations in the model.
Legal compliance and documentation	Ensure that the models comply with legal requirements and capture documentation about how these models work so they can share it with other stakeholders, auditors, and senior management.
Model improvement recommendations	Provide recommendations for improving the model.

IT Auditor

The IT auditor is responsible for analyzing system access activities, identifying anomalies and violations, preparing audit reports for audit findings, and recommending remediations. Their areas of focus include model governance, data integrity and management, AI applications security, ethical considerations, AI systems performance and scalability, and continuous monitoring.

HANDS-ON ROLEPLAY EXERCISE: ADOPTING NEW ROLES IN AN AI PROJECT

This exercise is to help everyone understand their new roles better and learn how these roles collaborate with each other.

TASK DESCRIPTION	TASK OWNERS (JOB FUNCTIONS)	DELIVERABLES
Introduction: Brief participants on the importance of AI/ML team and roles.	Facilitator	Understanding of AI/ML roles and importance
Role identification: List all required roles on Post-It notes.	Facilitator	Visual representation of roles
Skill mapping: Map primary skills required for each role.	Participants, facilitator	Skills identified for each role
Team assembly simulation: Simulate a hiring panel to select candidates for each role.	Participants in groups	Selected candidates for each role

continues

continued

TASK DESCRIPTION	TASK OWNERS (JOB FUNCTIONS)	DELIVERABLES
Discussion and justification: Discuss and justify the chosen candidates.	Participants in groups, facilitator	Agreed candidates, understanding of hiring criteria
Role interrelation activity: Understand how roles interact through a hypothetical scenario.	Participants in groups, facilitator	Understanding of team dynamics and collaboration
Document key learnings: Document insights and feedback for future reference.	Facilitator, possibly an HR representative	Documented insights to guide future hiring

WORKBOOK TEMPLATE: TEAM BUILDING MATRIX

Download the "Team Building Matrix" template from the download section of the book (www.wiley.com/go/EnterpriseAIintheCloud). use this template to build a skills and roles matrix for building your AI team. It will help you have all the necessary roles and skills needed to implement your AI project successfully.

SUMMARY

The chapter discussed the roles and responsibilities you need to fill for your project to take off and ensure the efficient development, deployment, and management of your AI systems. It also discussed the core roles and other noncore roles that you need to fill depending on the specific needs of your project. The discussion of these roles should help you build a blueprint for assembling a team of professionals who can navigate the complexities of AI development by taking on responsibilities and driving innovation. Remember to customize these roles according to your company's needs.

Understanding of these roles and how they interact with each other will help you plan the team structure, communicate the vision of the AI system, and ensure that the AI system is robust, secure, fair, and legally compliant.

In the next chapter, we will discuss setting up a robust enterprise AI cloud platform that will help you take your model from ideation to production quickly with the least amount of risk.

REVIEW QUESTIONS

These review questions are included at the end of each chapter to help you test your understanding of the information. You'll find the answers in the following section.

1. The primary responsibility of a machine learning engineer is
   A. Running models and drawing insights
   B. Ensuring the data pipeline is appropriately implemented
   C. Designing the overall AI strategy
   D. Deploying models into production

2. The primary role of a business analyst is
   A. Collecting, cleaning, and analyzing data
   B. Developing and validating assumptions and hypotheses
   C. Bridging the gap between business and technical teams
   D. Developing the project plan

3. What task does a model owner NOT perform?
   A. Algorithm selection and deployment
   B. Model maintenance
   C. Model testing and validation
   D. Performance metrics definition

4. Who ensures that the AI models comply with legal requirements and capture documentation?
   A. IT auditor
   B. Security engineer
   C. Model validators
   D. Software engineer

5. Which role is primarily responsible for the model's development, maintenance, governance, and performance?
   A. Security engineer
   B. Model validators
   C. Model owner
   D. IT auditor

ANSWER KEY

1.	D	3.	C	5.	C
2.	C	4.	C		

PART V
Setting Up Infrastructure and Managing Operations

In this part, you roll up your sleeves and get technical. Part V is like your DIY guide to building your own AI/ML platform. Here, I discuss the technical requirements and the daily operations of the platform with a focus on automation and scale. This part is a hands-on toolkit for those who are hungry to get geeky.

13

Setting Up an Enterprise AI Cloud Platform Infrastructure

Design is not just what it looks like and feels like. Design is how it works.

—*Steve Jobs*

In this chapter, you get your hands dirty by setting up an enterprise AI cloud platform infrastructure (see Figure 13.1). By now, you should have a good idea of the strategic vision, have aligned with the stakeholders on the AI/ML use cases and the business metrics, implemented change management processes, built a team, and may even have a good idea of the ML algorithm that you want to adopt.

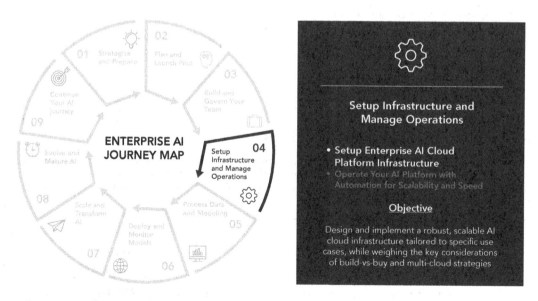

FIGURE 13.1: Setting up the enterprise AI cloud platform infrastructure

Building a production-ready, robust enterprise AI cloud platform infrastructure is important because it helps you take your models from ideation to production in the shortest possible time and with the least risk possible.

This chapter is not just about the theory; it's about integrating AI into business processes to automate, reduce costs, increase efficiency, and create new opportunities. To do this, you must create efficient models and build a repeatable, robust, stable, and secure enterprise AI system adaptable to changing conditions. The right infrastructure will serve as a solid foundation for serving models with good performance, scalability, and reliability and as a launchpad to transition from pilot projects to full-blown AI operations. See Figure 13.1.

In this chapter, you

➤   Review the typical reference architectures (AWS, Azure, and the Google Cloud Platform) for the most common use cases

➤   Review the general components of an ML platform

➤   Learn how to choose between building and buying a ready-made ML platform

➤   Learn how to choose between different cloud providers

➤   Review hybrid and edge computing and the multicloud architecture

REFERENCE ARCHITECTURE PATTERNS FOR TYPICAL USE CASES

There are close to 200 services provided by AWS and this number keeps growing. This becomes challenging for companies attempting to choose the correct tools for the right problem and map them to various use cases. This section reviews a few reference architecture patterns so you can use them to customize your implementation based on your specific project needs. This can help you create your future-state strategy and gain insights from big data processing, data warehousing, visualization, and AI/ML to prepare for the future. Those architectural patterns are related to the following five use cases:

➤   Customer 360-degree architecture

➤   Event-driven architecture with IoT data

➤   Personalized recommendation architecture

➤   Real-time customer engagement

➤   Data anomaly and fraud detection

Customer 360-Degree Architecture

Customer 360-degree architecture can be used to increase customer retention and profitability by improving customer service, increasing sales, and improving marketing campaigns. Building a 360-degree customer view involves aggregating data from multiple data sources into a single unified solution, from which you can draw the necessary insight about your customers.

Building this architecture, as shown in Figure 13.2, involves four steps.

STEP NUMBER	STEP NAME	DESCRIPTION	POSSIBLE AWS COMPONENTS
1	Data sources	Ingest the data from multiple sources into a single data source. Data can come from SAP, ERP, CRM, websites, Salesforce, Google Analytics, and so on.	AWS Data Migration Service, AWS Glue

STEP NUMBER	STEP NAME	DESCRIPTION	POSSIBLE AWS COMPONENTS
2	Knowledge graph system	Build a unified customer profile by implementing a graph-based knowledge system to identify new customer segments and build customer hierarchies.	Amazon Neptune
3	Intelligence layer	Build an intelligence layer by offloading the data into Amazon RedShift or S3 so that insights can be drawn using analytical tools such as Amazon Athena.	Amazon Redshift, Amazon S3, Amazon Athena
4	Activation layer	Use the insights from the intelligence layer and enrich it with recommendations or predictions from AI/ML to create the next best action and personalize customer experiences.	AWS Lambda, Amazon Personalize

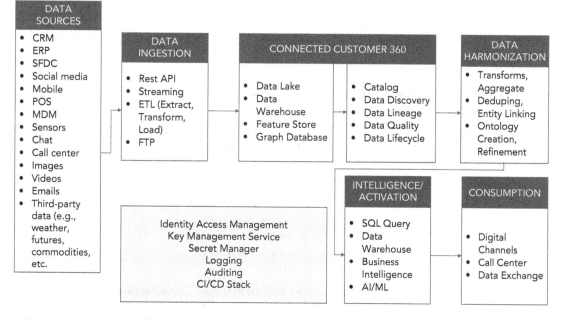

FIGURE 13.2: Customer 360-degree architecture

Figure 13.3 shows an implementation of the customer 360-degree architecture using AWS components. You should be able to build similar architecture using Google or Azure Cloud components.

> **NOTE** *The customer 360-degree architecture has four steps: data ingestion, knowledge graph system, intelligence layer for insights, and activation layer for personalized customer experiences.*

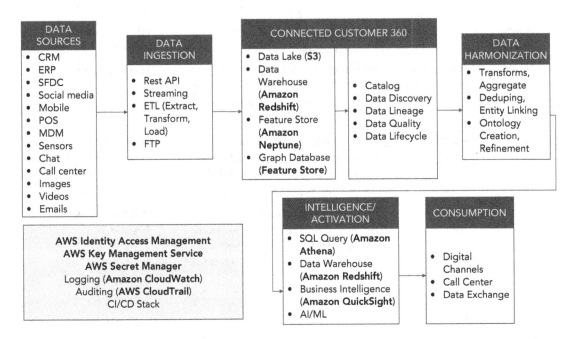

FIGURE 13.3: Customer 360-degree architecture using AWS components (AWS components shown in bold)

EXERCISE: BUILDING A CUSTOMER 360-DEGREE VIEW ARCHITECTURE USING AWS

This is an experiential learning exercise that allows the team members to apply their theoretical knowledge of AWS services into practice and acquire AWS skills.

STEP NAME	TASK OWNER	TASK DETAILS	DELIVERABLE
Set up data sources	Data engineer	Create mock data that represents different data sources (CRM system, web analytics, etc.)	Mock data files
Data ingestion	Data scientist	Ingest the data from multiple sources into a single data source on AWS using AWS Data Migration Service or AWS Glue.	AWS Data Migration Service or AWS Glue configuration

STEP NAME	TASK OWNER	TASK DETAILS	DELIVERABLE
Build knowledge graph system	Data scientist	Create a Graph DB using Amazon Neptune. Load the ingested data into this DB and explore the relations between different data entities.	Amazon Neptune DB setup, relations explored
Build intelligence layer	Machine learning engineer	Offload the data into Amazon RedShift or S3. Draw insights from the data using Amazon Athena.	Amazon RedShift or S3 setup, insights drawn using Amazon Athena
Build activation layer	Machine learning engineer and data scientist	Enrich the insights from the intelligence layer with predictions or recommendations from AI/ML to create the next best action and personalize customer experiences. Use AWS Lambda and Amazon Personalize for this.	AWS Lambda and Amazon Personalize setup, recommendations, or predictions generated
Report preparation	AI architect	Document the architecture built, problems encountered, solutions implemented, and insights drawn from the customer data. Include screenshots of the AWS console.	Report with necessary details and screenshots

Develop an Event-Driven Architecture Using IoT Data

The event-driven architecture shown in Figure 13.4 is focused on getting value by making near real-time decisions from the data. Some of these use cases are as follows:

➤ Data from medical devices used to provide personalized healthcare

➤ Data from equipment to prevent equipment failures or to impact employee training

➤ Data from autonomous vehicles to improve safety

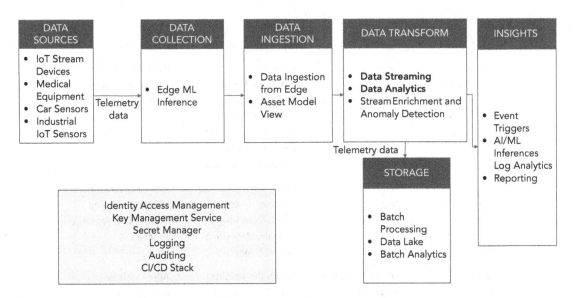

FIGURE 13.4: Event-driven near real-time predictive analytics using IoT data (AWS components shown in bold)

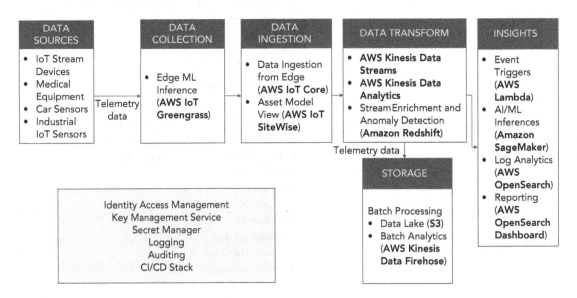

FIGURE 13.5: IoT-based event-driven predictive analytics using AWS components (AWS components shown in bold)

Figure 13.5 shows the IoT-based event driven architecture using AWS components. The following table shows the steps involved in setting up an Internet of Things (IoT)–based architecture that facilitates an end-to-end journey—from data collection to insight generation.

STEPS	DESCRIPTION	AWS SERVICES
Data collection	Data from IoT devices, such as medical devices, car sensors, and industrial equipment is collected.	AWS Greengrass
Data ingestion	The collected data is then ingested into the cloud platform.	AWS IoT Core, AWS IoT SiteWise
Stream transformation	The streamed data from these IoT devices is transformed using data from a data warehouse.	Amazon Kinesis Data Analytics
Data storage	The transformed data is then stored for further downstream analysis.	Amazon Redshift
Model training and deployment	The model is trained and deployed to generate inferences.	Amazon SageMaker
Event triggering	Inferences from the models trigger certain events.	AWS Lambda
Dashboard creation	Dashboards are created to visualize insights.	Amazon OpenSearch Service Dashboards

> **TIP** *IoT architecture leverages streaming data from IoT devices to make real-time decisions for use cases such as personalized healthcare, autonomous cars, and equipment monitoring.*

EXERCISE: BUILDING AN EVENT-DRIVEN ARCHITECTURE USING AWS AND IoT DATA

This is an experiential learning exercise that allows the team members to design and implement an event-driven architecture that collects, processes, and analyzes data from IoT devices in real time.

Prerequisites: You need a basic knowledge of AWS services, IoT devices, and some data science concepts.

Tasks: Use the steps outlined in the previous table to build this architecture. The details of building this architecture is outside the scope of the book, but it would be a good starting point if your use case involves processing IoT data.

Personalized Recommendation Architecture

Figure 13.6 shows a personalized recommendation architecture, and Figure 13.7 shows the architecture with AWS components.

In Figure 13.7, the first step is to gather click views and item view data from websites and upload them into Amazon S3. The data is then cleaned using Amazon Glue DataBrew.

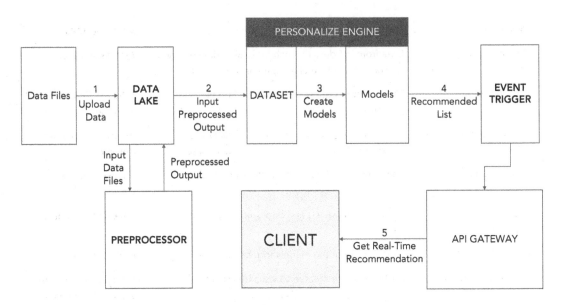

FIGURE 13.6: Personalized recommendation architecture

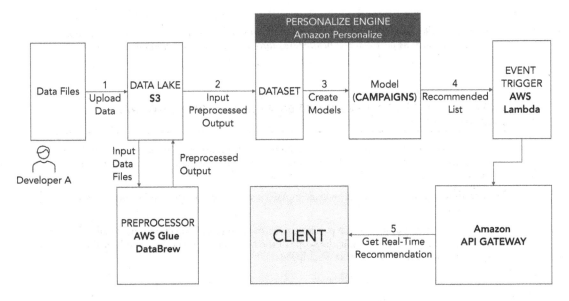

FIGURE 13.7: Personalized recommendation architecture using AWS components (shown in bold)

The second step involves training the model in Amazon Personalize to make real-time personalization recommendations. In this step, you use three types of data.

➤ Event data, such as the items the user clicks on, purchases, or browses

➤ Item data, such as the price, category, and other information in the catalog

➤ Data about the users, such as the user's age, location, and so on

The next step is to feed this data into the Amazon Personalize service and get a personalized private model hosted for you through the Amazon API Gateway. You can then use this API to feed the recommendations to your users in your business application.

> **NOTE** *To train a personalized model, you must gather event data, item data, and user data.*

EXERCISE: BUILDING A PERSONALIZED RECOMMENDATION SYSTEM USING AWS

This is an experiential learning exercise that allows the team members to develop a personalized recommendation system using Amazon Personalize.

Prerequisites: You need a basic knowledge of AWS services, data gathering techniques, data cleaning processes, and some machine learning concepts.

TASK NAME	TASK OWNER (SKILL SET)	TASK DETAILS	DELIVERABLE
Data gathering	Data engineer	Gather click views and item view data from websites. Store this data in Amazon S3.	Data stored in Amazon S3
Data cleaning	Data scientist/ data engineer	Use Amazon Glue DataBrew to clean and prepare the data for model training.	Cleaned data in Amazon S3
Model training	Machine learning engineer	Train a recommendation model in Amazon Personalize using event data, item data, and user data.	Trained recommendation model
Model hosting	Machine learning engineer	Host the trained model via Amazon API Gateway to make it accessible for the application.	API endpoint for model
Recommendation implementation	Software engineer/ full-stack developer	Use the API created in the previous step to integrate recommendations into the business application.	Application with integrated recommendation feature

Real-Time Customer Engagement

Figure 13.8 shows a real-time customer engagement reference architecture that implements use cases such as churn predictions, recommendations using customer segmentation, and engaging with customers by sending them messages based on real-time transactions.

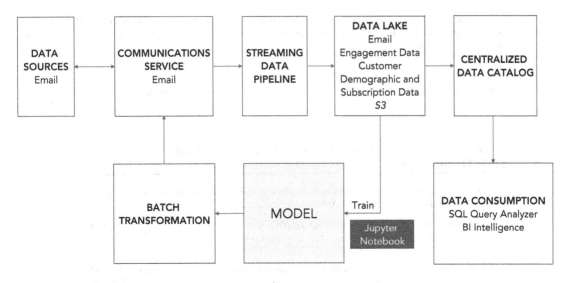

FIGURE 13.8: Real-time customer engagement architecture

The following steps implement the real-time customer engagement reference architecture using the AWS components shown in Figure 13.9:

STEP NAME	STEP DESCRIPTION	AWS SERVICES INVOLVED
Upload user data	First, you upload the users and their contact info, such as emails, into Amazon Pinpoint and collect data about customer interactions into S3.	Amazon Pinpoint, Amazon S3
Ingest data	You then ingest this data in Amazon S3 using either Amazon Kinesis Data Firehose or Amazon Kinesis data stream.	Amazon S3, Amazon Kinesis Data Firehose, Amazon Kinesis Data Stream
Train model	You then use this data in S3 to train a model in Amazon SageMaker to predict the likelihood of customer churn or gather customer segmentation data. You can create a SageMaker endpoint once the model is ready for production.	Amazon S3, Amazon SageMaker
Run inference and export results	You then run the inference in a batch manner and export the results into S3 and Pinpoint.	Amazon S3, Amazon Pinpoint
Combine data and gather insights	You can combine the data in Pinpoint with other data from your data lake and get insights using Amazon Athena.	Amazon Pinpoint, Amazon Athena
Visualize data	Finally, you can use Amazon QuickSight to visualize the data and share it with others.	Amazon QuickSight

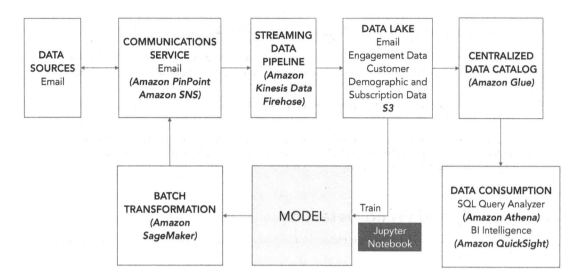

FIGURE 13.9: Real-time customer engagement architecture on AWS (AWS components shown in bold italics)

> **TIP** *By using Amazon SageMaker Pipelines, you can automate the steps to build, train, and deploy machine learning models and save time and effort.*

Figure 13.10 shows a customer engagement architecture that you can implement using Azure components.

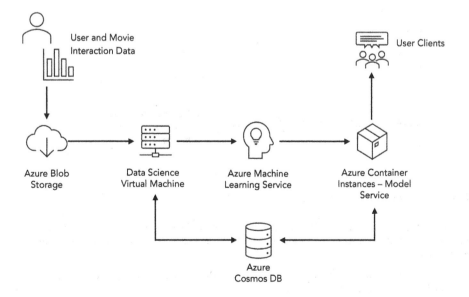

FIGURE 13.10: Real-time customer engagement architecture on Azure

---

EXERCISE: BUILDING A REAL-TIME CUSTOMER ENGAGEMENT SYSTEM

This is an experiential learning exercise that allows the team members to implement a real-time customer engagement system focusing on use cases such as customer churn, and personalized recommendations using customer segmentation.

Prerequisites: You need a basic knowledge of AWS services, IoT devices, and some data science concepts.

Tasks: Use the steps outlined in the table to build this architecture. The detail of building this architecture is outside the scope of the book, but it would be a good starting point if your use case involves engaging with customers.

Data Anomaly and Fraud Detection

The fraud detection architecture shown in Figure 13.11 helps detect fraud in transactions such as fake accounts and fraudulent payments.

NOTE *Use Amazon SageMaker Autopilot to automatically build, train, and deploy machine learning models for fraud detection.*

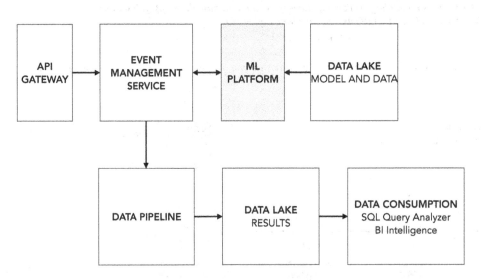

FIGURE 13.11: Fraud detection architecture

To build the fraud detection architecture using AWS components shown in Figure 13.12, you must first use the Amazon CloudFormation template to instantiate an instance of Amazon SageMaker with the sample dataset and train models using that dataset.

The solution also contains an Amazon Lambda function that invokes the two Amazon SageMaker endpoints for classification and anomaly detection using the sample data.

The Amazon Kinesis Data Firehose loads the transactions into the Amazon S3, which is used to make predictions and generate new insights.

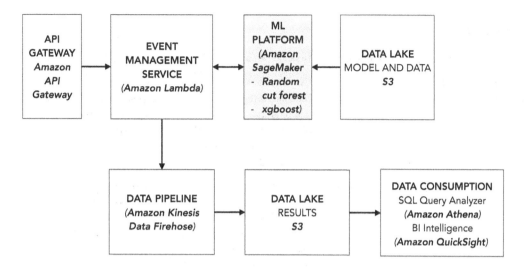

FIGURE 13.12: Fraud detection architecture on AWS (AWS components shown in bold italics)

EXERCISE: BUILDING A REAL-TIME CUSTOMER ENGAGEMENT SYSTEM

This is an experiential learning exercise that allows the team members to build a working fraud detection system that can automatically detect fraudulent transactions in real time.

Prerequisites: You need a basic knowledge of AWS services and some data science concepts.

STEP NAME	TASK OWNER	TASK DETAILS	DELIVERABLE
Initialize Amazon SageMaker	Data scientist	Use the Amazon CloudFormation template to create an instance of Amazon SageMaker equipped with a sample dataset for fraud detection.	Amazon SageMaker instance with sample dataset
Train models	Data scientist	Use Amazon SageMaker Autopilot to automatically build, train, and deploy machine learning models for fraud detection.	Trained machine learning models
Set up Lambda Function	AWS architect	Create an Amazon Lambda function that will invoke your Amazon SageMaker endpoints. This function should be able to feed new data to these endpoints and receive their predictions in return.	Working AWS Lambda function

continues

continued

STEP NAME	TASK OWNER	TASK DETAILS	DELIVERABLE
Set up Kinesis Data Firehose	AWS architect	Use Amazon Kinesis Data Firehose to create a real-time data streaming pipeline. This pipeline will load new transactions into Amazon S3.	Real-time data pipeline with Amazon Kinesis Firehose
Run inference on new data	Data scientist	As new transactions are loaded into Amazon S3, use your Amazon SageMaker models to make predictions. These predictions should indicate whether each transaction is likely to be fraudulent.	Working fraud detection system

FACTORS TO CONSIDER WHEN BUILDING AN ML PLATFORM

This section covers ML platform considerations such as building versus buying an ML platform, choosing a suitable cloud provider, and the MLOps maturity model.

The Build vs. Buy Decision

Building a platform to meet the needs of a healthcare ML platform can be a daunting task. You would need to customize the entire stack using best-of-breed, open-source, and out-of-the-box services and tools provided by cloud providers. It is vital for you to embrace the automation, instrumentation, and scalability of MLOps to achieve your platform goals. The logical question is whether to build or buy best-of-breed solutions. To answer this question effectively, carry out the tasks in the following exercise.

HANDS-ON EXERCISE: BUILDING VS. BUYING AN ML PLATFORM

This is a hands-on experiential learning exercise that allows the team members to make an informed decision on building versus buying an AI/ML platform based on the company's needs.

Using the table, execute the steps to deliver a recommendation to your leadership team for a build vs buy decision.

TASK NAME/ DETAILS	ROLE	BUY	BUILD	DELIVERABLE/ IMPORTANCE
Identify Organization's Needs List the specific requirements and constraints of your organization with respect to an ML platform.	Business analyst	Pay specific attention to the need for customization and configuration, integrate-ability, vendor expertise and support. Also factor in cost, scalability, and security requirements.	Consider factors like in-house expertise, cost, integration, scalability, training needs, and the need for control of data.	Comprehensive list of organizational requirements for an ML platform
Explore Available Options Explore various ML platforms both ready-made and open-source options and evaluate their pros and cons.	Data scientist	Factor in attributes to evaluate such as features, cost, community support, security and compliance. Also consider vendor support and skillsets, ease of use, scalability, integration ability, interoperability, training, and upgradability.	N/A	Comparative analysis report of different ML platforms
Assess In-house Talent Your success depends on your capacity to support either scenario.	HR manager	You must consider the vendor's AI/ML expertise and support. You need a smaller team to implement and maintain the system. Evaluate your inhouse skills and training needs.	You need AI/ML talent to build, maintain, and operate the platform and there is significant investment in training and development.	Report on the current state of in-house talent and training needs
Consider Interoperability Ensure the chosen AI/ ML services and solutions can work seamlessly with existing or planned systems is paramount.	IT architect	Evaluate the cloud provider's compatibility with other systems. Usually, it is easier to integrate within their ecosystem. Vendor lock-in is possible.	You can customize to ensure maximum compatibility with other systems, but it requires extra resources and time.	Assessment report on interoperability of potential ML platforms

TASK NAME/ DETAILS	ROLE	BUY	BUILD	DELIVERABLE/ IMPORTANCE
Evaluate Control over Platform For an AI/ML platform, the ability to tweak the algorithms or change the architecture can be crucial depending on your company's specific needs.	IT manager	Limited control over underlying AI/ ML algorithms and tools, and you may have to depend on vendor's upgrade/release cycle for new features.	You would have greater control over aspects such as adding or modifying features as needed.	Report on the degree of control provided by different options
Explore Open-Source Support Open-source tools provide greater community support and have frequent updates and hence is important to consider.	Data scientist	Vendor may not offer full support for open-source AI/ML tools. Some may work well only with their proprietary tools.	You could incorporate as many open-source components as necessary providing you with flexibility and innovation speed.	Report on the open-source support by different options
Estimate Time-to-Market You have to factor in the time urgency to choose between the two options.	Project manager	You can deploy faster due to prebuilt AI/ML capabilities but may still need customization and integration.	Custom development can be time-consuming, leading to slower deployment.	Estimated timeline for each option
Assess Cost You must factor in both the initial and ongoing costs when choosing to buy or build.	Financial analyst	You would have upfront costs, possibly with ongoing licensing or subscription fees.	Potentially high upfront development costs, ongoing costs for maintenance, upgrades, and potential modifications.	Cost assessment report for build versus buy

TASK NAME/ DETAILS	ROLE	BUY	BUILD	DELIVERABLE/ IMPORTANCE
Review Feature Requirements Your choice will depend on your specific business and functional requirements.	Business analyst	May not be as customizable. Might not meet all specific requirements.	It is usually possible to meet most specific business requirements.	Report on the alignment of feature requirements with available options
Examine Scalability and Flexibility As your business grows, your need to deal with large volumes of data and complex models will also grow.	Data engineer	The vendor should be able to scale to your growing data and model complexity.	You can build your platform with scalability in mind from the start and provide greater flexibility.	Report on the scalability and flexibility of each option
Assess Vendor Support and Upgrades AI/ML field is constantly evolving, and this is a key factor to consider from an innovation perspective.	IT manager	Vendors provide regular support and updates, but you are still dependent on their update cycle.	You have to take greater responsibility for support and updates, and this may require additional resources.	Assessment report on vendor support and upgrades
Analyze Security and Compliance Ensuring data security and meeting regulatory compliance are critical, regardless of whether the solution is bought or built.	IT security officer	AI/ML cloud providers should ensure that their solution meets industry and regulatory compliance standards such as HIPAA or GDPR.	You have greater control over the compliance process, but it also means you have to design with security and regulatory compliance in mind, potentially adding complexity.	Report on the security and compliance of each option
Make a Recommendation	Project lead	Make a recommendation on whether to build or buy the ML platform		Recommendation report on whether to build or buy the ML platform

> **TIP** *Consider factors such as talent, interoperability, control, open-source support, time-to-market, cost, feature requirements, scalability, vendor support, and security compliance when making the build versus buy decision.*

Choosing Between Cloud Providers

When choosing between cloud providers, you need to factor in a few considerations. The following exercise helps you to evaluate the appropriate criteria.

HANDS-ON EXERCISE: CHOOSING THE RIGHT CLOUD PROVIDER

The goal of this hands-on exercise is to help you gain a comprehensive understanding of the different cloud providers, including their strengths and weaknesses, and choose the right cloud provider or a combination of providers for different AI/ML services, platforms, and tools that best suit your company's needs.

Here are the steps needed to choose the best cloud provider:

TASK	TASK OWNER	EVALUATION CRITERIA	DELIVERABLE
Identify cloud providers.	Team lead	Shortlist the cloud providers you want to evaluate.	List of cloud providers
Evaluate AI/ML services and capabilities that are crucial for your AI and ML projects.	Data scientist	Check for the availability of AI and ML services for various aspects of the machine learning lifecycle, such as data processing, model training, testing, deployment, and monitoring. **Tip:** Look out for the availability of prebuilt models, frameworks, and development tools.	Report regarding AI/ML services and capabilities available for each cloud provider
Examine scalability and performance, which are essential for growing businesses.	Data engineer	Evaluate the scalability and performance including support for distributed processing, and compare their performances and latencies for large volumes of data and high-intensity ML workloads.	Report on scalability and performance for each cloud provider

TASK	TASK OWNER	EVALUATION CRITERIA	DELIVERABLE
Examine data management and integration, which are important when dealing with large or sensitive datasets.	Data architect	Compare in terms of their support for data processing, labeling, and data governance, as well as the ability to integrate with industry-specific data.	Report on data management and integration capabilities
Evaluate platform ecosystem and community, which are useful for faster development and troubleshooting.	Software engineer	Compare the availability of developer community, vendor support, and the development ecosystem such as APIs, SDKs, and development tools.	Report on platform ecosystem and community
Assess security and compliance, in particular for dealing with sensitive data.	Security analyst	Evaluate the cloud providers in terms of their support for encryption access controls, data privacy, and other industry certifications that they may have.	Report on platform support for security and compliance
Analyze pricing model and costs, which is important for budget management.	Financial analyst	Evaluate their pricing model and compare their costs for data storage, data processing, data transfer costs, compute costs, and ML service pricing.	Cost comparison report
Evaluate vendor support, which is required for smoother implementation and operation.	Project manager	Evaluate their documentation, training, product support, and the available developer and partner ecosystem.	Report on vendor support
Make a final recommendation.	Team lead	Make a recommendation based on your evaluations and choose a cloud provider or a combination thereof that suits your company.	Recommendation report

TIP *Consider the range of AI/ML services offered by the various cloud providers, including prebuilt models, development tools, and support for the entire ML lifecycle when choosing a cloud provider.*

KEY COMPONENTS OF AN ML AND DL PLATFORM

An ML platform's main components are enabling data ingestion, data preparation, model training, deployment, governance, and monitoring. Many organizations want to deploy their machine learning models in the cloud for the benefits discussed earlier. This is true for companies just beginning to deploy machine learning models and those who are advanced in this journey.

Organizations trying to get value from business applications or using curated data are looking at the underlying machine learning platform and infrastructure as a means to an end. By adopting AI services in the cloud, even developers with little or no skills in machine learning can build, train, and deploy complex models in production.

As you keep trying to adopt ML widely across your organization and as the requirements become increasingly complex, you must adopt a combination of cloud-based services, open-source tools, best-of-breed solutions, and your own proprietary custom solutions to build an enterprise-wide AI platform. This will give you fine-grained control over the entire platform but also take a lot of effort and cost. You can derive unique value from the platform software, infrastructure, and expertise, but you have to decide, based on the cost-benefit analysis, which approaches you want to take.

KEY COMPONENTS OF AN ENTERPRISE AI/ML HEALTHCARE PLATFORM

This section considers the use case of a healthcare company trying to build an enterprise AI/ML imaging platform. You can use this to guide your own AI/ML platform. The platform must have the following components:

COMPONENT	DESCRIPTION
Data ingestion	Ingest enormous amounts of medical data such as X-rays, CT scans, and MRIs from multiple sources.
Preprocessing and data cleaning	Automatically preprocess and clean the data such as reducing noise, adjusting contrast, and carrying out normalization.
Labeling	Label a subset of images to create a labeled dataset for subsequent model training. This may involve identifying and annotating abnormalities and identifying new feature sets.
Model training	Train the ML models using the labeled data to carry out machine learning tasks, such as anomaly detection classification and segmentation.
Model testing	Test the machine learning models by integrating them into a simulation environment that simulates real-life clinical scenarios. This helps with thorough performance analysis and evaluation of the models before they can be deployed in production.
Model deployment	Deploy the models in a production scenario, such as a specific hospital or a diagnostic center, to assist doctors and radiologists in accurately interpreting medical images.
Performance monitoring	Continuously monitor the performance of these models by measuring their accuracy recall and precision metrics in real time.

COMPONENT	DESCRIPTION
Alerting, dashboarding, and feedback reports	Generate alerts, dashboards, and feedback reports to assist healthcare professionals so that they can make further improvements to these models, as well as provide better patient care by suggesting alternative diagnoses, identifying better treatments, and providing better care overall.

> **NOTE** *Handling large amounts of data requires a robust and automated data ingestion and preprocessing pipeline.*

Figure 13.13 shows some core platform architecture components, each of which is covered in the following sections.

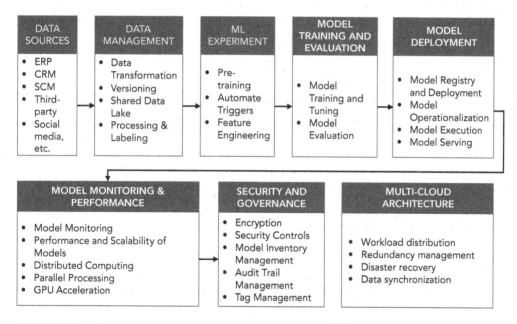

FIGURE 13.13: Basic components and their integrations in an AI/ML platform

Data Management Architecture

The data management components shown in Figure 13.14 are required for storing, ingesting, collecting, cleaning, and preparing data for model training. You also need data orchestration, distribution, governance, and access control tools.

Shared Data Lake

To use data for machine learning, you must store the data in one central location. It is recommended to set up a data lake for this purpose. Consider factors such as data volumes, data access patterns, and data lifecycle management requirements. You must choose data storage solutions such as Amazon S3, Google Cloud storage, and Azure blob storage based on your specific requirements.

Once you store large datasets in S3, other data processing and ML services can access that data. Storing data in one central location, such as S3, helps you manage data scientists' workflow, facilitates automation, and enables true collaboration and governance.

Creating the following folder structure with proper data classification will help you exercise access control and facilitate machine learning workflows, tracking, traceability, and reproducibility during experiments:

FOLDER	DESCRIPTION
Users and project teams folders	Individual data scientists and teams can use these folders to store their training, test, and validation datasets that they use for experimentation purposes.
Shared features folders	These folders can contain shared features such as customer data, product data, time series, and location data, which can all be used for model training across teams and models.
Training, validation, and test datasets folders	These are used for formal model training, testing, and validation purposes. Managing these folders is essential, as this can help you with the traceability and reproducibility of models.
Automated ML pipelines folders	These folders can be accessed only by automated pipelines, such as a WS code pipeline for storing artifacts related to the pipeline.
Models in production folders	These models should be actively monitored and managed through version control and play a key role in ensuring traceability.

Data Sources

Your data can come from one or more sources located in various locations or systems. It helps to treat them as enterprise-level assets rather than department-specific assets. The data sources can include databases, data warehouses, data lakes, external APIs, files, and even streaming data from IoT devices and sensors. These sources provide the raw data for the ML models during the training process.

Data Ingestion

Data ingestion is the process of loading the data from these data sources into the machine learning platform, which can be an automated or manual process. It includes techniques such as data extraction, integration, and loading.

Data Catalog

The data catalog acts as the central repository for all metadata about the datasets that are used in the ML system. It contains information related to data sources, dataset description, data quality metrics, schema information, data format, and usage statistics. Data scientists, analysts, and data engineers use this catalog to discover, understand, and access data related to their projects.

> **TIP** *Establish a shared, centralized data lake to promote governance, collaboration, and seamless data access across your company.*

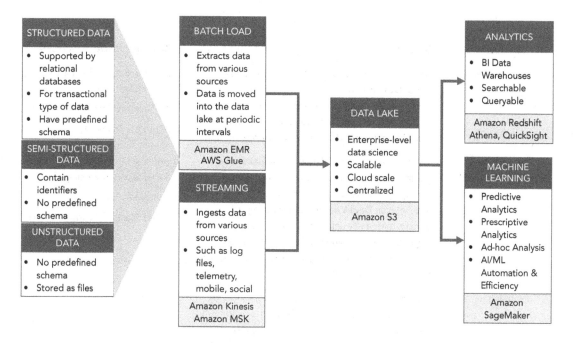

FIGURE 13.14: Data management architecture

Data Transformation

Data transformation is the process of getting the raw data in a format and structure ready to use in ML models. It involves cleaning the data, preparing it, feature transformation, data normalization, dimensionality reduction, and so on.

Data Versioning

Data versioning is the process of assigning versions to datasets and tracking any changes to the data used in the model. It helps you revert to the older version if necessary, and you can track the lineage of datasets used in different model training experiments. This can help you with the traceability and reproducibility of ML experiments.

Data Science Experimentation Platform

As shown in Figure 13.15, the data science or machine learning experimentation platform should provide comprehensive tools and services to help data scientists and teams conduct multiple individual or team-based experiments for their projects. Consider these factors:

FEATURE	DESCRIPTION	EXAMPLE TOOLS/SERVICES
Data querying and analysis	Teams must be able to explore data, analyze data, conduct SQL analysis or data transformations, and visualize results. For example, use Amazon Athena to query data in a data lake using SQL.	Amazon Athena Google BigQuery ML Dataflow Azure HDInsight, Azure Data Lake Analytics

continues

(continued)

FEATURE	DESCRIPTION	EXAMPLE TOOLS/SERVICES
Code authoring	Teams should be able to write and edit code using IDEs and notebooks. For example, Amazon SageMaker Notebook Instance and SageMaker Studio can be used for code authoring, data processing, model training, and experimentation.	Amazon SageMaker Notebook, SageMaker Studio AI Platform Notebook Azure ML Studio
Data processing	This includes tools for data preprocessing and transformation, such as data cleaning, data wrangling, and feature engineering. For example, use Amazon Data Wrangler for data import, transformation, visualization, and analysis. Amazon SageMaker processing can be used for large-scale data processing, including integration with Apache Spark and scikit-learn.	Amazon Data Wrangler, SageMaker Processing Google AI Hub Azure Machine Learning Studio
Pretraining	Pretraining is the process of training a model on a large, unlabeled corpus of data. It helps identify general patterns and features from the data using unsupervised or semi-supervised learning. This model can then be used on a smaller subset of labeled data to develop better predictions for specific tasks.	
Automate triggers	Events or triggers are set up in the machine learning experimentation project to automate various steps. For example, when new data is available, or a model has been updated, they can trigger another workflow for deploying a model in production or initiate the evaluation of a trained model.	
Feature store	Enables sharing common features across teams for model training and inference.	Amazon SageMaker Feature Store Vertex AI Feature Store Azure Machine Learning
Model training and tuning	Involves the ability to train and test using various techniques and algorithms, evaluate models, and conduct hyperparameter tuning. For example, use Amazon SageMaker training/tuning service.	Amazon SageMaker Training/ Tuning Service Google Cloud AutoML Vertex AI Azure ML Studio Azure Automated Machine Learning

FEATURE	DESCRIPTION	EXAMPLE TOOLS/SERVICES
Model evaluation	In a machine learning experimentation platform, model evaluation is a crucial step that helps you compare different experiments, conduct hyperparameter tuning, and choose the best model available for deployment. Compare the performance of different trained models using metrics such as accuracy, precision, F1 score, and recall based on the type of task and the problem domain. Model evaluation determines how well the model generalizes against the unseen data and solves the problem.	Amazon SageMaker Training/ Tuning Service Google Cloud AutoML Vertex AI Azure ML Studio Azure Automated Machine Learning
Containerization	The ability to build, test, and deploy models and workflows as containerized applications or services. For example, use Amazon ECR to store training, processing, and inference containers.	Amazon ECR Kubernetes Engine Azure Container Registry
Source code control	Managing code using source code control systems such as Git to enable tracking changes and collaboration between team members and ensure reproducibility. For example, Artifacts repositories are private package repositories used to manage library packages and mirror public library sites.	Git
Data science library access	Providing easy access to data science libraries such as NumPy, Pandas, scikit-learn, PyTorch, and TensorFlow to allow easy development and experimentation.	NumPy, Pandas, scikit-learn, PyTorch, TensorFlow
Self-service catalog	Using ML tools, services, and products to allow data scientists and team members to quickly access their ML needs.	Self-service catalog
Implement a self-service catalog	Developing a self-service catalog of various ML tools, services, and products so that other team members, such as data scientists, can provision tools such as SageMaker Studio or Canvas through the self-service portal.	Implement a self-service catalog

Hybrid and Edge Computing

Hybrid and edge computing are two different types of computing approaches in the world of machine learning that can be used to embrace the best of both worlds (see Figure 13.16).

Hybrid Computing Scenarios

In the case of hybrid computing, the following are some typical practices:

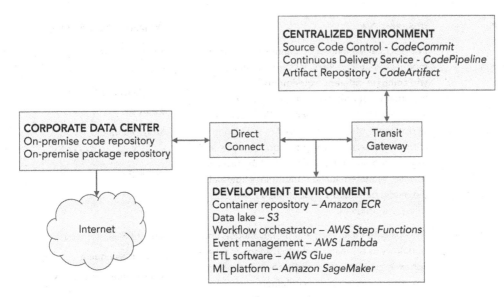

FIGURE 13.15: Components of an ML experimentation platform

➤ Deploy models in the cloud for increased scalability and performance and then deploy some models in the edge for increased security.

➤ You can carry out data storage, data preprocessing, and model training in your own on-prem infrastructure and offload distributed processing, large-scale training, and hosting the model to the cloud.

➤ Hybrid computing can help you with resource optimization, cost optimization, and data governance.

Edge Computing

Here are some considerations for edge computing:

➤ It brings data processing and model training to edge devices such as IoT devices, sensors, or edge servers closer to the point of data generation or data source.

➤ It can be handy for use cases that require real-time processing of data with exceptionally low latencies, reduced bandwidth, and increased security and privacy.

> **NOTE** *Hybrid and edge computing are especially useful in use cases such as remote healthcare monitoring, autonomous vehicles, and industrial IoT.*

Designing Models for the Edge

Designing models for the edge, you need to factor in some specific considerations, such as the following:

➤ **Model size:** The model should be small enough to fit on the edge device.

➤ **Model latency:** The model latency should be low enough to suit the requirements of the application.

➤ **Model accuracy:** The model should be accurate enough to meet the requirements of the application.

To meet these requirements, you may be required to adopt model compression techniques such as quantization and model pruning to reduce the model size. Moreover, the model should be designed to operate in offline or intermittent connectivity scenarios.

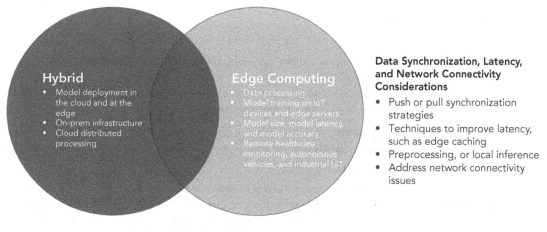

Data Synchronization, Latency, and Network Connectivity Considerations

- Push or pull synchronization strategies
- Techniques to improve latency, such as edge caching
- Preprocessing, or local inference
- Address network connectivity issues

FIGURE 13.16: Hybrid and edge computing in machine learning

➤ **Data synchronization, latency, and network connectivity:** In the case of hybrid and edge computing scenarios, data synchronization latency and network connectivity are crucial factors for the effective operation of machine learning models.

➤ **To keep the data consistent between the cloud and the edge devices:** Adopt a push or pull synchronization strategy. In the case of push synchronization, the cloud pushes the data to the edge device, or in the pull synchronization strategy, the edge device pulls the data from the cloud.

➤ **To improve latency:** You can adopt techniques like edge caching, preprocessing, or local inference to avoid round trips to the cloud.

➤ **To address network connectivity issues:** You can build fault-tolerant systems by using compression techniques or by optimizing data transmission protocols.

The Multicloud Architecture

The multicloud architecture aims to improve the scalability and reliability of the overall enterprise platform by leveraging the strength of the various cloud providers. However, it can be a complex endeavor, and you need to manage various aspects such as data synchronization, workload distribution, system redundancy, disaster recovery, and implement security protocols, as shown in the following table:

CATEGORY	DETAILS
Workload distribution	You can implement workload distribution in such a manner that you can choose one cloud provider for model training based on their infrastructure capabilities, such as specialized GPU instances, and choose another provider for real-time inference based on their low latency services. • You can also reduce the risk of service disruptions by distributing the workloads across multiple cloud providers. • Using geolocation services, you can distribute the workload to the users based on their locations. • You can also use load-balancing features to distribute the load across multiple cloud providers so that no one cloud provider is overloaded.

continues

(continued)

CATEGORY	DETAILS
Redundancy management	You can employ redundancy management to ensure no single point of failure. You can implement this by having data redundancy, infrastructure redundancy, application redundancy, load balancing, and service failover techniques. You can have either active-active or active-passive configurations set up to ensure continuity of services.
Disaster recovery	By implementing the redundancy management techniques discussed earlier, you can also ensure you have a sound disaster recovery system in place so that you can failover should the system go down.
Data synchronization	Keeping the data synchronized across multiple cloud environments is a critical step, and you must employ different techniques, such as real-time or scheduled synchronization. You must employ distributed databases, data synchronization, replication, and streaming techniques.
Security	You must employ a robust multicloud security strategy to protect data, applications, and networks. Security measures such as IAM, access controls, data encryption, network security, and monitoring are essential. Data flow between cloud environments should be encrypted, and security protocols across the different cloud environments should be synchronized.

> **NOTE** *Achieving a successful multicloud architecture helps you avoid vendor lock-in, but it can be a complex endeavor.*

WORKBOOK TEMPLATE: *ENTERPRISE AI CLOUD PLATFORM SETUP CHECKLIST*

Download the "Enterprise AI Cloud Platform Setup Checklist" template from the download section of the book (www.wiley.com/go/EnterpriseAIintheCloud). Use this template to ensure you not only have the needed resources, but also have secured and optimized the environment. Track your progress with setting up your enterprise AI cloud platform.

SUMMARY

This chapter laid the foundations for the rest of your AI journey. The infrastructure serves as the technical bridge between your initial strategic planning, team building, and the subsequent stages of data processing, model training, deployment, and scaling.

This chapter covered the complex components of an enterprise AI cloud platform and dived into five types of reference architectures that are most common. You also reviewed the considerations for buy versus build decisions and the criteria for choosing between cloud providers. The chapter delved into the specific components of the ML and DL platforms, data management architecture, and the nuances of the hybrid and edge computing and multicloud architecture.

Whether it is building an AI platform for healthcare or data synchronization in real time, this chapter provided the necessary knowledge and tools to benefit IT professionals, cloud architects, system administrators, data scientists, decision-makers, and technology strategists.

But your journey doesn't stop here. With your infrastructure now set, you will be processing your data, choosing the right algorithms, training your models, and ensuring they are deployed efficiently and ethically. Remember that the infrastructure plays a key role in scaling your AI efforts, deploying models seamlessly, and evolving and maturing your AI capabilities, all of which are covered in the remaining chapters of this book.

REVIEW QUESTIONS

These review questions are included at the end of each chapter to help you test your understanding of the information. You'll find the answers in the following section.

1. Name the AWS service used to collect data from IoT devices in the described architecture.
   A. AWS Greengrass
   B. AWS IoT Core
   C. Amazon Redshift
   D. Amazon S3

2. The _____ service is used to train a personalized recommendation model.
   A. Amazon S3
   B. Amazon Glue DataBrew
   C. Amazon Personalize
   D. Amazon API Gateway

3. The _____ service is used to automate the steps of building, training, and deploying machine learning models.
   A. Amazon Pinpoint
   B. Amazon S3
   C. Amazon SageMaker
   D. Amazon Athena

4. The biggest advantage of adopting machine learning in the cloud is that developers with little or no machine learning skills can:
   A. Only deploy pretrained models
   B. Only build simple models
   C. Build, train, and deploy complex models in production
   D. Only access curated data

5. _____ should be considered when deciding whether to build or buy solutions for an enterprise ML platform. (choose more than one answer)
   A. Availability of in-house talent
   B. Integration with third-party applications
   C. Cost of hardware and software licenses
   D. Time required for model training

6. True or False: It is more important to manage data than to improve models in machine learning.

7. _____ is NOT a technique for improving latency in hybrid and edge computing.
   A. Edge caching
   B. Preprocessing
   C. Local inference
   D. Round trips to the cloud

8. Which of the following statements are true regarding multicloud architecture?

   A. Workload distribution in multicloud architecture allows choosing different cloud providers based on their specialized infrastructure capabilities.

   B. Disaster recovery in multicloud architecture is not necessary as the risk of service disruptions is reduced.

   C. Data synchronization in multicloud architecture can be achieved only through real-time synchronization.

ANSWER KEY

1.	B	4.	C	7.	D
2.	C	5.	A, B, C, D	8.	A
3.	C	6.	True		

14

Operating Your AI Platform with MLOps Best Practices

The value of an idea lies in the using of it.

—Thomas Edison

Now that the AI platform has been built, your focus shifts toward operating the AI platform; ensuring the efficiency, reliability, and repeatability of the ML operations workflow; and enabling scale with automation (see Figure 14.1).

The target audience includes tech leads, operations managers, ML engineers, data scientists, systems administrators, and IT professionals looking to employ automation in daily operations.

Automation using MLOps isn't just a buzzword. It's the secret sauce to scaling rapidly, reducing manual errors, speeding up processes, and enabling adaptability in a dynamic business landscape.

In this chapter, you review various key components, from model operationalization and deployment scenarios to automation pipelines, platform monitoring, performance optimization, security, and much more. It includes actionable deliverables that will help you crystallize the MLOps ideas presented in this chapter.

This chapter serves as a pivotal transition point from setting up your AI infrastructure (Chapter 13) to actual data processing and modeling (Chapters 15–17), highlighting the role of MLOps in ensuring this transition is smooth, efficient, and automated.

CENTRAL ROLE OF MLOps IN BRIDGING INFRASTRUCTURE, DATA, AND MODELS

This section discusses the role that the MLOps best practices in this chapter play in ensuring automation and integration across the platform infrastructure, data, and model layers.

What Is MLOps?

MLOps stands for "machine learning operations," which is a set of practices, principles, and tools that unify machine learning (ML) development and operations (Ops). It focuses on automating the end-to-end machine learning lifecycle, from data preparation to model training to deployment and monitoring. It enables faster, more reliable, and scalable ML implementations, which is the focus of this chapter. MLOps is similar to DevOps in software development, but it is specifically geared towards automating ML workflows.

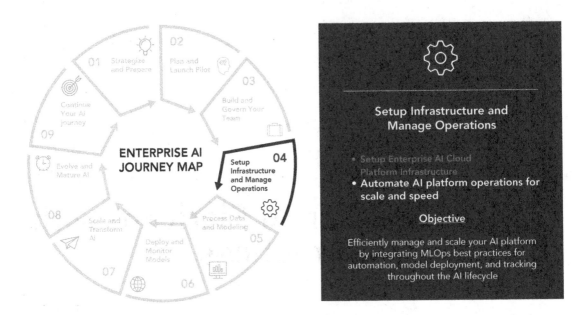

FIGURE 14.1: SETUP INFRASTRUCTURE AND MANAGE OPERATIONS: Automate AI platform operations for scale and speed

MLOps is about continuous integration and continuous delivery (CI/CD) of not just models, but also of data. The goal of MLOps is to automate and scale the tasks of processing and engineering data. Your goal must be to ensure that you employ the best practices in this chapter so that when processing data in Chapter 15, as new data comes in, it's processed and made available automatically for model training seamlessly.

In Chapters 16 and 17, you may try different algorithms and train and tune multiple models. Your goal must be to deploy the best practices in this chapter to ensure that each model version is tracked, stored, and can be rolled back or forward as needed. This also ties in with the concept of tagging and container image management, which will facilitate this process.

Once you have trained your models, they need to be evaluated. The practices outlined in this chapter and Chapter 19 can help automate this step. It ensures that as soon as the model is trained using the practices in Chapter 17, it's automatically evaluated and metrics are logged.

Finally, I want to emphasize the importance of having feedback loops. By that I mean the evaluations and insights obtained from the training, tuning, and evaluation of the models should be fed back into the system to refine the data processing methods in Chapter 15.

Automation Through MLOps Workflows

To achieve speed and scale, you must automate the different steps in the machine learning workflow, such as data collection, ingestion, cleaning, feature transformation, model training, testing, tuning, deployment, and monitoring. These steps should be done in an automated fashion in a specific sequence at predefined times. Automating routine tasks helps the data science team focus on value-added tasks such as developing new models or insights.

You can use tools like Apache Airflow or Google Cloud Composer to schedule and orchestrate your data pipeline tasks so they are executed in a given order and on time.

The following table shows various MLOps practices that can be adopted across the machine learning workflow with a particular focus on data management. It details the tools or applications that can be used along with use cases where applicable.

STEPS IN MACHINE LEARNING WORKFLOW	DESCRIPTION	TOOLS/APPLICATIONS	USE CASES
Data collection, ingestion, cleaning, feature transformation	Automate these steps in an ordered, predefined sequence.	Apache Airflow, Google Cloud Composer	N/A.
MLOps automation: model training, testing, tuning, deployment, and monitoring	You can create machine learning workflows using the CI/CD pipeline and a discipline known as MLOps, which evolved from DevOps, a common practice in software development.	Kubeflow, MLflow, AWS SageMaker pipelines, Azure Machine Learning pipelines, Google Cloud AI platform pipelines	You can retrain the model if it doesn't meet the performance thresholds, validate it, and redeploy it once it meets the performance criteria.
Using a feature store	A feature store is a key feature in the MLOps lifecycle. It speeds up machine learning tasks and eliminates the need to create the same feature multiple times.	Online and offline feature storage. Online feature storage is used for real-time inferences, while offline feature storage is used to maintain a history of feature values.	It is helpful for training and batch inferences. It helps machine learning engineers and data scientists create, share, and manage features during ML development and reduces the curation work required to create features out of raw data.
Continuous learning	When the model was released in production, it would have been trained on past data, but its performance may decline as time goes on. This is because customers' tastes, product lines, and many other variables change. In other words, while the world has changed, the model remains unchanged. This means you need to continuously monitor the model for its performance and retrain it in an automated manner. This process is known as continuous learning.	AWS SageMaker, Azure Machine Learning, Google Cloud AI Platform.	Taking the cooking analogy, just like a restaurant's menu needs to be updated with the customers' changing tastes, you need to keep your models up-to-date.

STEPS IN MACHINE LEARNING WORKFLOW	DESCRIPTION	TOOLS/APPLICATIONS	USE CASES
Data version control	Data version tracking is like a recipe book, where you capture all the ingredients, the process steps, and the meal created in the end. This list helps you re-create or tweak the meal because you know what was done precisely. In the context of machine learning, you maintain the list of datasets used, the models and their versions, and the parameters used to tune the model. All this information helps you in the future to either tweak the model for better performance or to troubleshoot the model to identify the root cause of its poor performance. If you get different results every time, you can assess whether the model, the data, or both contribute to the results.	You can use data version control tools like the Data Version Control (DVC) to manage the data versions and track the models with which they were used. DVC can integrate with other version control tools, such as Git, and handle large amounts of data.	One advantage of DVC is that you can maintain a record of all the data, code, and models used and share that data and models across other teams, reproduce experiments, and roll back changes, thus making your machine learning workflows collaborative, reproducible, and reliable.

> **TIP** *Use a machine learning workflow management tool that can automate the machine learning process to scale your ML operations*

MODEL OPERATIONALIZATION

Model operationalization is the process of taking a previously trained model and getting it ready for execution, hosting, monitoring, and consumption in production. It ensures that the model can be executed on new data, hosted on a scalable and reliable infrastructure, monitored for performance, and seamlessly integrated into applications and systems to draw business insights for further action. Remember that while training a model by itself is a significant achievement, its real value is only realized when it's operationalized. Let's look at each step of model operationalization in more detail:

STEP	PURPOSE	TOOLS/SERVICES
Model execution	The process of taking a previously trained model and integrating it into an existing application or system to take new data and make predictions in real-world scenarios.	Model execution can happen using two methods: one is online processing, and the other is batch processing. **Online processing:** In the case of online processing, one piece of data is fed into the model, as is the case with product recommendations. **Batch processing:** In the case of batch processing, a large batch of data is fed into the model for prediction, which is the case for fraud detection and risk management.
Model hosting	The ability to host models in production in a controlled environment to ensure functionality and performance testing before deploying it for widespread use. It involves setting up the necessary infrastructure and providing the necessary compute resources to run efficiently without a significant latency for high workloads.	Model hosting can be done using various approaches, such as deploying it on serverless computing, containers such as Dockers, and dedicated servers. In-house platforms can also host models but can be more expensive to maintain. Amazon SageMaker Hosting is an example of this.
Model monitoring	The process of continuously monitoring the deployed models for performance and behavior in a production environment. **Metrics:** It involves gathering the metrics such as model response time, prediction outputs, and other data to assess the model's accuracy, stability, and adherence to performance goals. It helps detect concept drift and model drift and identify anomalies to ensure the model performance does not degrade over time.	Metrics gathering tools, Amazon CloudWatch.

STEP	PURPOSE	TOOLS/SERVICES
Model consumption	The actual process of using the model to make predictions. You may need to integrate the model into downstream applications, systems or user interfaces, and other business processes or workflows so that users can make predictions using the model.	Model consumption can happen in two ways: by using an API for real-time prediction and a web service for batch predictions for large datasets.

> **TIP** *Implement continuous model monitoring to maintain quality and reliability of models in real-world scenarios.*

Automation Pipelines

Automation pipelines are the bedrock of enterprise AI. Through automation, you can enforce governance and standardization such as tagging and naming conventions and repeatability of the entire machine learning lifecycle, starting from data preparation model training, testing, deployment, and monitoring.

As shown in Figure 14.2, the automation pipeline consists of several components for model training and deployment, such as the following:

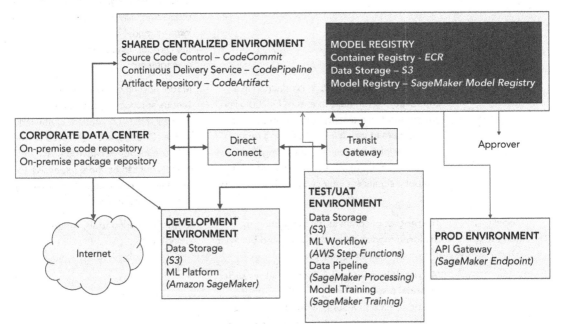

FIGURE 14.2: CI/CD flow for model training and deployment

The table below describes the various components included in Figures 14.2 and 14.3 for model training and deployment.

COMPONENT	DESCRIPTION	EXAMPLE SERVICES
Code repository	The starting point for an automated pipeline run, and it consists of several artifacts such as Docker files, training scripts, and other dependency packages required to train models, build containers, and deploy models.	Docker files, training scripts, dependency packages Azure OpenAI Code Repository, Google Artifact Registry
Code build service	A code build service can be used to build custom artifacts like the Docker container and push them to a container repository like Amazon ECR.	AWS CodeBuild, Jenkins Azure DevOps, Google Cloud Build, Kubernetes
Data processing service	A data processing service can be used to process raw data into training/validation/test datasets for model-training purposes.	Amazon SageMaker data processing, Dataflow, Dataproc, Azure Databricks
Model training service	The model training service gets the data from the data lake, trains the model, and stores the model output back into the output folder of the data storage, typically S3.	Amazon SageMaker training service, Google AutoML, Vertex AI, Azure Machine Learning Studio
Model registry	A model registry is used to manage the model inventory, and it contains the metadata for the model artifacts, the location, the associated inference container, and the roles.	AWS Model Registry, AI Hub, Vertex AI Model Registry, Azure OpenAI Code Repository, Azure DevOps, Azure Machine Learning Model Registry
Model hosting service	The model hosting service accepts the model artifacts from the model registry and deploys them into a serving endpoint.	AWS Model hosting service, Google AI Platform Prediction, Azure Kubernetes Service
Pipeline management	Orchestrates pipeline workflow using SageMaker pipeline or AWS Step Functions. At the same time, the AWS CodePipeline integrates with the AWS CodeCommit repository and AWS CodeBuild to build the code. AWS CodePipeline supports different deployment actions by integrating with AWS Lambda, AWS CloudFormation, and AWS Step Functions.	SageMaker pipeline, AWS CodePipeline, AWS CodeCommit, AWS Lambda, AWS CloudFormation, AWS Step Functions, Cloud Data Fusion, Azure Data Factory, Azure Machine Learning Pipelines

Figure 14.3 shows the implementation of a CI/CD pipeline using AWS components.

This pipeline architecture completely automates the machine learning workflow from code commit, pipeline start, container build, model building, model registration, and production deployment. In the case of AWS, you can use tools like CodeCommit, CodeBuild, CloudFormation, Step Functions, and SageMaker Pipelines.

Implementing automated pipelines is the secret sauce behind an enterprise AI platform, as it facilitates automation, standardization, and reproducibility in machine learning workflows.

> **TIP** *By automating the deployment of models in production it becomes possible for companies to scale their AI implementations across the enterprise.*

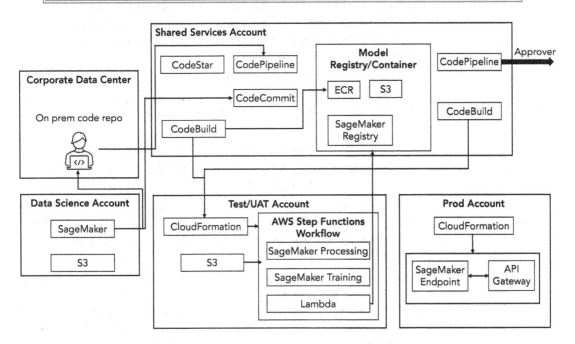

FIGURE 14.3: CI/CD pipeline for ML training and deployment on AWS

EXERCISE: DESIGNING AND IMPLEMENTING A DATA PIPELINE

The goal of this exercise is to give you an idea of the steps to design a data architecture and implement a data pipeline to gather, clean, and store data for machine learning experiments. In addition to automating the model training and deployment process, automating the data pipeline can help you scale.

TASK DESCRIPTION	TASK OWNERS (JOB TITLES)	DELIVERABLES
Identify data sources: List different data sources that will be utilized, including databases, APIs, filesystems, etc.	Data engineer	A list of different data sources
Design a data flow diagram: Create a visual representation of how data will flow through the system, including data gathering, transformation, and storage.	Data engineer	A diagram showing the data flow

TASK DESCRIPTION	TASK OWNERS (JOB TITLES)	DELIVERABLES
Implement an ETL process: Write a script or use a data pipeline tool to extract data from the identified sources, transform it (e.g., clean, aggregate), and load it into a data warehouse or database.	Data engineer	A script or tool configuration for the ETL process
Test the pipeline: Ensure that the data is correctly processed and stored in the desired format and create a report summarizing the results.	Data engineer	A report detailing the implementation and test results

Deployment Scenarios

In the previous sections, we discussed automating the data pipeline, model training and deployment steps. In this section, let us discuss creating different automation pipelines based on the deployment scenario. This section reviews these different scenarios. The deployment scenarios can range anywhere from comprehensive end-to-end pipelines that span from raw code production to production deployment, to more specialized scenarios like Docker build, or model registration pipelines.

➤ **End-to-end automated pipeline:** This involves taking the source code and data and training the model all the way to deploying it into production. It involves stages like building the Docker image, processing data, training the model, getting approval for deployment, and finally deploying the model.

➤ **Docker build pipeline:** This involves building the Docker image from the Docker file and pushing it into a container repository, such as Amazon ECR, along with associated metadata.

➤ **Model training pipeline:** This involves training the model using an existing Docker container and then optionally registering it into a model registry.

➤ **Model registration pipeline:** This pipeline registers the model in the ECR registry and stores the model in S3.

> **TIP** *Use a continuous integration/continuous delivery (CI/CD) pipeline to automate the process of building, testing, and deploying your machine learning models.*

➤ **Model deployment pipeline:** This pipeline deploys the model from the model registry into an endpoint.

Figure 14.4 shows a code deployment pipeline. These pipelines can be triggered by an event, or a source code commit or through the command line.

In Figure 14.4, a Lambda function is used to trigger the pipeline. The Lambda function can look for a change in an existing source code file or determine when a new file is deployed to trigger the pipeline accordingly.

Model Inventory Management

Another best practice of MLOps is implementing model inventory management for effective model risk management. As the number of models increases in your organization, it becomes important to manage them to ensure transparency, efficiency, and control over these assets. You can keep track of deployed models including their versions, metadata, and so on, and monitor and control their performance to ensure they are aligned with business objectives. The table shows the different model inventory management tools available from the major cloud providers.

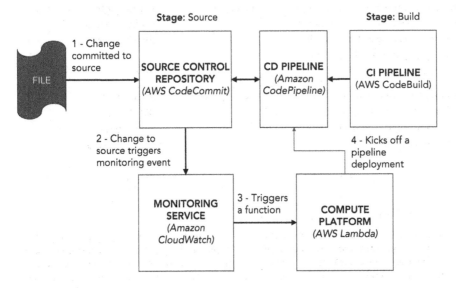

FIGURE 14.4: Code deployment pipeline

CLOUD PROVIDER	MODEL INVENTORY MANAGEMENT TOOLS	FEATURES AND USES
AWS	SageMaker Model Registry	Whenever a new model is developed, you can register it there, and every time it is trained, the latest version can be created. It supports
		➤ Model auditing
		➤ Model lineage tracking management of associated metadata
		➤ Creation of new model versions
Azure	Azure Machine Learning Model Management Service	➤ Attach metadata to models (model name, owner name, business unit, version number, approval status, and other custom metadata)
		➤ Manage the deployment of various versions in the organization across accounts and environments

CLOUD PROVIDER	MODEL INVENTORY MANAGEMENT TOOLS	FEATURES AND USES
Google	AI Platform Model Registry	➤ Register models and their versions
		➤ Deploy models to various environments and deployment targets
		➤ Create prediction services, deploy custom containers, or integrate with other Google services, such as the Kubernetes engine

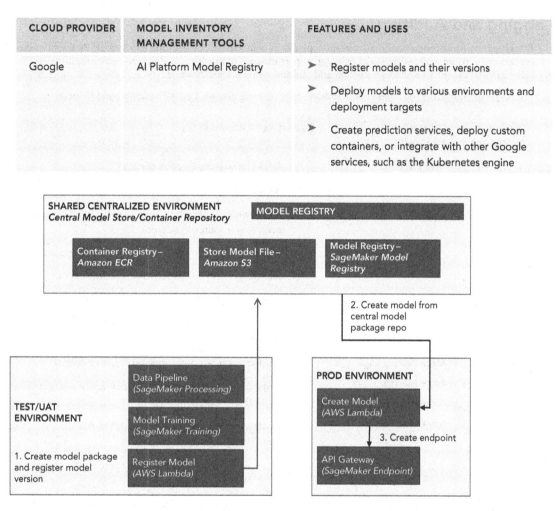

FIGURE 14.5: Centralized model inventory management

There are two main ways to implement model inventory management:

➤ **Distributed model management:** Models developed manually or generated by various automation pipelines can be stored in the respective accounts. For example, different organization units can have their models registered to their own ML UAT/test accounts.

➤ **Centralized model management:** As shown in Figure 14.5, the models developed by the automation pipelines can be stored in a shared services account. You can create a model package group to store the different versions associated with the model. At the time of deployment, a particular version is used to deploy from the package group.

> **NOTE** *Implement model inventory management to track model lineage, manage model metadata, and audit model use.*

Logging and Auditing

Tracking the operations carried out by various platform components for auditing is essential. By tracking the ML operations, you can assist with model debugging, performance monitoring, audits, and health monitoring of the ML platform. Figure 14.6 shows a logging and auditing reference architecture.

The following table lists the logging and auditing tool features provided by AWS, Azure, and Google:

CLOUD PROVIDER	LOGGING AND AUDITING TOOLS	FEATURES AND USES
AWS	AWS CloudTrail	➤ Tracks operations for AWS services. ➤ Stores logs in S3. ➤ Logs contain event name, user identity, event time, event source, and source IP address. ➤ Users can access logs directly from the AWS console. ➤ Integration with Splunk for downstream analysis. ➤ Tracks activities within the SageMaker instance. ➤ Good practice to create roles for each user for attribution during auditing.
Azure	Azure Activity Logs Azure Monitor Azure Storage Azure Sentinel	➤ Tracks operations performed on Azure resources. ➤ Logs can be sent to either Azure storage or Azure monitor for further analysis. ➤ Azure storage provides options such as Azure Blob Storage. ➤ Azure Sentinel provides advanced security monitoring, incident response, and reporting.
Google	Google Cloud Audit Logs Google Cloud Storage, Google Cloud Logging Google's Security Command Center	➤ Captures logs that are sent to other downstream systems for analysis. ➤ Stores logs in Google Cloud storage buckets. ➤ Logs can be analyzed using Google's centralist monitoring system, Google Cloud Logging. ➤ Security command center offers security and compliance monitoring, vulnerability scanning, and threat detection capabilities.

> **TIP** *Implement a robust auditing system to track all activity and monitor suspicious activity. Create roles for each user so that proper attribution can be made for these activities during auditing.*

Data and Artifacts Lineage Tracking

Tracking the data and artifacts lineage is essential, as it will help you reproduce the entire data processing, model building, and deployment processes to meet regulatory and compliance requirements. This section reviews the different artifacts that you need to track, as shown in Figure 14.7.

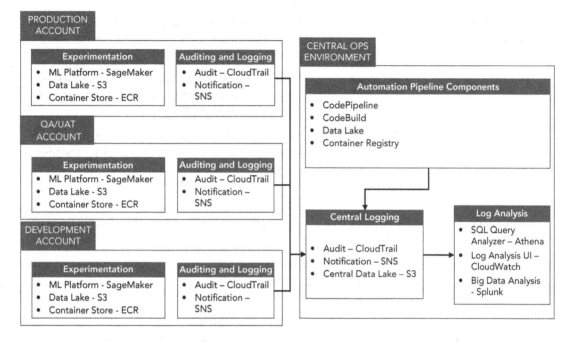

FIGURE 14.6: Logging and auditing architecture

This table lists the tools provided by AWS to track code, datasets, metadata, container, training job, model, and endpoint versions:

ARTIFACT	TRACKING TOOLS	DESCRIPTION
Code Versioning	GitLab, Bitbucket, CodeCommit	Code repositories help you track the versions of the code artifacts. You can check in and check out using a commit ID, which you can use to track the versions of the artifact.
Dataset Versioning	S3, DVC	You can track the versions of your dataset by using a proper S3 data partitioning scheme. When you upload a new dataset, you can add a unique S3 bucket/prefix to identify the dataset. DVC is another open-source dataset versioning system that can be integrated with source code control systems such as GitLab and Bitbucket when creating new datasets, and S3 can remain your backend store.
Metadata Tracking	SageMaker Lineage Tracking Service	Metadata associated with datasets can be tracked by providing details such as the dataset properties and the lineage.

ARTIFACT	TRACKING TOOLS	DESCRIPTION
Container Versioning	Amazon ECR (Elastic Container Repository)	Amazon ECR tracks the container versions using the image URL containing the repository URI and image digest ID.
Training Job Versioning	SageMaker	SageMaker's training job contains its ARN name and other metadata, such as URIs for hyperparameters, containers, datasets, and model output.
Model Versioning	Model Packages	Model versions can be tracked using model packages that contain their own ARN names and details such as the model URI and the container URI.
Endpoint Versioning	SageMaker	As part of creating the SageMaker endpoint, you can add other metadata, such as the model used to the endpoint configuration data

> **NOTE** *Implement a data and artifact lineage tracking system to understand how models work and identify potential problems.*

This table lists the tracking tools provided by Azure:

ARTIFACT	TRACKING TOOLS	DESCRIPTION
Code Versioning	Azure DevOps	Tracks code versions and integrates well with Git repositories.
Dataset Versioning	Azure Machine Learning Datasets	Used to track dataset versions.
Metadata Tracking	Azure Machine Learning Services	Helps track metadata such as model training metrics, dataset properties, and experiment configurations.
Container Versioning	Azure Container Registry	Keeps track of container images and their versions.
Training Job Versioning	Azure Machine Learning Services	Manages training job versions and other parameters such as hyperparameters, training data, and outputs.
Model Versioning	Azure Machine Learning Services	Tracks model versions. Models can be deployed as web services and metadata such as model properties, deployment configurations, and version information can be tracked.
Artifact Versioning	Azure DevOps, Azure Data Factory, Azure Data Catalog	Used to track the versions of artifacts throughout the machine learning lifecycle.

This table lists the tracking tools provided by Google:

ARTIFACT	TRACKING TOOLS	DESCRIPTION
Code Versioning	Git, Google Cloud Source Repositories	Supports integrating Git and Google Cloud source repositories to help track code versions.
Dataset Versioning	Google Cloud Storage	Datasets can be stored in Google Cloud Storage in versioned buckets, which allows you to track different versions of the datasets.
Metadata Tracking	Cloud Metadata Catalog	Can track different versions of model datasets and other artifacts by associating metadata such as properties, descriptions, and lineage.
Container Versioning	Google Cloud Container Registry	Can track different versions of container images.
Training Job Versioning	Google Cloud AI Platform	Can track different versions of training jobs, models, and endpoints.
Artifact Versioning	Kubeflow, Data Catalog, Dataflow	Provides services to track artifacts throughout the machine learning lifecycle.
Code Versioning	Git, Google Cloud Source Repositories	Supports integrating Git and Google Cloud source repositories to help track code versions.

Code Repository

Experiments
- Python notebooks and code

ML Training & Deployment
- Python code
- Docker files
- BuildSpec files
- CloudFormation templates

Model Registry

Images
- Data processing
- Model training
- Model deployment

Model Binaries
- model.tar.gz

Data Repository

Data Files
- Raw data
- Processed data
- Labeled data
- Training data
- Validation data
- Inference data
- Inference feedback

Manifest Repository

Release
- Container IDs
- Model name
- Model binary path
- Instance type and count
- Monitoring config

Build
- Container IDs
- Input data
- Data processing
- Compute
- Training
- Artifact registry
- Execution outputs

FIGURE 14.7: Data and artifacts lineage tracking

Google Cloud also provides services such as Kubeflow, Data Catalog, and Dataflow to track artifacts throughout the machine learning lifecycle.

Container Image Management

Container image management is a vital step to enable MLOps, because it ensures that the models are deployed in consistent environments. Container orchestration tools such as Kubernetes play a critical role in automating the deployment of ML models and platforms like AWS, Azure, and Google Cloud support this.

The following table lists several types of images that need to be managed:

TYPE OF IMAGE	STORAGE LOCATION/OWNERSHIP	DESCRIPTION
Public images	Docker Hub, GitHub, ECR Public Gallery	Publicly available images stored in public repositories.
Base images	Customer ECR Instance	Foundational images made from public images. They contain additional OS patches and other hardening.
Framework images	Central Team	Built on top of base images and represent stable versions of the environment. They may include specific versions of frameworks such as TensorFlow Serving.
Application frameworks	Application Teams	Created for specific environments and built on top of framework images. They contain additional sources, binaries, or model artifacts.

> **NOTE** *A secure container registry should allow you to store container images and provide image signing, vulnerability scanning, role-based access control, and image auditing features.*

The following are container management-related best practices using AWS to meet security and regulatory requirements:

BEST PRACTICE	TOOL/METHOD	DESCRIPTION
Security controls	Security patches	Implement security controls, consistent patching, and vulnerability scanning to meet security and regulatory requirements.
Organization	Namespace conventions	Organize repositories using namespace conventions to group repositories together.
Versioning	Image tags	Use image tags to indicate specific versions of containers, and unique tags can be used to track GitHub repository branches.

BEST PRACTICE	TOOL/METHOD	DESCRIPTION
Access control	Identity access management	Implement granular access control for containers by adopting resource-based and identity-based policies.
Container security	Regular scanning	Implement container security by regularly scanning vulnerabilities and patching.
Cross-account access	IAM policies	Enable cross-account access for repositories stored in shared accounts to users from other AWS accounts.

This table lists Azure-related security management best practices for containers:

BEST PRACTICE	TOOL/METHOD	DESCRIPTION
Image building	Azure Pipelines	Use Azure Pipelines, a CI/CD service, to build your images in an automated fashion.
Image storage	Azure Container Registry	Store your containers in Azure Container Registry, a secure and scalable repository.
Policy enforcement	Azure Policy	Use Azure Policy to enforce organizational security policies on your images.

This table lists Google-related security management best practices for containers:

BEST PRACTICE	TOOL/METHOD	DESCRIPTION
Image building	Cloud Build	Use Cloud Build to build your images.
Image storage	Google Container Repository (GCR)	Store your images in GCR.
Policy enforcement	Cloud Policy	Use Cloud Policy to implement security and compliance policies.
Image deployment	Google Kubernetes Engine (GKE)	Use GKE to deploy your images.

Tag Management

Tag management is another critical component of MLOps as it helps to track ML experiments and model versions. In addition to all the things discussed about using tags to manage resource usage, you can also use tags to manage other tasks, covered in this section.

Control SageMaker Endpoints and Studio Domain Creation

Using tags, you can control the creation of SageMaker endpoints and SageMaker studio domains (see Figure 14.8).

➤ **SageMaker endpoints:** The SageMaker endpoint functions as an API exposed to other endpoints to make the calls with the required input data to obtain predictions.

➤ **SageMaker studio domains:** These platforms help data scientists, machine learning engineers, and developers collaborate. They provide capabilities such as Jupyter notebooks, integrated debuggers, experiment environments, model registries, and Git integration.

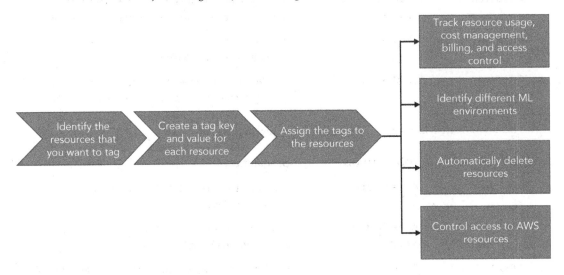

FIGURE 14.8: Using tags to track resource usage, cost management, billing, and access control

Cost Management and Billing

The following table reviews the tagging and cost management strategies of Azure and Google:

PROVIDER	TAGGING STRATEGY	COST MANAGEMENT STRATEGY
Azure	Azure resource manager tags help you attach metadata to various resources using tags to control their cost, usage, organization, and access control. You can assign these tags to virtual machines, storage systems, and ML platform components. These tags can be assigned based on organizational units, cost centers, environments, or projects. You can use the Azure Policy to mandate that the tag should be assigned to all resources, which can help you ensure governance, cost control, and enforce resource usage limitations.	The Azure cost management and billing service helps you control the usage of ML resources and manage its budget accordingly. The Azure machine learning service controls costs by setting up compute targets, for instance, types and sizes. Azure also provides cost management APIs that can help you retrieve costs and usage data related to various resources, which can be used in custom reporting for tracking purposes.
Google	Google provides similar resource labels to tag virtual machines, storage buckets, models, and other ML components. Using the Google Cloud policy, you can mandate that tags be associated with various resources, and these tags can be maintained at the organization, folder, or project level.	You can also control costs using Google's budget and billing alerts, AI platform auto-scaling, BigQuery cost control, and cloud billing API.

Tagging to Identify Different ML Environments

Tagging can differentiate between experimentation, automation, and production environment resources like SageMaker endpoints and model artifacts. Business tags can track ownership, monitor AWS spending, and create financial reports. Automation-related tags can be used to shut down specific resources during certain weeks while keeping other resources running.

> **TIP** *You can use tags to track resource ownership, automate tasks, and comply with regulations.*

Automatic Deletion of Resources

Tagging can be used to identify resources that need to be removed automatically. You can use this capability to delete resources as part of a workflow, put specific resources in quarantine, or delete noncompliant resources, such as those that are not tagged. You can automate the allocation and deallocation of resources using MLOps thus controlling costs optimally.

Controlling Access to AWS Resources

You can also enforce access to AWS resources by mandating that the resources have a specific tag to allow access. Security-related tags can be used to apply various levels of security controls based on their sensitivity. Role-based access is also critical in MLOps to ensure only authorized individuals can access and modify models and data.

HANDS-ON EXERCISE: SETTING UP AI PLATFORM WITH MLOps

This hands-on exercise aims to set up an enterprise AI platform with MLOps best practices that contains the major architectural components such as a data pipeline, model experimentation platform, MLOps environment, workflow automation and CI/CD pipeline, performance optimization, platform monitoring, security, and governance control practices.

Also note that the roles used here are for general guidance, and the actual roles used in our company will depend on your org structure, operating culture, and other considerations.

Finally, note that each of the following tasks depends on other tasks, and they have to come together holistically to contribute to the effective functioning of the platform as a whole:

TASK DESCRIPTION	TASK OWNER (SKILLS)	DELIVERABLES
Design Data Pipeline: Design a data pipeline to ensure that data is properly gathered, cleaned, and stored for use in machine learning experiments.	Data engineer	A list of different data sources; diagram showing data flow

continues

continued

TASK DESCRIPTION	TASK OWNER (SKILLS)	DELIVERABLES
Design your ML Experimentation Environment: Setting up an experimentation platform to conduct machine learning experiments, such as model training, testing, and validation. **Note:** MLOps solutions can streamline experimentation, making it easier to compare different model versions and experiments.	Data scientist	Detailed report on setup; diagram of interaction with data sources
Document MLOps setup: Documenting the steps to deploy trained models in a production environment, serving the models, and monitoring their performance. **Note:** The MLOPs setup is a critical step for automating model deployment, monitoring, and retraining.	ML engineer	Detailed report on model execution, serving, and monitoring; diagram illustrating model flow
Design Workflow Automation and CI/CD Pipeline Architecture: Designing the architecture to automate repetitive tasks and establish a continuous integration/continuous delivery pipeline.	DevOps engineer	Report describing the automation process; diagram of automation integration
Design Security Architecture: Designing the security architecture to ensure all data and models are secure, manage access controls, and meet regulatory requirements.	Security officer	Security architecture and plan outlining measures; diagram of integration of security measures
Configure Performance Optimization: Ensure the system works at optimal levels and makes the most of available resources.	Performance engineer	Report on performance optimization measures; diagram of how measures integrate into the system
Configure Platform Monitoring: Monitoring system performance and health, and document methods to send alerts if any issues arise.	System administrator	Report on monitoring system; diagram of how this system integrates into the system

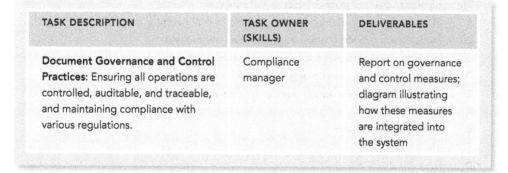

TASK DESCRIPTION	TASK OWNER (SKILLS)	DELIVERABLES
Document Governance and Control Practices: Ensuring all operations are controlled, auditable, and traceable, and maintaining compliance with various regulations.	Compliance manager	Report on governance and control measures; diagram illustrating how these measures are integrated into the system

WORKBOOK TEMPLATE: *ML OPERATIONS AUTOMATION GUIDE*

Download the "ML Operations Automation Guide" template from the download section of the book (www .wiley.com/go/EnterpriseAIintheCloud). Use this template to put together an operations automation guide to help scale AI in your enterprise. If done right, it can help you to reduce operational costs, increase efficiency, and increase productivity to allow employees to devote more time to innovation rather than maintenance.

SUMMARY

In the world of AI/ML production environments, three pillars stand out: efficiency, scalability, and reliability. To achieve those goals, automating the ML lifecycle is essential. MLOps is the secret sauce to achieve that automation, covered in this deep, technically intensive chapter. By enabling this automation, MLOps serves to bridge ML development and operations, thus bringing speed to deployment. This chapter focused mainly on cloud engineers and other IT professionals responsible for operating and automating as much of the ML lifecycle as possible. Moreover, business and technology strategists stand to benefit, given the accelerated speed to market and scale that MLOps brings.

The chapter covered a number of key concepts, such as container images and their management, using tagging for access control, tracking resource usage, and cost control. In addition, it explored platform monitoring, model operationalization, automated pipelines, model inventory management, data, and artifact lineage tracking. It discussed best practices using AWS, Azure, and Google Cloud platforms, covering topics such as security controls, organization, versioning, and access control.

The chapter provided hands-on exercises for setting up a modern enterprise AI platform incorporating the latest MLOps practices, encapsulating crucial architectural components like data pipeline, MLOps environment, CI/CD pipeline, and governance practices. These exercises structured around real-world roles like data engineer, data scientist, and ML engineer not only teach the MLOps methodology but also increase awareness around the roles and responsibilities of these roles.

This chapter is tailored toward professionals working in fields such as data engineering, machine learning, DevOps, and cloud architecture, providing both theoretical knowledge and practical tools to implement robust AI platforms. Whether a beginner or an experienced practitioner, you are likely to gain insights that will further your understanding of the complex landscape of modern AI infrastructure.

In the next chapter, let's discuss how to process data and engineer features.

REVIEW QUESTIONS

These review questions are included at the end of each chapter to help you test your understanding of the information. You'll find the answers in the following section.

1. The components involved in model operationalization are
   A. Model execution, model monitoring, and model deployment
   B. Model hosting, model evaluation, and model consumption
   C. Model training, data preprocessing, and feature selection
   D. Data visualization, model tuning, and model evaluation

2. Which of the following components is not part of an automated pipeline for machine learning?
   A. Code repository
   B. Data processing service
   C. Model training service
   D. Data visualization tool

3. The Lambda function is used in the pipeline architecture for which of the following?
   A. Building the Docker image and pushing it to a container repository
   B. Training the model using an existing Docker container
   C. Registering the model in the ECR registry and storing it in S3
   D. Triggering the pipeline based on a change in source code or deployment of a new file

4. Which of the following is NOT a benefit of platform monitoring?
   A. Improved accuracy
   B. Improved reliability
   C. Improved speed
   D. Reduced costs

5. _____ is NOT a benefit of using a model inventory management system.
   A. Improved model lineage tracking
   B. Improved model metadata management
   C. Improved model auditing
   D. Reduced model development costs

6. Which of the following is NOT a method or tool used for tracking data and artifacts lineage in machine learning?
   A. Code repositories such as GitLab and Bitbucket
   B. Dataset versioning using S3 data partitioning
   C. Azure DevOps for tracking code versions
   D. Kubeflow, Data Catalog, and Dataflow in Google Cloud

7. Which of the following tasks can be managed using tags in cloud platforms like AWS, Azure, and Google Cloud?
   A. Controlling access to AWS resources
   B. Deploying containers using Azure Pipelines
   C. Managing DNS settings in Google Cloud
   D. Monitoring network traffic in AWS

8. _____ is NOT a technique for improving latency in hybrid and edge computing.
   A. Edge caching
   B. Preprocessing
   C. Local inference
   D. Round-trips to the cloud

ANSWER KEY

1.	A	**4.**	A	**7.**	A
2.	D	**5.**	D	**8.**	D
3.	D	**6.**	D		

PART VI
Processing Data and Modeling

Data is the lifeblood of AI. Part VI is where you get your hands dirty with data and modeling. I teach you how to process data in the cloud, choose the right AI/ML algorithm based on your use case, and get your models trained, tuned, and evaluated. It is where science meets art.

15

Process Data and Engineer Features in the Cloud

The world is one big data problem.

—Andrew McAfee

In the world of AI, the true essence lies not just in sophisticated algorithms, but in the quality and structure of data. As most AI practitioners would attest, raw data is rarely ready to be used as is. This is where cloud-based data processing comes in. It refers to the process of collecting, ingesting, storing, preprocessing, engineering, and processing data for use in machine learning models through cloud-based data technologies from AWS, Azure, and Google.

So why is data so vital? Simply put, the most sophisticated model is only as good as the data on which it is trained. Incorrectly processed data or poorly engineered data can lead to inaccurate predictions and decisions costly to your business.

As companies try to embrace the scalability and power of the cloud, learning how to process data in the cloud becomes paramount. Cloud provides several benefits, including scalability, performance, security, flexibility, and cost-effectiveness.

In this chapter, you learn about exploring your data needs and the benefits and challenges of cloud-based data processing, and you dive into hands-on exercises, including feature engineering and transformation techniques.

This chapter underscores the importance of data augmentation, showcases methods to handle missing data and inconsistencies, and presents the art and science of feature engineering, all happening in the cloud. See Figure 15.1.

This chapter addresses many topics, including data storage and exploration, data storage architectures, and distributed data processing. Always remember, in the end, data is king—it is not just the starting point, but the foundation for everything else when it comes to AI.

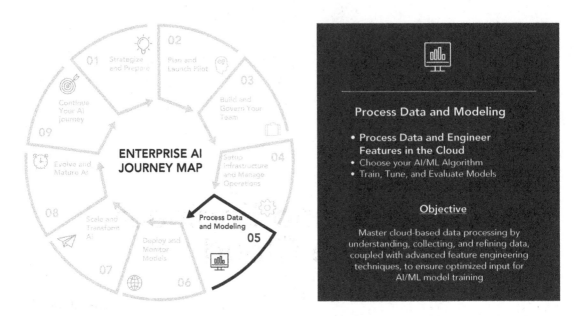

FIGURE 15.1: PROCESS DATA AND MODELING: Process data and engineer features in the cloud

UNDERSTANDING YOUR DATA NEEDS

You are now at a critical stage in your ML project, where you have a good idea of the business problem you need to solve. For example, consider a use case of a retail company. Assume you are working for them and trying to predict the next quarter's sales so they can plan their inventory, staffing, and other resources. To predict the sales, you need to develop a machine learning model. Armed with this information, you can now carry out these steps in the following hands-on exercise.

HANDS-ON EXERCISE: UNDERSTANDING YOUR DATA NEEDS

Problem Statement: The management of a retail chain store is facing problems in predicting the sales for the upcoming quarter. In the past, inaccuracies in the forecasts have resulted in either overstocking or understocking resulting in inefficient resource allocation or missed revenue opportunities. The management wants to leverage the company's past data to develop a machine learning model that can predict sales more accurately for the next quarter across their retail stores. They need this prediction a few weeks before the start of the quarter to allow effective inventory planning, staffing, and other resource planning. The goal is to minimize waste and increase profitability.

Here are the steps your team can follow:

STEP	TASK	EXAMPLE	TASK OWNER (SKILL SETS)	DELIVERABLES
Understanding the business problem	First you need to consult stakeholders to get a clear understanding of what they want to predict their time frame.	Stakeholders want to predict sales a few weeks before the start of the next quarter.	Project manager, business analyst	A clear statement of the problem, goals, and objectives of the project
Identifying data needs	You can now start understanding the data needs, such as what kinds of data are required and the potential sources for the same. List what types of data you might need for such a prediction and possible sources.	Past sales data is essential, along with data related to promotional offers, seasonal trends, price changes, customer reviews, competitor data, economic indicators, and so on.	Data scientist, data analyst	A comprehensive list of required data and potential data sources
Gathering data	You then try to identify the data sources and decide to gather the past sales data from the company's databases, promotional offers, and seasonal data from the marketing team, customer reviews from the website, economic indicators from the public databases, and competitor data from industry reports. Do not underestimate the amount of effort needed to clean this data.	Collect data from company's databases, marketing team, publicly available economic data, industry reports, etc.	Data engineer, data analyst	Collected raw data from different sources

STEP	TASK	EXAMPLE	TASK OWNER (SKILL SETS)	DELIVERABLES
Data cleaning	Once you gather the data, the next step is to clean the data, which may have missing values, outliers, and other inconsistencies.	Handle missing sales figures, correct inconsistencies in promotion categorization, remove outlier values in sales figures.	Data scientist, data analyst	Cleaned and standardized dataset
Exploratory Data Analysis (EDA)	Explore the data for seasonal trends, and the relationships between various data elements. This will eventually help you choose the suitable ML model and guide you in preparing the data for your model.	Identify patterns in sales based on promotions, holidays, competitor activities, economic indicators, etc.	Data scientist, data analyst	Report on the findings of the EDA, including visualizations and initial insights
Feature engineering and model building	Based on EDA, brainstorm potential new features that could improve your model's performance. Prepare the data for consumption in machine learning models.	Create features like frequency of promotions, duration since last promotion, average spending per visit, etc.	Data scientist, machine learning engineer	New features added to the dataset, ML model prototypes

> **NOTE** *While data may be available internally, one point that is often overlooked is the suitability of the data for consumption by the required algorithms.*

BENEFITS AND CHALLENGES OF CLOUD-BASED DATA PROCESSING

Processing data in the cloud has its own benefits and challenges, each discussed next.

Benefits of Cloud-Based Data Processing

Some of the benefits are large computing capacity, data integration, and preparation capabilities:

➤ **Computing capacity:** Regarding processing large amounts of data, it is crucial to have a large computing capacity to process data efficiently and quickly. Unlike the on-premises servers, which may be limited in capacity, cloud-based services provide scalable and robust cloud servers.

➤ **Data integration:** Note that your data sources may also be distributed in disparate sources. For example, sales data may be stored in S3, customer reviews in Google Cloud storage, and economic indicators in a public database hosted in Azure. Each cloud service has several tools that allow these data to be integrated and processed quickly. For example, you could use AWS Glue for extract, transform, and load (ETL) and Amazon Athena to query data directly from S3. Google Cloud's BigQuery can run SQL queries on the customer review data.

➤ **Data preparation:** Cloud-based tools such as AWS Glue can be used to clean the data for missing values, re-engineer features, and prepare the data to be used in the ML models.

> **TIP** *Cloud-based tools like AWS Glue can clean the data, handle missing values, engineer features, and prepare data for the ML model.*

Challenges of Cloud-Based Data Processing

Handling data in the cloud can pose security challenges and raise cost concerns. Consider these issues:

➤ **Security and compliance:** When the data is stored in the cloud, it is essential to ensure it is securely stored and processed and complies with privacy regulations like GDPR or CCPA. While cloud providers may provide many tools, such as access control and data encryption, you must have in-house skills to implement them appropriately.

➤ **Cost control:** Another factor to consider is the aspect of cost control, because even though the cloud providers provide a pay-as-you-go model, the cost can pile up as large volumes of data are being processed. Managing costs is especially important when dealing with Gen AI models.

Handling Different Types of Data

Another challenge when preparing the data is to handle different types of data, as shown in Figure 15.2. You can think of the predictions as the meal, the different AI, ML, and deep learning models are the cooks, and the data is the ingredients. No matter how good the models are, the predictions will be good only if the data is correct.

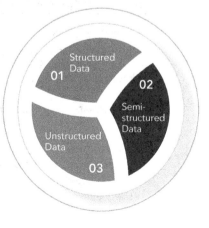

FIGURE 15.2: Data types

As noticed in the previous case study about the retail company, there are different data types, such as structured, unstructured, and semi-structured data. Each data type has a different purpose, format, and suitable models, as shown in the following table:

DATA TYPE	EXAMPLE	PURPOSE	FORMAT AND PROCESSING	SUITABLE MODEL
Structured data	Historical sales data	Helps identify sales trends and seasonality	Comes as CSV file or a SQL database	Regression models for predicting future sales
Unstructured data	Customer reviews	Provides insights into customer preferences or sentiments	Can be messy, requires natural language processing for feature extraction	Deep learning models to identify patterns in customer sentiment
Semi-structured data	Economic indicators	Helps assess how economic indicators impact sales	Comes as XML or JSON files, predefined structure but not as rigid as in a table	Decision trees to evaluate impact of economic indicators on sales

Different ML models can use this data, such as a regression model for predicting future sales that uses structured sales data well. However, a deep learning model can be used on unstructured customer review data to identify patterns in customer sentiment. On the other hand, a decision tree may work well with *semi-structured data,* such as economic indicators, to assess how economic indicators impact sales.

> **TIP** *Match the data types with the most suitable models and processing techniques.*

Going back to the meals analogy, the better the quality and variety of the ingredients used, the better the meal—in this case—the predictions.

HANDS-ON EXERCISE: HANDLING DIFFERENT DATA TYPES

This hands-on exercise can help make this concept of handling different data types clearer.

Problem Statement: A retail company is facing challenges dealing with handling multiple data types such as structured, unstructured, and semi-structured data to use in the ML models. Your task is to guide them to build a clean, consolidated dataset to use in their ML models.

STEP NAME	DESCRIPTION	TASK OWNER (SKILL SETS)	DELIVERABLES
Process structured data (such as historical sales data).	First you can import the historical sales data from the company's database into a CSV file or SQL database.	Data analyst, data scientist	An organized CSV file or SQL database of historical sales data

STEP NAME	DESCRIPTION	TASK OWNER (SKILL SETS)	DELIVERABLES
Process unstructured data (such as customer reviews).	For unstructured data, you can use NLP techniques to extract features from customer reviews data.	Natural language processing expert, data scientist	A processed dataset of customer reviews with relevant features extracted
Process semi-structured data (such as economic indicators).	Then for semi-structured data such as economic indicators, you can clean and process them. This data is crucial to understand the macroeconomic trends that might influence sales.	Data analyst, data scientist	A processed dataset of economic indicators
Align datasets.	Now ensure that all the structured, unstructured, and semi-structured datasets are aligned properly and aggregate them as needed.	Data analyst, data scientist	Datasets that are aligned based on time, e.g., daily, weekly, or monthly
Match datasets.	Identify differences in the datasets and try to match them as needed. For example, if you have sales data that is based on stores but the economic indicators are based on region, then try to match the store to the correct region.	Data analyst, data scientist	Matched datasets that are correlated to each other by the right entities, such as store, region, etc.
Consolidate datasets.	Once the data has been aligned and matched, you can consolidate them into a single table or a single database with multiple tables depending on the complexity and data size.	Data analyst, data scientist	A single, consolidated dataset ready to be cleaned

continues

continued

STEP NAME	DESCRIPTION	TASK OWNER (SKILL SETS)	DELIVERABLES
Check and clean datasets.	Perform a quality check for missing values, outliers, and other inconsistencies and correct them.	Data analyst, data scientist	A high-quality dataset free of missing values, outliers and other inconsistencies and is ready for machine learning model training

THE DATA PROCESSING PHASES OF THE ML LIFECYCLE

This section discusses the data processing phases of the ML lifecycle. The data processing workflow involves data collection and ingestion and then data preparation.

Data Collection and Ingestion

Once you have identified the data needs, the next step is to collect and ingest the data from various sources. Figure 13.3 shows the various activities involved in the collection phase. These activities are labeling, ingesting, and aggregating.

The following table explains some of the data collection methods:

STAGE	DESCRIPTION
Labeled data	Data about which you already know the target answer. If the label is missing, the activity involves labeling the missing data either manually or using automated means.
Data collection	Depending on the use case, data can be collected from various sources, such as sensors, time-series data, event data, IoT data, and social media.
	In the retail company case study, you may need to use an API or a SQL query to store the past sales data, pricing data, or promotional offers data in a cloud storage such as S3.
Web scraping	Use *web scraping* to gather the review data and handle real-time ingestion for customer reviews, as review data is continuously trickling in. The marketing data can come as semi-structured data such as an XML, JSON, or CSV file, which you need to ingest into the cloud environment.
Direct downloads	In the case of economic indicators data, you can use the APIs offered by the financial institutions or the government bodies or a direct download to extract data and use different methods to ingest data into the cloud.
Data ingestion methods	Collected data must be ingested into storage facilities, through either real-time or batch processing.

Figure 15.3 shows the activities involved in a data collection process.

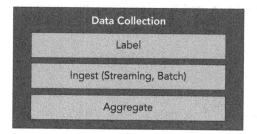

Data Collection
- Label
- Ingest (Streaming, Batch)
- Aggregate

FIGURE 15.3: Data collection process

> **NOTE** *Data can be collected from various sources such as sensors, time-series data, event data, IoT data, and social media using API or SQL query, web scraping, or direct downloads.*

Data that's collected must be ingested into various storage facilities using real-time or batch processing. The following table compares the pros and cons of the two methods:

DATA INGESTION METHOD	DESCRIPTION	EXAMPLE USE CASE	PROS	CONS
Real-time data ingestion	For real-time data ingestion, you must use a real-time processing system such as Apache Kafka or AWS Kinesis.	Customer reviews can be smaller in volume but high in velocity as new reviews keep coming in. For this scenario, a real-time ingestion method is appropriate.	Handles high velocity data; ensures data is current	Requires specific tools and systems and is not suitable for large volume data.
Batch data processing	Processes large volumes of data at specific time intervals.	The velocity with which the data comes in can vary; for example, sales data can come in large quantities but be updated once a day or weekly. In such situations, you may use a batch ingestion process.	Handles large volume data; doesn't require immediate processing	Data may not always be current and is not suitable for high velocity data.

> **NOTE** *Choose real-time or batch ingestion methods and tools based on the velocity and volume of data. Unless you are positive that you are doing one-time pulls of data from a source, consider automation as an important part of your AI/ML journey.*

Data Storage Options

After collecting your data, you need to store the data for further processing and analysis. You have many options to store such data depending on the data type. Data storage options vary and can be any of the following:

- Transactional SQL databases
- Data lakes
- Data warehouses

The following table lists the pros and cons of these options:

STORAGE OPTION	PROS	CONS
Transactional SQL databases	Ideal for structured data and supports real-time processing	Not ideal for handling large volumes of data.
Data lakes	Useful for storing a vast amount of raw data in its native format	Data may need further processing before it can be used.
Data warehouses	Optimized for analyzing structured data and performing complex queries	Might not be the best choice for unstructured or semi-structured data.

The following table lists the storage options from various cloud providers:

STORAGE OPTION	DESCRIPTION	PROS	CONS
Amazon S3	In the retail company example, you can store the sales and promotional events data in Amazon S3 (Simple Storage Service), which is highly scalable and grows with your needs.	• It is scalable. • It can also seamlessly integrate with other AWS services that you use to carry out further processing.	• The trade-off with S3 is its cost because even though it is reasonably priced, it can rise if you have to handle large volumes of data more frequently. • Moreover, it may need to integrate better with other non-AWS services.
Google Cloud Storage	Google Cloud Storage is another option, as it's also scalable, like S3, and integrates well with other Google Cloud services such as Natural Language Processing.	• It is scalable. • It has good Google Cloud services integration.	• It can also become expensive. • It may need to integrate better with non-Google Cloud services. • It is also not considered as comprehensive or mature as S3, although it's been catching up in recent years.

STORAGE OPTION	DESCRIPTION	PROS	CONS
Azure Blob Storage	Azure Blob Storage can also be a good choice due to its scalability and integration ability with Azure Cloud services.	• It is scalable. • It has good Azure Cloud services integration.	• It can also become more expensive. • Integration with non-Azure services can be challenging. • It is also less user intuitive than S3 or Google Cloud Storage.

> **TIP** *When choosing a data storage option, it's crucial to consider factors such as cost, user-friendliness, integration with other services, in-house skill sets, tiered storage, disaster recovery, and data type and volume.*

When choosing these storage options, you should evaluate them against the following factors:

➤ Cost

➤ User-friendliness

➤ Integration ability with other services

➤ In-house and easily acquirable skills

➤ The ability to have tiered storage where you can store infrequently accessed data to lower cost storage

➤ Multiregional storage for disaster recovery

UNDERSTANDING THE DATA EXPLORATION AND PREPROCESSING STAGE

Once your data is stored in the cloud, the next step is to explore and clean it and then ensure it is ready for model building. This is similar to how you clean your ingredients before they go into the pot for cooking.

According to one of the data science surveys, more than 66 percent of a data scientist's time is spent cleansing and loading data and doing the visualization activities, as shown in Figure 15.4.

Data Preparation

Data preparation is the process of preparing the collected data for further analysis and processing. Data preparation includes data preprocessing, exploratory data analysis, data visualization, and feature engineering.

Figure 15.5 shows a data processing workflow. Note that your project may have different workflows with different steps.

➤ **Data preprocessing:** Data preprocessing is the stage where data is cleaned to remove any errors or inconsistencies.

➤ **Exploratory data analysis:** Data exploration or exploratory data analysis is about looking at what's in your dataset. It is part of data preparation and can be used to understand data, carry out sanity checks, and validate the quality of the data.

➤ **Methods used:** It involves generating summary statistics, visualizing the distribution of data and variables, and identifying relationships between variables. You can use out-of-the-box features provided by various cloud ML platforms, data visualization tools such as Tableau and Google Data Studio, and software libraries such as Pandas and Matplotlib in Python.

➤ **Example:** In this case study example, you can explore summary statistics such as mean, median, and range of sales per day or product. You can create histograms to visualize this data or create scatterplots to identify relationships between sales and other variables such as price and promotional events.

➤ **Feature engineering:** Feature engineering is the phase where new features are created from existing data to improve the performance of the models.

➤ **Data visualization:** Data visualization can help with exploratory data analysis by providing visual representations of data to better understand patterns, trends, and correlations.

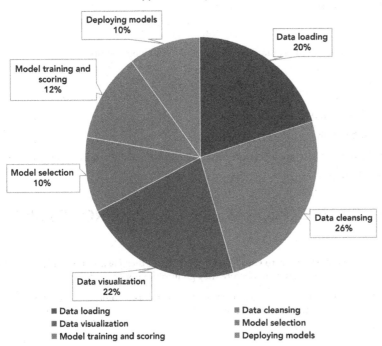

FIGURE 15.4: Average time spent in ML tasks

> **TIP** *When preparing data, ensure thorough data preprocessing for cleaning, exploratory data analysis for understanding, feature engineering for model performance enhancement, and data visualization to discern patterns and correlations.*

Data Preprocessing

Data preprocessing is about preparing the data to be in the right shape and quality for model training. Figure 15.6 shows the different strategies available for data preprocessing.

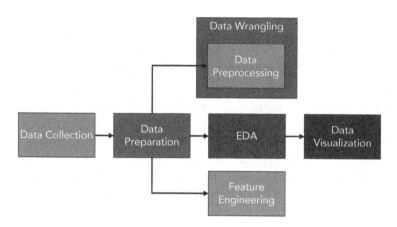

FIGURE 15.5: Data processing workflow

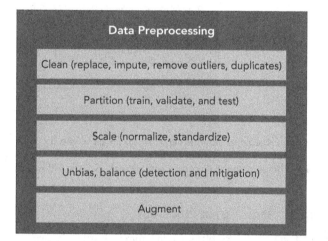

FIGURE 15.6: Data preprocessing strategies

Data wrangling is part of the data preparation process. It involves the process of transforming and mapping data from one "raw" format into another to allow subsequent analysis and consumption.

Using tools such as SageMaker Data Wrangler will help you prepare data using its visual interface to access data, perform EDA, perform feature engineering, and then seamlessly import the data into the SageMaker pipeline for model training.

SageMaker Pipeline comes with about 300 built-in transforms, custom transforms using Python and PySpark, built-in analysis tools such as scatterplots, histograms, and model analysis capabilities such as feature importance, target leakage, and model explainability.

Data Cleaning Techniques

Your next step is to clean up the data. You look for missing values, outliers, and inconsistent formatting.

Dealing with Missing Values

Missing values, such as missing sales data for some days, can result in your algorithms producing inaccurate results or failing. For missing values, either you can replace them with the imputation techniques, or you can simply remove the record. If you're using imputation techniques, you can fill the missing data with mean or median values, use the regression method, or use multiple imputation by chained equations (MICE) techniques.

DATA ISSUE	DESCRIPTION	TECHNIQUES USED	RETAIL CASE STUDY
Missing values	Missing values in the data can lead to inaccurate results or algorithm failure.	Imputation	**Problem:** A retail store finds missing sales data for some days in its sales tracking system.
	These gaps in the dataset need to be dealt with effectively to maintain the integrity of the data analysis.	Regression method	**Action:** They decide to fill the missing values to maintain the continuity and reliability of the data.
		MICE	**Technique Used:** They use a regression model based on the historical pricing or promotional events data to fill in the missing sales data.
		Mean/median Imputation	Alternatively, they replace missing sales price data with the average sales price to impute the missing data.

Handling Outliers

In the case of outliers, you have to identify if there's an error or an extreme value. If it is an error, you try to resolve the error, and if it is an extreme value, you can decide to keep it but try to reduce the impact of it by using techniques such as normalization. Data normalization helps keep the data on a similar scale. See the following table for more details:

DATA ISSUE	DESCRIPTION	TECHNIQUES USED	RETAIL CASE STUDY
Handling outliers	Outliers are data points that deviate significantly from other observations.	Normalization	**Problem:** A retail store notices that its sales quantity data can vary from hundreds to thousands, while product price ranges from $1 to $50.
		Min-max scaling	**Action:** To avoid giving more importance to sales quantity data due to its higher value, they normalize the data to bring it to a similar scale.
	They can be errors or extreme values and can lead to skewed or misleading	Standardization	**Technique Used:** They apply min-max scaling, where they transform the data to fit within a specified range, typically 0 to 1. This reduces the impact of outliers.
	results in data analysis.	Z-score normalization	They also apply standardization (Z-score normalization) to handle outliers as it's less sensitive to them. This process makes the mean of the data 0 and standard deviation 1.

> **TIP** *Be sure to clean up data by handling missing values using imputation techniques like mean or median values, regression, or MICE, and take care of outliers using normalization techniques like min-max scaling or standardization.*

Data Partitioning

It is important to split data into training, validate, and test datasets so that the models do not overfit, and you can evaluate the models accurately. You need to ensure that there is no leakage of test datasets into training datasets. One way to achieve this is to remove duplicates before splitting.

Data Scaling (Normalize, Standardize)

Consider the example of predicting the sales of various products in the store. Say you have collected a dataset with the following features:

➤ Average customer footfall per day, ranging from 100 to 400

➤ Average income level, ranging from $50,000 to $200,000

➤ Average price of the product, ranging from $1 to $100

Normalization

To calculate the normalized value, you take each value, subtract the minimum value from it, and then divide it by the range. So, for a footfall value of 200, your normalized value is 200 – 100/300 = 0.33.

You do the same for the income level and the price. By normalizing all the values, the vast difference in the absolute values is minimized, and therefore your algorithm will give equal weightage to all these features.

FEATURE	ORIGINAL RANGE	NORMALIZATION METHOD	NORMALIZED EXAMPLE
Average customer footfall/day	100–400	(value-min)/range	For a customer footfall value of 200, normalized value is (200–100)/300 = 0.33.
Average income level ($K)	50–200	(value-min)/range	For an income of 100, normalized value is (100–50)/150 = 0.33.
Average price of product ($)	1–100	(value-min)/range	For a product price of 50, normalized value is (50–1)/99 = 0.49.

Standardization

If you didn't scale these values, income levels would have an unfair advantage in influencing the predictions, making your results inaccurate. Note that standardization is preferred for handling outliers, as it's less sensitive to them.

Unbias and Balance (Detection and Mitigation)

This section discusses detecting and mitigating bias in data. Say you are trying to predict your customers' spending habits and using features such as age, income, purchasing habits, and location. When you train the model and discover that it has different accuracies for different age groups, that is an example of bias. For example, this might happen if most of your data belongs to middle-income, middle-aged customers, so your model may be very good at predicting those segments. However, it might not be suitable for lower-income, younger groups, or high-income, older groups.

Sometimes the bias can come from the algorithm itself. For example, if it has the predisposition to predict favorably for larger group segments, and if you're running a discount program using this model, it might give more discounts to the middle-aged, middle-income groups.

You can mitigate bias by adopting data level, algorithm level, post-deployment level including continuous monitoring techniques, as shown in the following table:

BIAS MITIGATION TECHNIQUES	DESCRIPTION	EXAMPLE
Data level	You can build a balanced dataset by undersampling the overrepresented groups and oversampling the underrepresented groups.	You could attempt to balance your dataset by including more data from lower-income, younger groups, or high-income, older groups.
Algorithm level	1. Try different algorithms. 2. Change the parameters of the chosen algorithm. 3. Use an ensemble method that combines the predictions of multiple models.	You can test different algorithms or adjust the parameters of your chosen algorithm to see if they perform better for underrepresented groups. You could also use ensemble methods to combine the predictions of several models.
Post-processing level	1. Conduct a fairness audit of the model. 2. Do a fairness correction to adjust the model's output until the bias is reduced.	First you must check if the model is predicting accurately across multiple groups. Then, you can experiment by adjusting the model's output to reduce any identified bias.
Continuous monitoring	1. Monitor the model's performance across all groups. 2. Make corrections to the model as needed.	To begin with, regularly monitor the model's performance across all customer groups and adjust as necessary. This can help ensure that the model continues to make accurate predictions for all customer groups.

NOTE *You can detect and mitigate bias in machine learning models by using tools like Sage-Maker Clarify, AWS Machine Learning Interpretability Toolkit, Azure Fairlearn, and GCP Explainable AI.*

Using SageMaker Clarify, you can monitor for bias at the data preparation stage before the training starts and during each stage of the ML lifecycle. This can also detect bias after deployment and provides detailed reports that quantify different types of bias and provide feature importance scores to explain how the model made its predictions. It explains the data, model, and monitoring used to assess predictions.

Azure provides the Azure Machine Learning Interpretability Toolkit and Azure Fairlearn, and Google provides GCP Explainable AI to detect and mitigate bias and provide explanations for predictions.

Data Augmentation

Another technique you can use is data augmentation. This involves creating new data from existing data. It is often used in deep learning. See the following table for more details:

STEPS	TECHNIQUES AND METHODS	RETAIL CASE STUDY EXAMPLE
Creation of new data	This involves creating new data from the existing data.	In a retail setting, you could create synthetic new customer reviews to augment your existing dataset.
Adding noise to data	Adding noise to data can help improve the robustness of the model.	You could add noise to the sales data. This could allow your model to handle a broader range of data and possibly improve its performance.

Handling Inconsistent Formats

In the case of inconsistent formats, you can use either text processing or parsing techniques. For example, you can rectify the incorrect date formats using dateUtil libraries or regular expressions.

FEATURE ENGINEERING

Each unique attribute of data is a feature. Feature engineering is about selecting the right attributes for the model to become more accurate and generalizable for new data. You choose different features based on the type of model.

Feature engineering consists of the components shown in Figure 15.7.

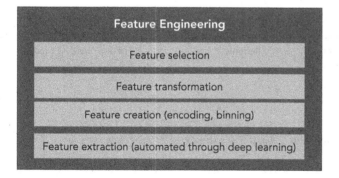

FIGURE 15.7: Feature engineering components

Feature Types

This section explains the various feature types that you can create for your models. The following table lists these feature types, their suitable models, and some examples:

FEATURE TYPES	DESCRIPTION	USEFUL MODELS	CASE STUDY EXAMPLE
Time-series features	Time-series features capture temporal information such as day of the week, month, holiday season, or if it's a weekend.	ARIMA, Prophet	The fluctuating sales throughout the week or the sales promotions during the holiday season.
Ratio-based features	Ratio-based features represent relationships between different numerical variables. For instance, the relationship between the current price and the average price.	Decision trees (XGBoost and random forests), regression models	Comparison of the price of an item among its competitors.
Categorical features	Categorical features represent categories or discrete values such as the type of promotion.	Classification models such as logistic regression, support vector machines	Promotion type can be a key feature, for instance, "Buy one get one" versus "20% off."
Binary features	Binary features take on two possible values like yes/no or 1/0.	Various models	Whether or not a sales promotion was running.
Sentiment scores or topic features	These features are derived from text data like customer reviews. Sentiment scores or topics extracted using NLP techniques.	Deep learning models such as RNNs, transformers	Sentiment scores or topics obtained from the analysis of customer reviews.
Interaction features	Interaction features represent dependencies between other features, such as the interaction between price and promotions.	Useful for any model that might miss these relationships	For instance, a feature representing the effect of a promotion on a high-priced item.

> **TIP** *Use domain knowledge to create features that are relevant to the problem you are trying to solve.*

Feature Selection

Feature selection is the process of selecting the attributes that are more relevant to predicting the results. Consider the use case of predicting a customer's spending habits. Assume the dataset contains features such as the customer's age, income, location, purchase habits, number of children, job title, education level, and frequency of store visits.

When selecting the features to predict the customer's spending habits, you have to decide which feature is going to be more relevant to predict this spending habit, and you have to decide which one is irrelevant, a duplicate, or even counterproductive.

Feature Importance Scores

One method used to determine the relevancy of the features to the target is to train the model and examine the feature importance scores. Algorithms like decision trees and their ensembles, such as random forest and gradient boosting, natively provide these feature importance scores. By training these models, you may find that occupation titles and education levels do not impact spending habits as much as income levels, purchasing history, and store visits do.

Correlation Matrix

Another metric that can help you select features is the correlation matrix, a table showing the relationship between the target variable and the feature. A high value implies that it plays a greater role in predicting the target, in this case, the spending habits. You can also use this correlation metric to eliminate features that have a high correlation. For example, suppose income and occupation title are highly correlated. In that case, you may retain the income and remove the occupation title from the dataset, because the income may correlate more to the target variable, namely, the spending habit.

The advantage of feature selection is that you can reduce the size of the datasets by removing redundant and irrelevant features. The smaller dataset will result in less overfitting of the model in addition to higher performance and simplicity, which makes it easier to interpret.

> **NOTE** *Use feature selection techniques like examining feature importance scores and correlation matrices to select relevant features, reduce overfitting, improve accuracy, and reduce training time. This results in higher performance and simplicity, leading to better interpretability.*

Feature Extraction

Feature extraction involves techniques that combine the existing attributes to create new ones. This is done to reduce the dimensionality of the dataset and retain the original information. Figure 15.8 shows some examples of those techniques.

Principal Component Analysis

The principal component analysis (PCA) technique creates new features, which are linear combinations of the original features. They try to capture as much of the variance in the original data as possible.

In the case study, this technique may combine products that are brought together, such as paints and paint brushes, and combine them under a new category called Painting Essentials.

Independent Component Analysis

Unlike the principal component analysis, which tries to maximize the variance in the dataset, independent component analysis (ICA) chooses attributes that are independent.

In the retail case study, this technique may choose attributes such as customers who buy gardening tools along with those who buy baby products because they're usually independent of each other.

> **NOTE** *Use feature extraction techniques like PCA, ICA, and linear discriminant analysis (LDA) to create new features. This reduces the dimensionality of the dataset while retaining the original information.*

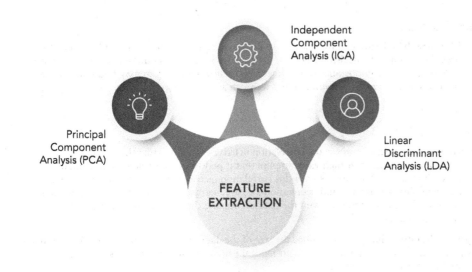

FIGURE 15.8: Feature extraction techniques

Linear Discriminant Analysis

Linear discriminant analysis uses a supervised learning technique using the class information to select a linear combination of the features.

For example, if you choose to have different classes for high and low spenders, this technique may find the selection of products that separate the low spenders from the high spenders.

Feature Creation

Feature creation helps you add new relevant variables to your dataset to improve your model's performance. Still, you must be careful to ensure that it does not add noise or complexity to the model. The following table explains the different feature creation techniques with examples:

FEATURE CREATION TECHNIQUES	DESCRIPTION	EXAMPLE
One-hot encoding	One-hot encoding involves converting the categorical variables into a form that can be fed into the model for better predictions.	You can convert the preferred shopping day category into two binary categories: the prefers_weekday or prefers_weekend feature. Each feature takes a value of 0 or 1, depending on whether the customer prefers to shop during the weekend or weekday.
Binning	Binning is a technique that combines similar items to create numerical or categorical bins.	You can create groups of ages such as 16 to 25, 26 to 35, 36 to 45, and so on. It increases the accuracy of the prediction by reducing the impact of minor differences between ages.

FEATURE CREATION TECHNIQUES	DESCRIPTION	EXAMPLE
Splitting	Splitting involves creating two or more features from one feature.	You can split an address into different features, such as city, state, and street, which can help you discover spending patterns based on these new features.
Calculated features	Calculated features are new features that you can create by performing calculations on existing features.	You can create a new feature, such as average spending per visit, by adding all the spending over the year and dividing it by the number of customer visits in that year.

> **TIP** *Evaluate the performance of your model with different sets of features.*

Feature Transformation

Feature transformation helps ensure the data is complete, clean, and ready for use in a model. The following table explains the different feature transformation techniques available with examples:

FEATURE TRANSFORMATION TECHNIQUE	DESCRIPTION	EXAMPLE
Cartesian products of features	By calculating the cartesian products of two features, you can create a new feature with greater meaning to the end result.	Suppose you have two features: average spending per visit and total number of visits per month. In that case, multiplying these two will give you the monthly spending, which may have more relevance to solving your problem.
Nonlinear transformations	The nonlinear transformation will help you understand the nonlinear effects of data.	A good example is binning numerical values into categories. For example, you can create a group of categories using the age feature, such as age groups between 16 to 25, 26 to 35, 36 to 45, and so on. This categorization will help you assist with the impact of age on spending habits from a nonlinear perspective.
Domain-specific features	These are new features that you can create based on your domain knowledge.	If you know that some customers buy organic-only products, you know these are high spenders, and you can create a new feature named organic buyers.

> **TIP** *Use a variety of transformation techniques, such as scaling, normalizing, and transforming. Start with a small number of transformation techniques and add more as needed.*

Feature Imputation

Feature imputation is the process of handling missing data using different imputation methods depending on the feature type, as shown in Figure 15.9.

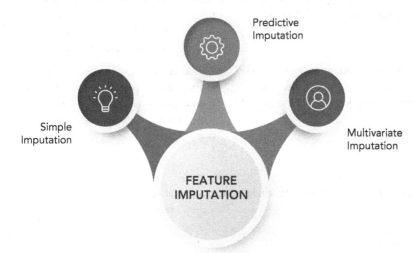

FIGURE 15.9:   Feature imputation techniques

Simple Imputation

Simple imputation involves replacing the missing values with mean, median, or mode values. For example, if you have a feature named "number of visits per month," you can fill in the missing values with the median number of visits for all customers per month.

Predictive Imputation

Predictive imputation involves predicting the missing values using other features. For example, you can predict the missing value for income by training a model using other attributes such as occupation and education levels.

Multivariate Imputation

Multivariate imputation is used when there are relationships between features. Missing values are filled by running a model using other features in the round-robin fashion. You can use methods like MICE to fill in missing values in different features by predicting them from other features in a round-robin fashion. This results in multiple datasets, which can then be combined to account for uncertainty in the missing data.

For example, in a dataset that contains three variables such as Math score, English score, and Attendance, and if the values for Math and English scores are missing, instead of imputing them separately, you can use the Attendance record to predict the Math score and then use the predicted Math score and the Attendance record to predict the English score.

> **NOTE** *Choose the right imputation method based on the type of missing data—such as simple imputation, predictive imputation, or multivariate imputation—to reduce bias based on available resources.*

WORKBOOK TEMPLATE: *DATA PROCESSING & FEATURE ENGINEERING WORKFLOW*

Download the "Data Processing & Feature Engineering" template from the download section of the book (`www.wiley.com/go/EnterpriseAIintheCloud`). Use this template to put together a workflow chart for data processing and feature engineering. You can use this as a roadmap for the various stages that the data goes through from collection to being ready for model training.

SUMMARY

This chapter covered a wide range of topics related to cloud-based data processing and feature engineering and essential steps in the machine learning lifecycle that are crucial to professionals in cloud engineering, data engineering, and machine learning. The detailed insights into the data collection techniques, preprocessing methods, and feature engineering combined with the hands-on exercises should give you the skills and knowledge to start data processing. You also learned how cloud providers such as AWS, Microsoft, and Google play a vital role in making data scalable, secure, and cost-effective.

Beyond the technology factor, you also learned how the human element comes into play for making decisions around data partitioning, augmentation, balancing, and handling inconsistent values.

REVIEW QUESTIONS

These review questions are included at the end of each chapter to help you test your understanding of the information. You'll find the answers in the following section.

1. Which of the following is true about data processing in the cloud?
   A. Local servers are more scalable than cloud servers.
   B. Data from multiple sources cannot be processed easily using cloud tools.
   C. AWS Glue can be used for ETL and Amazon Athena for data query in S3.
   D. Data stored in the cloud does not have rigorous security requirements.

2. Which of the following is an example of structured data?
   A. Customer reviews
   B. Economic indicators in XML or JSON files
   C. Sales trends or seasonality
   D. None of the above

3. Which of the following is true regarding the data processing workflow?
   A. Data processing workflow includes only data collection and does not include data preparation.
   B. Labeled data indicates information that has no target.
   C. Exploratory data analysis is part of data preparation and can be used to understand data.
   D. Data cannot be collected from sources such as sensors, time-series data, event data, or IoT data.

4. Which of the following is true about real-time and batch data ingestion?
   A. Real-time data ingestion cannot handle high-velocity data.
   B. Apache Kafka and AWS Kinesis are used for real-time data ingestion.
   C. Batch data ingestion is the preferred method to keep data current.
   D. The choice between the real-time and batch ingestion methods does not depend on the velocity and volume of data.

5. Select the technique used to handle missing values.
    A. Normalization
    B. Standardization
    C. Regression
    D. Outlier removal

6. Which technique minimizes the difference in absolute values of features in a dataset?
    A. Regression
    B. Normalization
    C. Outlier removal
    D. Standardization

7. What is true about feature engineering?
    A. It is about selecting random attributes from the dataset.
    B. Ratio-based features are better suited to ARIMA models.
    C. Sentiment scores from NLP are useful for RNNs and Transformers.
    D. Interaction features identify the differences between variables.

8. Which of the following is true about feature selection?
    A. Feature selection involves choosing all the variables for maximum accuracy.
    B. Feature selection involves selecting the most appropriate variables.
    C. Feature selection has no impact on model accuracy.
    D. Feature selection depends on feature importance scores and less on correlation matrices.

9. Which of the following is NOT a feature extraction technique commonly used in machine learning?
    A. Component analysis (PCA)
    B. Independent component analysis (ICA)
    C. Linear discriminant analysis (LDA)
    D. Random component analysis (RCA)

10. Which of the following techniques is NOT related to feature creation in a machine learning model?
    A. One-hot encoding
    B. Binning
    C. Splitting
    D. Principal component analysis

11. Which of the following is NOT a feature transformation technique?
    A. Cartesian products of features
    B. Nonlinear transformations
    C. Domain-specific features
    D. One hot encoding

12. What does the acronym ETL stand for in the context of data pipelines?
    A. Export, transform, load
    B. Extract, test, load
    C. Extract, transform, load
    D. Export, test, load

13. Which of the following statements is true about data warehouses and data lakes?

 A. Data warehouses hold highly structured data, while data lakes hold structured and unstructured data.

 B. Data warehouses are like a farmer's market, while data lakes are like well-organized grocery stores.

 C. Data warehouses provide scalability and flexibility, while data lakes allow for higher performance and easy data analysis.

 D. Data warehouses and data lakes are interchangeable terms for storing big data.

14. What is the main purpose of a feature store in MLOps?

 A. To maintain a history of model performances

 B. To provide a platform for hosting machine learning models

 C. To create, share, and manage features during machine learning development

 D. To orchestrate and schedule data pipeline tasks

15. What is the main purpose of data version control in machine learning?

 A. To store multiple versions of data, track the models with which they were used, and reproduce experiments

 B. To keep track of all the models in production and monitor their performance

 C. To orchestrate and schedule data pipeline tasks

 D. To provide a platform for hosting machine learning models

16. What is the purpose of data lineage tracking in machine learning?

 A. To create versions of your data and model artifacts to protect from deletion

 B. To track the changes the data has undergone throughout the machine learning lifecycle and identify any unintended changes

 C. To enforce security by developing a plan to reduce the exposure of data and the sprawl of data

 D. To protect data privacy and ensure compliance with data protection regulations

ANSWER KEY

1.	C	7.	C	13.	A
2.	C	8.	B	14.	C
3.	C	9.	D	15.	A
4.	B	10.	D	16.	B
5.	C	11.	D		
6.	B	12.	C		

16

Choosing Your AI/ML Algorithms

The only source of knowledge is experience.

—Albert Einstein

Data, as pivotal as it is, still requires algorithms to become actionable and give life to your AI initiatives. Choosing the right AI/ML algorithm is like choosing the right tool for a job. This chapter covers different machine learning algorithms and explores aspects such as how they work, when to use them, and what use cases they can be employed for (see Figure 16.1).

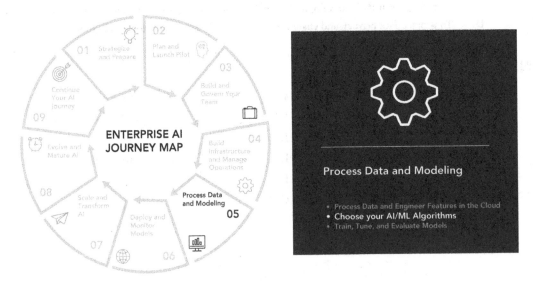

FIGURE 16.1: PROCESS DATA AND MODELING: Choose your AI/ML algorithm

Note that the choice of a machine learning algorithm is not a straightforward process, and the relationship between the algorithms and models is many to many; the same use case can be served by more than one algorithm, and the same algorithm can solve many use cases and business problems.

This chapter explores different categories of machine learning, such as supervised learning, unsupervised learning, and deep learning. You'll discover a plethora of algorithms such as linear regression, decision trees, neural networks, and more.

Along the way, I discuss factors to consider when choosing an algorithm, ensuring that you have a robust methodology to align your choice with the problem at hand. By the end of this chapter, you'll have a firm grasp on how to pick the right algorithm.

BACK TO THE BASICS: WHAT IS ARTIFICIAL INTELLIGENCE?

Artificial intelligence is a broad, umbrella term that refers to the collection of technologies enabling computers to mimic human intelligence. The dictionary definition of intelligence is "the ability to acquire knowledge and skills and apply them."

Artificial intelligence refers to a machine's ability to perform the human mind's cognitive functions, such as perceiving, reasoning, learning, interacting, solving problems, and even showing creativity. Anything that a machine does, for example, listening to someone and responding in human words, such as Alexa, is artificial intelligence. Artificial intelligence is also when a machine looks at the surroundings using computer vision and helps a car navigate. The technologies involve the following:

➤ Radars and sensors

➤ Devices that take in all data and feed it to the car so that it can take appropriate action

Artificial intelligence includes those collections of technologies, such as natural language processing, speech recognition, and computer vision. Figure 16.2 shows the range of technologies and applications that fall under the broad umbrella of artificial intelligence.

Here's Gartner's definition of AI:

> Artificial intelligence (AI) applies advanced analysis and logic-based techniques, including machine learning, to interpret events, support and automate decisions, and take action.
> (Source: www.gartner.com/en/topics/artificial-intelligence)

Machine Learning: The Brain Behind Artificial Intelligence

The next question is, then, what is machine learning? *Machine learning* is often used interchangeably with artificial intelligence. An excellent way to answer that question is to take the driverless car example. Again, the sensors, radars, and other systems in the car take in all the data from the environment and move the car around. But, how is the car moving autonomously?

There is a machine learning model that takes in the data and predicts the outcome. The model's output tells the car to go left, right, stop, move fast, and accelerate.

Machine learning is about crunching all the data, processing it, identifying the patterns, and, based on that, returning a prediction.

Artificial intelligence is an umbrella term for all the technologies that try to mimic human intelligence. But the actual process by which large amounts of data are crunched to come up with insights is through machine learning.

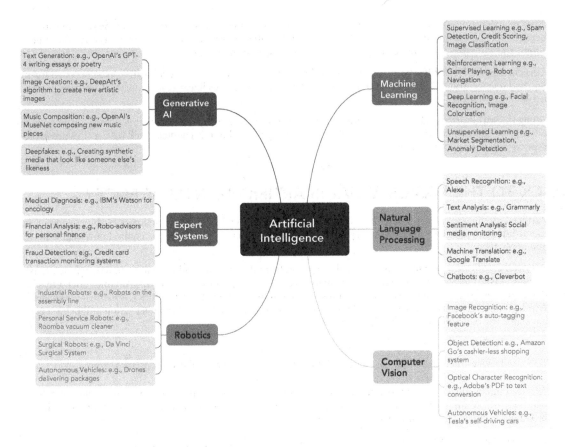

FIGURE 16.2: Umbrella of AI technologies

Features and Weights of Predictive Algorithms

An algorithm has two key components—features and weights. *Features* are parts of a dataset identified as essential to determine an outcome. The features may also be known as columns or attributes in a dataset.

You can think of features as essential attributes to predicting an outcome. For example, if you are trying to predict the price of a home, the features could include the number of bedrooms, square footage, location, and so on.

However, you also need to know the context of the attribute impacting the outcome, in other words, how important that attribute is to predict an outcome. That's where the *weights* come in. These weights are assigned as part of training, and if, say, it is highly influential to the outcome, the system might assign a higher weight, say 0.8. The training process uses the dataset to assign the weights to different factors to predict the outcome with a certain level of accuracy.

FACTORS TO CONSIDER WHEN CHOOSING A MACHINE LEARNING ALGORITHM

This section walks through an example scenario to understand the steps in choosing a machine learning algorithm. Suppose your company has asked you to use machine learning to increase sales. You have a large amount of data such as customer purchase history, demographic information, website behavior information, and so on.

FACTOR	DESCRIPTION
Identify the type of problem.	The first thing to do is identify the problem you need to solve. In this case, you're trying to increase sales, which means you're trying to identify customers who are likely to purchase from your site. This is the classification problem because you're trying to identify who will buy and who will not.
Assess the size of the dataset.	The next step is to assess the size of the dataset. If you have a large dataset, using complex algorithms such as deep learning is possible. However, if the dataset is smaller, you can use simpler algorithms such as linear regression.
Decide on the interpretability of the model.	The algorithm choice also depends on whether the model needs to be *interpretable*, meaning is it required to explain how the model came up with its prediction? If you have to explain how the model predicts the outcome, you cannot use complex algorithms such as deep learning.
Decide on the performance metrics.	It is also vital to decide on the metrics you'll use to evaluate the model's performance. In this case, you can use accuracy, precision, and recall, thereby evaluating how well the model predicts which customer will likely make a purchase.
Plan for scalability.	It would help if you also planned for the scalability of the model. In this case, given that you have a large dataset, it may be a good idea to plan for a distributed machine learning algorithm such as Apache Spark.

> **TIP** *When choosing a machine learning algorithm, carefully consider the problem type, dataset size, interpretability requirements, appropriate performance metrics, and the need for scalability to ensure an effective and efficient solution.*

HANDS-ON EXERCISE: SELECTING A MACHINE LEARNING ALGORITHM

This is a strategic hands-on exercise focused on choosing the right machine learning algorithm for your project's use case. It is a critical step because choosing the right algorithm will decide the accuracy of the model and therefore drives the outcome of your overall project.

It will help you to think critically about various phases of machine learning such as identifying a problem, assessing data, interpreting models, measuring performance, and considering scalability requirements. This exercise mirrors the thought process that goes into planning a data analysis or modeling project.

Goal: Assume that you have been hired as a data scientist for an e-commerce company that has trusted you with the responsibility of leveraging the customer data to gain a competitive advantage to address the stiff competition the company has been facing. The marketing team has told you that they would like to predict which customers are likely to purchase next month so they can plan their marketing campaigns accordingly. They have given you a dataset that contains the customers' past purchases as well as other demographic information such as age, location, browsing behavior, and so on. Now your task is to identify a suitable algorithm to solve the problem.

continues

continued

STEP	DESCRIPTION
Identify the type of problem.	Decide what type of machine learning problem this is; in this case, this a classification problem as this is trying to identify the customers who are likely to buy vs those who may not.
Assess the size of the dataset.	If the dataset is very large, you may need a deep learning algorithm, else a simpler algorithm would suffice.
Check whether the model needs to be interpretable.	If the model needs to be interpretable, you will need a simpler model.
Choose appropriate performance metrics.	Choose the appropriate performance metrics based on the model; for example, in this case it's a classification problem, so you can choose accuracy, precision, and recall.
Check out the scalability requirements.	If the dataset is large and likely to grow, you should explore machine learning algorithms that are compatible with distributed processing such as those offered by Apache Spark.
Write a report regarding the finalized algorithm.	Prepare a report with the type of algorithm, how it meets the requirements, as well as the challenges, limitations with this approach, and other alternatives if available.

DATA-DRIVEN PREDICTIONS USING MACHINE LEARNING

Machine learning is a branch of artificial intelligence that allows computers to learn from data without explicit programming. They achieve this by identifying common patterns and then using probabilistic distributions to make predictions. In other words, they develop the conditional probability of an output variable based on a set of input variables.

You feed in a dataset containing input-output pairs to the model, and the model tries to discern patterns. Using this insight, the model makes predictions on a new, unseen dataset of input variables. Machine learning adopts the probabilistic reasoning approach, which aims to determine the probability of a particular outcome based on the evidence available.

The data can be in the form of text numbers, images, or any data. Machine learning uses different types of algorithms to make these predictions, for example, supervised learning, unsupervised learning, and so on. These algorithms are based on statistical methods.

> **NOTE** *An essential characteristic of machine learning is that these models keep improving over time because they learn from the existing data and can make better predictions over time.*

Different Categories of Machine Learning

You can classify machine learning problems into three categories: supervised learning, unsupervised learning, and reinforced learning. Figure 16.3 shows how different tasks can employ supervised or unsupervised learning and how certain tasks can be implemented using supervised or unsupervised learning techniques.

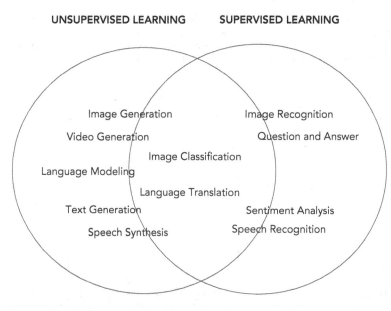

FIGURE 16.3: Use cases of supervised and unsupervised learning tasks

The next few sections discuss the different algorithms shown in Table 16.1.

TABLE 16.1: Supervised and Unsupervised Machine Learning Algorithms

SUPERVISED LEARNING	UNSUPERVISED LEARNING
Linear regression	Autoencoder
Logistic regression	K-means clustering
Linear/quadratic discriminant analysis	Gaussian mixture model
Decision tree	Hierarchical clustering
Naïve Bayes	Recommender system
Support vector machine	Manifold learning
Random forest	
AdaBoost	
Gradient boosting trees	
Simple neural network	

Note that the main point of this discussion of different applications is for you to be able to understand these different types and then go back to your organization and apply these to your different problems.

Using Supervised Learning

This section discusses supervised learning, including when to use it, how it works, and typical use cases.

Supervised learning is a type of machine learning where the model is trained on labeled data. Labeled data implies that every training data sample should have a predefined output. It is also known as *ground truth labels*.

One good example is the case of email spam applications, whereby you have a set of training data in which you know which emails are spam and which ones are not. For each spam email, you also know the corresponding features that identify that email as spam. Machine learning uses an algorithm that trains itself based on this data to create a model. The model uses these features to predict the outcome, which in this case, is to predict whether an email is spam.

> **TIP** *When using supervised learning, ensure you have a large, labeled, well-formatted, and clean dataset for accurate training and prediction.*

Let's discuss the supervised learning process shown in Figure 16.4.

Labeling
01

02
Training

Prediction

03

A human labels
the input data

The algorithm is
then trained on
the labeled input
data

The algorithm is
applied to new
data to predict
the outcome

FIGURE 16.4: How supervised learning works

> ➤ **Labeling:** A human labels the input data by identifying the input and output variables. In the case of identifying spam, they would identify the input fields such as subject, to, and from fields and define the output variable as spam or not spam.

> ➤ **Training:** The algorithm is then trained on the labeled input data to understand the patterns between the input variables and the output.

> ➤ **Prediction:** Once the training is complete and when you determine that the algorithm is pretty accurate, the algorithm is applied to new data to predict the outcome. See Figure 16.5.

Classification

Within supervised learning, you have two types of algorithms, classification and regression (see Figure 16.6). In the case of classification, you are trying to predict whether the outcome belongs to a particular type of category. In contrast, you're trying to predict a continuous value in the case of regression.

System learns by identifying patterns in the data previously labeled by humans

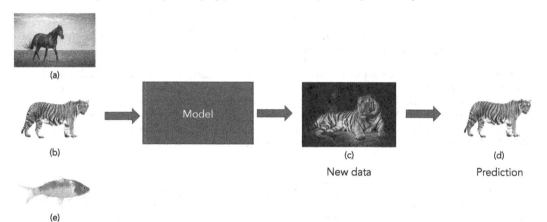

FIGURE 16.5: How supervised learning works
Source: (a) Kate / Adobe Systems Incorporated, (b) anankkml / Adobe Systems Incorporated, (c) Quality Stock Arts / Adobe Systems Incorporated, (d) anankkml / Adobe Systems Incorporated, (e) khumthong / Adobe Systems Incorporated

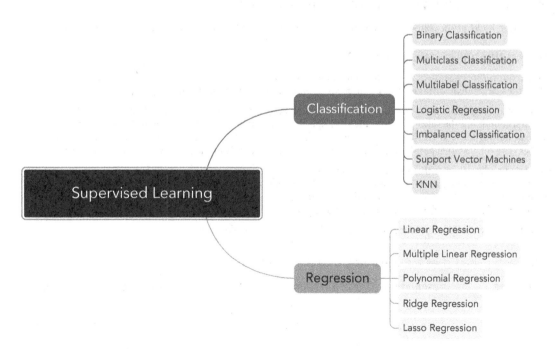

FIGURE 16.6: Types of supervised learning

Within classification are binary classification or multiclass classification:

➤ **Binary classification:** The outcome can be one of two values, such as whether the email is spam.

➤ **Multiclass classification:** You can have more than two outcomes, such as when you're trying to classify a set of animal images. For example, it could be a cat, dog, horse, and so on.

Another example of a classification problem involves an Amazon fulfillment center. There are millions of boxes. They have hundreds of items in each box, and some items may be missing or damaged. You can use machine learning to identify which boxes are damaged and then send warehouse representatives to address the issue. Note that classification can also be further subdivided into multilabel classification, imbalanced classification, ensemble methods, support vector machines, KNN, and so on. Logistic regression, SVM, and decision tress are types of binary classification, and neural networks, random forests, and naïve Bayes multivariate are types of multiclass classification.

Regression Problem

This section looks at the example of a regression problem that focuses on predicting a continuous value. One such example is forecasting the demand for a product based on past historical time-series data. In this case, the output of the regression problem is the number of products the customers will buy. You can even use regression to predict a product's price based on its historical data and other factors. Regression can be further subdivided into linear regression, multiple linear regression, polynomial regression, ridge regression, lasso regression, and so on.

> **NOTE** *Regression is different from classification because it is focused on predicting continuous numerical values based on the input variables. Classification is focused on categorizing data into specific classes or categories based on input variables.*

Types of Supervised Learning Algorithms

This section looks at the following ML algorithms that are available in the category of supervised learning.

Predicting the Value Using Linear Regression

Linear regression is a statistical method that can identify the relationship between one or more independent variables and a dependent variable. There can be an infinite number of values for the dependent output variable.

Say you want to predict a car's sales price based on age. First, you need to collect the data for the last few months or years, containing the sales price and the car's age. Typically, you use a software algorithm to carry out the analysis, but for the sake of simplicity, say you are using an Excel sheet for this analysis. You first start by capturing this data on a scatter plot by plotting the car's age on the x-axis and the price of the car on the y-axis.

You then fit a line so that the distance between the line and the data points is minimal, as shown in Figure 16.7. This line should minimize the sum of the squared distances between the actual and predicted prices denoted by the line. This line is the *regression line* and represents the best-fit line through the data. Using this line, you can now predict the price of the car based on the age, by using the slope and intercept on the line.

Table 16.2 shows a list of potential use cases for linear regression algorithms.

TABLE 16.2: Use Cases for Linear Regression Algorithms

USE CASE	DESCRIPTION	INDUSTRY	DATA TYPE	PREDICTIVE OUTPUT
Sales forecasting	Assist with demand planning, inventory management, and resource allocation	Retail, e-commerce	Sales data Marketing data	Sales forecast

USE CASE	DESCRIPTION	INDUSTRY	DATA TYPE	PREDICTIVE OUTPUT
Customer analytics	Improve customer retention and increase sales	Retail Finance Insurance Telecommunications	Customer data Behavior data	Customer lifetime value Churn purchase propensity
Financial analysis	For data-driven investment decisions, market analysis, and risk management	Finance Investment	Market data Financial data	Stock prices Asset values
Demand forecasting	To optimize inventory management and supply chain operations	Retail Supply chain	Sales data Market data External factors	Demand forecast
Performance optimization	For process optimization, resource allocation, and cost reduction	Manufacturing Supply chain Logistics	Production data Supply data	Process optimization
Price optimization	For maximizing revenues and market competitiveness	Retail Manufacturing	Pricing data Sales data	Pricing strategy
Risk assessment	Make better lending decisions and reduce the risk of financial losses	Insurance Finance	Risk data Historical data	Defaulting on a loan
Fraud detection	Prevent fraud and protect losses	Financial services Retail	Transaction data	Fraud
Energy consumption analysis	To implement energy saving measures, optimize resources	Energy Sustainability	Energy data Building data	Energy consumption analysis

Other factors can impact the price of the car, such as the car's condition, make and model, local market conditions, competition, advertisement, and so on. Although this is a trivial example, it serves to help you understand how linear regression works. Note that you will be using linear regression algorithms provided by different frameworks in the real world.

Linear regression is a commonly used tool in various fields and industries, including finance, manufacturing, statistics, economics, psychology, and so on. It can be used to optimize price points and estimate product-price elasticities.

You can use linear regression in the following situations:

USE CASE	DESCRIPTION	SUITABLE ALTERNATIVE(S)
Linear relationship	Linear regression is most effective when there is a linear relationship between the input and output variables.	
No multicollinearity	Linear regression is appropriate when there is no multicollinearity (linear relationship) between the independent variables. Multicollinearity can result in unstable results.	Ridge regression, lasso regression
Small number of independent variables	Linear regression is a good choice when the number of independent variables involved is small.	Support vector decomposition, random forest, gradient boosting
Simplicity of relationships	Linear regression may not be suited for capturing complex relationships between the independent variables.	Neural networks or other complex algorithms

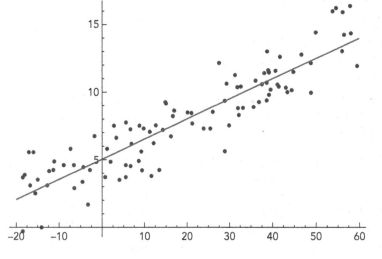

FIGURE 16.7: Example of linear regression with one independent variable

> **TIP** *When using linear regression, ensure a linear relationship between variables, avoid multicollinearity, and limit the number of independent variables. For complex relationships, consider advanced models such as neural networks.*

Predicting Categorical Outcomes Using Logistic Regression

Logistic regression is helpful when you want to predict the outcome of an event; in other words, the outcome variable is categorical. The value of the output variable is binary (e.g., yes or no, black or white) rather than continuous as in the case of linear regression.

Categorical values represent different categories or groups and are represented by labels. They can be further divided into nominal or ordinal types.

VARIABLE TYPE	DESCRIPTION	INHERENT ORDER	EXAMPLES
Nominal	Represent different categories or groups and are represented by labels. These categories do not have any inherent numerical meaning and are mutually exclusive.	No	Gender (male, female), color (red, green, blue)
Ordinal	Have a specific order or ranking.	Yes	Education levels (high school, bachelor's degree, master's degree), customer satisfaction levels (poor, fair, good, excellent)

Consider an example where you want to predict whether a customer will churn. In this case, you collect all the data that will contribute to this event, such as how many products they bought, how often they bought, how much they spent, and how often they canceled their subscription. You should be able to get all this information from a customer loyalty program.

Once you train the logistic regression model using this data, this software will draw a logistic regression line fitting this data, and you can use this line to understand the relationship between the various independent variables and their probability of whether the customer will churn, as shown in Figure 16.8.

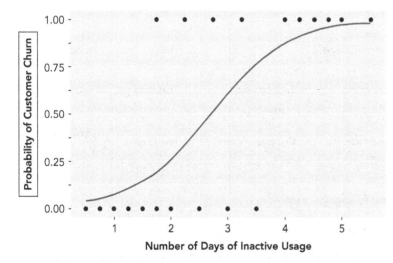

FIGURE 16.8: Example logistic regression graph showing the probability of customers churning based on the number of days not using the service

This algorithm is useful in many use cases in healthcare, finance, and marketing, as shown in Table 16.3. Some of these use cases are whether a customer will default on a loan, whether a prospect will buy a car, and whether a customer will churn.

TABLE 16.3: Use Cases for Logistic Regression

USE CASE	DESCRIPTION	INDUSTRY	DATA TYPE	PREDICTIVE OUTPUT
Customer churn prediction	Reduce customer churn and increase retention	Retail Finance Insurance Telecommunications	Customer data Behavior data	Customer churn probability
Loan default prediction	Improve lending decisions and prevent losses	Financial services	Customer data Behavior data	Default probability Creditworthiness
Fraud detection	Prevent fraud and avoid financial losses	Retail Finance Insurance Telecommunications	Transaction data	Fraud probability
Email spam filtering	Reduce spam and increase email deliverability	Technology Email Security	Email data Metadata	Spam/not spam
Medical diagnosis	Improve patient care and diagnosis	Healthcare	Medical data	Disease prediction
Product recommendation	Improve product recommendation and increase sales	Retail	Customer data	Propensity to buy a product
Sentiment analysis	Make data driven decisions	Social media Marketing	Text data	Sentiment label
Image classification	Object and facial recognition	Computer vision apps	Image data	Image label

You can use logistic regression in the following situations:

USE CASE REQUIREMENT	DESCRIPTION
Classification problems	When the outcome variable is binary, the outcome can be yes or no, true or false, and so on. In other words, it's a classification problem.
Large datasets	When the dataset is small, the model is likely to overfit. It is ideal for large datasets, as it can lend itself to computational efficiency and more statistical power to make more accurate predictions.

USE CASE REQUIREMENT	DESCRIPTION
Interpretability	When you want the model to be interpretable, meaning you want to understand how the outcome is predicted based on the inputs.
Efficiency	When you want an efficient algorithm that can perform fast with fewer computational resources.

> **TIP** Overfitting *means the model has almost memorized the outcomes and cannot be generalized for new data. It performs poorly on new data even though it works perfectly on training data.*

Using Decision Trees

Decision trees are machine-learning algorithms that can be used for classification and regression. In other words, it is a supervised learning type of algorithm. They work by breaking down the dataset recursively into smaller subsets based on specific criteria until you reach a point where the outcome can be determined.

Say you want to identify the customer who is likely to default on a loan. You collect the dataset of past loan applicants and their information, such as their income, loan amount, credit rating, age, employment, and so on. Then you start by identifying the feature on which to break this dataset. That depends on which feature gives you the highest information gain. You may break the dataset based on the credit score rating in this case.

You then analyze if the customer will default based on their credit rating. If you find that to be true, you create a leaf node that predicts that the customer will default when their credit rating is below that level.

On the other hand, if there is no clear pattern, you choose a different feature, such as their income. You continue with this process until you reach a point where all the data points under a specific subset belong to a particular class, meaning either they have or have not defaulted. Or they stop at some predetermined point, such as a specific tree depth or any other criteria you agree on.

You can then use the prediction on new data once you finalize the decision tree, as shown in Figure 16.9.

The benefits of the decision tree are that it can operate on numerical and categorical data, handle outliers well, and is also visual, making it easy for people to understand. On the other hand, it is susceptible to bias and inaccuracies if it's not developed properly. Therefore, alternative approaches should be explored if necessary.

Table 16.4 shows various use cases for decision trees.

TABLE 16.4: Use Cases for Decision Tree Algorithms

USE CASE	BENEFITS	INDUSTRY	DATA TYPE	PREDICTIVE OUTPUT
Customer segmentation	Personalized marketing campaigns and strategies, improved customer satisfaction	Retail Finance Insurance Telecommunications	Customer data Behavior data	Customer segments

continues

(continued)

USE CASE	BENEFITS	INDUSTRY	DATA TYPE	PREDICTIVE OUTPUT
Fraud detection	Identifying and preventing fraudulent activities, minimizing financial losses, enhancing security	Finance Insurance	Transaction data User data	Fraudulent/ nonfraudulent
Credit risk assessment	Informed lending decisions, assessing creditworthiness, minimizing default risk	Banking Finance	Credit data Applicant data	Credit risk assessment
Fault diagnosis	Identifying system faults, troubleshooting guidance, reducing downtime	Manufacturing IoT	Sensor data, system parameters	Fault diagnosis
Customer service routing	Efficient customer support, improved response times, enhanced customer satisfaction	Customer service	Customer queries, service data	Service routing
Demand forecasting	Optimized inventory management, production planning, and supply chain operations	Retail Supply chain	Sales data, market data	Demand forecast
Medical diagnosis	Enhanced decision support for healthcare professionals, improved accuracy in diagnoses	Healthcare	Patient symptoms, medical records	Potential medical diagnoses
Equipment maintenance	Proactive maintenance scheduling, reduced downtime, optimized equipment performance	Manufacturing IoT	Sensor data, maintenance records	Equipment maintenance needs

This section covers the situations when decision trees can be adopted.

CONDITION	DESCRIPTION	EXAMPLE
Interpretability	Decision trees provide interpretability, which means you can explain how the model predicts based on given inputs.	Understanding the decision-making process of the model

CONDITION	DESCRIPTION	EXAMPLE
Both numerical and categorical data	Decision trees can handle both numerical and categorical data types.	Dataset that contains both numerical values like age, income, and categorical values like gender, nationality
Handling missing data	Decision trees can handle missing data by assigning probabilities based on the available data.	Imputing missing data based on the relationships in available data
Large datasets	Decision trees are efficient for large datasets.	Processing datasets with high volume
Ensemble models	Decision trees can be combined with other algorithms to build ensemble models.	Building a random forest or gradient boosting model
Better performance	Decision trees can be tuned to develop high performing models.	Improving the prediction accuracy or reducing error rates

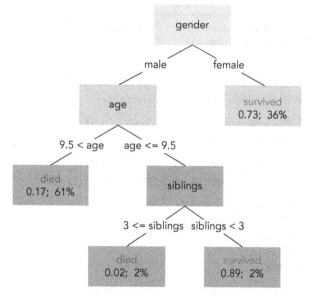

Survival of passengers on the Titanic

FIGURE 16.9: Decision tree that shows the survival of passengers on the *Titanic*. Figures under the leaves show the probability of survival and the percentage of observations in the leaf.
Source: Wikipedia

> **TIP** *Consider decision trees for large, mixed-type datasets that need to be well-understood by stakeholders and for handling missing data and use ensemble models for enhanced performance.*

HANDS-ON EXERCISE: BUILDING A DECISION TREE

The goal of this exercise is to build a decision tree model to predict whether a loan applicant will default.

Prerequisites: This is a high-level overview, but to actually execute this exercise, you should be familiar with Python, pandas, and the scikit-learn library.

Access to a loan dataset that contains data such as applicant name, age, income, and so on, and whether they defaulted.

STEP NAME	TASK OWNER	INSTRUCTIONS	DELIVERABLES
Dataset preparation	Data analyst/ scientist	Load the loan dataset into a pandas dataframe. Clean and format the data as needed.	A cleaned and formatted dataset
Exploratory data analysis (EDA)	Data analyst/ scientist	Examine the dataset to understand the distribution of variables and evaluate the ratio of defaulters to non-defaulters.	Data insights
Preprocessing	Data analyst/ scientist	Encode categorical variables, handle missing values, scale numerical variables, etc.	A preprocessed dataset ready for model training
Splitting the data	Data analyst/ scientist	Divide the dataset into a training set and a testing set.	A training set and a testing set
Model selection	Data analyst/ scientist	Choose a decision tree algorithm for the task.	Selected model algorithm
Training the model	Data analyst/ scientist	Train the selected model using the training dataset.	A trained decision tree model
Model evaluation	Data analyst/ scientist	Evaluate the model using the test dataset. Use relevant metrics such as accuracy, precision, recall, F1 score, or AUC-ROC.	Evaluation results
Model interpretation	Data analyst/ scientist	Visualize the decision tree and interpret its decision rules.	Model visualization and interpretation
Model tuning	Data analyst/ scientist	If the model performance is not satisfactory, consider tuning the parameters or try using a more sophisticated algorithm.	A fine-tuned model with improved performance

Using Random Forests for Classification and Regression

Random forests are helpful for both classification and regression types of problems. You can think of a random forest as an improvisation of a decision tree because it is a collection of multiple decision trees built based on random subsets of data and features. Figure 16.10 shows a simplified view of a random forest.

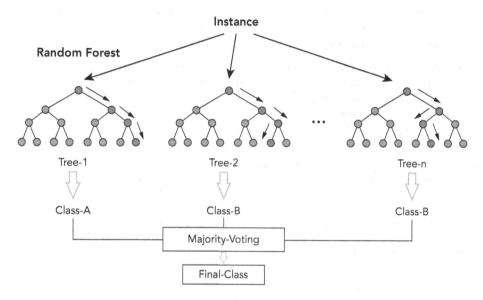

FIGURE 16.10: A simplified view of a random forest

Source: `https://en.wikipedia.org/wiki/Random_forest#/media/File:Random_forest_diagram_complete.png`

The methodology and benefits of using Random Forest are outlined in the following table:

STAGE	DESCRIPTION	IMPORTANCE
Training	You break down your dataset into a training and test dataset and then divide the dataset to build multiple decision trees, each using a random subset of data and features.	By doing this, you can eliminate some of the drawbacks of your decision tree, such as overfitting and avoiding bias. The final decision is arrived at by combining the outcomes of the individual trees.
Testing	To evaluate the model's performance, you then test the model against the test dataset and compare the predictions to the actual outcomes using metrics, such as accuracy, precision, recall, and F1 score.	Helps evaluate the performance of the model and improve its accuracy.
Accuracy	When you need accuracy in the predictions, this method is good because you are using multiple decision trees, which is more accurate.	Essential for making reliable predictions and minimizing errors.

continues

(continued)

STAGE	DESCRIPTION	IMPORTANCE
Robustness	When you need robustness in the model predictions, this method is good because it uses multiple decision trees and issues such as overfitting are avoided.	Enhances the stability of the model and its ability to handle a variety of data inputs.
Interpretability	When interpretability is required, even though these models are not as interpretable as linear regression models, they still provide visibility into how they came up with the predictions.	Important for understanding how the model works and explaining its predictions.

Random forests are especially suited for customer churn prediction, fraud detection, image classification, recommendation systems, predictive maintenance, demand forecasting, and credit risk assessment.

> **TIP** **Random forests** *are helpful for both classification and regression types of problems because they use multiple decision trees to enhance the stability of the model and its ability to handle a variety of data inputs.*

Using Naïve Bayes

Naïve Bayes is a machine learning algorithm used for classification purposes. It uses the Bayes theorem to calculate the probability of an outcome based on given evidence. The following table illustrates the steps involved in implementing a naïve Bayes classifier:

STEP	DESCRIPTION	PURPOSE
Building the classifier	You're building a classifier that identifies different types of fruits, and you have several features such as color, texture, size, and shape.	Helps in categorizing data based on independent features. Note: This is called a *naïve* theorem because in the real world features are usually not independent.
Creating a base model	Calculate the probability of the different labels based on the training dataset.	The base model serves as the initial representation of the problem, which can then be improved through further training and adjustments.
Prediction	You then use the new data against this model to make predictions.	Applying the model to new data allows you to predict outcomes based on the learned relationships from the training data.

The Naïve Bayes theorem is a powerful tool that can be used to identify spam, classify text and images, categorize documents, analyze customer reviews, classify news articles, detect fraud, diagnose medical issues, perform sentiment analysis, and perform facial recognition.

The following table captures the conditions under which the Naïve Bayes theorem is recommended:

CONDITION	DESCRIPTION	EXAMPLE
Text data	Naïve Bayes works well when the data is text type.	Useful for sentiment analysis, topic classification, and spam detection
Categorical data	Naïve Bayes works well when the data is categorical.	Useful when dealing with colors, demographic information, product classification, etc.
High dimensionality	Performs well on large datasets with many features.	Applicable in scenarios with many input variables or features
Real-time inference	Naïve Bayes is a simple and fast algorithm, suitable for real-time applications.	Beneficial for applications requiring real-time predictions or decisions
Limited labeled data	Naïve Bayes works well with limited labeling in the dataset.	Useful in situations where there's limited labeled data for training

> **TIP** *Consider using Naïve Bayes for classification tasks involving text or categorical data, especially in high-dimensional spaces. Its simplicity and efficiency make it a strong candidate for real-time prediction tasks.*

Using Support Vector Machines

Support vector machines (SVMs) can be used for classification and regression analysis. They create a hyperplane separating the two outcomes with the most significant margin possible.

Say you want to identify spam based on the length of the emails and the number of punctuations used in an email. You then plot the email length on the x-axis and the punctuation on the y-axis. SVM would then find the line that separates the spam versus nonspam classification types in the two-dimensional space. You can then use this model to predict the outcomes, as shown in Figure 16.11. This figure shows a support vector machine that chooses a separating hyperplane for two classes of points in 2D. H1 does not separate the classes. H2 does, but only by a small margin. H3 separates them with the maximum margin.

In the cases where the features are not linearly separable, the SVM algorithm chooses a kernel to transform the data into a higher dimensional space where it is linearly separable. For example,

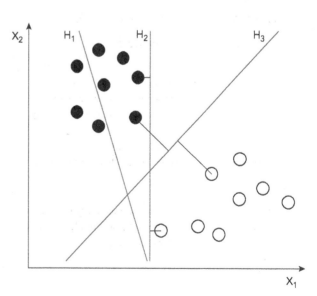

FIGURE 16.11: Support vector machine trained from two samples

the model would add a third feature, such as the frequency of certain words in the email, and transform the two-dimensional data into three dimensions.

SVM can also choose several other types of kernel functions, such as linear, polynomial, and radial base functions.

The following table captures the conditions under which support vector machines can be adopted:

CONDITION	DESCRIPTION	EXAMPLE
Linear and nonlinear data	Support vector machines are helpful for classification use cases, but more important, they are useful for both linear and nonlinear data due to the use of kernel functions.	Suitable for various classification problems, regardless of linearity
High-dimensional data	SVMs can be helpful for high-dimensional data (many features) use cases with large amounts of data.	Useful when dealing with many features or large amounts of data
Limited data	SVMs work well with limited data, avoiding overfitting and improving generalization.	Ideal for scenarios with limited training data
Complex classifications	Because SVMs can handle nonlinear use cases better, they are helpful for complex classification scenarios.	Suitable for complex or intricate classification tasks
Outliers and noise handling	SVMs are efficient at handling outliers and noise in the data.	Good fit for datasets that may contain noise or outliers

Table 16.5 lists some of the use cases suited to support vector machines.

TABLE 16.5: Use Cases for Support Vector Machines

USE CASE	DESCRIPTION	INDUSTRY	DATA TYPE	PREDICTIVE OUTPUT
Image classification	Identify objects in images, categorize images into predefined classes, and computer vision apps	Retail Healthcare Manufacturing	Image data	Image labels
Text classification	Identify the topic of a document, sentiment of a text, detect spam	Finance Customer service Marketing	Text data	Document labels
Anomaly detection	Detection of outliers or unusual patterns in data, identify potential security breaches	Cybersecurity IoT	Sensor data System logs	Anomaly labels

SVMs can also be used for handwriting recognition, fraud detection, customer sentiment analysis, spam email detection, medical diagnosis, and market trend prediction.

> **TIP** *Consider using SVMs for classification tasks involving both linear and nonlinear data. They are especially useful when dealing with high-dimensional or limited datasets and capable of handling complex classifications and outliers effectively.*

Using Gradient Boosting

Gradient boosting is helpful for both classification and regression tasks. The name implies it's focused on iteratively improving a weak learner by adding new models to the ensemble and correcting the previous model's errors.

Say you are trying to predict the price of houses using a certain number of features, such as the square foot area, the number of bedrooms, and so on.

To build the tree ensemble, you would train a decision tree and then calculate the errors between actual and predicted prices. Then, you would run another decision tree that addresses the errors in the previous model. The new model will be added to the ensemble, and you will continue the process by training another decision tree to correct the errors in the second decision tree.

You continue this process until you reach a point where you have high accuracy. The ensemble model would perform better than any of the individual decision trees and would be less prone to overfitting. The final model would be a weighted combination of the individual models based on their performance on the validation set.

Gradient boosting is a robust algorithm that provides highly accurate models for large datasets and is helpful in click-through rate prediction, customer churn prediction, demand forecasting, credit risk assessment, financial modeling, fraud detection, and image recognition use cases.

Here are the situations in which a gradient boosting model is a good candidate:

CONDITION	DESCRIPTION	EXAMPLE
Large and complex datasets	Particularly useful for large and complex enterprise-level datasets.	Useful when dealing with a complex dataset with many variables
High accuracy	Useful for high accuracy requirements.	Ideal when high precision is essential
Complex feature engineering	Can handle various input features, including categorical and numerical features.	Applicable in scenarios that require intricate feature engineering
Noise and outliers	Since this is an ensemble model, it can handle complex scenarios, making it more robust to noise and outliers.	Good fit for datasets that may contain noise or outliers
Real-time inferences	Ensemble models can be trained very quickly and therefore are ideal for time-sensitive applications and real-time inferences.	Beneficial in scenarios that require real-time predictions

> **TIP** *Consider using gradient boosting for complex, large datasets requiring high accuracy because it corrects previous model errors, handles intricate features, noise and outliers, and helps with real-time inferences.*

Using K-Nearest Neighbors (KNN)

K-nearest neighbors (KNN) is helpful for both classification and regression problems. It can be used on
both categorical and numerical outcomes. It works
by identifying the K closest data points for a given
input data point and then using the outcomes of
those data points to come up with the outcome
(see Figure 16.12). The dark circle corresponds to
K=3, and the outcome is red triangles because you
have more triangles than squares. The dotted circle
corresponds to K=5, and the outcome would be blue
squares since they outnumber the red triangles.

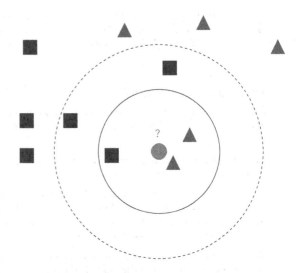

Say you want to predict the price of a house based on
its features, such as number of bedrooms, square feet
area, and so on.

You start by assuming a value for K. Usually, this
value for K is obtained through trial and error.
You need to learn some metrics, such as utility and
distance, to measure the distance between the actual
houses in the dataset and the new house for which
you need to make a prediction.

FIGURE 16.12: Example of K-NN classification
Source: Wikipedia / CC by 3.0 / Public Domain

Once you identify the five closest houses, you can take
the average price to come up with a new prediction. Of course, this prediction assumes that houses with similar
features will have similar pricing.

When the value of K is small, it's possible that your price is susceptible to the outliers and noise in the dataset. If
you choose a higher value for K, the outcome may be influenced by houses dissimilar to your new house.

In practice, KNN is an excellent algorithm to be chosen for applications such as product recommendations, image
classification, and anomaly detection.

KNN is a good candidate under the following conditions:

CONDITION	DESCRIPTION	EXAMPLE	ALTERNATIVES
Labeled, structured data	The dataset should be labeled and ideally have structured data.	Ideal for datasets where each instance is tagged with a label	Unsupervised learning algorithms for unlabeled data
Small and medium sized datasets	Works best with small to medium-sized datasets; larger datasets can become computationally intensive.	Not recommended for very large datasets due to high computational cost	Decision tree, random forest, or gradient boosting for large datasets
Classification and regression only	Suitable for problems that involve classification or regression.	Not suitable for problems that don't involve classification or regression tasks	Deep learning or reinforcement learning for complex tasks

CONDITION	DESCRIPTION	EXAMPLE	ALTERNATIVES
Not for real-time inference	Suitable for situations where you can train offline and deploy it online. If real-time online performance is essential, other models should be explored.	Not ideal for situations requiring real-time predictions	Random forests or gradient boosting machines (GBMs) for real-time predictions
Explainability	A good model when explainability is required, as predictions can be easily traced.	Helpful when it's necessary to explain the decision-making process	Decision tree, logistic regression for explainability

> **TIP** *Use KNN in classification or regression tasks for small to medium-sized, structured, and labeled datasets. It is essential to select an appropriate value for K to balance between noise sensitivity and the included dissimilar data points.*

Data Analysis and Predictive Modeling Using Neural Networks

Here are the conditions under which neural networks are recommended:

CONDITION	DESCRIPTION	EXAMPLE
Large data	Suitable for very large amounts of data	Data-intensive fields like genomic research or social network analysis
Complex pattern analysis	Particularly well suited to analyze complex patterns in data	Image or speech recognition tasks
Predictive modeling	Well suited for predictive modeling to make accurate predictions based on historical data	Predictive maintenance or forecasting sales
Real-time CNN use cases	Can be used for convolutional neural network (CNN) use cases that require real-time decisions	Autonomous vehicles or real-time financial trading
Large-scale cloud AI	Well suited for large-scale enterprise cloud AI implementations	Allows workload distribution across multiple servers and GPUs for speedier training and inference

Refer to the section "Deep Learning" in this chapter for more details.

> **TIP** *Consider using neural networks for large datasets, complex pattern analysis, predictive modeling, real-time CNN tasks, or large-scale cloud AI deployments.*

Using Unsupervised Learning to Discover Patterns in Unlabeled Data

Next is unsupervised learning, where the data is not labeled, and therefore, it is up to the algorithm to find common patterns, as shown in Figure 16.13.

There are two types of unsupervised learning applications: clustering and anomaly detection.

Machine discovers and creates the labels itself.

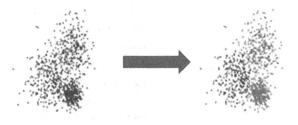

Original Data   Clustered Data

FIGURE 16.13: How unsupervised learning works

Clustering

An excellent example of a clustering application is when you have a large amount of customer data. You use this algorithm to break the data into multiple segments based on buying patterns and other attributes. You could then analyze those different segments and identify one of those as college students or moms, and so on, and then tailor your products and services based on which customer segments you are marketing to.

Another example of clustering applications is *topic modeling*. For example, you can feed the content from multiple books into this algorithm, generate topics, and classify those books into different categories.

Anomaly Detection

Anomaly detection is used to detect anomalies in data. In other words, look for patterns that do not conform to expected behavior. It is of great use in the case of fraud detection in customer transactions, such as an unusually large number of purchases in a foreign country or abnormal patient readings indicating a potentially serious health condition. The following table summarizes the different types of unsupervised learning algorithms:

UNSUPERVISED LEARNING APPLICATION	DESCRIPTION	EXAMPLE
Clustering	Clustering algorithms divide a dataset into groups or clusters, based on similarity in the data features.	Customer segmentation or topic modeling
Anomaly detection	Anomaly detection algorithms identify outliers in the data that do not conform to the expected patterns.	Fraud detection or abnormal patient readings in healthcare

> **TIP** *Use unsupervised learning when dealing with unlabeled data to discover hidden patterns. Clustering helps with grouping similar data, while anomaly detection uncovers outliers useful in fraud detection or health diagnostics.*

Segmentation Using K-Means Clustering

K-means clustering is an unsupervised algorithm that groups data points into clusters, as shown in Figure 16.14.

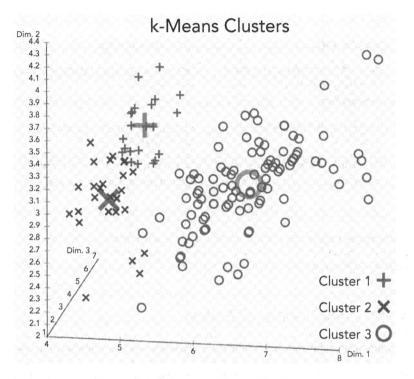

FIGURE 16.14: K-means clusters created from an Iris flower dataset
Source: Wikipedia

The algorithm starts by randomly assigning K cluster centers and then attaching the remaining data points to one of the clusters closer to it. Then the cluster centers are recomputed by calculating the mean of all the data points attached to that cluster center. The process is then repeated until the cluster centers do not change anymore.

K-means clustering is helpful for image segmentation, customer segmentation, fraud detection, and anomaly detection.

These are the conditions under which means clustering can be adopted:

SITUATION	DESCRIPTION	USE CASE EXAMPLE
Large data	You have a large amount of data to be processed.	Analyzing massive user datasets in social media platforms
Unlabeled data	The data is not labeled.	Segmenting a database of consumer details without pre-established categories
Pattern analysis	When you want to identify patterns in the data.	Identifying common buying patterns in retail consumer data
Segmentation use cases	There is a need for segmentation of customers, products, or any other entity.	Segmenting customers into distinct groups based on purchasing behavior

continues

(continued)

SITUATION	DESCRIPTION	USE CASE EXAMPLE
Process optimization	You want to optimize processes by identifying inefficiencies or areas of improvement.	Identifying inefficient processes in a manufacturing line
Uncorrelated data	Useful when the data is not highly correlated.	Clustering unrelated blog posts based on topics
Unknown number of clusters	Ideally, the number of clusters is not known.	Organizing news articles into categories without pre-established groups

> **TIP** *Use K-means clustering for large, unlabeled datasets where the number of clusters is unknown and the data is not highly correlated. It's useful for tasks like customer segmentation and process optimization.*

Reducing Dimensions Using Principal Component Analysis

Principal component analysis reduces the dimensionality of a large dataset by identifying the underlying patterns and reducing the number of features. It does this by transforming the original features into a new set of uncorrelated variables called *principal components*. And it does this without losing much of the original information in the dataset. Since it deals with data that does not have labeled examples or explicit target variables, it is appropriate for exploratory data analysis and feature extraction.

> **NOTE** *Given that PCA doesn't use labels, it is considered an unsupervised learning technique.*

Say you have product data served with a lot of information, such as sales history and specifications of the product, such as its color, size, shape, and so on. Each row represents a product, and each column is an attribute of the product. However, the dataset is so large that making any sense of that data is becoming difficult. Follow these steps to use PCA:

STEP	DESCRIPTION	USE CASE EXAMPLE
Calculate the covariance matrix.	The first step is to use PCA to calculate the covariance matrix of the data. This matrix tells you how correlated the different variables are. If two variables are highly correlated, they will have a high value for covariance value, and if they are negatively correlated, they will show a negative covariance value.	For a dataset with variables like age, income, and purchasing history, the covariance matrix will reflect how these variables correlate with each other.

STEP	DESCRIPTION	USE CASE EXAMPLE
Identify the principal components.	Next, you use the covariance matrix to identify the principal components in the data. These components are the linear combination of variables that capture the significant patterns in the data. The first principal component is the one that explains the most variance in the data, followed by the second.	In a customer dataset, the principal components might be combinations of variables that explain the most variability, such as a combination of age and income.
Retain the top N components.	After identifying all the principal components, you can choose to retain the top N components and discard the rest and thus reduce the number of dimensions. After doing the principal component analysis, you discover that the top three principal components account for 90 percent of the data variance, as shown in Figure 16.15. You can therefore retain those three dimensions instead of the ten or more you had.	If the top three principal components account for 90 percent of the data variance, these can be retained while the rest are discarded, simplifying the data from 10 dimensions to 3.

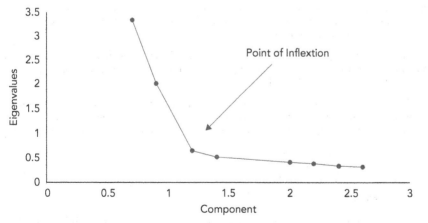

FIGURE 16.15: Interpreting the PCA: The start of the bend indicates that three factors should be retained.

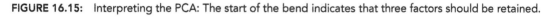

NOTE *A screen plot is a line plot of the eigenvalues of factors or principal components used in PCA to identify the significant factors.*

Here are some use cases of the principal component analysis:

USE CASE	DESCRIPTION
Dimensionality reduction	Used to reduce the dimensions in the data, thus helping to simplify complex datasets with numerous variables
Pattern analysis	Helps to reveal underlying patterns in the data by focusing on the principal components that explain the most variance
Dataset compression	Used to compress a dataset by retaining only the most informative dimensions, which can be beneficial for saving storage and improving computational efficiency
Noise reduction	Removes noise from a dataset by focusing on the components that explain the most variance and ignoring components associated with noise
Clustering	Useful in a clustering scenario where it can be used to visualize clusters in a lower-dimensional space after reducing the dimensionality of the data

> **TIP** *Use PCA for high-dimensional data to simplify the dataset and is beneficial for noise reduction, data compression, and improving cluster visualization.*

Feature Extraction and Dimensionality Reduction Using Singular Value Decomposition

Singular value decomposition (SVD) is a mathematical technique used in dimensionality reduction and feature extraction tasks. Its usage in unsupervised tasks depends on the algorithm in which it is included. SVD is a factorization method that breaks the matrix into three separate matrices: U, Σ, and V. Breaking it into its constituent parts, you can understand the matrix's structure and properties intuitively.

Say you have a dataset of all the customer purchases in a grocery store. You want to conduct a customer insight analysis, but it is too complex to draw that insight. You can apply SVD to create three smaller components: a left singular matrix, a diagonal matrix, and a suitable singular matrix.

The *left singular matrix* represents the customer and their purchases, and the *suitable singular matrix* represents the purchases and the items bought. The *diagonal matrix* represents the strength between those relationships. Armed with this kind of data, you can identify the group of customers based on their purchases or identify which products are purchased together.

SVD can be used under the following conditions:

USE CASE	DESCRIPTION
Large dimensionality	When you have large dimensionality in the data and you want to reduce the computational resources reducing the dimensions.
Identifying essential features	SVD can be used to identify the most essential features in a dataset.
Collaborative filtering	SVD can be used for product recommendations, such as collaborative filtering, to identify which products the users are likely to purchase based on their historical behavior.

USE CASE	DESCRIPTION
Image and signal processing	In image and signal processing tasks, SVD can be employed to manipulate and analyze data effectively. This includes tasks like image compression, noise reduction, and signal enhancement.

> **TIP** *Utilize SVD for efficient dimension reduction and feature extraction in large datasets, making it useful for recommendation systems and image processing tasks.*

Using Autoencoders

An *autoencoder* is a type of artificial neural network that is primarily used in unsupervised learning and for dimensionality reduction. It solves many problems, such as facial recognition, feature detection, and anomaly detection, and it can generate meanings of words and in generative models to create new data that is like the input training data.

> **NOTE** *Autoencoders are versatile tools that can be used for both supervised and unsupervised learning.*

The autoencoder is focused on creating the most compact representation of the input data, effectively reducing the dimensionality of the data.

The autoencoder has an input layer that's connected to an encoder, which is a series of hidden layers that reduce the dimensionality of the input data. It contains two functions. It contains an encoding function that transforms the input data into a lower-dimensional latent space representation, also known as an *encoding*. Figure 16.16 shows how an autoencoder works.

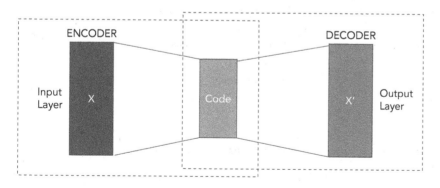

FIGURE 16.16: Schema of a basic autoencoder

The encoded data is then passed to a *decoder*, which is a series of hidden layers. The decoder layer uses a decoder function that re-creates the input data from the encoded representation. The output layer is compared to the input layer and the error is used to train the autoencoder.

Autoencoders can be used for the use cases listed in Table 16.6.

TABLE 16.6: Use Cases for Autoencoders

USE CASE	DESCRIPTION	INDUSTRY	DATA TYPE	PREDICTIVE OUTPUT
Dimensionality reduction	Autoencoders learn lower-dimensional representations of high-dimensional data. It results in efficient storage and computation.	Data compression, image processing	Numerical data Categorical data Image data Audio data Video data	Lower-dimensional encoded representation Image compression Feature extraction
Feature extraction	Autoencoders can extract important features from input data learning meaningful representations for downstream tasks.	Natural language processing Computer vision	Text data Image data Sensor data	Salient features Embeddings Classification Clustering
Anomaly detection	Autoencoders reconstruct normal data and in the process identify outliers.	Network security Fraud detection	Numerical data Categorical data	Anomaly score Outlier detection
Data denoising	Autoencoders re-create clean data by removing unwanted variations.	Speech recognition Image denoising	Noisy Numerical data Image data	Clean data Image denoising Audio restoration
Data generation	Autoencoders can generate new data.	Image generation Text generation	Image Text	New data similar to input data

> **TIP** *Leverage autoencoders in unsupervised learning tasks for efficient dimensionality reduction, feature extraction, and anomaly detection.*

Using Hierarchical Clustering

Hierarchical clustering is a clustering algorithm used in unsupervised learning to group similar data points into clusters based on their similarities or differences. It offers several advantages, such as the ability to identify clusters at different scales, and it preserves the full hierarchy of the clustering solutions.

Hierarchical clustering is a bottoms-up approach where it treats each data point as a cluster and then groups them together to form clusters that form a hierarchical structure. It uses different linking techniques, such as single linkage, complete linkage, and average linkage.

Hierarchical clustering is used in various domains, including biology, social sciences, image analysis, market segmentation, customer segmentation, and so on. It can be used to cluster customers into micro-segmented groups using various criteria, such as customer loyalty and social media data.

Personalized Recommendations Using Recommender Systems

Recommender systems are used in e-commerce, music, books, social media, and other domains to help users find items that are relevant or interesting to them. These systems try to predict the preferences or ratings that the user would give to an item based on the user's interests, preferences, or past behavior.

There are two different types of recommender systems: content-based systems and collaborative filtering systems.

Collaborative systems work by recommending items to users based on the ratings or preferences of other users who have similar interests. For example, if you liked a movie, the system may recommend movies that other users who liked that movie also liked. Figure 16.17 shows how a collaborative filtering system works.

	TV	Binoculars	Book	Laptop
Tom	Like	Dislike	Like	Like
Nancy		Like	Dislike	Dislike
Alfred	Like	Like	Dislike	
John	Dislike		Like	
Laura	Like	Like	?	Dislike

FIGURE 16.17: Collaborative filtering based on a rating system

Content-based filtering is based on the content of the item itself. For example, if you liked a book, the system may recommend books that are like the book that you liked.

Recommender systems are used in the following areas:

USE CASE	DESCRIPTION	EXAMPLE
Product recommendation	To suggest products to users based on their past purchase and browsing history	Amazon
Movie recommendation	To suggest movies to users based on their viewing history and ratings	Netflix
Social media	To suggest friends, groups, or posts based on a user's social interactions	Facebook
News personalization	To recommend news articles based on a user's reading history and topic preferences	Google News
Travel recommendations	To suggest hotels, flights, and other travel arrangements based on a user's past search and travel history	Expedia

continues

(continued)

USE CASE	DESCRIPTION	EXAMPLE
Course recommendations	To suggest courses, books, and other educational resources based on a user's search and educational history	Coursera
Personalized patient care	To suggest treatments, medications, and other healthcare services based on a patient's medical history	IBM Watson

> **TIP** *To deliver relevant recommendations at scale, leverage recommender systems that apply collaborative filtering or content-based algorithms.*

Nonlinear Dimensionality Reduction Using Manifold Learning

Manifold learning is also known as *nonlinearity dimension reduction* and is used to find low-dimensional representations of high-dimensional data while preserving its essential characteristics.

Some popular manifold learning algorithms are t-Distributed Stochastic Neighbor Embedding (t-SNE), Isomap, Locally Linear Embedding (LLE), and Laplacian Eigenmaps.

Here are some good use cases for nonlinearity dimension reduction:

USE CASE	DESCRIPTION
Customer segmentation	To segment customers based on their purchase history, demographics, and other factors to target their marketing campaigns effectively
Fraud detection	To identify fraudulent transactions
Risk management	To assess the risk of a customer defaulting on a loan or failing to meet a contract
Product recommendation	To make product recommendations to customers based on their past purchases
Enterprise AI	From an enterprise AI perspective, you can use manifold learning for dimensionality reduction, data visualization, feature extraction, and anomaly detection

Reinforced Learning: Learning by Trial and Error

Reinforced learning is a type of machine learning that allows an agent to learn by interacting with its environment via trial and error.

The agent is given a reward for taking actions that lead to favorable outcomes and a penalty for taking actions that lead to negative outcomes. Over time, the agent learns to maximize its rewards. See Figure 16.18.

Reinforcement learning is used under the following situations:

➤ **Dearth of data:** When there is not a lot of training data available.

➤ **The end state is not known:** The desired end state is not known.

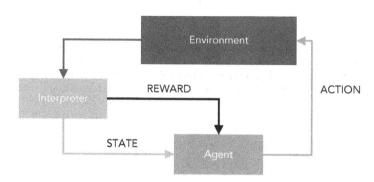

FIGURE 16.18: Reinforcement learning is when an agent takes action in an environment, which leads to a reward and is fed back to the agent.

Here are some good use cases for reinforcement learning:

USE CASE	DESCRIPTION
Robotics	RL can be used in robotics applications, such as picking and placing objects in a warehouse, navigating through cluttered environments, and even playing sports.
Finance	Can be used in finance to develop algorithms to predict stock prices and to automatically place trades.
Customer service	Used to create chatbots to place orders and troubleshoot problems.
Self-driving cars	Optimizes the behavior of self-driving cars.

> **TIP** *For problems with limited training data or undefined end states, consider a reinforcement learning approach where algorithms learn through trial-and-error interactions.*

EXERCISE: REINFORCEMENT LEARNING

Let's assume you have a robot that needs to be programmed to pick and place objects in various locations.

Here are the high-level steps you can follow. Actual details are beyond the scope of the book, but you can find additional resources from Open AI Gym, GitHub, and so on.

Step 1	Create a reinforcement learning environment using a software library such as Open AI Gym.
Step 2	Define the actions the agent can take.
Step 3	Define the rewards the agent will receive.
Step 4	Train the reinforcement learning algorithm using one of the methods available.
Step 5	Test the reinforcement learning algorithm by giving the agent a new set of tasks and check its performance.

Deep Learning

Deep learning is a subset of machine learning, and it uses the concept of neural networks, which mimic how the human brain works. It's a way of training computers to learn and improve independently without being explicitly programmed. Just like our brains learn from experience, these deep learning models learn by training on large amounts of data. Figure 16.19 shows how deep learning works and how it's different from traditional and other machine learning algorithms.

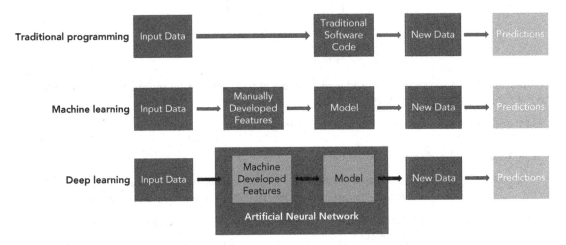

FIGURE 16.19: Deep learning is different from machine learning and traditional programming.

Neural networks consist of layers of interconnected nodes, where each node processes the data and sends it to the next layer. This helps the neural network represent the data and generalize the patterns in that data. These multiple layers allow these deep learning models to learn more complex data representations.

This ability to learn complex data makes these deep learning models good candidates for speech and image recognition, natural language processing, and gaming use cases.

> **TIP** *One advantage of deep learning is that you do not have to do manual feature extraction because the system can do that on its own.*

From an enterprise AI perspective, deep learning can improve the quality of customer service interactions because of its ability to improve the accuracy of speech and image recognition. Deep learning can also be used to detect anomalies in financial transactions and fraud detections and improve supply chain operations by predicting demand and optimizing inventory levels.

Deep learning can process a wider range of data resources, requires less preprocessing from humans, and produces more accurate results than traditional machine learning approaches.

Implementing deep learning in an enterprise does come up with its own nuances.

> **TIP** *Because of the intensive nature of the neural networks, you need a robust data storage, processing, analytics infrastructure, and specialized hardware such as GPUs for proper training and inference.*

You also need strong data scientists and engineers who can design, build, and train deep learning models and deploy them in production. They need to understand the different types of deep learning models available to use the appropriate model to solve the business problem at hand. A proper understanding of the business requirements to develop technical specifications to adopt deep learning is also required.

Convolutional Neural Networks

Convolutional neural networks (CNNs) are a type of artificial neural network designed to handle structured grid-like data such as images, videos, and time series. They are well suited for image classification and object detection use cases due to their ability to learn spatial relationships in data.

As shown in Figure 16.20, CNNs operate by applying a series of convolution operations to the input data. A *convolution operation* is a mathematical operation that takes in two functions as inputs and produces a third function. The two inputs are the data and the filter, which is a small matrix of weights used to extract features from the input data.

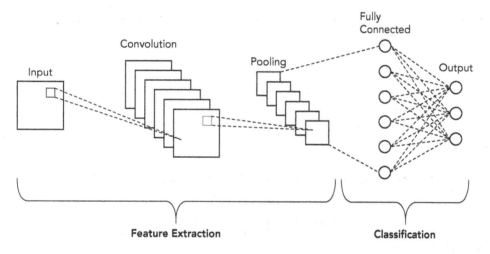

FIGURE 16.20: Typical CNN architecture

The convolution operation is then applied to the input data in a sliding window fashion. They filter across the input data, one pixel at a time. The output of a convolution operation is a *feature map*. Feature maps can then be used to classify the data or detect objects in the input data.

CNNs are useful under the following conditions:

SITUATION	EXPLANATION
Grid-like data structure	When the data has a grid-like structure such as images.
Spatial relationships	When the data has spatial relationships where the position of the features is important for classification.
Large data	When the amount of data is large. Since CNNs learn in a hierarchical manner, they can learn from large amounts of data without overfitting.
Noisy data	When the data has a lot of noise. Since CNNs learn in a hierarchical manner, they can learn features despite noise in the data.

CNNs are used in several applications, including the following:

APPLICATION	USE CASE
Object detection	Utilized in self-driving cars to detect objects such as other cars, pedestrians, and cyclists
Image classification	Employed in Google Photos to automatically label the photos based on what's in the image
Natural language processing	Adopted by Amazon to categorize customer reviews as positive or negative
Medical imaging	Leveraged by doctors to detect cancer in mammograms or identify Alzheimer's disease in brain scans
Financial trading	Used by investment firms to predict stock prices or identify patterns in market trends

> **TIP** *For machine learning problems involving image, video, audio, or time-series data, leverage CNNs to automatically learn spatial relationships and features.*

EXERCISE: BUILDING A CONVOLUTIONAL NEURAL NETWORK FOR IMAGE CLASSIFICATION

The goal is to develop a CNN model that can accurately classify images in a predefined dataset. But the larger intention is for the team to gain insights into the end-to-end process of developing, training, and deploying a deep learning model.

STEP NAME	TASK OWNER	INSTRUCTIONS	DELIVERABLES
Dataset collection	Data scientist	First, you must gather a labeled dataset of images for the CNN to classify.	A labeled dataset of images
Preprocess data	Data scientist	Clean and preprocess the data. As part of cleaning, you might need to resize images, normalize pixel values, and split the dataset into training and testing subsets.	A preprocessed dataset ready for model training

STEP NAME	TASK OWNER	INSTRUCTIONS	DELIVERABLES
Model selection and design	Data scientist	You should then choose a suitable CNN architecture. Start first with a simple architecture and then progressively add complexity. You can use transfer learning with pretrained models if needed.	Selected model architecture
Model training	Data scientist	Train the selected model using the training dataset. During this step, choose an appropriate loss function and optimizer. Use techniques such as data augmentation, dropout, or batch normalization to improve performance and reduce overfitting.	A trained CNN model
Model evaluation	Data scientist	Test the model's performance using the test subset of the dataset. Measure accuracy and review the classification report. You should plot and review the confusion matrix.	Evaluation results
Parameter tuning	Data scientist	If the model's performance is not satisfactory, continue with tuning the parameters of the model or the training process. You can adjust the learning rate, batch size, or the architecture of the CNN.	A fine-tuned model with improved performance
Model deployment	Data scientist/ ML engineer	Once the model performance is satisfactory, go ahead and deploy the model for real-world image classification tasks.	Deployed CNN model for image classification

Recurrent Neural Networks

Recurrent neural networks (RNNs) are artificial neural networks designed to process sequential or time-series data. RNNs can learn long-term dependencies in data, which makes them suitable for natural language processing and speech recognition tasks.

RNNs use a feedback loop to connect the output from one layer to the input of the next layer. This allows the network to learn relationships between data points that are not immediately next to each other.

Some of the key features of RNNs are sequential processing to analyze patterns in the data, recurrent connections to allow data to be passed from one step to the next, hidden state that acts as a memory, and backpropagation to help them learn and adjust the weights based on the sequence of inputs.

RNNs are suitable under the following situations:

➤ **Sequential data:** When the data is sequential, such as audio, speech, and text

➤ **Long-term dependencies:** When the data has long-term dependencies, such as when the meaning of a word depends on the context

➤ **Noisy data:** When the data is noisy

RNN can be used for the following use cases:

USE CASE	DESCRIPTION
Translation	To translate between languages such as in Google Translate.
Speech recognition	To recognize speech as in Alexa.
Forecasting	To forecast. For example, a bank may use it to predict the price of gold in the next month
Object detection	To identify objects such as in self-driving cars.

> **TIP** *For sequential or time-series data like text, audio, or sensor streams, RNNs are well-suited to learn temporal relationships.*

Transformer Models

A *transformer* is an advanced neural network used for natural language processing tasks such as machine translation, text generation, text summarization, natural language understanding, speech recognition, and question answering.

Transformers work based on the attention mechanism, which allows them to learn long-term dependencies in text. They calculate similarity scores between each input token and output token. Similarity scores are then used to compare the weights of the input tokens to the output token, which the transformer then uses to cater to different parts of the input to generate the output text.

The transformer model can learn long-range dependencies because of the use of the attention mechanism and is also more efficient because it is not as computationally intensive as the recurrent neural network.

Transformer models are suitable under the following conditions:

USE CASE	DESCRIPTION
Translation	By capturing the relationship between words in different languages, they helped translate between languages.
Contextual meaning	By capturing the contextual meaning of the words, they have been effective in sentimental analysis, text classification, named entity recognition, and text summarization.
Question answering	They have been able to help answer questions based on context.

USE CASE	DESCRIPTION
Chatbots	Useful for building conversational chatbots.
Recommendation systems	Useful for building recommendations systems by analyzing the user preferences, historical data, and item features.
Image processing	Helpful for image classification, object detection, image generation, and image captioning.
Speech recognition	Used in speech to text and text to speech conversions.
Information extraction	Useful in assisting with extracting key information from documents, document classification, summarization, and information retrieval.
Text generation	Useful in text generation for chatbots, story generation, content creation for marketing, and so on.

Here are some examples of use cases for transformer models:

USE CASE	DESCRIPTION
Translation	By capturing the relationship between words in different languages, they helped translate between languages.
Contextual meaning	By capturing the contextual meaning of the words, they have been effective in sentimental analysis, text classification, named entity recognition, and text summarization.
Question answering	They have been able to help answer questions based on context.
Chatbots	Useful for building conversational chatbots.
Recommendation systems	Useful for building recommendation systems by analyzing the user preferences, historical data, and item features.
Image processing	Helpful for image classification, object detection, image generation, and image captioning.
Speech recognition	Used in speech-to-text and text-to-speech conversions.
Information extraction	Useful in assisting with extracting key information from documents, document classification, summarization, and information retrieval.
Text generation	Useful in text generation for chatbots, story generation, content creation for marketing, and so on.

> **TIP** *Use transformers to provide state-of-the-art performance on problems such as translation, question answering, sentiment analysis, and dialogue.*

Generative Adversarial Networks

Generative adversarial networks (GANs) are a type of machine learning model that is used to generate new data like the data that it is trained on. GANs have been used to create audio, text, and images that look realistic but do not exist in real life.

GANs consist of two neural networks—one is the generator and the other is the discriminator—as shown in Figure 16.21.

➤ **Generator:** The generator is trained to create new data that is as realistic as possible.

➤ **Discriminator:** The discriminator is trained to distinguish between real and fake data.

As you train them, both get better at their respective tasks.

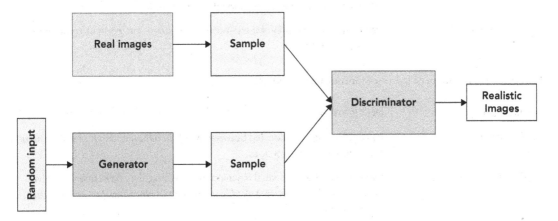

FIGURE 16.21: GAN model

GANs are suitable in the following scenarios:

➤ **Large data:** When there is a large amount of data

➤ **Multimodal models:** When the data is complex with multiple modals such as audio, text, and images

➤ **Limited labeled data:** When the data is not labeled or has limited labeling

➤ **Realistic content:** When the requirement is to create new realistic content

Here are some use cases for GANs:

USE CASE	DESCRIPTION
Image and video editing	The image and video editing capabilities of GAN can be used to generate realistic images and videos in the entertainment, marketing, and advertising industries.
Text generation	The text generation capabilities of GAN can be used to create content for websites, social media, as well as new forms of art and literature.
Music composition	The music composition capabilities of GAN can be used to create songs, soundtracks, entire music albums, as well as for music in TV and movies.

USE CASE	DESCRIPTION
Drug discovery	GANs can be used to create new drug molecules with the potential to treat diseases.
Financial data generation	GANs can be used to create realistic financial data, such as stock prices and economic indicators, which can be used to make financial decisions and forecast economic trends.
Climate control	GANs can be used in climate control by generating realistic climate models to gain a better understanding of climate change.
Artificial intelligence	GANs can be used in artificial intelligence to create training data for other models to improve their accuracy.
Facial reconstruction	GANs can be used in reconstructing a face from incomplete or degraded images that can be used in forensics, entertainment, and virtual character creation.

> **TIP** *For generating realistic synthetic data like images, audio, and text, consider using GANs.*

THE AI/ML FRAMEWORK

The AI/ML framework is a set of tools and resources that developers can use to build and train machine learning models.

Say you want to build a machine learning model to identify customers likely to default on a loan. You must collect data, clean it before using it in a model, train the model, test the model, and deploy the model. All of this requires code, and as a developer, instead of building this code from scratch, you can use prebuilt libraries from frameworks such as TensorFlow, PyTorch cafe, and so on.

> **TIP** *AI/ML frameworks provide prebuilt components for data preprocessing, model architecture, building, and deployment, allowing you to focus more on the functionality and business problem.*

TensorFlow and PyTorch

While TensorFlow is an open-source framework developed by Google, PyTorch is an open-source framework that was developed by Facebook. These frameworks are powerful tools used to create new products and services, transform industries, and build new markets. Table 16.7 compares these two frameworks.

TABLE 16.7: TensorFlow vs. PyTorch ML Frameworks

ATTRIBUTE	TENSORFLOW	PYTORCH
Released on	November 9, 2015	October 7, 2017
Developed by	Google	Facebook

continues

(continued)

ATTRIBUTE	TENSORFLOW	PYTORCH
License	Apache 2.0	Apache 2.0
Supported programming languages	Python, C++, Java	Python, C++, Lua
Focused on	Large-scale machine learning	Deep learning
Community support	Large and active	Growing and active
Available documentation	Extensive and well-written	Good, but not as extensive as TensorFlow's
Ease of use	Learning curve involved	User-friendly
Performance	Very fast	Fast
GPU supported	Yes	Yes
Deployment	Supports a variety of deployment options, including TensorFlow Lite	Supports a variety of deployment options, including PyTorch Lightning and PyTorch Mobile
Distributed computing	Yes	Yes
Visualization	Good visualization tools, including TensorBoard	Good visualization tools, including the PyTorch Debugger, Visdom
Community support	Large and active community	Growing community
Overall	A powerful and versatile framework for large-scale machine learning	A flexible and easy-to-use framework for deep learning

Keras

Keras is a high-level neural network API built to run on top of other frameworks, such as TensorFlow and Theano. Keras aims to make model development user-friendly on top of complex frameworks such as TensorFlow and Theano.

Keras has a user-friendly interface for beginners, but even experienced developers can use it to build models and experiment with deep learning. It reduces the number of user actions, provides clear error messages, and makes it easier to develop documentation and guides. It makes it easy to define and train deep learning models and is helpful for complex tasks such as image classification, NLP, and speech recognition. It helps researchers and scientists develop iterative prototypes and drives faster innovation through experimentation.

Caffe

Caffe stands for Convolutional Architecture for Fast Feature Embedding. It is a deep learning framework developed by the Berkeley Learning and Vision Center. It is maintained by the community and is written in C++ with the Python interface. Since it is developed in C++, it is more user-friendly for beginners. It is less user-friendly than TensorFlow or PyTorch. It has extensive documentation and is intended to be fast and flexible, as it can be extended to support new tasks.

> **NOTE** *Caffe is helpful for large-scale, complex tasks such as image recognition, object detection, semantic segmentation, and speech recognition.*

MXNet

MXNet is a robust deep-learning framework developed as open source by the University of Washington and the University of Hong Kong. It is used by Baidu for its search algorithms and is developed in C++. It is tricky for beginners and is not as user-friendly as TensorFlow and PyTorch.

> **NOTE** *MXNet is an open-source solution developed by the Apache Software Foundation and is a powerful tool for developing high-performing models.*

Scikit

Scikit stands for *scientific kit*. It's written in Python and is a powerful and versatile machine-learning library for beginners. It includes classification, regression, clustering algorithms, support vector machines, and random forests, and K-means.

Scikit is intended to work with other Python libraries—NumPy and SciPy. It's free software released under the BSD license. It is a good choice for beginners who want to learn machine learning.

Chainer

Chainer is a powerful open-source deep learning tool used to develop many deep learning models written in Python on top of other libraries such as NumPy and CuPy. It can be used for classification, object detection, and NLP use cases. It was developed by the Japanese venture company called Preferred Networks in collaboration with IBM, Intel, NVIDIA, and Microsoft.

Many more AI/ML frameworks exist, such as CNTK, DLib, and so on.

WORKBOOK TEMPLATE: *AI/ML ALGORITHM SELECTION GUIDE*

Download the "AI/ML Algorithm Selection Guide" template from the download section of the book (`www.wiley.com/go/EnterpriseAIintheCloud`). Use this template to choose the right AI/ML algorithm for your AI/ML project. You can use this to improve the quality of the predictions or classifications, the quality of data, and the amount of computation needed.

SUMMARY

You took a comprehensive trip into the world of AI and ML algorithms. Tailored for experienced data scientists and beginners alike, this chapter demystified the process of selecting the right algorithms based on use cases. The chapter dived into the basics of artificial intelligence, reviewed different types of machine learning, discussed the nuances between models and algorithms, and provided hands-on exercises to help you choose the right algorithms.

Understanding these algorithms is akin to processing the keys that unlock the vast potential hidden in the data. While choosing the algorithms, note that the choice of an algorithm is rooted not only in the data but also in the business problem you are trying to solve. In subsequent chapters, you can look forward to diving deeper into the training, tuning, evaluating, and deploying models. Your journey continues!

REVIEW QUESTIONS

These review questions are included at the end of each chapter to help you test your understanding of the information. You'll find the answers in the following section.

1. What are the types of data that machine learning algorithms can use?
    A. Text data
    B. Images
    C. Only structured data
    D. All kinds of data

2. What is the primary purpose of AI?
    A. To automate business processes
    B. To improve customer service
    C. To mimic human intelligence
    D. To monitor events and take action

3. The purpose of labeled data in supervised learning is
    A. To identify input variables
    B. To predict continuous values
    C. To create a model
    D. To define the output variable

4. Which one of the following is a regression problem?
    A. Identifying spam emails
    B. Forecasting product demand
    C. Recommendation systems
    D. Classifying images

5. The purpose of reinforcement learning is to
    A. Classify data into labels
    B. Predict continuous values
    C. Learn from interactions and rewards
    D. Automate process interactions

6. Random forests are useful for which types of problems?
    A. Classification
    B. Regression
    C. Both classification and regression
    D. None of the above

7. How does KNN work?
    A. It uses deep learning to work.
    B. It calculates the mean of all data points to make predictions.
    C. It identifies the K closest data points and uses their outcomes to make predictions.
    D. It randomly assigns clusters to data points.

8. Principal component analysis is useful for
   A. Classification problems
   B. Regression problems
   C. Dimensionality reduction
   D. Real-time CNN use cases

9. What is a singular value decomposition?
   A. Clustering algorithm
   B. Dimensionality reduction technique
   C. Image processing technique
   D. Classification technique

10. A key advantage of deep learning compared to traditional machine learning is which of the following?
    A. Can work with smaller amounts of data
    B. Can work with less human intervention
    C. Produces less accurate results
    D. Performs better on small datasets

11. CNNs are particularly good for
    A. Image data
    B. Text data
    C. Sequential data
    D. Tabular data

12. RNNs are particularly good for
    A. Image data
    B. Text data
    C. Sequential data
    D. Tabular data

13. Transformer models are useful for
    A. Image classification
    B. Text generation
    C. Anomaly detection
    D. Generative adversarial networks

14. This AI/ML framework is written in C++ and is less user-friendly than TensorFlow or PyTorch.
    A. Keras
    B. Caffe
    C. MXNet
    D. scikit-learn

15. _____ is known for its versatility and includes algorithms for classification, regression, and clustering use cases.
    A. Keras
    B. Caffe
    C. scikit-learn
    D. Chainer

ANSWER KEY

1.	D	**6.**	C	**11.**	A
2.	C	**7.**	C	**12.**	C
3.	D	**8.**	C	**13.**	B
4.	B	**9.**	B	**14.**	B
5.	C	**10.**	B	**15.**	C

17

Training, Tuning, and Evaluating Models

Success is not final; failure is not fatal: It is the courage to continue that counts.

—*Winston Churchill*

Traveling the AI journey is like solving a jigsaw puzzle. In the previous chapter, we got one step closer to solving this puzzle by learning how to choose the most apt AI/ML algorithm, a critical step in transitioning data into actionable intelligence. This chapter builds that up to get into the actual act of modeling, which brings these algorithms to life.

This chapter delves into the three pillars of modeling: training, tuning, and evaluation (see Figure 17.1). The focus is on ensuring these models are secure, efficient, and high performing. We begin by looking at the intricacies of model building and the likely challenges during the training process. From distributed processing to container code, we dive into the tools and techniques of model development. You learn about optimizing models for high performance using hyperparameters and model tuning. Evaluation and validation will help you align with your enterprise objectives when dealing with real-world data and ensure the models are robust and ready to achieve tangible, transformative outcomes.

MODEL BUILDING

Model building is an iterative process, and it is the first step in the process that sets up the model for training to begin. Figure 17.2 shows the model development lifecycle.

The purpose of model building is to build a working model that can be used to make predictions on new data. It is the process of defining the model's structure, parameters, and hyperparameters. Taking the cooking analogy, model building is like building a recipe to build your meal.

BEST PRACTICE TIPS FOR PICKING AN ALGORITHM

Start by selecting an algorithm suited to your data type and problem. However, always be open to trying different algorithms based on model performance and the insights gained during the training phase.

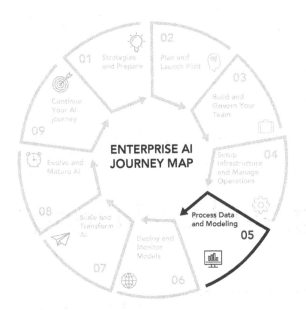

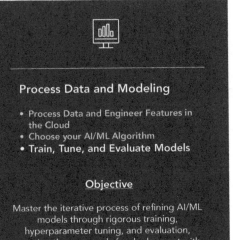

FIGURE 17.1:   Training, tuning, and evaluating models

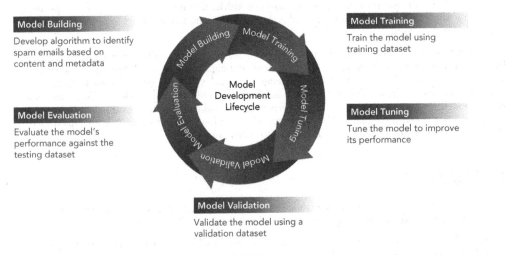

FIGURE 17.2:   Phases of a model development lifecycle

You will be using various tools and frameworks such as TensorFlow, PyTorch, scikit-learn, and so on.

Structure, Parameters, and Hyperparameters

The **structure** refers to the algorithm or architecture used, such as linear regression, decision tree, or neural network. The **parameters** refer to the internal variables related to the model, such as weights and biases. These values are estimated from the data during training. You can think of the model as the hypothesis and the parameters as the customization of the hypothesis to predict from a specific dataset. **Hyperparameters** refer to the external settings configured by the user before training the model, such as learning rate, batch size, and regularization.

Figure 17.3 lists the training and tuning components discussed in this chapter.

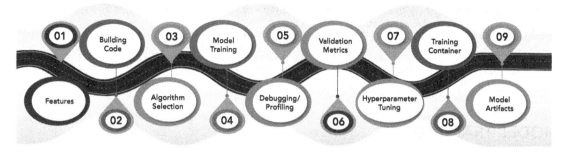

FIGURE 17.3: Model training and tuning components

Steps Involved During Model Building

Model building involves the following steps:

1. Choosing an appropriate algorithm, such as a decision tree, linear regression, or neural network based on the problem to be solved

2. Defining the features and the label that needs to be predicted

3. Choosing the loss function such as mean squared error

4. Building the model architecture if required

Model building is all about experimenting with different algorithms, features, and hyperparameters iteratively until a satisfactory performance is achieved. As part of this process, you may be required to carry out some data preprocessing, such as scaling, encoding, or feature engineering.

> **TIP** **Model architecture** *refers to the algorithm or framework that is used to predict. It can refer to the layers, nodes, activation functions, loss functions, and optimization algorithms that are arranged and configured in a certain way. Some common machine learning model architectures are linear regression, decision trees, neural networks, convolution neural networks, and recurrent neural networks.*

Developing the Algorithm Code

As a machine learning engineer, you can write your algorithm code in different languages, such as Python, R, or Java, depending on your preferences or environment. Your code will need to do the following:

➤ Import the data

➤ Clean the data

➤ Split the data

➤ Train the model

➤ Make predictions

Selecting the Right Algorithm

During this model building process, you will be experimenting with different algorithms and parameters to short-list the right algorithm. You will be evaluating the models based on different parameters such as training/prediction time, accuracy, explainability, memory requirements, and so on.

For our case study, you may choose classification algorithms such as logistic regression, naïve Bayes, and support vector machines as possible candidates to build the model.

> **NOTE** *Refer to Chapter 16 on algorithms to learn more about various algorithms and when to use which one.*

MODEL TRAINING

Once you have shortlisted a model during model building, the next step is to train your model with the training dataset. Model training is a crucial step in machine learning that results in a working model, which you can validate, test, and deploy. Using the cooking analogy, model training is like actually starting to cook the meal using the recipe you came up with during the model building process.

> **NOTE** *A model is a set of rules or equations that the machine can use to learn from data to make predictions. Depending on the type of problem, these predictions could be about identifying if an email is spam or classifying images as different types of animals.*

During this step, you will feed the training data into the model and begin the training process. The training process teaches the machine how to make its predictions. During this process, the weights (parameters) of the algorithm get updated to reduce the loss, which is the difference between the prediction and the actual labels. In other words, the training process helps to increase the accuracy with which the machine makes its predictions.

> **TIP** *Keep a close eye on metrics such as accuracy, precision, and recall to check if the model is performing well or needs adjustment.*

Distributed Training

When dealing with a lot of data or a complex model, your training process can take a long time, sometimes even days or hours. It is where distributed training comes to our rescue. Distributed training involves using multiple machines to train your model.

You have two types of distributed training, namely, data parallelism and model parallelism.

Model Parallelism

Model parallelism involves splitting the model into smaller parts to predict different features and assigning each part to different machines. The models are then combined to form the final model.

Model parallelism is more complex than data parallelism but is more suited for models that cannot fit into one device. You can also combine model parallelism with other techniques such as data parallelism to improve training efficiency.

Data Parallelism

Data parallelism involves splitting the training dataset into mini batches evenly distributed across multiple nodes.

For example, if you have 1,000 emails to identify spam, you can divide them into 10 groups of 100 emails each and assign each group to a different computer. Therefore, each node trains on only a fraction of the dataset. You will update the model with the results from the other machines to make the final model.

> **NOTE** *An* **optimization algorithm** *helps update the parameters of the model to reduce a loss function, such as mean squared error. A good example is the gradient descent algorithm, which adjusts the parameters iteratively in the direction of the steepest descent of the loss function.*

Problems Faced When Training Models

When training your models, you are going to face a number of problems, some of which are listed in Figure 17.4. We will review these challenges in this section.

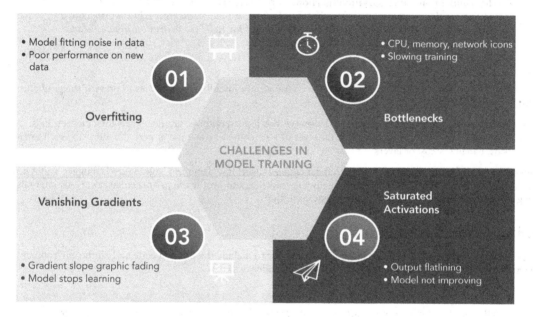

FIGURE 17.4: Problems faced when training models

Overfitting and Underfitting

Overfitting happens when you are training the model with a lot of training data. Your model starts to memorize the labels and is unable to generalize to new data. It happens when the model captures every noise or irrelevant pattern in the data. The model becomes too complex and is unable to predict against new data. It can lead to errors and inaccuracies in your model predictions on validation or test data.

Underfitting is the reverse of overfitting. In this case, the model is too simple and does not capture important patterns or relationships that are relevant for the prediction.

System Bottlenecks

When your system faces a bottleneck, it can bring down the entire process performance regarding memory, CPU disk space, or network bandwidth.

Saturated Activation Functions

Saturated activation functions mean the output does not change even if the input changes, which means the neural network cannot learn anymore. It happens when the activation functions, namely, sigmoid and tanh, have reached their minimum or maximum levels. When this happens, we say the activation functions are saturated. ReLU is an alternative in such situations.

Vanishing Gradients

Vanishing gradients happen when the gradients or the incremental changes to the neural network weights are minimal or close to 0 during backpropagation. When this happens, the neural network will not learn much from the data. It can happen when using sigmoid or tanh, as well as when the gradients are not propagated back through the network.

> **TIP** *Think of* **saturated activation functions** *as rusty gears in a machine. If they are not moving, neither is your model's learning. Similarly, vanishing gradients are like whispers in a noisy room and your model is not hearing them. Opt for RelU for activation functions and proper weight initialization to address these issues.*

To resolve this situation, you can either use ReLU or use weight initialization schemes to prevent the gradients from becoming too small.

You can use a debugger tool to keep track of the network's inputs, outputs, gradients, weights, metrics, logs, errors, and so on. The tool can also capture the state of a machine learning job at periodic intervals, such as various epochs, batches, steps, or layers.

Some examples of a debugger are the PyTorch debugger, TensorFlow debugger, SageMaker Debugger, and Azure Machine Learning debugger. ML debuggers help you to debug and profile the performance at various intervals using breakpoints, alerts, watches, visualizations, and filters.

Training Code Container

A training code container comes in handy when you want to include the training code and all the environmental dependencies into one package to take care of code dependencies.

> **TIP** *Building training code containers is an essential step in the machine learning process to build and deploy models quickly and reliably at scale.*

Suppose you're trying to build a model to predict customer churn. You have collected all your data and used the logistic regression model to predict customer churn. And now, you have written some Python code in your local machine to train the model. You have integrated your code with other frameworks and libraries such as scikit-learn and pandas.

Now, you are all set to deploy your working code into production using the cloud. Unfortunately, this is where you are going to face some issues, such as the following:

➤ Your code may not run due to differences in the hardware, software, and operating system configuration.

➤ Your code may not be able to access the data that is stored in the cloud platform.

➤ You may need to scale up or down your compute and storage resources depending upon the workload.

Here comes your training container to your rescue. You will start by creating a container image with the training code and the entire dependent stack, such as the libraries, framework, tools, and environment variables for your model to run. You can then train the model quickly and deploy it on another platform at scale because now your code is running as part of a self-contained unit with all the dependencies taken care of.

Creating a Training Code Container

To create a training code container, you need the following:

➤ **A Docker file:** This file contains the instructions to build the image.

➤ **train.py:** This file contains the training code for the machine learning model.

➤ **requirements.txt:** This file contains the dependencies such as scikit-learn and pandas for the machine learning model to run.

You can then use the Docker file to build the container image and push it to a container registry such as the Docker Hub or the Google Container Registry.

Using the Training Code Container

The container image can be pulled to train the model onto any machine that has docker installed. You need to specify the data sources, compute resource requirements, and set other parameters for the training job. You can save the file once the training is completed and you have chosen the right hyperparameters.

Using that file for real-time predictions, you can then deploy the model on any other machine.

Model Artifacts

You need to realize that the final model is one of many outputs you will get when training a model. There will also be other model artifacts, such as the trained parameters, model definition, and metadata. These model artifacts are essential pieces of the puzzle to understand, use, reproduce, and improve upon your model. Figure 17.5 shows the artifacts.

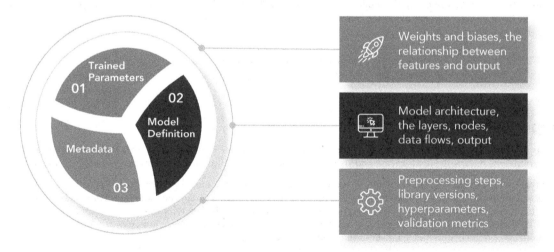

FIGURE 17.5: Model artifacts outputted during model training

Trained Parameters

In the case of predicting the price of a house, you had trained parameters such as the weights and biases that your model learned during the model training process. These parameters define the relationship between the features and the price of the house. They basically determine how the model works.

Model Definition

Model definition defines the architecture or structure of the model. It defines how the data flows into the model, the layers, the nodes, and how they interact. In the case of the house pricing prediction model, this could define the structure of the neural network in all the regression models. It would detail how the inputs (house features) are processed to produce the output (predicted price).

Other Metadata

This could be any information that you may have used during the model training process, such as the preprocessing steps that you used to prepare the data, the versions of the libraries, the hyperparameters to tune the model, and the validation metrics that you used to evaluate the model, and so on.

> **TIP** *It is vital to keep track of the model artifacts as they will help in reproducibility, governance, explainability, troubleshooting, lineage tracking, and centralized artifacts management.*

MODEL TUNING

Model tuning involves fine-tuning the parameters not optimized during the training process. Model tuning helps to modify the structure of the model itself. During model training, the internal trainable parameters, such as weights and biases of the neural networks, are trained using the training data.

In the case of model tuning, the focus is on tuning hyperparameters. Those hyperparameters are structural settings that are set before fitting the model and are not learnable from the training data. These are parameters such as the learning rate, number of epochs, regularization strength, and so on.

> **TIP** *Think of model tuning as sharpening your pencil. While training sets the foundation, tuning is where you achieve perfection.*

Hyperparameters

Suppose you are a chef trying to create a recipe to bake bread. While creating your bread, you can change a few parameters, such as the temperature and the baking time. You can think of these parameters as *hyperparameters*.

Hyperparameters control how the model works and help optimize the model performance on training and validation datasets. It helps to avoid overfitting or underfitting. These values cannot be estimated from data and are often configured by a practitioner. Hyperparameters help to control the behavior of the algorithm or the model and control how fast the training occurs and how complex the model is. Hyperparameters are set before the model gets trained, and they guide how the model learns its trainable parameters.

I next discuss the learning rate, regularization, batch size, number of epochs, hidden layers, and hidden unit hyperparameters, as shown in Figure 17.6.

Learning Rate

Learning rate is the rate at which the model parameters are updated at each iteration of the gradient descent.

You can think of the learning rate as the baking temperature. A high temperature can speed up the baking, but it can get spoiled by overheating. Similarly, a high learning rate speeds up the convergence to minimize the loss function. However, it can also cause instability or overshooting. A low learning rate can ensure stability but can take a long time to converge and potentially get stuck in local minima.

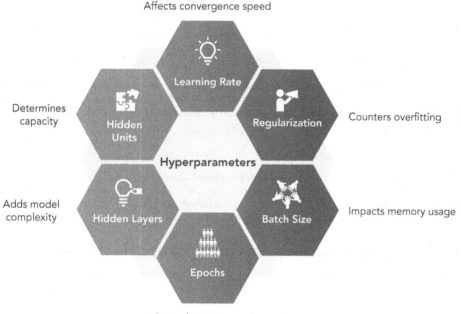

FIGURE 17.6:   Tuning hyperparameters for optimal model performance

Regularization

Regularization is adding a penalty to the loss to reduce the complexity or magnitude of the parameters. While this approach may reduce the variance and help avoid overfitting, it can introduce bias. Using the cooking analogy, compare the situation of overfitting to having added more salt. To reduce this saltiness, you would add more water. You can think of regularization in a similar manner.

Batch Size

Batch size is the number of data points in each dataset used to train the model for each iteration of the gradient descent.

A large data size can reduce the variance in the parameter updates and noise, but it takes a long time to compute and uses a lot of memory. Smaller batch size is the reverse effect: it reduces the time taken to compute and uses less memory. However, it increases the noise and variance in the parameter updates.

Number of Epochs

The number of epochs stands for the number of times the entire training dataset is fed to the model for training. A higher number means the model runs the risk of overfitting, while a lower number may lead to underfitting of the model.

To find the sweet spot for the number of epochs, you can resort to techniques such as early stopping in the case of overfitting and adopt techniques such as cross-validation to get better results.

Hidden Layers

Hidden layers are the layers that are not visible to the user in a neural network.

> **NOTE** *The hidden layer is an important parameter that can decide the complexity of the model.*

Simple layers can catch broad features, and deeper layers can catch more intricate, specific details. A higher number of hidden layers can result in overfitting, while a lower number can lead to underfitting. To identify the right number of hidden layers, you can try grid search or random search techniques to evaluate the performance using different numbers of hidden layers.

Hidden Units

Hidden units are the number of neurons in a layer in a neural network. They determine the representational capacity of the neural network. A higher value can lead to overfitting, and a lower value can lead to underfitting. You can identify the correct optimal number of hidden units using techniques such as a grid or random search to evaluate the network's performance using different numbers of hidden units.

Choosing the Right Hyperparameter Optimization Technique

You can employ manual or automated model-tuning techniques such as grid search, random search, or Bayesian optimization (see Figure 17.7).

FIGURE 17.7: Grid versus random searches

You can use your intuition or experience when choosing the hyperparameters to manually tune a model. Your goal is to choose the model with the best validation performance. While using an automated approach, the grid search provides the best possible model. In contrast, the random search approach is more efficient.

> **TIP** *If you're running on, you will choose the random search approach, but if you're looking for accuracy, you will choose the grid search approach.*

Grid Search vs. Random Search

Say you're trying to predict whether a patient has cancer, and you're using a random forest model that contains two hyperparameters, namely, the depth of the tree and the number of trees in the model. See Figure 17.7.

To use grid search to tune the hyperparameters, you can set the maximum depth of the decision tree to 10, 20, 30, 40, and 50. You can set the number of trees in the random forest to 100, 200, 300, 400, and 500.

When you use grid search, the system will try all 25 combinations of the hyperparameter values, which will take a long time but will provide the best model.

If you used random search, the system would randomly sample the maximum depth of the tree from a uniform distribution between 1 and 50 and randomly sample the number of trees from a uniform distribution between 100 and 500.

> **NOTE** *While random search will not give the best possible model, it will be faster than the grid search approach.*

Bayesian Search

Bayesian search is a hyperparameter optimization technique well suited to noise or use cases that are more complex for a grid or random search. It is more efficient than grid or random search but can be complex to implement and may need some knowledge of Bayesian statistics.

> **TIP** *Bayesian search can be used for any machine learning model but may not be as effective as a grid or random search for more straightforward objective functions.*

The Bayesian search uses Bayesian statistics to find the best hyperparameters and works by building a probabilistic model of the objective function being optimized. It has been successfully used in many applications such as spam filtering and credit card fraud detection.

MODEL VALIDATION

This section discusses how to validate the models and the metrics that you have to use.

Choosing the Right Validation Techniques

You will need to validate your model using the validation dataset during the training phase when it is being developed and optimized. The goal of the model validation process is to compare the predictions of the model with the actual outputs of the new dataset. You will use techniques such as holdout validation and cross-validation. This evaluation aims to test the model's generalization ability, identify any issues with the model, and choose the best model among the candidates. Its focus is to avoid overfitting the training data. Model validation happens during the training phase, while model evaluation happens after the model is deployed in production.

There are several cross-validation techniques—the two most popular ones are K cross validation and leave-one-out cross validation (see Figure 17.8).

Cross-validation techniques are more expensive and time-consuming but are very accurate. If you're short on time, you should go for holdout validation, but when accuracy is critical, you will use cross-validation techniques.

Holdout Validation

Holdout validation involves breaking the dataset into a training dataset and a test dataset. You will use the training dataset to train the model and then use the model to test the dataset using the test dataset. By comparing the results with the actual dataset, you can evaluate how accurate the model is.

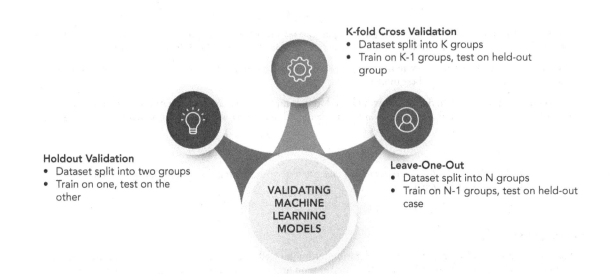

K-fold Cross Validation
- Dataset split into K groups
- Train on K-1 groups, test on held-out group

Holdout Validation
- Dataset split into two groups
- Train on one, test on the other

VALIDATING MACHINE LEARNING MODELS

Leave-One-Out
- Dataset split into N groups
- Train on N-1 groups, test on held-out case

FIGURE 17.8:   Validating machine learning models

K Cross-Validation

This involves breaking down the validation set into K folds and training and testing the model on each fold. Then you will compare the performance average across all folds with other models.

Leave-One-Out Cross Validation

Leave-one-out cross validation involves splitting the data into n data folds where n is the number of data points. You would then train the data in $n - 1$ folds and evaluate the model against the fold not used in training.

> **TIP** *Using the leave-one-out cross-validation technique helps you test the data against all the data points, which is very accurate.*

Validation Metrics

As shown in Figure 17.9, validation metrics are used during the different phases of a model development lifecycle.

During Model Building

For example, during the model build phase, validation metrics can be used to choose the suitable model for classification-type problems based on a validation metric such as area under the receiver operating characteristic curve (AUC-ROC). In the case of regression type problems, use metrics such as mean absolute error or R-squared.

> **TIP** *Always select metrics aligned with your model's objectives.*

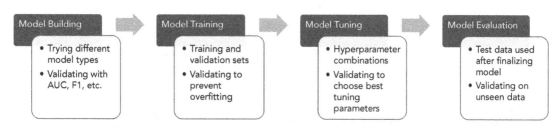

FIGURE 17.9: Validation across ML model development phases

During Model Training

During the model training phase, you can break down the dataset into training and validation datasets. Once the training is completed using the training dataset, you can validate the model on the validation dataset and optimize the model parameters accordingly to prevent overfitting.

During Model Tuning

During the model tuning process, you will choose the combination of the hyperparameters using techniques such as a grid or random search that optimizes the validation metrics.

During Model Evaluation

Once the model is trained and tuned, you can then evaluate the model using the validation metrics on the test dataset. It helps you to understand how well the model will perform on new, unseen data.

> **TIP** *Validation metrics are used to measure the model performance in a quantifiable manner during different phases of the model development lifecycle. During model building, use them to choose the right model; during training, use them to ensure learning is on the right track; during tuning, use them to choose the right hyperparameters; and during evaluation, use them to finalize the model.*

Validation Metrics for Classification Problems

This section discusses some validation metrics for classification problems, such as accuracy, precision, recall, and F1 score, as shown in Figure 17.10.

> **TIP** *No single metric will tell you the whole story. While accuracy may be very impressive, it can be misleading if your classes are imbalanced. That's why you need to look at other metrics such as precision, recall, and F1 score.*

Accuracy

Accuracy is the percentage of the correctly predicted labels out of all predictions calculated as follows:

Accuracy = Number of correct predictions / Total number of predictions

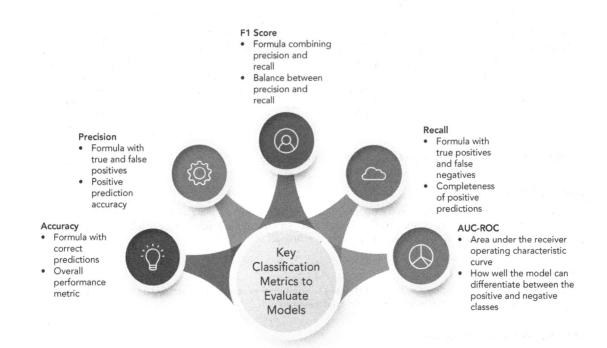

FIGURE 17.10: Validation metrics for classification problems

Precision

Precision is the percentage of the correctly predicted positive labels out of the total positive predictions.

$$\text{Precision} = \text{Number of true positives} / (\text{Number of true positives} / (\text{Total number of true positives} + \text{Total number of false positives}))$$

Recall

Recall is the percentage of the correctly predicted positive labels out of the total actual positive predictions.

$$\text{Recall} = \text{Number of true positives} / (\text{Number of true positives} / (\text{Total number of true positives} + \text{Total number of false negatives}))$$

F1 Score

F1 score is the harmonic mean of the precision and recall.

$$\text{F1 Score} = 2 \times \text{Precision} \times \text{Recall} \left(\text{Precision} + \text{Recall} \right)$$

AUC-ROC

AUC-ROC stands for area under the receiver operating characteristic curve, and it helps to determine how well the model can differentiate between the positive and negative classes. Its value ranges from 0 to 1. A value of 0.5 implies random guessing, and 1 implies its perfect classification. It plots the true positive rate (recall) against the false positive rate (1 – specificity) for various threshold values.

Since these predictions are probabilities, we must convert them into binary values using the threshold concept. So, for a threshold of .5, if the predicted probability is greater than .5, it means it's positive, and any value less than .5 is treated as negative.

> **NOTE** *AUC-ROC is a measure of how well a model can distinguish between two classes, ranging from 0 to 1.*

Confusion Matrix

Confusion matrix is a table that summarizes the number of true positives (TPs), true negatives (TNs), false positives (FPs), and false negatives (FNs) for a given class.

Consider the scenario for predicting customer churn. Table 17.1 shows The confusion matrix.

TABLE 17.1: Sample Confusion Matrix

	ACTUAL NO CHURN	ACTUAL CHURN
Predicted No Churn	TN	FN
Predicted Churn	FP	TP

Assume your model returns the results shown in Table 17.2.

TABLE 17.2: Sample Results Predicted by the Model

CUSTOMER ID	ACTUAL LABEL	PREDICTED PROBABILITY	PREDICTED LABEL
1	0	0.2	0
2	1	0.8	1
3	0	0.6	1
4	1	0.4	0

You can build the confusion matrix as shown in Table 17.3.

TABLE 17.3: Confusion Matrix with Values

	ACTUAL NO CHURN	ACTUAL CHURN
Predicted No Churn	90	10
Predicted Churn	20	80

Using the formula, your validation metrics will be as follows:

➤ Accuracy = (90 + 80) / (90 + 10 + 20 + 80) = 0.85

➤ Precision = 80 / (80 + 20) = 0.8

➤ Recall = 80 / (80 + 10) = 0.89

➤ F1-score = 2 * 0.8 * 0.89 / (0.8 + 0.89) = 0.84

➤ AUC-ROC = 0.93

These metrics reveal that this model is fairly accurate, but still, there is some scope to improve as it still has some false predictions. You can use these metrics to choose between different models or algorithms. You can also use these metrics to choose between different hyperparameters, such as regularization or threshold value, as part of the model-tuning process.

MODEL EVALUATION

After training a model, the next important step is to evaluate the model for its performance and accuracy. Think of model evaluation as your final examiner that validates if the model is ready for the real world.

As part of the evaluation, you have to take care of three things.

➤ Ensure the model can generalize well for new unseen data.

➤ Ensure the model satisfies the business rules, objectives, and expectations. Otherwise, it's like a ship without a compass.

➤ Ensure it can accommodate different scenarios and handle different trade-offs. The fact is no model can handle every situation perfectly.

Model evaluation will help you to address these challenges. As part of it, you will select the suitable model after a lot of experimentation, followed by validating the model and fine-tuning it with the correct hyperparameters.

> **NOTE** *Note that the model evaluation can take place using offline or online data.*

Offline data evaluation will be done using holdout data, while online evaluation will take place in real time in production, which can be risky but more effective.

Figure 17.11 shows the various components of the model performance evaluation pipeline. Model evaluation involves testing the model against a test dataset not used for training or validation. It helps to test the final accuracy and quality of the model. You will use evaluation metrics such as accuracy, precision, recall, and F1 score.

During this phase, you will look for potential bias and discrimination in the model and also try to explain how the model works using a feature importance score or confusion matrix.

> **TIP** *Model evaluation is a critical step to ensure your model is robust, fair, aligned with your business objectives, and ready for the real world.*

BEST PRACTICES

This section reviews some practices you can implement during the model development lifecycle to streamline workflows, secure your platform, enhance model robustness, improve performance, and reduce costs.

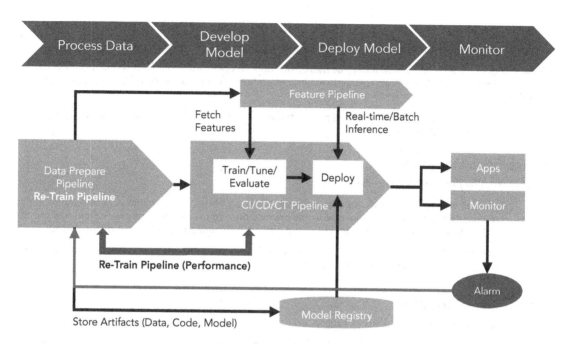

FIGURE 17.11: Performance evaluation pipeline

Streamlining Your ML Workflows Using MLOps

This section reviews the operational best practices you can employ during model training, tuning, and performance evaluation to ensure streamlined and efficient ML workflows. Your goal must be to constantly monitor these systems and continually improvise upon the processes and procedures.

Harness the Power of MLOps Through IaC and CaC

Infrastructure as code (IaC) and configuration as code (CaC) are two vital techniques to automate cloud infrastructure management. IaC helps you define your infrastructure in code, while CaC helps you capture your code configurations. Implementing IaC and CaC will provide you with two benefits:

➤ Implementing IaC will ensure consistency in the infrastructure across staging and production environments and help you avoid the tedious, error-prone manual process.

> **TIP** *IaC and CaC will lead to more predictable deployments and fewer manual errors.*

➤ Implementing CaC will ensure the traceability of different data and model artifacts across multiple environments and configurations. It will help you troubleshoot issues and avoid the manual, tedious process of managing configurations across multiple environments.

> **TIP** *IaC and CaC help manage versions, making rolling back changes easier. They are lifesavers to scale ML operations.*

You can use AWS CloudFormation, Terraform (open source), and AWS Cloud Development Kit to implement IaC.

Establish Scalable Ways to Access Public ML Libraries and Resources

When working with public libraries in an enterprise setup, you'll likely encounter some challenges.

First, you must ensure that the ML library or framework fully complies with your company's policies and is approved for use. Second, you must ensure these libraries and frameworks are compatible with your machine-learning environment.

You need to be able to share the latest and approved libraries across multiple environments, teams, and projects to prevent disparities across teams.

Embrace Containerization

Containerization provides the following benefits:

➤ **Governance and Compliance:** By packaging the ML code, libraries, and frameworks into the container and ensuring that these are approved by the organization, you can ensure compliance and compatibility with environments as well as share these containers across multiple teams within the organization.

➤ **Standardization:** It will ensure standardization of the machine learning infrastructure and code, in addition to enabling governance across the enterprise.

Use an Artifact Repository

Here are some benefits of using an artifact repository.

➤ **Centralized storage:** Storing the model, data, and libraries in an artifact repository helps to ensure that all teams are accessing the same, approved resources.

➤ **Version control:** Repositories help you to track the versions of these artifacts easily and roll back changes in case of issues.

➤ **Enhanced collaboration:** Central repositories make it easier to share artifacts across multiple projects, teams, and data scientists so that they can build upon each other's work.

> **TIP** *Implementing MLOps best practices will not only streamline your ML development process but also ensure consistency, governance, and collaboration, which are foundational pillars for an agile, reliable, and scalable AI implementation.*

Securing Your ML Platform

This section discusses some of the best practices to ensure the security of your models, data, infrastructure, and other assets, as listed in Figure 17.12.

Protect from Transfer Learning Risks

Transfer learning is a technique in machine learning that leverages the learning gained by a pretrained model when solving a specific business problem to solve another similar problem by fine-tuning it. When doing so, we run the risk that the weights inherited from the pretrained model may not produce the correct predictions.

> **TIP** *To avoid transfer learning risk, you can use the AWS SageMaker Debugger to detect any bias in the new predictions.*

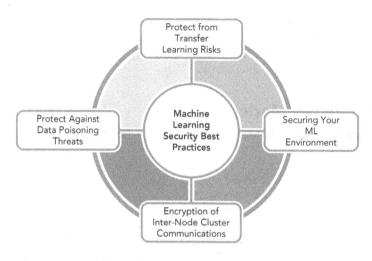

FIGURE 17.12: Machine learning security best practices

Secure Your ML Environment

To secure your ML environment, follow these best practices:

➤ **Encryption:** Use encryption to secure your data at transit and at rest.

➤ **Active monitoring:** Monitor your ML environment for suspicious activity.

➤ **Incident response:** Have a plan to respond to security incidents quickly.

➤ **Access controls:** Break down your ML workloads by organizational units and environments so that you can provide appropriate access controls.

➤ **Environment access:** Limit infrastructure access to administrators based on the dev, staging, and production environment.

➤ **Container security:** Secure your model training and containers.

➤ **Jupyter Notebook access:** Implement a restricted Jupyter Notebook access policy through a centralized management system and enable self-provisioning.

Enable Encryption of Inter-Node Cluster Communications

When using distributed training, you need to enable data transfer encryption between the nodes for sensitive ML operations. You can do this by enabling inter-node encryption in Amazon SageMaker or enabling encryption in transit when you're using EMR.

Protect Against Data Poisoning Threats

Data poisoning is a serious threat where attackers try to gain access to training data and inject harmful data to influence the model outputs. Here are some steps you can take:

➤ **Anomaly detection:** Use anomaly detection to check for tampering with training data.

➤ **Change tracking:** Keep track of all the changes made to the training data and the models and maintain a baseline.

➤ **Diversify data sources:** Use more than one data source to train your models so the impact of compromise to a single data source is minimized.

➤ **Audit and oversight:** Have an audit process in place to check for unusual changes and ensure alignment with corporate security.

Building Robust and Trustworthy Models

You can enhance model robustness and trustworthiness by following these recommendations shown in Figure 17.13.

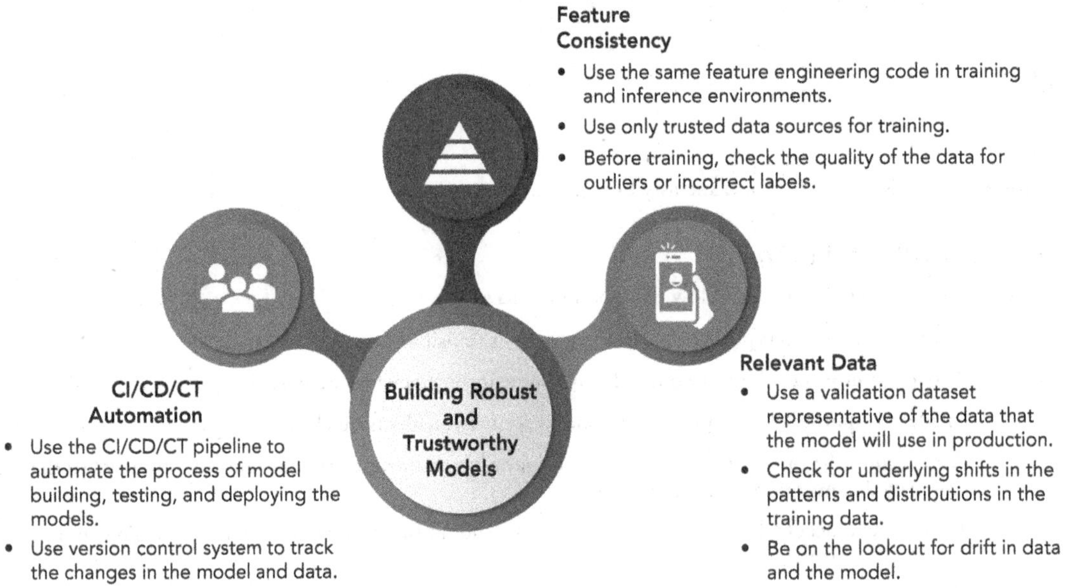

Feature Consistency
- Use the same feature engineering code in training and inference environments.
- Use only trusted data sources for training.
- Before training, check the quality of the data for outliers or incorrect labels.

Building Robust and Trustworthy Models

CI/CD/CT Automation
- Use the CI/CD/CT pipeline to automate the process of model building, testing, and deploying the models.
- Use version control system to track the changes in the model and data.

Relevant Data
- Use a validation dataset representative of the data that the model will use in production.
- Check for underlying shifts in the patterns and distributions in the training data.
- Be on the lookout for drift in data and the model.

FIGURE 17.13: Reliability best practices

Ensure Feature Consistency Across Training and Inference

Here are some best practices to ensure feature consistency:

➤ **Unified feature engineering:** Use the same feature engineering code in training and inference environments.

➤ **Trusted data sources:** Use only trusted data sources for training.

➤ **Audit trails:** Implement a robust audit process to replay the activity based on who did it and at what time.

➤ **Data quality assurance:** Before training, check the quality of the data for outliers or incorrect labels.

Ensure Model Validation with Relevant Data

Here are some best practices for validating data:

➤ **Representative validation data:** Use a validation dataset representative of the data the model that will be used in production.

➤ **Detect data shifts:** Check for underlying shifts in the patterns and distributions in the training data, which might affect model reliability.

➤ **Drift monitoring:** Be on the lookout for drift in data and the model and address them appropriately to ensure accuracy.

➤ **Automated validation checks:** Implement automated validation checks using relevant and updated data to ensure the model works as expected.

Enable ML Automation and Traceability

Here are some best practices to implement automation and traceability in the ML process:

➤ **Implement CI/CD/CT pipeline:** Use the CI/CD/CT pipeline to automate the process of model building, testing, and deploying the models.

➤ **Version control and traceability:** Combining it with a version control system to track the changes in the model and data will ensure the traceability and reproducibility of the model.

Ensuring Optimal Performance and Efficiency

The following sections discuss some of the performance-related best practices.

Optimize Training and Inference Instances

Ensure you're using appropriate instance types for training and inference purposes for optimal performance and cost-efficiency.

> **TIP** *Using SageMaker Debugger, you can capture real-time training metrics that you can use to optimize performance.*

Explore Multiple Algorithms and Structures to Improve Performance

This is to reiterate what was already discussed: to explore different algorithms to best fit the problem, hyperparameters for better performance, and preprocessing data techniques to improve performance continuously.

Establish a Model Performance Evaluation Pipeline

Having a model performance evaluation pipeline will help you to assess performance continuously, detect any deterioration in performance proactively, and send automated alerts so that you can address them immediately.

Establish Feature Statistics

Having feature statistics will help you identify the distribution of the features and improve performance by choosing the right algorithms accordingly.

Conduct Performance Tradeoff Analysis

Conduct a performance trade-off analysis to ensure that you're using your resources efficiently and yet not compromising on the performance.

Utilizing Cost Optimization Best Practices

The following sections discuss some of the steps you can take to optimize the cost of your ML implementation (see Figure 17.14).

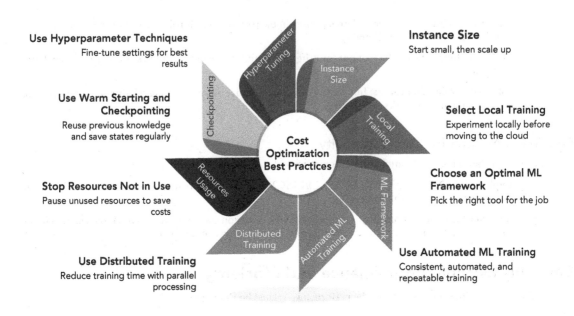

Use Hyperparameter Techniques
Fine-tune settings for best results

Use Warm Starting and Checkpointing
Reuse previous knowledge and save states regularly

Stop Resources Not in Use
Pause unused resources to save costs

Use Distributed Training
Reduce training time with parallel processing

Instance Size
Start small, then scale up

Select Local Training
Experiment locally before moving to the cloud

Choose an Optimal ML Framework
Pick the right tool for the job

Use Automated ML Training
Consistent, automated, and repeatable training

FIGURE 17.14:   Cost optimization best practices

Select Optimal Instance Size

Choosing the correct type of instances for training and inference will help you save costs. Use debugging capabilities to assess the resource requirements during training. Simple models may not train fast enough on larger instances; hence, you can start with small instances and then scale them up gradually. SageMaker Experiments can help here.

Select Local Training

For training small-scale ML workloads, you can resort to local training and experiment with different algorithms first before moving on to the cloud.

HANDS-ON EXERCISE: SELECTING OPTIMAL INSTANCE SIZE AND LOCAL TRAINING

Goal: Understand how to choose the correct instance size for a given problem and then experiment with local training before scaling.

TASK DESCRIPTION	TASK OWNER	DELIVERABLES
Start Small: Begin by training a simple model (e.g., linear regression) on a small dataset using a small EC2 instance or even your local machine.	Data scientist	Trained model on a small instance, initial performance metrics

TASK DESCRIPTION	TASK OWNER	DELIVERABLES
Scale Up: Gradually increase the instance size, observing the training time and performance metrics. Note down the changes.	Data scientist	Performance report including training time and metrics at various instance sizes
Analyze: Compare the results to identify the optimal balance between instance size and performance.	Data scientist	Optimal instance size report, cost-benefit analysis
Local to Cloud Transition: Experiment with training the model locally first, then transitioning to the cloud for further tuning. Compare costs and efficiency.	Data scientist	Comparison report of local versus cloud training, efficiency analysis, local-to-cloud transition plan

Choose an Optimal ML Framework

Choosing the proper ML framework is essential to save costs depending on your use case. SageMaker Experiments can help you choose the right one. You can also choose deep learning AMIs and containers optimized for specific ML frameworks. Some come with pre-installed TensorFlow, PyTorch, Apache MXNet, Chainer, Gluon, Horovod, and Keras.

Use Automated ML Training

Resorting to automated ML training can help you optimize costs because they are built using a consistent, automated, and repeatable manner. They can choose the best algorithm, test different solutions quickly, and identify the best parameters.

HANDS-ON EXERCISE: AUTOMATE MODEL TRAINING AND HYPERPARAMETER TUNING WITH SAGEMAKER

Goal: Use AWS SageMaker to automate the training process and optimize hyperparameters.

TASK DESCRIPTION	TASK OWNER	DELIVERABLES
Set Up SageMaker Configure a SageMaker experiment using a predefined algorithm suitable for your problem (e.g., XGBoost for regression).	Data scientist	Configured SageMaker experiment, algorithm selection
Automate Training Implement automated training by utilizing SageMaker's automatic model tuning feature.	Data scientist	Automated training setup, initial model output

continues

continued

TASK DESCRIPTION	TASK OWNER	DELIVERABLES
Tune the Hyperparameters Define a range for hyperparameters and let SageMaker find the optimal values. Observe how the system tests various combinations and settles on the best one.	Data scientist	Range of hyperparameters, optimal hyperparameter values, comparison report of different combinations
Analyze Results Review the best models, their parameters, and how they were chosen. Compare this with manual tuning if desired.	Data Scientist	Report on best models, analysis of how they were chosen, comparison with manual tuning (if applicable), final model

Use Distributed Training

Distributed training can also help reduce the training time, provided the algorithm allows it. The distributed data-parallel library in Amazon SageMaker can break down the model across multiple GPUs and speed up the process.

Stop Resources Not In Use

It may be an obvious thing, but it is essential to stop resources that are not in use. It includes the Jupyter networks that you are using to run small models. Remember to stop the computing and storage services as well. You can use an AWS CloudWatch Billing Alarms when the usage exceeds the threshold. Use the SageMaker lifecycle configuration to start and stop Jupyter Notebooks when idle.

Use Warm Starting and Hyperparameter Checkpointing

Warm starting can help you to avoid the need to train a model from scratch. Instead, you can load from a previously tuned model along with its hyperparameters and reuse the knowledge gained from it.

Hyperparameter checkpoints are snapshots of a model's state during training, including the model's parameters, optimizer state, and hyperparameters.

You can save your model's state regularly, such as after an epoch or every few epochs. Restarting from checkpoints can help you save time and cost.

Use Hyperparameter Optimization Techniques

Use hyperparameter optimization techniques to speed up the process of tuning your hyperparameters. For example, SageMaker automatic model tuning runs multiple training jobs on the dataset, just as the best model uses the hyperparameter ranges you specify.

WORKBOOK TEMPLATE: *MODEL TRAINING AND EVALUATION SHEET*

Download the "Model Training and Evaluation" template from the download section of the book (www.wiley .com/go/EnterpriseAIintheCloud). Use this template to track the metrics and methods used during the training and evaluation phases. It will help you to ensure that the model meets the required quality standards before it is deployed.

SUMMARY

In this chapter, you began a comprehensive journey through training, tuning, and evaluating machine learning models. You examined the various stages, including model building, model training, model tuning, model validation, and model evaluation. You also learned about some best practices in areas such as security, reliability, performance, and cost management.

This chapter serves as a foundational guide for data scientists, machine learning engineers, and leaders to continue to explore machine learning and the model-building process in particular. As we close this chapter, it is essential to remember that this is a continuous process, and the challenges and opportunities will continue.

In the next chapter, let's discuss how to deploy models in production to ensure the models function optimally and responsibly.

REVIEW QUESTIONS

These review questions are included at the end of each chapter to help you test your understanding of the information. You'll find the answers in the following section.

1. What is one of the benefits of building models in the cloud?
    A. Scalability
    B. Security
    C. Privacy
    D. None of the above

2. What is the purpose of model building?
    A. To build a working model that can be used to make predictions on new data
    B. To train the model
    C. To tune the model
    D. To validate the model

3. _____ is the primary step in machine learning that results in a working model that can be validated, tested, and deployed.
    A. Model training
    B. Model building
    C. Model tuning
    D. Model evaluation

4. What is the difference between the model build process and the model training process?
    A. The model build process focuses on discovering patterns in the training dataset and selecting the best-performing model, while the model training process focuses on adjusting the model's parameters to improve its performance.
    B. The model build process focuses on adjusting the model's parameters to improve its performance, while the model training process focuses on discovering patterns in the training dataset and selecting the best-performing model.
    C. The model build process and the model training process are the same.
    D. None of the above.

5. What is data parallelism?

    A. Using more than one computer or device to train the model

    B. Splitting the model into smaller parts to predict different features and assigning each part to different devices or computers

    C. Combining models to form the final model

    D. None of the above

6. What is model parallelism?

    A. Using more than one computer or device to train the model

    B. Splitting the model into smaller parts to predict different features and assigning each part to different devices or computers

    C. Combining models to form the final model

    D. None of the above

7. What is the role of hyperparameters in machine learning models?

    A. They guide the model learning process.

    B. They are automatically learned from data.

    C. They control the loss function.

    D. They are the trainable parameters of the model.

8. How does a high learning rate affect model convergence in gradient descent?

    A. It slows down convergence.

    B. It stabilizes the convergence.

    C. It speeds up convergence but might cause instability.

    D. It does not affect convergence.

9. What is the purpose of regularization in a machine learning model?

    A. It helps to speed up model training.

    B. It adds a penalty to the loss function to reduce model complexity.

    C. It increases the learning rate of the model.

    D. It increases the number of epochs in model training.

10. What is the focus of the data prepare pipeline?

    A. To prepare a clean and consistent dataset ready for feature engineering

    B. To store, retrieve, and copy features into and from an online or offline feature repository for use in a model

    C. To validate and test the model before releasing it into production in various environments

    D. To deploy and monitor the model's real-time performance in production.

11. Which phase involves tweaking the data, hyperparameters, and model parameters based on evaluation results?

    A. Model training

    B. Model selection

    C. Model fine-tuning

    D. Model validation

12. Which of the following steps is not involved in the model evaluation process?

    A. Model selection

    B. Model validation

C. Model fine-tuning

D. Model training

13. What is the benefit of implementing infrastructure as code (IaC)?

A. Consistency across different infrastructures

B. Traceability of different data and model artifacts

C. Both A and B

D. Neither A nor B

14. What is one of the risks associated with transfer learning?

A. The inherited weights from the pretrained model may not produce the correct predictions.

B. The fine-tuned model may take longer to train than a new model.

C. The pre-trained model might not have been trained on relevant data.

D. All of the above.

15. What is the purpose of conducting a performance trade-off analysis in machine learning?

A. To find a balance between model complexity and accuracy

B. To ensure optimal utilization of resources without compromising performance

C. To compare the performance of different models

D. Both A and B

ANSWER KEY

1.	A	6.	B	11.	C
2.	A	7.	A	12.	D
3.	A	8.	C	13.	A
4.	A	9.	B	14.	D
5.	A	10.	A	15.	D

PART VII
Deploying and Monitoring Models

Hooray! It is launch time. Part VII guides you through the process of deploying the model into production for consumption. I also discuss the nuances of monitoring, securing, and governing models so they are working smoothly, safely, and securely.

18

Deploying Your Models Into Production

Do not wait to strike till the iron is hot but make it hot by striking.

—William Butler Yeats

Having navigated through data processing, algorithm selection, model training and fine-tuning, you are now on the verge of an important step: model deployment. This is an essential chapter for data scientists, ML engineers, IT professionals, and organizational leaders involved in deploying models into production using the cloud.

The true value of an AI model is not just in its design or accuracy but in its real-world use. This chapter dives deep into the nuances of deploying your model, from understanding the challenges in model deployment, monitoring, and governance to deciding between real-time and batch inferences.

Model deployment isn't just about pushing a model live. It involves strategic decisions, systematic processes, and synchronized architecture. Keep in mind that you will not just be launching models into production; you will also be ensuring that the models are functioning optimally and responsibly within your larger AI ecosystem. See Figure 18.1.

The focus of this chapter, though, is to have a successfully deployed model that is making the impact that it was meant to have during the design process to achieve continuous innovation and growth.

STANDARDIZING MODEL DEPLOYMENT, MONITORING, AND GOVERNANCE

Here are some considerations for your model deployment, monitoring, and governance process:

> **Automate deployment:** You should automate the deployment process and make it repeatable and standardized. This will ensure that the model is deployed consistently across multiple environments.

> **Automated performance monitoring:** You need to ensure that the model is performing well over a period of time. The monitoring process needs to be automated so that you can proactively identify and address any issues promptly. You need a robust monitoring system to measure the model's performance metrics, such as accuracy, precision, recall, latency, and throughput.

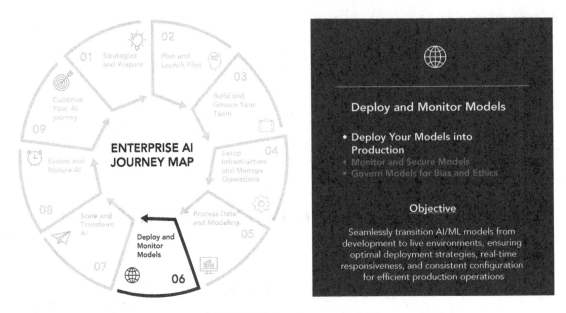

FIGURE 18.1: DEPLOY AND MONITOR MODELS: Deploy your models into production.

➤ **Ethical use and responsibility:** You need to ensure that the model is used responsibly and ethically in a production environment without discriminating against its users. To enforce governance, you must define policies and procedures integrated into your organization's overall governance framework and establish systems to detect bias proactively and address them in real time.

> **TIP** *Adopt deployment best practices such as automatically deploying through CI/CD pipelines, deployment scripts, version control, continuous performance monitoring, ethical use, proactive bias detection, and establishing a model governance framework.*

Challenges in Model Deployment Monitoring and Governance

There are several challenges when deploying models and ensuring they are implemented ethically and responsibly in production, discussed next.

Model Deployment Challenges

Consider these deployment challenges:

➤ **Scalability:** Models may not scale well enough to handle large amounts of data in production.

➤ **Operational efficiency:** Poor operational efficiency and data silos may result from a lack of integration of the models with backend processes, systems, and data storage systems.

➤ **Latency:** High latency of the models can render them useless for practical use.

➤ **Reproducibility:** Over time, reproducing these models for retraining and redeployment becomes impossible because of numerous changes in the underlying hardware, software libraries, and other dependencies.

Model Monitoring Challenges

Here are some monitoring-related challenges:

➤ **Dynamic data:** The world is constantly changing, and therefore, the data feeding the models also changes, which can cause issues when monitoring the model performance.

➤ **Model complexity:** Most of these models are complex, and it becomes difficult to understand how they work because of the black-box nature of the algorithms. It poses a challenge to enforcing governance of the models because of the need for model explainability and interpretability.

➤ **Talent shortage:** There is not enough talent and resources to focus on model deployment and monitoring.

➤ **Unified framework:** You may find that the methods adopted to develop and deploy models are not standardized across teams.

➤ **Data lineage tools:** There is also a lack of transparency in the data quality and lineage.

Model Governance Challenges

Finally, these are governance challenges:

➤ **Bias control:** Since these models reinforce existing biases in the data, controlling biases is a challenge.

➤ **Data privacy and regulation:** Data privacy and security should be carefully protected during training and prediction to comply with legal regulations such as GDPR, CCPA, and HIPAA.

➤ **Industry regulations:** Navigating regulations in industries such as healthcare or finance can be an issue.

➤ **Model inventory:** Models tend to increase rapidly across business units in large enterprises, and keeping track of inventories becomes tough.

➤ **Change logs:** Keeping track of changes in AI models is not easy because you have to track the changes in the code and the changes in data, hyperparameters, and models.

➤ **Accountability:** The question of who is accountable or responsible when the model fails is also tricky.

> **TIP** *Solving these challenges requires a mix of technology initiatives such as MLOps, pipelines, explainability techniques, governance policies, data use policies, regulatory guidelines, and culture.*

DEPLOYING YOUR MODELS

This section dives into the model deployment process. It is often underestimated in the model development lifecycle. However, it is the most crucial step from a user perspective because it makes the model available for user consumption. The following sections review some best practices.

Pre-deployment Checklist

First, you must ensure the model is fully trained and tested. Second, ensure that you have fully optimized the model using the best practices discussed in the previous chapter. Third, perform dry runs in a staging or sandbox environment to uncover unforeseen issues.

Deployment Process Checklist

As shown in Figure 18.2, the deployment process involves the following:

➤ **Features:** Retrieve the features from the feature store.

➤ **Artifacts and dependencies:** Retrieve the model from the model registry and other artifacts required for the model to run.

➤ **Inference code container:** Retrieve the inference code container, which contains the code required to make the predictions against the model. The inference code container is typically retrieved from the container registry using a docker pull command.

➤ **Deployment:** Once the features, the artifacts, and the inference code container are retrieved, the model is deployed into the production environment.

➤ **API access:** Making it available as a Restful API using a web service framework like Flask or deploying it in a cloud platform such as AWS SageMaker, GCP, or Azure Machine Learning.

➤ **Application integration:** Integrating it with other applications if necessary.

➤ **Monitoring:** Periodically review the model's output with the actual values to ensure the model performs properly using a manual or an automated governance process.

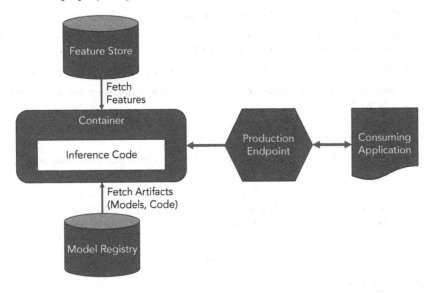

FIGURE 18.2: Model deployment process

Choosing the Right Deployment Option

As part of your architecture design discussion, you need to decide which one of the model deployment options is the best fit for you. As shown in Figure 18.3, you have four options: cloud deployment, on-premises deployment, edge deployment, and hybrid deployment.

Cloud Deployment

Here are some considerations for cloud deployment:

➤ **Scalability:** Cloud is the best option if you have many users to serve and if the load fluctuates. It allows you to process large amounts of data using a large computing capacity, and to store large amounts of data.

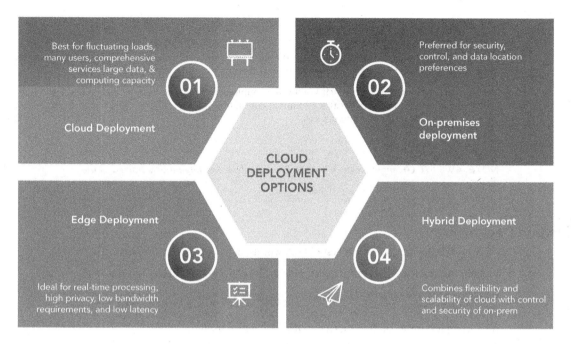

FIGURE 18.3: Model deployment options

> **Service integration:** The cloud providers also provide several services that make deploying and managing your model easy. For example, you can leverage services for computing, storage, and networking.

> **Data security:** The cloud allows you to connect to sensitive data using robust network security protocols offered by the cloud providers.

For these reasons, the cloud option is often the most popular option.

On-Premises Deployment

Some companies may resort to on-premises deployment of their models using their own servers, storage, and networks in their data centers.

> **Security requirement:** It is preferred when security is a primary requirement, and you want to keep your data in your own locations.

> **Infrastructure control:** It also gives more control over their infrastructure. However, you need to regularly update your hardware and software, have robust backup and disaster recovery, and regularly monitor for bottlenecks.

> **Expensive:** However, it can be more expensive and resource intensive to manage.

Edge Deployment

Here are some considerations for edge deployment:

> **Model performance and latency:** If your model performance and latency are important, then you would resort to deploying the model at the edge where the data resides and action happens. Your edge devices could be smartphones, IoT sensors, tablets, or industrial machines.

➤ **Real-time processing:** It allows you to process data in real time, provides greater privacy, and has fewer bandwidth requirements.

➤ **More complex:** However, this can be the most complex deployment type because managing and updating models across multiple devices can take time and effort.

➤ **Other considerations:** Remember that you need to implement device management to manage software updates, may encounter issues because of limited computing power, and may need to synchronize data between central servers/cloud and devices.

> **NOTE** *AWS IoT Greengrass can run models in edge devices using models trained in the cloud.*

Hybrid Deployment

People use a hybrid deployment to get the best of both worlds, namely, cloud and on-prem deployments.

➤ **Flexible and scalable:** This approach can provide flexibility and scalability of cloud deployment.

➤ **Greater control and security:** This approach can provide greater control and security through an on-prem deployment.

➤ **More complex:** It can be challenging to implement and manage.

With Amazon SageMaker, you can run the models on the cloud and at the edge. It has a compiler that can read models from various frameworks and compile them into binary code to run the model in the target platform. It also enables the "train models once and run anywhere" concept.

> **TIP** *Think long term and ensure that your deployment method suits your future growth potential. Avoid vendor lock-in and factor in regulatory requirements.*

Choosing an Appropriate Deployment Strategy

To reduce the risk involved in model deployment, there are several deployment strategies that you can adopt, as shown in Figure 18.4. The following sections discuss them.

Blue/Green Deployment

Consider these characteristics of blue/green deployment.

➤ **Environment consistency:** In the blue/green deployment approach, you have two identical production environments running in parallel. You will continue the live traffic on the blue production environment, and the green environment will be used for the deployment. When a new version of the model is ready for deployment, you will deploy it first in the green environment to test it. Once it has been tested and found to be working fine, you will start directing the live traffic to the green environment. The blue environment will now become the backup.

➤ **Rapid rollback:** The benefit of this approach is that you can roll back your changes if the model is not working correctly. It is scalable and requires minimal downtime.

➤ **Resource management:** But the disadvantage is that it has additional infrastructure costs due to the need to maintain two production environments in parallel. It is more complex to implement and needs additional resources.

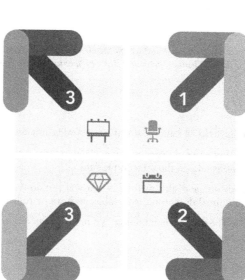

Shadow
Deployment

Run old and new
versions side-by-side for
testing. Real-life testing
environment, scalable

Blue/Green
Deployment

Test on green, switch
live traffic upon success.
Scalable with minimal
downtime

A/B Testing

Split users randomly
and serve old and new
versions. Allows data-
driven decisions

Canary
Deployment

Release to a small
group initially. Monitor
and scale up traffic if
successful

FIGURE 18.4:   Choosing a deployment strategy

Canary Deployment

Consider these characteristics of canary deployment:

➤ **Segmentation:** You release the model to a small group of users.

➤ **Continuous monitoring:** It allows you to monitor the model's performance closely, and once you find it satisfactory, you can slowly ramp up the traffic to 100 percent.

➤ **Live testing:** The benefit of this approach is that you can test the model in a live, fully controlled environment.

➤ **Rollback:** It allows you to roll out a new model without impacting all the users and can roll back if there is an issue with the new model.

➤ **Small sample size:** The disadvantage is that you are testing it against a small sample size, and not all errors may be caught. It won't be easy to target a suitable set of users and assess the full impact of the new model.

A/B Testing

Here are some characteristics of A/B testing:

➤ **Controlled variables:** You split the users into two groups in a random fashion and then test them with the old and new versions of the model to compare their performance. The first group is called the *control group* and is served the old model, and the other group is called the *treatment group* and is served the new model.

➤ **Statistical relevance:** The benefit of this approach is that it allows you to make data-driven decisions. It allows you to test different features and configurations.

➤ **Planning:** It takes a lot of planning to avoid biases. It will need to run for a substantial amount of time or need a substantial amount of traffic to reach statistical significance.

➤ **Targeting:** It is also difficult to target the right set of users and therefore understand the full impact of the model.

> **NOTE** *AB testing is similar to canary deployment. However, it requires a more significant number of users and will take longer, typically days or weeks, to reach a conclusion.*

Shadow Deployment

With shadow deployment, you have the old and new versions running side by side.

➤ **Data synchronization:** While the old version serves the users, the new version is used purely for testing and analysis. Both versions take in the same input data.

➤ **Real-life testing:** The advantage of this method is that you can do real-life testing in a real-life environment, which involves minimal downtime, is scalable, and can be rolled back in the case of an issue.

➤ **Additional complexity:** The cost of maintaining two models may require additional resources and are more complex to implement.

> **TIP** *Regardless of the deployment strategy used, always ensure that the infrastructure is robust, scalable, and have well-defined rollback plans.*

Choosing Between Real-Time and Batch Inference

Another critical decision you must make is to choose between real-time and batch inferences. Your choice will depend on the business need and the use case.

Your decision to choose between real-time and batch inference will depend on balancing immediacy, cost, and technical feasibility.

CONSIDERATION	REAL-TIME INFERENCE	BATCH INFERENCE
Business requirement	Requires instant feedback (e.g., fraud detection).	Result isn't immediately necessary (e.g., monthly reports).
Infrastructure and cost	Needs robust infrastructure for 24/7 uptime and scalability. Can be more expensive.	Tuned for large-scale processing. Generally, more cost-effective.
Latency	Requires quick decisions (e.g., algorithmic trading).	Can tolerate delayed results (e.g., daily analytics).
Data consistency	Handles sporadic or inconsistent streaming data.	Deals with consistent, structured datasets.
Error handling	Needs instant alerts and quick correction mechanisms.	Requires checkpoints and logging for post-facto error detection.
Resource allocation	High availability and redundancy are critical.	Needs significant storage and compute during processing.

CONSIDERATION	REAL-TIME INFERENCE	BATCH INFERENCE
Reliability	Should have failover mechanisms.	Ensure reliability based on processing frequency.
Hybrid approaches	Possible to combine for immediate predictions with deeper analytics.	Can be combined with real-time for comprehensive insights.

> **TIP** *Batch inference is not valuable for use cases where real-time predictions are essential.*

Implementing an Inference Pipeline

When you want to make predictions based on incoming data in real time, you should explore the option of using inference pipelines. For example, an inference pipeline helps predict customer churn in real time or make real-time product recommendations on your website.

As shown in Figure 18.5, the inference pipeline can consist of several steps, such as data preprocessing, feature extraction, model inference, and post-processing. It takes in data in real time and converts them into predictions in real time. It can consist of any ML framework, built-in algorithm, or custom containers and works on both real-time and batch inference requests.

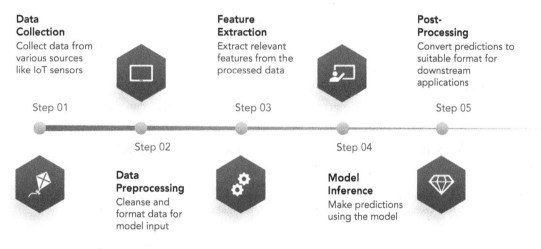

Data Collection
Collect data from various sources like IoT sensors

Step 01

Data Preprocessing
Cleanse and format data for model input

Step 02

Feature Extraction
Extract relevant features from the processed data

Step 03

Model Inference
Make predictions using the model

Step 04

Post-Processing
Convert predictions to suitable format for downstream applications

Step 05

FIGURE 18.5: Different steps in an inference pipeline

Data Collection

During this step, the data from various sources, such as IoT sensors, is collected and stored in data storage. However, this data is not ready yet for use in the model.

> **TIP** *Leverage reliable and scalable storage systems.*

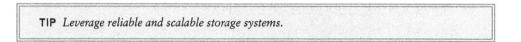

Data Preprocessing

During the data preprocessing step, the incoming data is cleansed and converted into a suitable format to be fed into the model. The data may need to be resized, normalized, standardized, or augmented. It is an essential step because it will determine the accuracy with which the model predicts, as it depends on the accuracy and consistency of the input data.

> **TIP** *Automate the cleansing process.*

Feature Extraction

The pipeline extracts the relevant features from the input dataset during this step. Again, this is an important step that ensures accuracy in the model performance. For example, in the case of image processing, this may involve edge detection, object segmentation, and other techniques to extract meaningful information from the raw image.

> **TIP** *Leverage domain-specific expertise and refine features periodically.*

Model Inference

This is the most critical part of the inference pipeline and is the core because this is where the actual prediction happens. This step may provide meaningful insights to drive subsequent actions.

> **TIP** *Use optimized models for faster inference and retrain models as necessary.*

Post-processing

The predictions are converted into the format for other downstream applications during this step.

> **TIP** *Standardize output formats and ensure downstream application compatibility.*

You can see that implementing an inference pipeline can improve efficiency, latency, and accuracy in real time. However, it can be a complex process that requires careful planning, design, and implementation.

> **NOTE** *Amazon SageMaker Inference Pipeline has 2 to 15 containers to process inference requests.*

EXERCISE: IMPLEMENTING AN INFERENCE PIPELINE

Goal: Implement an end-to-end inference pipeline to predict customer churn.

TASK DESCRIPTION	TASK OWNERS	DELIVERABLES
Collect and preprocess data: Gather data from various sources and preprocess it to make it suitable for the model (e.g., resizing, normalizing).	Data collection team	Preprocessed data ready for feature extraction
Extract features: Utilize statistical or machine learning techniques to extract relevant features from the preprocessed data.	Feature engineering team	Extracted features ready for model inference
Implement model Inference: Employ a pretrained model to make predictions or inferences based on the extracted features.	Model implementation team	Predictions or inferences made by the pretrained model
Add post-processing steps: Format the predictions or inferences so they can be used by downstream applications (e.g., convert to required data formats).	Post-processing team	Formatted predictions ready for consumption by other applications or services
Test the pipeline: Evaluate the entire inference pipeline using real-time data to ensure it functions as expected.	Testing and QA team	A fully functioning inference pipeline validated with real-time data, including a testing report

SYNCHRONIZING ARCHITECTURE AND CONFIGURATION ACROSS ENVIRONMENTS

You must ensure that the model performs consistently across multiple environments, such as development and production.

> **NOTE** *Sometimes even a minor change in the architecture configuration can result in different inferences in different environments.*

You must also ensure the model shows the same accuracy range across development, staging, and production environments. Any model that fails to show this level of accuracy should not be deployed in production. It becomes imperative as you scale your operations across multiple geographies and product lines.

Ensuring Consistency in the Architecture

You can leverage infrastructure as code to ensure consistency in the architecture for both AWS and third-party components. Using AWS CloudFormation, you can manage the infrastructure as one unit and deploy them across multiple environments. It allows you to create, update, and delete an entire stack as one unit.

Ensuring Identical Performance Across Training and Production

Synchronizing the architecture across environments alone isn't enough. You must also ensure the model performs identically across the training and production environments. You can achieve this validation through the use of AWS SageMaker Model Monitor. If you find a difference in the model's accuracy between production and training environments, you can start troubleshooting the cause and try to address the issue.

Looking for Bias in Training and Production

SageMaker Clarify can also detect bias either during training or in production. SageMaker Clarify can help you understand how these models predict using a feature attribution approach. It also keeps monitoring the model in production and looks for any bias or feature attribution drift.

Generating Governance Reports

You can use the governance reports generated by SageMaker Clarify to share with your stakeholders, such as audit teams, regulators, risk and compliance teams, and other business stakeholders.

EXERCISE: DETECT BIAS USING SAGEMAKER CLARIFY

Goal: Monitor the model for bias during training.

TASK DESCRIPTION	TASK OWNERS	DELIVERABLES
Identify bias metrics: Define and select the specific metrics that will be used to measure and identify bias in the training data.	Data science team	List of selected bias metrics tailored to the specific use case and data.
Configure SageMaker Clarify: Set up SageMaker Clarify by specifying the configuration settings such as preprocessing and post-processing scripts.	Machine learning engineers	Configured SageMaker Clarify environment for detecting bias.
Run bias analysis: Execute the bias detection process using SageMaker Clarify, analyzing the training data against the defined metrics.	Machine learning engineers	Raw output of bias analysis, including identified biases and related statistical measures.

TASK DESCRIPTION	TASK OWNERS	DELIVERABLES
Analyze bias results: Interpret the results of the bias analysis, understanding the underlying causes and potential impact on model performance.	Data science and analytics team	In-depth analysis report highlighting the findings, causes, and potential remedies for detected biases.
Implement remediation strategies: Based on the analysis, apply mitigation strategies to reduce or eliminate the identified biases in the training data.	Data science team	Revised training data and model training approach, minimizing the identified biases.
Monitor bias in production: Implement continuous monitoring of the deployed model to detect any bias that might emerge in production.	Monitoring and analytics team	Continuous monitoring setup, with regular reports on identified biases in the production model.
Generate and share reports: Prepare comprehensive reports on the detected biases and share them with stakeholders such as audit teams, regulators, etc.	Compliance and reporting team	Comprehensive bias reports, ready for distribution to internal and external stakeholders, ensuring alignment with regulations and policies.

MLOps AUTOMATION: IMPLEMENTING CI/CD FOR MODELS

The previous section talked about using an inference pipeline to automate the process of converting input data into a prediction for subsequent follow-up action.

Implementing CI/CD for models is a similar automation concept but is focused on automating the process of deploying models into production. It involves automating the process of training, testing, and deployment of the model into production, which is a complex process given the nature of data, the model parameters, and the configuration versions (see Figure 18.6).

Ensure you follow some best practices such as maintaining model versions, automated testing for data preprocessing, feature extraction, validation testing; also ensure environmental consistency across dev, staging, and production, and many other practices outlined in this part of the book.

> **TIP** *Implementing CI/CD can introduce a lot of efficiency and scale, especially when managing large enterprise AI implementations with many models to manage.*

Model Development	Continuous Integration	Continuous Deployment
• Code repository (e.g., Git) • Model versioning • Data preprocessing scripts • Feature extraction scripts	• Automatic code pull (upon push to the repository) • Data preprocessing and feature extraction • Model training • Validation testing	• Deployment to development environment • Deployment to staging environment • Deployment to production environment

FIGURE 18.6: Implementing CI/CD for models

The following list covers some of the CI/CD tools:

➤ **Amazon SageMaker** is a fully managed service from AWS that provides end-to-end lifecycle implementation support, including continuous integration and continuous deployment.

➤ **Jenkins** is an open-source automation server that can be used in model deployment to run the scripts necessary to train, test, and deploy models.

➤ **GitLab CI/CD** is another software automation tool that can automate training, testing, and deployment and is particularly useful for version control of the model artifacts.

➤ **Azure DevOps** is a set of development tools that includes Azure Pipelines, which can be used to create CI/CD workflows for models.

➤ **Kubeflow and MLflow** are open-source platforms for orchestrating machine learning workflows.

➤ **TensorFlow Extended (TFX), Azure Machine Learning, and Google Cloud AI Platform** are end-to-end platforms to build, train, and deploy machine learning models.

EXERCISE: IMPLEMENTING CI/CD FOR MODELS USING JENKINS

Goal: Automate the process of training, testing, and deploying a model using Jenkins.

TASK NAME	TASK DESCRIPTION	TASK OWNERS
Set up a Jenkins Pipeline	Install and configure Jenkins to create a continuous integration and deployment pipeline.	DevOps team
Write Scripts	Develop scripts for training, testing, and deploying the model as part of the CI/CD process.	Development and data science team
Configure the Pipeline	Integrate the written scripts into the Jenkins pipeline and set triggers, parameters, etc.	DevOps and configuration team

TASK NAME	TASK DESCRIPTION	TASK OWNERS
Monitor and Ensure Success	Continuously monitor the pipeline, detect any issues, and ensure the successful deployment of the model.	Monitoring and QA team

WORKBOOK TEMPLATE: *MODEL DEPLOYMENT PLAN*

Download the "Model Deployment Plan" template from the download section of the book (www.wiley.com/go/EnterpriseAIintheCloud). Use this template to plan the model deployment process and ensure that the model performs well when it is integrated into the business processes.

SUMMARY

This chapter discussed the intricate process of deploying models. It started with an introduction to model deployment followed by considerations and challenges in model deployment. It then discussed choosing the right deployment option from cloud to on-premises, edge, and hybrid setups, and choosing an appropriate deployment strategy, including blue/green, canary, A/B testing, and shadow deployments. It addressed the choice between real-time and batch inference and discussed the pros and cons of each approach. It also discussed other deployment best practices such as synchronizing architecture and configuration across environments, striving for identical performance between training and production, and generating insightful governance reports.

In the next chapter, let's discuss how to monitor models for data quality, data drift, concept drift, model performance, bias drift, and feature attribution drift.

REVIEW QUESTIONS

These review questions are included at the end of each chapter to help you test your understanding of the information. You'll find the answers in the following section.

1. Which of the following is NOT a common challenge in model deployment?
   A. Models may not scale well to handle large data volumes.
   B. Lack of integration with backend processes can create data silos.
   C. Models become more explainable and interpretable over time.
   D. Reproducing models for retraining and redeployment can become difficult due to changes in dependencies.

2. Which deployment option can be the most complex because managing and updating models across multiple devices can take time and effort?
   A. Cloud deployment
   B. On-premises deployment
   C. Edge deployment
   D. Hybrid deployment

3. Which of the following is a disadvantage of real-time inference?
   A. It is not scalable for large datasets.
   B. It requires more resources and is expensive to implement.

    C.   It is not valuable for use cases where real-time predictions are essential.

    D.   Predictions can't be stored in a database for later access.

4.   Which step in an inference pipeline converts predictions into a format suitable for other downstream applications?

    A.   Data collection

    B.   Data preprocessing

    C.   Feature extraction

    D.   Post-processing

5.   What do TensorFlow Extended (TFX), Azure Machine Learning, and Google Cloud AI Platform have in common?

    A.   They are open-source platforms.

    B.   They are end-to-end platforms to build, train, and deploy machine learning models.

    C.   They are specifically designed for version control.

    D.   They are data collection tools used in the data preprocessing stage of model development.

ANSWER KEY

1.	C	3.	B	5.	B
2.	C	4.	D		

19

Monitoring Models

What gets measured gets managed.

—*Peter Drucker*

This chapter deals with the critical components of monitoring, including making informed decisions around real-time and batch monitoring. It delves into checking the health of model endpoints, selecting appropriate performance metrics, and ensuring model freshness. To ensure the AI systems remain agile and responsive, you learn how to review and update features, automate endpoint changes, and scale on demand (see Figure 19.1).

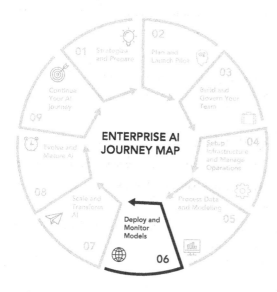

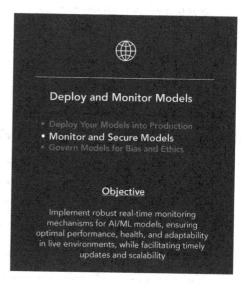

FIGURE 19.1: Monitoring models

MONITORING MODELS

Monitoring models is an essential aspect of MLOps to ensure that the model performs well and that the data used is high quality.

Importance of Monitoring Models in Production

Models are trained based on historical data, and we expect them to work in the same fashion on new data. However, in the real world, things are constantly changing, and hence there is a need to monitor the model and keep it updated. Here are some of the reasons to monitor the models:

➤ Data drift can happen due to changes in input data with respect to training data.

➤ Concept drift can happen due to changes in model performance.

➤ Detect unfair bias introduced by the model.

➤ Changing business needs may require a model to be updated. For example, a retailer may introduce new product lines that require a product recommendation model to be retrained.

➤ New regulations require the model to be retrained.

➤ Model performance can decay over a period of time due to changes in the underlying data distribution.

➤ Ensure the model is robust against all use cases in the real world.

➤ Feedback from the model performance evaluation process requires retraining the model or even choosing a new model.

➤ There are regulatory and compliance requirements to monitor models.

➤ New technological advancements such as the advent of a new or improved algorithm may require you to update models.

> **TIP** *It is important to monitor the models for any changes and update them with new data, algorithms, or any other changes required.*

Challenges Faced When Monitoring Models

Monitoring models in production can be tricky because of a number of factors, some of which are listed here:

➤ Data drift can be hard to determine, and it needs evaluating data distributions.

➤ Degradation can happen slowly and go unnoticed.

➤ When you have multiple models in production, and especially when they interact with each other, it can become complicated.

➤ Edge case scenarios that occur infrequently can be missed.

➤ Black-box models can be difficult to explain.

➤ Monitoring involves overheads, and troubleshooting can be time-consuming.

Addressing these challenges requires a mix of monitoring strategies, tools, infrastructure, and analysis techniques, covered in this chapter.

KEY STRATEGIES FOR MONITORING ML MODELS

You need to employ a combination of strategies to effectively implement model observability to track a model all the way from data to decision-making to performance. I review them here in brief and then cover them in greater detail in the subsequent sections of this chapter.

➤ **Detecting and addressing data drift:** Monitoring statistics such as feature distribution, missing values, data quality issues, and so on

➤ **Detecting and addressing concept drift:** Detecting if relationships between data elements are changing

➤ **Monitoring bias drift:** Detecting unequal performance for various user segments

➤ **Feature attribution drift:** Detecting drift in the feature attribution values resulting from a drift in the distribution of the live data in production

➤ **Tracking key model performance metrics:** Tracking key model performance metrics like accuracy, F1, recall, and so on

➤ **Model explainability:** Explaining model behavior using interpretability techniques

➤ **Ground truth testing:** Evaluating predictions against true outcomes to validate accuracy

➤ **Deployment testing:** A/B testing, shadow deployments, canary deployments, and building validation into CI/CD pipelines

> **TIP** *Do a phased rollout by starting with shadow deployments, and then move to canary before a full-scale deployment.*

The following sections discuss these monitoring strategies in more detail.

Detecting and Addressing Data Drift

For a model to perform well, the data must be complete and accurate. You need to differentiate between data quality and data drift because both impact model performance. When the data is of poor quality, it could mean two things.

➤ The data itself is bad, out of range, or erratic.

➤ The feature engineering code is not working correctly.

While monitoring data quality involves ensuring that the data used to train and deploy machine learning models is of high quality, monitoring for data drift involves detecting changes in the distribution of data used to train and deploy machine learning models.

Data drift can be caused by changes in how data is collected, processed, or stored. Poor data quality can result from errors during data entry, data corruption, or data inconsistencies. While poor data quality can lead to inaccurate results, data drift can lead to decreased model accuracy.

An example of data drift is a model that predicts if a customer will default on a loan. It may have been trained five years ago based on customers with good credit. But over time, the model performance may decrease because customers with poor credit ratings have started to apply in more significant numbers, and your data distribution is no longer the same.

> **TIP** *You need to clearly distinguish between data drift and data quality issues because the resolution is different. For data drift issues, you would need to retrain the model using new data, while for data quality, you would need to clean the data or remove outliers. You can use unsupervised learning algorithms to train the model so that it can adapt to the changing data by changing the hidden structures dynamically.*

There are several methods to detect data drift, such as the following (see Figure 19.2):

➤ Population stability index (PSI), which compares the expected probability distribution in the present dataset with that of the training dataset

➤ Kolmogorov-Smirnov test

➤ Kullback-Leibler divergence

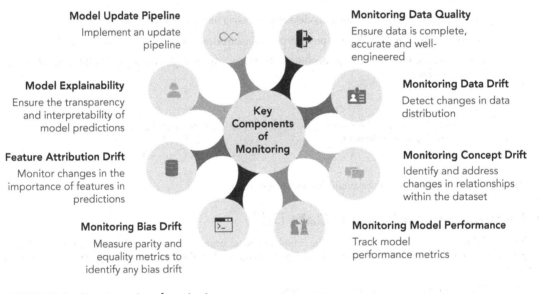

Model Update Pipeline
Implement an update pipeline

Monitoring Data Quality
Ensure data is complete, accurate and well-engineered

Model Explainability
Ensure the transparency and interpretability of model predictions

Monitoring Data Drift
Detect changes in data distribution

Key Components of Monitoring

Feature Attribution Drift
Monitor changes in the importance of features in predictions

Monitoring Concept Drift
Identify and address changes in relationships within the dataset

Monitoring Bias Drift
Measure parity and equality metrics to identify any bias drift

Monitoring Model Performance
Track model performance metrics

FIGURE 19.2: Key strategies of monitoring

> **TIP** *Implement a comprehensive monitoring system that automates the monitoring process to ensure models work accurately.*

Detecting and Addressing Concept Drift

Using the same loan example, say the bank started offering a new type of loan with different characteristics, such as different interest rates or repayment terms. In this case, the relationship between the various features in the dataset to the default behavior would have changed, which is considered concept drift.

You can address concept drift using these steps:

1. Use neural networks to train the model to identify new relationships.

2. Try classification algorithms to capture the new relationships.

3. Use an ensemble of model instead of a single model to reduce the impact of concept drift.

Here are some steps to detect concept drift:

1. Monitor the accuracy and performance of the model to check if the performance is deteriorating over time.

2. Calculate the average confidence score of the model and check if it's deteriorating.

3. Check the data distribution of the training dataset and the new dataset, and if there is a significant difference, then a concept drift may have occurred.

> **TIP** *Plan for periodic retraining of models when significant concept drift is detected.*

Monitoring Bias Drift

Bias drift can happen when the distribution of the data changes. For example, in the case of a product recommendation model, the model has been trained using data for high-income groups; it will perform poorly for lower-income groups. The model will also show bias when the underlying data is also biased.

> **TIP** *To detect bias drift, you must measure metrics such as demographic parity, equal opportunity, and equal odds.*

SageMaker Clarify can help detect bias in the models and is also integrated with SageMaker Model Monitor, which can help detect data and concept drifts.

Watching for Feature Attribution Drift

Feature attribution drift refers to the change in the importance attributed to the feature toward a prediction. If the importance of the feature changes, the model will no longer perform well. It's likely to happen when the model is trained with new features or when the data distribution changes.

> **TIP** *To monitor feature attribution drift, you must track metrics such as featuring importance score and feature correlation.*

An example of feature attribution drift is for a customer churn model; it might have been that the number of years the customer has been with the company may have been the most critical feature, but when a competitor introduces a new product, the customers may churn. Their stay with the company will no longer be a significant factor.

While it is true that implementing a comprehensive monitoring system can be very intensive, it can automate the monitoring effort and save you a lot of manual effort and time to ensure the models are working accurately.

> **TIP** *SageMaker Model Monitor can help detect data and model drifts in real time by evaluating the inputs and outputs and sending you alerts.*

Model Explainability

Model explainability is about explaining how the model makes its predictions so that it can be trusted. It is essential as it helps you understand the root causes of a specific prediction and avoid biases. You need to know how each feature contributes to the prediction and whether the prediction is in line with the existing domain knowledge. It requires measuring metrics related to model quality, fairness, and drift.

> **TIP** *Where possible, opt for models that are inherently more interpretable. Leverage tools like LIME or SHAP to understand complex model behaviors.*

TRACKING KEY MODEL PERFORMANCE METRICS

The choice of model performance metrics depends on the type of problem that you are trying to solve. Figure 19.3 is a brief look at some of those categorized by the type of problem.

Classification Metrics

The previous chapter discussed classification metrics, including accuracy, precision, recall, F1 score, AUC-ROC, and confusion matrix.

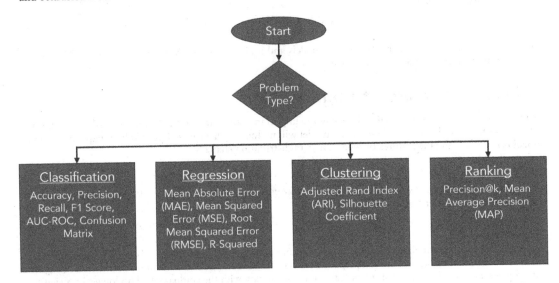

FIGURE 19.3: Choosing model performance metrics

Regression Metrics

Consider these regression metrics:

➤ **Mean absolute error (MAE):** This gives an idea of how wrong the predictions were and is calculated by taking the average of the absolute differences between the predicted and actual values.

➤ **Mean squared error:** This is similar to MAE except that the differences are squared before averaging, so they accentuate the more significant errors more than the MAE.

➤ **Root mean squared error:** As the name suggests, it is the square root of the MSE.

➤ **R-squared:** Also known as the coefficient of determination and is the proportion of the variation in the dependent variable that is predictable from the independent variable(s).

Clustering Metrics

Adjusted Rand index and silhouette coefficient are two clustering metrics.

➤ **Adjusted Rand index (ARI)** measures the similarity between two data clusters.

➤ **Silhouette coefficient** identifies a model that has better-defined clusters. It provides a visual way to assess clusters.

Ranking Metrics

Precision@k and mean average precision are two metrics used to measure rankings.

➤ **Precision@k** measures how many of the first k recommendations are in the set of true positive items. True positive is when the actual and predicted values are the same.

➤ **Mean average P(MAP)** is used to measure the ranking of the recommended items.

> **TIP** *Set reasonable ranges for metrics, and when the performance falls out of range, trigger a review or retraining process.*

REAL-TIME VS. BATCH MONITORING

You can monitor your models either in real time or as a batch process. Your choice will depend upon several factors, some of which are mentioned next.

When to Use Real-Time Monitoring

In the case of real-time monitoring, data is collected in real time and analyzed in real time. Real-time monitoring is required if your model is used in healthcare or finance use cases, where you need to respond quickly to data changes or take quick action in response to predictions. The real-time option is the way to go if you have stringent latency requirements.

When to Use Batch Monitoring

Batch monitoring is appropriate when the requirement is to get a comprehensive view of the model's performance. Data is collected over a period of time and is analyzed at a later time.

> **NOTE** *If the data under consideration is extensive, real-time monitoring may not be an option. Real-time monitoring is also more expensive.*

TOOLS FOR MONITORING MODELS

This section describes some commonly used tools to monitor models. We can broadly classify them into three types: cloud provider tools, open-source libraries, and third-party tools. Note that this is not an exhaustive list.

Cloud Provider Tools

The following tools are available from major cloud providers:

➤ **Amazon SageMaker Model Monitor** is specifically designed to monitor models to detect and remedy model quality issues and does not require any manual intervention.

➤ **Azure Machine Learning and Azure Application Insights** tracks web apps for performance and failures.

➤ **Google Cloud's AI platform and Google Cloud Operations suite** monitors Google cloud services.

➤ **IBM Watson OpenScale** provides a similar functionality.

Open-Source Libraries

In this category, you have the following options:

➤ **Evidently, Prometheus,** with **Grafana** monitor model performance, data, and fairness.

➤ **Amazon Deequ** is a validation library for Apache Spark.

➤ **Tensorboard** tracks TensorFlow models.

Third-Party Tools

A number of third-party tools such as Whylabs, Arize, Datadog, Monte Carlo, Labelbox, and Seldon are worth checking out.

> **TIP** *Choose cloud provider tools for scale, open-source tools for customizability, and third-party tools for an end-to-end integrated solution.*

BUILDING A MODEL MONITORING SYSTEM

You need to consider some things before deploying your model in production from a monitoring standpoint (see Figure 19.4).

1	2	3	4	5
Decide on the Model Metrics	**Set Up the Thresholds**	**Employ a Monitoring Service**	**Set Up Alerts**	**Conduct Periodic Reviews**
Monitor infrastructure health, endpoint responses, track model versions and data	Establish statistical, business, and adaptive thresholds	Use monitoring services like Amazon CloudWatch and AWS Cost Profiler to track metrics	Configure alerts for issue detection	Perform regular checks and adjust metrics and thresholds

FIGURE 19.4: Monitoring the health of your endpoints

Determining the Model Metrics to be Monitored

First, you must decide on the metrics you should monitor for your model endpoint once the model is deployed. You should do the following:

➤ Monitor metrics to measure the health of the infrastructure hosting the endpoint. The metrics used to measure the health of the underlying compute resources are memory and CPU/GPU usage, ML endpoint invocations, and latency.

> **NOTE** *You can use Amazon SageMaker Model Monitor to monitor the quality of the models and send metrics data to CloudWatch.*

➤ Monitor the health of the endpoint responses. The metrics used to monitor the model responses are the accuracy and number of errors in the model response. You can use Amazon SageMaker Clarify to identify bias and feature attribution drift.

➤ Track and trace these metrics to the model's version or the data used for these predictions.

Setting Up the Thresholds for Monitoring

Thresholds determine whether a metric is acceptable within a specific range, and alerts are triggered when exceeded.

You can set **statistical thresholds** for triggering alerts if the average prediction accuracy over time falls below a certain percentage. You can also set **business thresholds** based on business impact, where the threshold level may vary depending on the criticality of the metric. In other cases, you might have an **adaptive threshold,** where the threshold varies depending on certain factors, such as the time of day.

Ensure you review the thresholds periodically because the models and data change and the thresholds may have to be changed accordingly.

Employing a Monitoring Service with Dashboards

You must employ a monitoring service that provides dashboards and reports to track these metrics. For example, you can use Amazon CloudWatch to track the metrics of your SageMaker deployments. You can use Amazon EventBridge to automate event responses and AWS Cost Profiler to keep tabs on expenses.

Setting Up Alerts

You should also set up alerts to be notified in case of an issue, such as increased memory utilization, a sudden increase in latency, and so on. Integrate them with other notification systems such as emails, SNS, SMS, and even Slack.

> **TIP** *Ensure the alerts also have the necessary information as to what went wrong and possibly the root cause so that you can act on them.*

Conducting Periodic Reviews

Finally, conduct periodic reviews to ensure you have the right metrics and thresholds and make necessary changes as needed.

MONITORING MODEL ENDPOINTS

Model endpoint best practices such as automating endpoint changes, implementing a recoverable endpoint, and autoscaling endpoints ensure models perform reliably and help identify opportunities to improve predictions, reduce costs, and avoid failures.

Automating Endpoint Changes Through a Pipeline

Every time you change the model, you must manually deploy that change to the endpoint. It is an error-prone, time-consuming process. A better way to do that is to use a pipeline that does the following:

➤ Checks out the latest version of the model code

➤ Builds the model

➤ Deploys the model to the endpoint

By integrating the endpoint into the change management system, you can track every time a new model is deployed to the endpoint. When you face a problem during a deployment, you can roll back to the older version. This process is not only automatic, but it also reduces downtime. You could use a change control system such as Git and CI/CD pipeline management tools like Jenkins, GitLab, or AWS CodePipeline.

> **TIP** *By automating the model deployment to the endpoint, you can eliminate the errors and reduce the downtime, which will reflect in the improved accuracy of your model, thus helping you achieve your business objectives.*

Implementing a Recoverable Endpoint

It is vital to have a recoverable endpoint and a solid version control strategy if your system goes down because of errors or any other reason. You must ensure all components relevant to the hosting model endpoint are version controlled and the relationships between these components are maintained in a lineage tracker system. Maintaining all the versions will help you maintain backups of all these components, and maintaining the relationships will help you roll back when the situation demands. Figure 19.5 shows the different steps involved to implement a recoverable endpoint.

Consider how to achieve this using AWS services.

➤ You can implement **Amazon SageMaker Pipeline** to automate the development, training, and deployment of the models and switch between versions seamlessly.

➤ Using **SageMaker Projects,** you can enable collaboration between the data scientists and the developers by bringing all the necessary components to build an end-to-end ML solution under one umbrella. These components could include the pipeline executions, the registered models, the ML code, the datasets, and the endpoints.

➤ At the same time, we can use the **AWS CloudFormation** tool to manage the infrastructure as code to manage different versions of the infrastructure and revert to different versions if necessary. You can store the code in **AWS CodeCommit** repositories.

➤ You can use **Amazon's ECR** as a container registry to manage different versions of the containers and revert to different versions as needed.

➤ Finally, you can use **AWS SageMaker Lineage** to track the relationships between all these components and troubleshoot issues quickly.

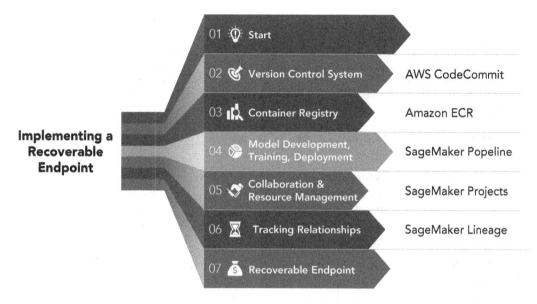

FIGURE 19.5: Implementing a recoverable endpoint

> **TIP** *Plan for scale and prepare for the unexpected and leverage tools to automate pipelines, control versions, centralize components, track lineage, and adopt autoscaling.*

Implementing Autoscaling for the Model Endpoint

As you start taking more and more workload, ensuring that your model endpoint can serve customers with the same quality of service is essential. You can achieve this by implementing autoscaling of your model endpoint.

Configure Automatic Scaling Using SageMaker Endpoint

SageMaker Endpoint can automatically increase or decrease the number of EC2 instances attached to the model endpoint based on the workload or the number of inference requests. The advantage of this approach is that there is no need for manual intervention.

Leverage Amazon Elastic Inference

Another thing that you can do is, in addition to configuring the right-sized EC2 instances with the required CPU and memory power, is configure Amazon's Elastic Inference, which helps the system choose the correct number of GPU-powered inference accelerations to serve the load.

> **EXERCISE: MACHINE LEARNING OPERATIONS (MLOps) EXERCISES**
>
> The field of MLOps is complex and requires a combination of technical skills, strategic thinking, and effective implementation. This chapter contains a set of hands-on exercises that cater to different aspects of a machine learning pipeline, reflecting real-world scenarios. From
>
> *continues*

continued

setting up alerts and monitoring dashboards to automating deployment and ensuring scalability, these exercises are reflective of most MLOps responsibilities. It is vital that the different task owners in these exercises collaborate with each other to deploy these configurations. Of course, in your specific organization, these titles may vary, and therefore I recommend you tailor them accordingly.

TASK NAME	TASK DESCRIPTION	TASK OWNERS	DELIVERABLES
Setting up thresholds	Define and simulate alerting thresholds including statistical, business, and adaptive thresholds.	Monitoring team	Alerting rules, simulation script, and documentation of thresholds
Monitoring service with dashboards	Set up CloudWatch for monitoring SageMaker deployments and create widgets for specific metrics.	DevOps team	CloudWatch dashboard, monitoring configurations, and response documentation
Setting up alerts	Integrate alerts with email or Slack using Amazon SNS and create conditions for alerts.	Alerting team	SNS topic, subscription setup, alerting script, and integration documentation
Conducting periodic reviews	Create a review schedule for a hypothetical model and define the review process.	Model review team	Review schedule, review process documentation, and potential change recommendations
Choosing model performance metrics	Implement various metrics for classification, regression, clustering, and ranking using sample data.	Data science team	Code for calculating metrics, comparison report of different metrics
Updating model regularly	Simulate the updating of a model with new data and algorithms, demonstrating data drift handling.	ML engineering team	Updated model, data drift simulation, and update documentation

TASK NAME	TASK DESCRIPTION	TASK OWNERS	DELIVERABLES
Keeping models fresh with scheduler	Implement a retraining pipeline using tools like Apache Airflow or AWS Step Functions.	Pipeline team, DevOps team, MLOps team	Retraining pipeline, schedule, and performance tracking over time
Automating endpoint changes	Automate the deployment of a model using Jenkins, GitLab, or AWS CodePipeline.	Deployment team, DevOps team, MLOps team	CI/CD pipeline, automated deployment script, and rollback procedures
Implementing a recoverable endpoint	Use AWS services to create a version-controlled, recoverable endpoint.	Recovery team, DevOps team, MLOps team	Version-controlled endpoint, recovery procedure, and lineage tracker system setup
Implementing autoscaling	Configure autoscaling for a SageMaker endpoint and simulate different loads.	Scalability, DevOps team, MLOps team	Autoscaling configuration, load simulation script, and Elastic Inference setup

OPTIMIZING MODEL PERFORMANCE

It is vital to ensure optimal levels of model performance by continuously evaluating various aspects of models such as data, features, and hyperparameters. Some of these techniques include the following:

➤ Reviewing features periodically

➤ Implementing model update pipeline

➤ Keeping models fresh with schedulers

➤ Monitoring data distributions

➤ Performing A/B testing

➤ Checking for skewed distributions

➤ Applying data balancing

➤ Detecting outliers and anomalies

➤ Tuning hyperparameters

This section delves into reviewing features periodically, implementing model update pipelines, and keeping models fresh with scheduler pipeline (see Figure 19.6).

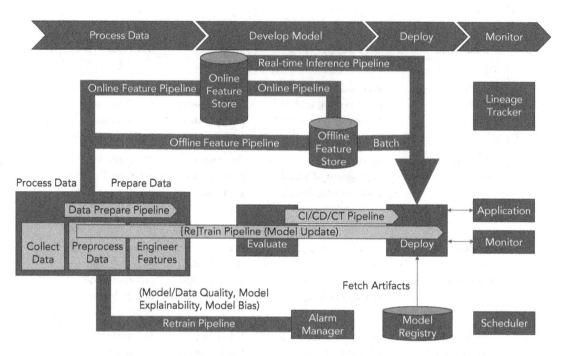

FIGURE 19.6: ML lifecycle

Reviewing Features Periodically

Depending on the changes in your business environment, you must schedule a periodic review of your features used in the model. This will help you ensure that your model is performing accurately. As part of this process, you must not only review for new features that are impacting your model performance but also explore the opportunity to improvise upon the existing feature sets in your model.

You can use AWS Data Wrangler to look for features that were not used in the original model as well as to review existing features for improvement opportunities.

How frequently you review the features will depend upon how frequently your business environment changes.

Implementing a Model Update Pipeline

You need to have a model update pipeline in place, which gets triggered in the case of any violations in the performance of the model. This pipeline should activate the data prepared pipeline, the feature pipeline, and the CI/CD/CT pipeline.

This retraining process will ensure that the new data is cleansed before feeding into the model and new features are engineered, if required, in the CI/CD/CT pipeline, ensuring that the model is trained and tested before deploying into production. This way, the model is continuously retrained with new data and can continue to make accurate predictions.

Keeping Models Fresh with a Scheduler Pipeline

The scheduler pipeline plays a vital role in keeping the AI models fresh. When new data comes into the model, the data distribution and patterns can change, impacting the accuracy of the model predictions. When that happens, it is essential to retrain the model so that its predictions reflect the input data.

For example, the patient's health may depend on several factors. However, these factors can change with time, a phenomenon known as **concept drift**. There may have been a disease outbreak that caused a change in these factors. Under such situations, you need to retrain your model; this is where a scheduler pipeline can greatly help. The scheduler pipeline retrains the model at predefined business intervals, which helps keep the model always reflective of the latest data patterns.

The data preparation pipeline gets activated when the scheduler pipeline activates the retraining process. The data preparation pipeline collects and cleans the new data for use in a model.

At the same time, the feature pipeline gets activated, which extracts the important or relevant features from the prepared data to feed into the model.

Once the model gets retrained with the new features and when done, the CI/CD/CT pipeline gets activated. During this process, the trained model gets integrated with the rest of the system, is then deployed to the production environment, and then tested to ensure its functionality and performance are intact.

> **TIP** *A scheduler pipeline ensures that the model is constantly kept up-to-date even if the data or model drift happens.*

WORKBOOK TEMPLATE: *MODEL MONITORING TRACKING SHEET*

Download the "Model Monitoring Tracking Sheet" template from the download section of the book (www .wiley.com/go/EnterpriseAIintheCloud). Use this template to ensure that the model is delivering the expected results and is in line with the business goals. Keep track of key performance indicators, issues, and necessary updates.

SUMMARY

This chapter discussed monitoring models and the key components of monitoring, such as monitoring data quality, data drift, concept drift, model performance, bias drift, and feature attribution drift. It discussed real-time versus batch monitoring and the tools for monitoring models.

To ensure resilience and recovery, the chapter also covered advanced topics such as automating endpoint changes through a pipeline, implementing recoverable endpoints, and autoscaling to handle variable workloads.

At this point, you should be equipped with the knowledge and strategies to not just deploy but also to monitor your models to ensure reliability, scalability, and performance. Needless to say, this is just the beginning of your learning journey, but I hope this chapter has given you a good start.

In the next chapter, let's deal with model governance nuances such as ethics, bias, fairness, explainability, and interpretability.

REVIEW QUESTIONS

These review questions are included at the end of each chapter to help you test your understanding of the information. You'll find the answers in the following section.

1. What is the main purpose of monitoring model performance?
   A. To ensure that the model performs above a certain threshold
   B. To detect bias in the model's predictions
   C. To monitor the distribution of the data used to train the model
   D. To predict future changes in the model's accuracy

2. Which of the following performance metrics for regression problem gives an idea of how wrong the predictions were?

    A. Mean absolute error (MAE)

    B. Mean squared error

    C. Root mean squared error

    D. R-squared

3. Which clustering metric measures the similarity between two data clusters?

    A. Mean average precision (MAP)

    B. Adjusted rand index (ARI)

    C. Silhouette coefficient

    D. Precision@k

4. What is the concept drift in the context of AI models?

    A. The idea that the factors impacting the output of a model may change over time

    B. The phenomenon that AI models become outdated if not updated regularly

    C. A situation where the model's accuracy improves over time

    D. The occurrence of errors in AI models as a result of excessive retraining

5. How can you identify sensitive data such as personally identifiable information (PII) and intellectual property in your system?

    A. By enabling data access logging

    B. By classifying your data using tools such as Amazon Macie

    C. By monitoring data to look for any anomalous incidents

    D. By using threat detection services

ANSWER KEY

1.	A	3.	B	5.	B
2.	A	4.	A		

20

Governing Models for Bias and Ethics

In matters of truth and justice, there is no difference between large and small problems, for issues concerning the treatment of people are all the same.

—*Albert Einstein*

This chapter dives into governing models, explaining why they are more than just a regulatory concern and are an integral part of responsible AI. This chapter serves as your guide to deal with nuances such as ethics, addressing bias, ensuring fairness, and diving into making models explainable and interpretable (see Figure 20.1).

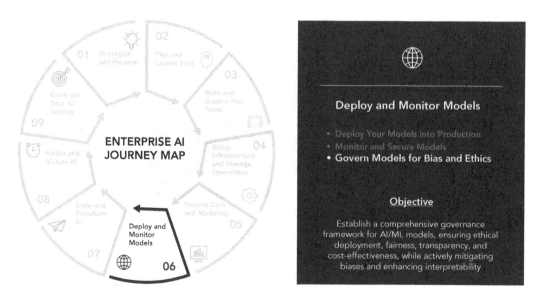

FIGURE 20.1:   DEPLOY AND GOVERN MODELS: Govern models for bias and ethics

Whether you are implementing augmented AI for human review, managing artifacts, controlling costs, or setting up an entire AI governance framework, this chapter can guide you.

IMPORTANCE OF MODEL GOVERNANCE

You know that AI is a powerful technology, but ensuring that innovation happens responsibly is also essential. Consider these reasons why governance is critical:

➤ Ensuring that the models are deployed and governed ethically and responsibly and employed in a non-discriminatory manner is critical for society.

➤ We need to ensure that the models protect data privacy and comply with various regulations such as HIPAA. GDPR, and CCPA.

➤ Models unintentionally perpetuate bias, and it's essential to conduct periodic audits and take corrective actions where needed.

➤ We need to implement measures so that we can explain and interpret how models make their predictions.

➤ We can build customer trust by adopting strict governance and compliance processes.

➤ By complying with regulations, we can also avoid potential financial penalties.

STRATEGIES FOR FAIRNESS

This section explores different strategies to ensure fairness in your models. See Figure 20.2.

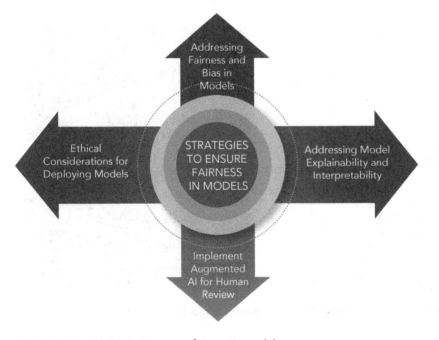

FIGURE 20.2: Strategies to ensure fairness in models

Addressing Fairness and Bias in Models

Bias and fairness are used interchangeably. Bias is a statistical concept of a model, and it refers to the difference in its predictions for specific groups or populations. Fairness is a much broader and subjective concept, and it refers to the absence of any discrimination against a particular group of people.

Consider these steps for mitigating bias:

1. First, you need to check if any groups are overrepresented or underrepresented and also look for labels or features with inherent biases.

2. You can correct bias using resampling techniques or generating synthetic data to balance their representation.

3. You can also deliberately adopt algorithms with built-in fairness mitigation constraints used during training.

4. You can update the model's thresholds during inference to equal error rates across different groups.

5. Lastly, you'll adopt tools such as SHAP, LIME, or tools like Amazon SageMaker Clarify to understand how these models work so you can address bias accordingly.

> **TIP** *Schedule periodic bias audits, preferably by a third-party to ensure an unbiased review.*

EXERCISE: ANALYZING FAIRNESS AND BIAS

Goal: To understand and mitigate biases in a given dataset.

TASK DESCRIPTION	TASK OWNER	DELIVERABLES
Select a dataset: Choose a public dataset that might contain biases related to gender, race, or other factors.	Data analyst	Chosen dataset
Analyze for bias: Utilize techniques such as statistical tests to identify any inherent biases.	Data scientist	Bias analysis report
Mitigate bias: Apply resampling or synthetic data generation to balance the representation.	Data scientist	Balanced dataset
Report findings: Document the process and findings in a detailed report.	Data analyst/team lead	Detailed report of process and finding

Addressing Model Explainability and Interpretability

Model explainability and interpretability are interrelated but with subtle differences. Interpretability is about understanding the model's inner workings in terms of how it came up with its predictions based on the input features.

Model explainability is about trying to make sense of the model's outputs, irrespective of whether the model is interpretable. Model explainability especially comes into play when dealing with neural networks where it is simply impossible to interpret how the model is working due to its complexity.

For model explainability, you can use feature importance scores, partial dependence plots, or more advanced methods like Local Interpretable Model-Agnostic Explanations (LIME) or Shapley Additive Explanations (SHAP).

> **TIP** *Consider setting up a central repository to store model decision explanations that can be referenced later during audits or inquiries.*

Implementing Explainability for Your Models

When working in highly regulated industries such as finance and healthcare, it is essential to ensure that you can explain how the model came up with its predictions.

To begin with, you need to document the explainability needs of your business. For example, you need to decide why you want the model to be explainable. Is it because you want to build trust in your model with your customers by explaining how you came up with a particular decision, or do you want to comply with your regulators?

Next, you need to understand the relationship between the complexity of the model and the difficulty in explaining them. This understanding will help you choose the right model type and develop the proper set of evaluation metrics. That way, you can come up with a performant and explainable model.

You can use SageMaker Clarify to explain the model's predictions. It uses feature attribution to explain which feature contributed to those predictions, and it can also help you to keep track of any drift that arises due to changes in the incoming data distribution and, consequently, the drift in the feature attribution.

SageMaker Clarify can also generate governance reports, which can be helpful to share with your regulators and your risk and compliance teams so they can understand how these predictions were made to ensure the model's fairness and explainability.

Ethical Considerations for Deploying Models

As shown in Figure 20.3, when deploying models in production, you need to factor in a few considerations, such as the following:

➤ Bais and fairness

➤ Transparency and explainability

➤ Data privacy and security

➤ Robustness and reliability

➤ Accountability

➤ Inclusivity

> **TIP** *Regularly discuss with ethicists or an ethics review board and get their sign-off before deploying a model in production.*

FIGURE 20.3: Ethical considerations when deploying models

Implementing Augmented AI for Human Review

Another best practice is to establish a QA system to monitor the performance of your model in production. Set up a team of domain experts who are responsible to evaluate these predictions, especially those that have a low confidence score.

You can use Amazon's A2I, which redirects predictions of low confidence score team for review. It can also randomly sample a set of predictions and forward them to the QA team to review. This approach ensures high accuracy and performance of the model.

> **TIP** *Leverage augmented AI to provide valuable feedback to the AI team that built the model to improve the model parameters when needed.*

OPERATIONALIZING GOVERNANCE

The previous section discussed different strategies to ensure fairness in your models. This section dives into some of the best practices to operationalize governance in the model's lifecycle, from creation to monitoring. It involves tracking the models, including its owners, lineage, versions, artifacts, and costs, and establishing an ethics governance framework.

Tracking Your Models

The following sections cover various steps involved in tracking your models.

Tracking Models, Owners, and Usage for Governance

Tracking the models, the owners, and usage will not only help you in organizing your operations but will also help you with governance. Here are some recommended actions:

➤ **Track all the models** that are developed and deployed using unique identifiers. It will help you to track their usage and performance over time.

➤ **Track the owners** of the model depending upon its stage in the lifecycle. Models may have different owners for development, deployment, monitoring, and performance as well as their governance and usage.

➤ **Track the usage** of the model, how many predictions it made, how often it is used, what are the underlying resources it consumed, and the business outcomes it achieved.

> **TIP** *Store all tracking information in a central repository for access by others for transparency and ease of governance.*

EXERCISE: MODEL TRACKING

Goal: Tracking a model through its entire lifecycle.

TASK DESCRIPTION	TASK OWNER	DELIVERABLES
Create a model lifecycle: Document a full lifecycle of a model from data collection to deployment.	Model architect	Lifecycle design document
Implement lineage tracking: Use tools like AWS SageMaker or MLflow for tracking.	Data engineer/ML engineer	Implementation of tracking tools
Analyze lineage: Analyze the tracked information to understand how a model evolved, how it was built, and how predictions were made.	Data scientist	Lineage analysis report
Write report: Write a report detailing the benefits and challenges of lineage tracking.	Data analyst/project manager	Detailed report on benefits and challenges

Implementing Version Control

You've read about this already, but not from a governance perspective. Make sure you maintain the versions of different model artifacts, which will help you to roll back in case of any issues as well as during troubleshooting. You must track not only the models but also the underlying data, code, model parameters, hyperparameters, and underlying infrastructure.

Adopt nomenclature best practices such as when naming versions, and make sure to include the order of the versions, timestamps, and semantic versions.

Use tools like MLflow, Data Version Control (DVC), and even Git for version control.

> **TIP** *Clean up versions regularly to optimize storage and improve clarity.*

Tracking Model Lineage

Model lineage tracking is the ability to track the model through its lifecycle, and it has many advantages. Here are some of the benefits of model lineage tracking:

➤   It helps to reproduce a model when required.

➤   Knowing exactly how it was built will help explain it to the auditors and regulators.

➤   Knowing how the model was built and how it came up with its predictions will help build trust with the customers and other stakeholders.

➤   Tracking the lineage will help manage the different versions of the model and revert if required due to poor performance.

➤   For the same reasons, it can help with debugging and troubleshooting.

Here are some actions to implement lineage tracking:

➤   Leverage MLOps tools such as AWS SageMaker, MLFlow, KubeFlow.

➤   Leverage version control systems such as Git.

➤   Maintain a tracker of your experiments in a central repository.

➤   Track the metadata such as what model, which data, what hyperparameters, and so on. Implement automation where possible to log your experiments.

➤   Implement access control to ensure collaboration and reuse.

> **TIP** *Ensure lineage data is backed up for future audits.*

Managing Model Artifacts

An essential aspect of MLOps is to manage the artifacts to allow collaboration, reproducibility, troubleshooting, governance, efficiency, and overall better MLOps.

The Importance of Managing Artifacts

This section examines some of the reasons that you need to manage artifacts, as listed in Figure 20.4.

➤   **Reproducibility:** Managing the artifacts will help to reproduce the experiments and train any inferences. Knowing how the model was created, what data was used, and how the inferences were made will help with troubleshooting, explainability, and compliance reasons.

➤   **Collaboration and reusability:** It'll also help machine learning engineers, data scientists, data engineers, and software engineers to collaborate and reuse the models, build upon previous work, avoid duplicate work, and save time.

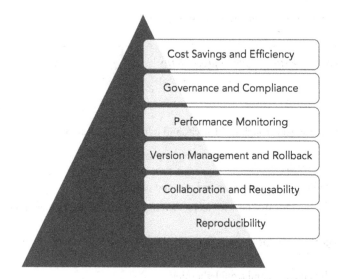

FIGURE 20.4: Different benefits of artifacts management

➤ **Version management and rollback:** Maintaining the versions of these artifacts and their relationships will help you to roll back to a previous version, which will be handy for troubleshooting and auditability.

➤ **Performance monitoring:** When the model performance starts to dwindle, you can try to compare different versions to understand what changed that caused this performance degradation.

➤ **Governance and compliance:** It is important to keep different versions of the artifacts simply for governance and compliance reasons so that we can provide the required documentation to the regulators.

➤ **Cost savings and efficiency:** By implementing an efficient artifact management process, we can remove or archive old files, avoid duplicate files, save costs, and improve efficiency.

> **TIP** *Organize periodic knowledge sharing sessions to familiarize teams with existing models and artifacts.*

Types of Artifacts to Be Stored

This lists describes the types of artifacts that need to be properly managed (see Figure 20.5).

➤ Preprocessed dataset that can be used for future training

➤ Training dataset to reproduce the training process

➤ Test dataset for testing purposes

➤ Validation dataset for validation purposes

➤ Model parameters such as the weights to re-create the training model

➤ Model configuration, such as the hyperparameters, to re-create the training process

➤ Evaluation metrics to evaluate model performance

➤ Logs to help with troubleshooting and performance optimization

➤ Feature engineering artifacts such as feature dictionaries, encoders used, scalars, and so on

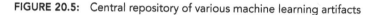

FIGURE 20.5: Central repository of various machine learning artifacts

Best Practices for Artifact Management

Here are some best practices to implement for artifact management:

➤ Implement version control using unique IDs to track different artifacts.

➤ Store the artifacts in a reliable storage system such as Amazon S3 or Google Cloud storage.

➤ Maintain a central catalog or repository of all the model artifacts along with the metadata, such as who trained it, when it was trained, and so on.

➤ Implement proper access control using IAM roles and policies.

➤ Ensure traceability between the model and the data, and the code that was used.

➤ Implement proper retention and archival policies to ensure all data is deleted in a timely manner.

Controlling Your Model Costs Using Tagging

Over a period of time, your costs to host your models can increase, and you would need to manage them proactively. You will need to identify how models are being spent across different environments, such as retraining and posting, as well as across different business units, owners, environments projects, purpose, and so on.

You can implement AWS tagging to keep a tab on these expenses. For example, you can tag AWS instances as retraining or hosting depending upon the purpose for which they are used.

You can then run billing reports based on the tags and understand how these models are used across these dimensions. This visibility will help you control costs by working with various stakeholders.

The visibility of costs using these tags can help not only control the costs but also plan for future expenses based on the cost of running the models and the benefits from them.

Setting Up a Model Governance Framework

Ensuring that a model is deployed ethically and responsibly is not just a technical endeavor but also requires some process initiatives, such as setting up a governance framework.

Setting up a model governance framework involves the steps outlined in Figure 20.6. I provided a hands-on exercise to help you get started.

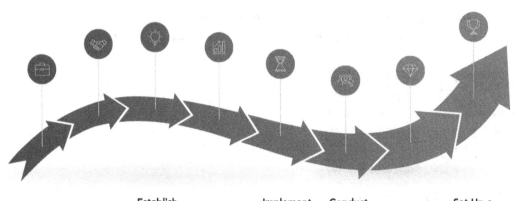

Define Ownership	Establish Policies	Establish Review Processes	Ensure Traceability	Implement Continuous Monitoring	Conduct Periodic Audits	Impart Training	Set Up a Feedback Loop
Establish ownership throughout model's lifecycle	Set policies across the model lifecycle	Implement manual and automated review processes	Ensure traceability for auditing and compliance	Continuously monitor model performance	Periodically audit the governance framework	Impart training on the governance framework	Establish a feedback loop for continuous improvement

FIGURE 20.6: Setting up a model governance framework

> **TIP** *Be inclusive of stakeholders from various departments to get a holistic view when drafting an ethics policy.*

HANDS-ON EXERCISE: SETTING UP A MODEL GOVERNANCE FRAMEWORK

Goal: Promote transparency, governance, compliance, quality, trust, and alignment with organizational objectives through a model governance framework.

TASK	TASK DESCRIPTION	TASK OWNER	DELIVERABLES
Define ownership	Start by establishing the ownership of the model for various stages throughout its lifecycle.	Model governance team	Ownership documentation
Establish policies	Establish policies across the model lifecycle such as fairness, bias, interpretability, explainability, responsible AI, data privacy, security, etc., in line with industry regulations and company guidelines.	Compliance/ regulatory team	Policy documentation

TASK	TASK DESCRIPTION	TASK OWNER	DELIVERABLES
Establish review processes	Establish manual and automated review processes to ensure the model works without bias and with fairness.	Review team	Review process guidelines
Ensure traceability	Ensure traceability by tracking the model's activities across its lifecycle for troubleshooting, auditing, and regulatory compliance.	Audit & compliance team	Traceability report
Implement continuous monitoring	Implement continuous monitoring of the models using tools such as AWS SageMaker Model Monitor to ensure they work within prescribed ranges.	Monitoring & operations team	Continuous monitoring implementation and report
Conduct periodic audits of the governance framework	Ensure adherence to the governance framework through periodic audits.	Internal audit team	Audit reports
Impact training	Impart proper training and awareness about the governance framework and have clarity around everyone's roles and responsibilities.	Training and development team	Training materials and attendance records
Set up a feedback loop	Establish a feedback loop to ensure the governance framework is a living document that gets constantly updated and improved upon.	Feedback and improvement team	Feedback mechanism implementation and improvement plan

WORKBOOK TEMPLATE: *MODEL GOVERNANCE FOR BIAS & ETHICS CHECKLIST*

Download the "Model Governance for Bias & Ethics" template from the download section of the book (www .wiley.com/go/EnterpriseAIintheCloud). Use this template to ensure that the model is not biased and is ethical so that the results are not skewed or discriminatory in any way.

SUMMARY

This chapter delved into the governance of models. Ethical considerations were emphasized, and you explored the topics of fairness, bias, explainability, and interpretability, as well as the implementation of augmented AI for human review. You learned about model tracking, from ownership to version control and lineage, and discussed managing model artifacts and controlling costs through tagging. The chapter concluded with practical steps to establish a robust model governance framework.

REVIEW QUESTIONS

1. Which of the following services is useful for detecting threats like data leaks or unauthorized access?
   A. Amazon S3
   B. Amazon Macie
   C. Amazon GuardDuty
   D. AWS CodeCommit

2. What is the primary difference between model explainability and interpretability?
   A. Explainability is about understanding the model's inner workings, while interpretability is about making sense of the model's outputs.
   B. Explainability is about making sense of the model's outputs, while interpretability is about understanding the model's inner workings.
   C. There is no difference; they mean the same thing.
   D. Both concepts do not exist in model development.

3. Which of the following is NOT typically considered an artifact to be stored and managed in machine learning operations?
   A. The preprocessed dataset used for training
   B. Evaluation metrics to evaluate model performance
   C. Temporary files generated during data cleaning
   D. Model configuration, such as the hyperparameters

4. What is the first step in setting up a model governance framework?
   A. Establish review processes
   B. Implement continuous monitoring
   C. Define ownership
   D. Conduct periodic audits

ANSWER KEY

1.	C		3.	C
2.	B		4.	C

PART VIII
Scaling and Transforming AI

You have built it, so now you can make it even bigger! In Part VIII, I present a roadmap to scale your AI transformation. I will discuss how to take your game to the next level by introducing the AI maturity framework and establishing an AI center of excellence (AI COE). I will also guide you through the process of building an AI operating model and transformation plan. This is where AI transitions from a project-level to an enterprise-level powerhouse.

21

Using the AI Maturity Framework to Transform Your Business

The greatest danger in times of turbulence is not the turbulence—it is to act with yesterday's logic.

—*Peter Drucker*

Having laid the foundation blocks for integrating AI into your business workflows, you will now venture into a pivotal phase: scaling and transforming your business through AI.

This chapter signifies a transformative shift from merely deploying AI systems to aspiring to become a genuinely AI-first company. But then, how do you know you are ready to make the transition? Enter the AI Maturity Framework (see Figure 21.1).

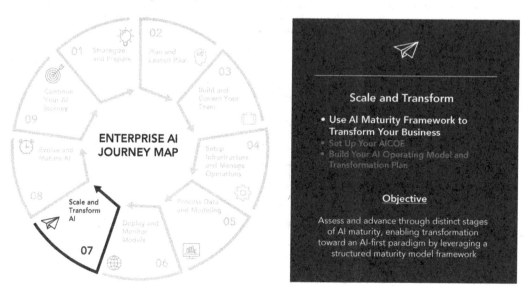

FIGURE 21.1: SCALE AND TRANSFORM: Use the AI Maturity Framework to transform your business

As you navigate this chapter, you will find the AI Maturity Framework to be an indispensable tool. This chapter walks you through the five stages of maturity, starting with the initial discovery, then pilot, operationalization, scaling, and culminating at the Transforming stage, where AI is not an addition but is core to your business strategy and operations.

> **TIP** *Understanding your company's vision and goals so you can conduct a maturity assessment helps identify gaps and enables you to create an AI transformation plan. This, in turn helps you move from pilot to production and makes AI a core part of your business strategy.*

This chapter focuses on leveraging the AI Maturity Framework, a vital tool tailored to guide your business through the transformational journey of AI integration. By understanding where your organization stands in its AI maturity and recognizing the stages ahead, you can strategically plan, execute, and optimize your AI-driven solutions.

SCALING AI TO BECOME AN AI-FIRST COMPANY

Now that you have deployed the pilot in production, it is time for the team to explore expanding AI adoption across the enterprise by identifying more use cases. You will soon realize that you can fully scale your AI efforts only if a few foundational elements are in place. To elevate your AI efforts to the next level, I recommend these three things:

➤ Setting up an AI center of excellence (AI COE)

➤ Developing the AI operating model

➤ Developing the AI transformation plan

These are interrelated, as you will learn after reading the rest of this chapter. The AI COE is responsible for building the AI operating model, a framework for adopting AI. The AI COE is also responsible for developing the AI transformation plan, which is used to implement the AI operating model. See Figure 21.2.

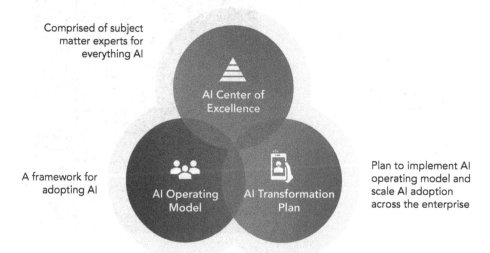

FIGURE 21.2:   Strategic pillars for an AI-first strategy

This section explains how to set up an AI center of excellence to implement AI at the enterprise level. Typically, companies face many challenges during the first six months of setting up an AI COE, so following some of the best practices outlined in this section is wise.

> **NOTE** *Setting up an AI COE is a strategic endeavor and needs careful thought and leadership support.*

Why Do You Need a Maturity Model Framework?

Companies such as Deloitte, Accenture, PwC, and Gartner have researched and concluded that only around 20 percent of companies have been able to go beyond the Envision or Launch phase. One of the reasons is that these companies have found it challenging to align the business, strategy, people, data, platform, governance, and operational capabilities to implement and realize the true business impact of AI. This maturity framework helps you measure where you are in the various stages of AI adoption across various dimensions, such as strategy, platforms, and data. It helps you to put in place the measures to implement AI in production and optimize in the long term for maximum business impact. See Figure 21.3.

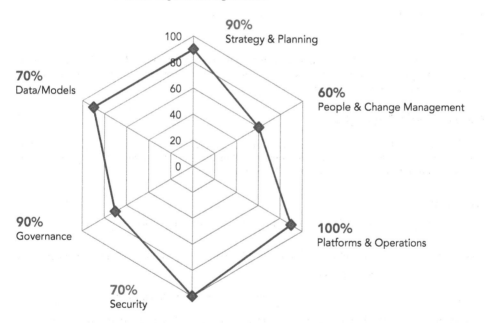

FIGURE 21.3: Sample AI Maturity Framework result

Note that AI is more than just a technology; it is a new way of thinking and operating. To succeed with AI, organizations must become digital at the core.

> **TIP** *To succeed with AI, you must measure AI maturity continuously and address gaps to become more data-driven and AI-enabled, ultimately leading to new products, services, and business models.*

Measuring AI maturity and addressing the gaps will help you assess and scale your business impact from AI systems. As you must have gathered from some of the case studies I presented earlier in Chapter 2, your initial focus will be improving your operations to achieve your business goals. Eventually, your focus will move toward making AI a core part of your organizational strategy, ultimately leading to defining new products, services, and business models.

THE AI MATURITY FRAMEWORK

AI is a complex and multifaceted technology that requires multiple dimensions to work together, and this AI Maturity Framework will help you do that. There are six organizational dimensions and five stages, resulting in a five-by-six matrix that you can use to assess your organization. These six dimensions are as follows:

➤ Strategy and planning

➤ Governance

➤ People and change management

➤ Data/models

➤ Platforms and operations

➤ Security

It is essential to make progress across all dimensions. Otherwise, it's not possible to make good progress overall with AI. For example, even if you make good progress with your platform, people, and operations, you may not succeed if you lack a strong business case for AI.

The Five Stages of Maturity

The five stages of maturity are Discovery, Pilot, Operationalizing, Optimizing, and Transforming. The best way to leverage this model is to assess where your company is in those dimensions and then identify the dimensions that will make the most significant impact when addressed. See Figure 21.4.

The Discovery Stage

You can identify your maturity level based on the following characteristics in the Discovery stage:

Understanding AI	Organizations are just beginning to hear about AI and trying to understand how it can help them.
AI adoption plans	Organizations have yet to make any clear plans to adopt AI.
Business use cases	This is typically handled by those focused on building business use cases and understanding costs and benefits.

During the next stage, they are becoming good at identifying good AI opportunities and start putting together a roadmap to define AI solutions.

Case Study Example

A retail company identified hundreds of potential AI projects but, upon deeper analysis, found that most of them were addressable through traditional programming options. They evaluated the remaining use cases for feasibility, viability, and desirability. This process eventually helped them to develop a strategy and a vision for AI setting them up for the next stage, the Pilot stage.

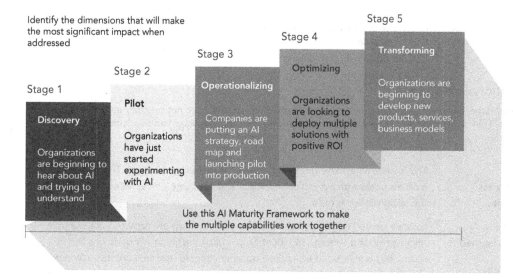

Identify the dimensions that will make the most significant impact when addressed

Stage 1

Discovery

Organizations are beginning to hear about AI and trying to understand

Stage 2

Pilot

Organizations have just started experimenting with AI

Stage 3

Operationalizing

Companies are putting an AI strategy, road map and launching pilot into production

Stage 4

Optimizing

Organizations are looking to deploy multiple solutions with positive ROI

Stage 5

Transforming

Organizations are beginning to develop new products, services, business models

Use this AI Maturity Framework to make the multiple capabilities work together

FIGURE 21.4: Five stages of the AI Maturity Framework

> **TIP** *Use the AI Maturity Framework to conduct self-assessment, perhaps annually, bi-annually, or as needed to identify areas of strength and improvement areas.*

The Pilot Stage

You can identify this stage based on the following characteristics:

Initial experimentation	The organization has just started experimenting with AI and may have done a proof of concept but have yet to put it into production.
Learning and iteration	The organization is still learning and iterating.
Identifying blocks and enablers	The organization's focus is on identifying the blocks and enablers of AI.
Identifying potential projects	The organization is trying to identify which projects can be put into production and how they will measure success.
AI governance	The organization is focusing on AI governance aspects such as reliability and accountability.

Case Study Example

An insurance company wanted AI to enable their claims processing division to add scale. They implemented a proof of concept using deep learning optical character recognition and predictive techniques to improve the process. They curated test data and evaluated metrics to evaluate the project's success. They eventually developed a model that improved their processing rates and saved cost, thus enabling them to work toward putting it into production, which is the next stage—operationalizing.

> **TIP** *Post assessment, chart out a roadmap for the next phase, but be ready to pivot based on your progress and external landscape.*

The Operationalizing Stage

During this stage, companies are trying to formalize their AI efforts and have put together an AI strategy and a roadmap. They are putting their proof of concepts into production. This stage can be identified based on these criteria:

Focus on business outcomes	The focus is on achieving business outcomes for business impact. There are clear business cases with agreed upon metrics and adequate processes and tools to ensure the responsible use of AI.
Capture lessons learned	Lessons learned to improve operations and technology are captured; for example, refining the data strategy and identifying improvements to AI operations and technology are included as a follow-up action item for the next iterative plan and execution.
Get leadership sponsorship	More complex use cases require leadership sponsorship for budget and mandates and ensuring the responsible use of AI.

Case Study Example

A healthcare company wanted to reduce the number of patients missing appointments, as it was causing a lot of operational and financial issues. A proof of concept was conducted, and the number of missed appointments was reduced by 25 percent. They worked with administrative staff and doctors to come up with the requirements for the model. As they gathered metrics on the model's performance and continued to improve, they became satisfied with its performance and confident to deploy it into production.

The Optimizing Stage

During this stage, the companies have put their proof of concepts into production and are scaling AI solutions, measuring their impact, and optimizing AI by making the necessary adjustments. Figure 21.5 and the following table capture some of the key elements that signify this stage.

AI solution deployment	By now, the organization has deployed at least one AI solution in production and is looking to deploy multiple solutions with positive ROI.
Component and model reuse	As more solutions are being deployed now, there is a greater opportunity for component and model reuse, and organizational alignment is important.
Infrastructure and operational challenges	Deploying multiple AI solutions causes additional challenges in managing infrastructure and operations, which requires additional investment and stakeholder buy-in.

Operational maturity	In the final stages, the organization has achieved maturity in development and deployment operations.
Ethics framework	The organization has developed an ethics framework for the responsible use of AI across the company.
C-level support and alignment	The organization has obtained C-level support for multiple AI deployments and achieved organizational alignment.

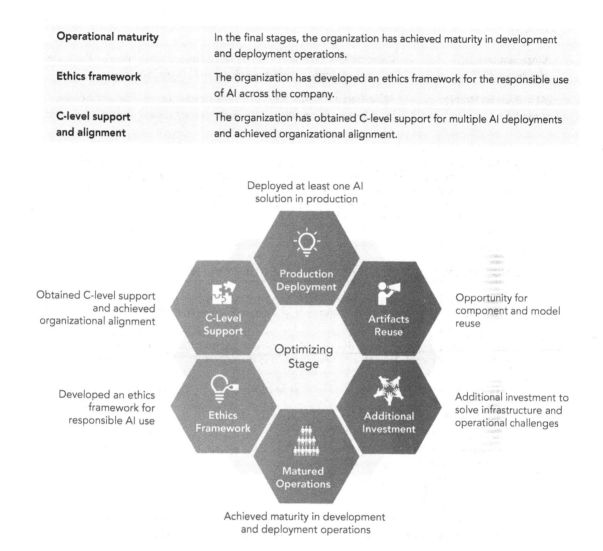

FIGURE 21.5: Key elements of the Optimizing stage

Ensure that ethics is ingrained in your AI strategy.

The Transforming Stage

During this stage, companies are transforming their businesses with AI and have the following characteristics:

New products and services development	They are beginning to develop new products, services, and business models.
AI in budget decisions	AI is a key factor during budget decisions, and executives make their decisions based on AI-driven data and insights.

continues

(continued)

Organizational silo changes	Organizational silos have been broken down to further integrate the teams across data, infrastructure, operations, and business functions.
AI in business strategy and ethics	AI has become fundamental to how business strategy is defined, and the focus is more on deploying AI in an ethical and socially responsible manner.

> **NOTE** *Very few organizations have reached this stage. The companies that have reached this stage either were born with AI from the start, such as Uber and Airbnb, or were digital-first companies that eventually shifted to become AI-first. These are companies such as Amazon and Google. Other traditional companies are trying to become digital at their core before becoming completely transformational through AI.*

HANDS-ON EXERCISE: DEVELOPING AN AI MATURITY PLAN

This exercise will help your implementation team develop a clear understanding of the opportunity areas to advance your AI maturity level and create a plan to improve it.

The following table provides the steps your team can take from self-assessment to tracking progress continuously. At the end of this exercise, every team member should have a clear understanding of their role in advancing your company's maturity level.

TASK DESCRIPTION	TASK OWNERS	DELIVERABLES
Discovery: Ask each member to individually assess the current AI maturity level and document areas of gaps or concerns using the five stages of AI maturity and the six organizational dimensions.	Strategy team	AI maturity assessment document
Group discussion: Hold a team meeting to discuss the gaps and areas of concerns openly to arrive at a consensus. Encourage open dialogue.	Team leads and department heads	Meeting minutes and identified gaps
Goals identification: Based on the consensus, define goals for each of the six dimensions based on where your team wants to be at the end of a defined period (e.g., quarterly, six months, one year).	Management team	Defined goals document
Document action items: Document clear action items or initiatives for those six dimensions to achieve the goals agreed upon.	Planning and strategy teams	Action items list

TASK DESCRIPTION	TASK OWNERS	DELIVERABLES
Assign task owners: Assign a team member who would be responsible for the action items or initiatives.	Project manager	List of task owners for each action item
Develop a plan with timelines: Attach definite start and completion dates for the tasks or initiatives.	Project management office (PMO)	Project timeline and schedule
Progress tracking: Track the progress regularly toward meeting the goals previously agreed upon and make the necessary changes.	Monitoring and control teams	Progress reports and updates

The Six Dimensions of AI Maturity

To be successful with AI, organizations must improve their maturity in all the six dimensions, namely, Strategy and Planning, People and Change Management, Platforms and Operations, Data/Models, Governance, and Security.

> **TIP** *AI maturity is not just about implementing AI projects but is more about getting maximum value from AI.*

Strategy and Planning

AI strategy is about having a plan in place to achieve the desired level of maturity in the organization. Strategy is the most important of all dimensions, and it helps the organization to understand what it is, why it is doing this, and where and when it needs to happen. Without having a proper AI strategy in place, organizations often find it difficult to have a sense of direction and the business justification needed to proceed with AI. It balances the long-term and short-term goals of the organization. Having clarity in this dimension provides momentum in the other areas of the maturity model and helps the organization move forward more confidently with AI.

Table 21.1 summarizes the maturity stages and explains each one, along with the next steps involved.

TABLE 21.1: The Stages of AI Maturity for Strategy and Planning

MATURITY STAGE	DEFINITION	NEXT STEPS
Discovery	There is no clearly defined strategy for AI. AI is looked upon as a nice-to-have tool. The efforts tend to be either too narrow or too broad, having little to no value to the organization. Internal experts are enthusiastic to try some projects on the side with a view to learning but no value to the organization as such.	Align the business and technical leaders with the need and value of having an AI strategy.

continues

TABLE 21.1: *(continued)*

MATURITY STAGE	DEFINITION	NEXT STEPS
Pilot	Strategy for AI is just beginning to emerge. Some initial use cases are being identified, but still, there is no clear understanding of how AI can add value. Some proof of concepts are being explored with limited funding from one business unit or a team. The onus still lies with the project owner to prove the benefits of AI.	Try to gather leadership support based on the success of the initial POCs.
Operationalizing	A clear strategy for AI has been developed and communicated throughout the organization. There is a shared understanding of what benefits AI can give to the organization and use cases have been prioritized based on their potential impact. Executive support is available for the effort allowing the organization to unlock the budget and provide a mandate to execute its strategy.	Document AI strategy for the organization to establish a shared understanding. Gain a budget and secure C-Suite sponsorship for AI projects.
Optimizing	There's a clearly defined AI strategy for the organization, and their strategy is integrated with the business strategy. There are established processes to manage AI projects. The organization is actively monitoring and measuring the impact of AI on the organization.	Align AI strategy with other organizational roadmaps. Discover opportunities to execute across other BUs or functional teams for maximizing business impact.
Transforming	The organization is continuously refining its AI strategy based on the results and impact. AI is significantly driving value to the business, and there is a culture of innovation and risk-taking.	Sustain momentum by continuing to experiment and innovate with new ideas.

People

This dimension involves having the leadership support and the skills, roles, profiles, and performance measures required to both implement and operate AI successfully (see Figure 21.6).

Chapter 7 discussed the importance of leading people and how to go about building a change acceleration strategy, as well as all the different deliverables that you have to deliver during the four phases in an implementation. It discussed leadership support and defining job roles, responsibilities, and personas. It talked about building the AI training courses and curriculums, as well as transforming the workforce through a talent program. Table 21.2 covers how to measure the maturity of this dimension along the five stages of a maturity model.

Platforms and Operations

This dimension deals with having the right platforms, tools, and operations set up to implement AI.

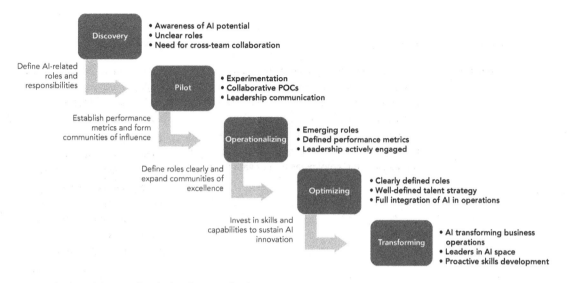

FIGURE 21.6: Maturity levels for the people dimension

TABLE 21.2: The Stages of AI Maturity for People

MATURITY STAGE	DEFINITION	NEXT STEPS
Discovery	Employees are aware of the potential of AI but do not know how to apply it to the business. Organizations do not know how to define roles and responsibilities to implement AI initiatives. Business teams need help from their AI counterparts on how to apply AI to solve business problems while the data science teams need help from the business to understand the business problems that are suitable for AI solutions.	Develop AI literacy for both business and technical teams so they can gain confidence. Obtain help from internal and external AI experts. Encourage collaboration and knowledge sharing between teams.
Pilot	Organizations are trying to experiment with AI using different roles and responsibilities. They should resist the temptation to allow AI teams (data scientists, BI, or data analysts) to operate independently but should encourage them to use the POC to identify the gaps in other technical and non-technical roles and responsibilities. The leadership should communicate their AI vision to the teams and ensure that different teams and experts are enlisted to be involved in these experimental projects.	Cross-functional and matrix teams across technical and nontechnical departments should own the AI POC effort. Organize learning activities such as hackathons, virtual training, demos. Identify AI career paths and explore implications to workforce planning.

continues

TABLE 21.2: *(continued)*

MATURITY STAGE	DEFINITION	NEXT STEPS
Operationalizing	New roles and responsibilities are emerging. Performance metrics are defined to track AI performance of employees. Centers of excellence and communities of influence are being established to fill up resources for these new roles. Leadership is actively engaged in communicating the vision to the employees to motivate them to participate in the new vision.	Organizations need to clearly define who's responsible for leadership, budget, team structure, and rules. Organizations need to have clearly defined rewards and recognition programs to recognize excellence in performance as well as have clearly defined performance evaluation programs acknowledge AI contributions. Encourage centers of excellence and communities of influence to engage employees outside the formal org structure to facilitate collaboration and knowledge sharing.
Optimizing	Organizations have clearly defined roles and responsibilities for AI. Communities of influence and community centers of excellence have expanded mandates including reaching out to the external AI ecosystem. There is a well-defined talent strategy to enable learning for employees. Leaders are very actively engaged to facilitate organizations through the change. AI is fully integrated into all business operations and employees are skilled in working with AI and are actively contributing to the development and optimization of AI solutions.	Include the AI organization in the discussions for strategy at the executive table with the accountability to achieve enterprise level KPI for AI. Establish formal learning journeys for those involved in implementing and using AI.
Transforming	AI solutions are transforming business operations and the individuals involved in AI are recognized as leaders in this space. The organization is proactively investing in the skills and capabilities of the employees and the leaders to sustain innovation and optimization in the organization.	Empower HR talent teams to use AI as a business transmission tool. Communicate and encourage self-driven AI learning paths to employees to continue their learning journey.

TABLE 21.3: The Stages of AI Maturity for Platform & Operations

MATURITY STAGE	DEFINITION	NEXT STEPS
Discovery	Platforms either do not exist or are disconnected. Operational processes do not exist.	Research new AI platforms and understand the need for CI/CD for AI projects.
Pilot	Some tools are in place for AI and some CI/CD processes are there but not standardized.	Standardize tools and platforms. Establish processes for deploying and monitoring AI.
Operationalizing	Platforms and tools are standardized along with established operational processes that are followed.	Continuously monitor the platforms and tools and ensure scalability and reliability of AI deployments.
Optimizing	Advanced tools are used to monitor models and there is seamless integration between platforms and operations.	Focus on automation and keep exploring emerging AI platforms, tools, and operations best practices.
Transforming	Platforms are self-evolving, and operations are mostly automated. AI projects are deployed automatically with minimal manual involvement.	Foster innovation allowing teams to experiment with new platforms and operational strategies.

Data/Models

In this dimension, you focus on ensuring the data is clean, unbiased, reliable, and available. The models need to be scalable, accurate, ethical, optimized, and relevant.

TABLE 21.4: The Stages of AI Maturity for Data/Models

MATURITY STAGE	DEFINITION	NEXT STEPS
Discovery	Data is siloed and is of poor quality, and few models, if any, have been developed.	Centralize storage of data and set up data cleaning processes. Start with simple models to understand data patterns better.
Pilot	Data pipelines have been started in development. Models have been developed in pilots but not in production yet.	Streamline data pipelines and focus on putting models into production and validation of models.
Operationalizing	Data is regularly cleansed, and data pipelines are implemented. Models are in production but need to be monitored.	Focus on getting consistent data quality and implementing model versions.
Optimizing	You have a robust data infrastructure. Models are regularly updated and optimized for performance.	Explore A/B testing and automated feature engineering updates for performance optimization.
Transforming	Data is seen as a valuable asset and models are at the core of the decision-making process.	Encourage a data-driven decision-making culture and continuously retrain models with new data.

Governance

This dimension deals with the ethical use of AI and the alignment of AI projects with the business goals.

MATURITY STAGE	DEFINITION	NEXT STEPS
Discovery	No formal governance structures are in place.	Understand the importance of governance structures and set up initial processes.
Pilot	Initial processes are set but are not enforced or standardized.	Review guidelines regularly and refine them to align with business goals.
Operationalizing	AI governance is clearly communicated, and there are regular audits of AI projects.	Keep refining governance structures based on feedback.
Optimizing	Governance is integrated into AI projects and ethical concerns are paramount.	Ensure governance processes are being adapted to changing situations.
Transforming	Governance is proactive and is changing rapidly in response to changes to the AI landscape.	Continue to foster ethics in all AI projects and regularly review and adapt.

Security

This dimension deals with securing the platforms, tools, infrastructure, models, and data.

MATURITY STAGE	DEFINITION	NEXT STEPS
Discovery	Little to no focus on security.	Try to understand the need for security and initiate some security measures.
Pilot	Some security measures are in place but are not enforced or standardized.	Prioritize data encryption and access controls. Review potential security issues.
Operationalizing	AI security measures are clear and communicated. But there may still be some security lapses or concerns.	Conduct regular security audits to address gaps and ensure all personnel are well trained in security.
Optimizing	Robust security infrastructure is in place and threats are being regularly monitored.	Implement advanced security and threat detection techniques and be proactive rather than reactive.
Transforming	Security is integrated in the DNA of AI projects. Security protocols are continuously monitored and evaluated.	Adopt the latest security techniques and ensure a culture of security first in all AI projects.

HANDS-ON EXERCISE: MLOps MATURITY ASSESSMENT

The goal of this hands-on exercise is to help your team assess the maturity level in MLOps based on various areas such as data management, model development, deployment, monitoring, and team collaboration.

Note that this is an iterative process, and you need to conduct this exercise periodically to improve over time with effort and focus.

TASK NAME	TASK OWNER	TASK DETAILS	DELIVERABLE
Identify Key Areas for assessment	Team leads across various disciplines	Identify the key focus areas in the ML workflow that need to be assessed, for example, data management, model development, model deployment, model monitoring, and collaboration among teams.	A list of key focus areas in ML workflow
Assess Maturity Level	ML team leads and the teams	Assess your organization's maturity level for each identified area. Use a scale such as Discovery, Pilot, Operationalizing, Optimizing, Transforming.	A report indicating the current maturity level in each identified area
Define Improvement Plans	ML team leads and management team(s)	Based on the assessed maturity levels, define plans to improve each area. For instance, implement a new data cataloging tool or develop better data validation procedures for data management.	A detailed improvement plan for each focus area
Prioritize Improvements	ML team leads and management team(s)	You should then prioritize these action items based on their potential impact on your ML process. I suggest you have data management take precedence over model improvements.	A prioritized list of improvement plans

WORKBOOK TEMPLATE: *AI MATURITY ASSESSMENT TOOL*

Download the "AI Maturity Assessment" template from the download section of the book (www.wiley.com/go/EnterpriseAIintheCloud). Use this template to evaluate how advanced your organization is and to identify areas of strength and improvement.

SUMMARY

This chapter covered the various steps you take as you move from the Align phase to the Launch phase and eventually the Scale phase. You used the AI Maturity Framework to evaluate your progress in strategy, people, data/models, platforms, governance, and security dimensions. It is a comprehensive framework to transform your business by adopting AI at the enterprise level. The chapter also discussed how you can take your company from the Launching to Optimizing to Transforming stages by evaluating your progress in these dimensions.

The heart of the chapter was a hands-on exercise to develop an AI maturity plan. It can guide your team from self-assessment to continuous progress tracking.

REVIEW QUESTIONS

These review questions are included at the end of each chapter to help you test your understanding of the information. You'll find the answers in the following section.

1. Conducting a company's AI maturity assessment during the Align phase helps
   - **A.** To identify gaps in the company's vision and goals
   - **B.** To assess the company's AI adoption across various dimensions
   - **C.** To create a proof of concept during the Launch phase
   - **D.** To optimize the company's AI efforts by expanding the adoption of AI

2. Identify the dimension in the AI Maturity Framework that is not discussed in this chapter.
   - **A.** Strategy and planning
   - **B.** Governance
   - **C.** Finance and accounting
   - **D.** People and change management

3. A company is just beginning to hear about AI and trying to figure out how AI can help them. Which stage of maturity are they in?
   - **A.** Pilot
   - **B.** Operationalizing
   - **C.** Optimizing
   - **D.** Discovery

4. What identifies the Optimizing stage?
   - **A.** Improving AI operations and technology
   - **B.** Maximizing business impact
   - **C.** Deploying multiple AI solutions
   - **D.** Developing an ethics framework

5. What identifies the Transforming stage?
   - **A.** Improving AI operations and technology
   - **B.** Maximizing business impact
   - **C.** Deploying multiple AI solutions
   - **D.** Developing new products

ANSWER KEY

1.	B	3.	D	5.	D
2.	C	4.	C		

Setting Up Your AI COE

Great things in business are never done by one person: they're done by a team of people.

—*Steve Jobs*

As you navigate your journey through enterprise AI transformation, you might realize that creating and deploying models into production is just one step of the larger journey toward becoming AI-first. For your company to fully transition into enterprise-wide AI, it needs a holistic approach to integrating AI into its core. And this holistic approach is the crux of this chapter.

This chapter delves into the compelling reasons to establish an AI Center of Excellence (AI COE), one of the three pillars to scale and transform your business with AI. You learn about its team structure, multifaceted roles, and the symbiotic relationship between the COE business and platform teams (see Figure 22.1).

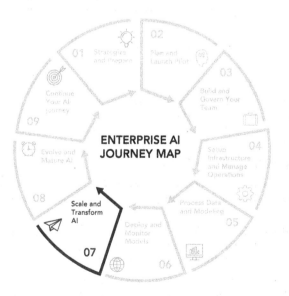

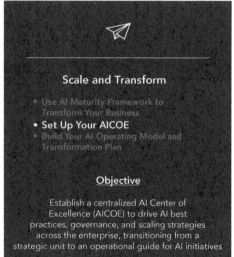

FIGURE 22.1: SCALE AND TRANSFORM: Set up your AI COE

The AI COE serves as an engine, propelling your organization through its transformation phases, and also acts as the AI evangelist to promote AI adoption. This chapter dives into how to evolve the AI COE's role from strategy to operations and its transition from being a central unit to an enterprise-wide advisor.

SCALING AI TO BECOME AN AI-FIRST COMPANY

Now that you have deployed the pilot in production, it is time for the team to explore expanding AI adoption across the enterprise by identifying more use cases. You will soon realize that you can fully scale your AI efforts only if a few foundational elements are in place. To elevate your AI efforts to the next level, I recommend these three things:

➤ Setting up an AI COE

➤ Developing the AI operating model

➤ Developing the AI transformation plan

These are interrelated, as you will realize after reading the rest of this chapter. The AI COE is responsible for building the AI operating model, a framework for adopting AI. It is also responsible for developing the AI transformation plan, which is used to implement the AI operating model.

This section explains how to set up an AI center of excellence to implement AI at the enterprise level. Typically, companies face many challenges during the first six months of setting up an AI COE, so following some of the best practices outlined in this section is wise.

Setting Up an AI Center of Excellence

The AI COE first focuses on transforming your organization from a traditional company into an AI-first company. Typically, you start with a small pilot team, and once you find success, you then start scaling it into a much larger COE. Setting up a full-fledged AI COE can take anywhere from six months to one year or more and requires leadership commitment.

Remember that setting up a COE could also be part of your AI transformation plan to establish an AI operating model in the long term.

> **TIP** *Before starting an AI COE, ensure everyone is clear about its objectives—to foster innovation, streamline operations, or optimize customer experiences.*

Why an AI COE Is Important for Scaling AI Across the Enterprise

Establishing the AI center of excellence is an iterative and time-consuming process, but it is worth the effort. It can help set up the AI/ML infrastructure in addition to defining the AI strategy and vision, planning a portfolio, and establishing the governance aspects of an AI initiative.

Your organization will have its own approach to the AI journey, but here are some basic guidelines and best practices you can follow. The primary function of your AI COE is to be the subject-matter expert on all things AI, which includes the cloud, data, models, governance, infrastructure, operations, and security.

It acts like a central team of experts from various disciplines who can guide the rest of the organization by adopting AI technologies and practices. With the help of the COE, you can ensure that AI is implemented consistently across the enterprise. The AI COE also acts as the central hub for the dissemination of knowledge and skill sets in addition to imparting training to your employees.

The AI COE can also help mitigate the risks associated with AI, such as ethics, social responsibility, bias, and data privacy concerns.

Finally, it can also act as an engine for innovation by promoting a culture of experimentation and innovation by helping to identify new use cases as well as adopting new technologies and approaches.

> **TIP** *Clearly communicate the goals, progress, and achievements of the AI COE to the rest of the organization to build trust and foster a culture of AI adoption.*

AI COE Team Makeup

The AI COE is a multidisciplinary team focused on AI strategy, governance, best practices for AI architecture, implementation, and operations that the rest of your organization can adopt. You should start by having an AI sponsor responsible for the COE's success and ensuring that the team's KPIs are aligned with your AI strategy and business goals.

> **NOTE** *The Center of Excellence team may sometimes also be known as the AI capability team, AI practices team, and so on.*

You should include stakeholders from the business and the technology as part of this AI COE; you could call them the AI business and platform team. You could have people with titles such as IT manager, finance manager, digital ops manager, operations manager, systems architect, systems administrator, application developer, database administrator, DevOps manager, AI engineer, ML engineer, data scientist, data analyst, and BI analyst. You can even have managers from various lines of business, such as finance, human capital, marketing, sales, operations, supply chain, and so on.

> **TIP** *Having a diverse mix of AI experts, data scientists, cloud architects, business analysts, and representatives across various departments is critical to get a holistic view of your organization's needs and challenges.*

AI COE Team Responsibilities

Your business stakeholders have to provide strategy, program management, and governance skills. On the other hand, your technology stakeholders will focus on platform engineering, security, and operations. This team should be able to make quick decisions, and their focus should be to define at least six or so goals, KPIs, key metrics, and core services to be achieved within the next six months.

COE Business and Platform Team Responsibilities

Figure 22.2 shows the various responsibilities that fall under the AI business and platform teams.

ESTABLISHING AN AI CENTER OF EXCELLENCE

This section reviews the various steps you need to execute to form and maintain an active, high-performing center of excellence.

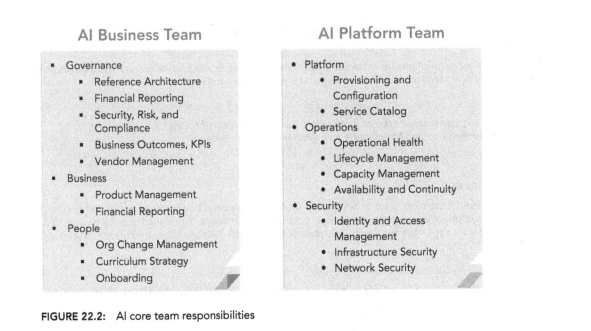

FIGURE 22.2: AI core team responsibilities

From Centralized Unit to Enterprise-wide Advisor

Your AI center of excellence team should be responsible for driving standards for AI across the enterprise. They should start as a centralized unit with a limited set of three to five A-class players who can guide the organization with generic standards. As your organization starts to adopt AI, your AI COE team will also mature. Eventually, your AI COE team should get into an advisory role to promote the best practices across the organization. As part of their efforts, they should develop your company's AI operating model and socialize it across the organization so that various teams can adopt it.

> **TIP** *Empower your AI COE to make quick decisions that will help AI projects and accelerate AI adoption.*

Evolving from Strategy to Operations Focus

Your center of excellence team can shift their focus from strategy to operations over a period depending upon the phase of AI within the organization. To begin, their objectives can be the following:

➤ Strategy

➤ Training

➤ Pilot projects

➤ Scaling

➤ Operating AI

Figure 22.3 shows how your AI COE starts as a centralized unit to becoming an enterprise-wide advisor and shifts its focus from strategy to operations. This is a good visual that you could use in your discussions about AI COE within your company.

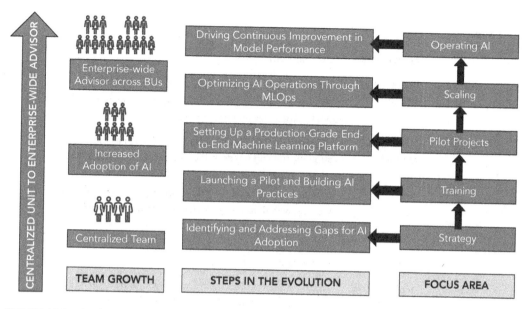

FIGURE 22.3: Evolution of an AI COE

> **TIP** *Embracing an agile approach can help your AI COE adapt quickly to changes and improve iteratively.*

The steps to form an AI COE team are covered next in the form of a hands-on exercise.

HANDS-ON STRATEGIC AND OPERATIONAL PLANNING EXERCISE: SETTING UP AN AI CENTER OF EXCELLENCE

This is a strategic and operational planning exercise focused on setting up an AI Center of Excellence in your company.

It has a series of steps requiring active participation from your team in making decisions, planning, execution, and review. It has components such as forming a team, assigning roles, managing a project, developing strategy, implementing technology, and reviewing performance.

PHASES	ACTIVITY	DESCRIPTION
Phase 1	Gathering the requirements	Gather your team and discuss the need for an AI COE. Document the gaps that can be addressed by this AI COE especially with regard to adoption. Discuss the team make up and identify potential members.

continues

continued

PHASES	ACTIVITY	DESCRIPTION
Phase 2	Planning the AI COE	Plan the roles and responsibilities of the team members. Prepare a charter for the AI COE explaining its purpose, goals, processes, and procedures.
Phase 3	Scoping the AI COE	Identify the initial scope for the AI COE such as the strategy, training needs, pilot projects, scaling strategies, and other operational aspects. Identify training needs and develop the course curriculum working with third-party vendors and internal training teams. Identify the KPIs that will be used to evaluate the performance of the AI COE.
Phase 4	Implementing the pilot project	Identify a pilot project that can help you to develop AI practices that can be adopted for future projects. The goal is to build agile practices and develop sets of AI policies for scaling AI. Implement the project and document the lessons learned. Your team must gain hands-on experience through pilots and demo labs.
Phase 5	Setting up the ML platform	Develop the plan for the ML platform. Implement a production grade, end to end ML platform integrated with data collection systems and appropriate access controls. Different environments such as development, staging, QA, and production are set up, and budget management and cost control practices and governance are also established.
Phase 6	Implementing MLOps	Set up MLOps with automated operations, code repositories, model version control, performance monitoring, notifications, and escalation policies. The team must also be involved in financial tracking, ML model deployment policies, and ensuring that any workload deployed for consumption is production ready.

PHASES	ACTIVITY	DESCRIPTION
Phase 7	Reviewing and Improving	Review the AI COE's performance, its operations, and identify areas of improvement and make necessary adjustments.
		Track the model performance and detect bias, data drift, and concept drift and put measures in place to address them with processes, people, and technology.
		The team must focus on automating everything, tracking everything through a portal, tracking costs, KPIs, and continuous training.

WORKBOOK TEMPLATE: *AI CENTER OF EXCELLENCE (AICOE) SETUP CHECKLIST*

Download the "AI Center of Excellence Setup" Checklist template from the download section of the book (www .wiley.com/go/EnterpriseAIintheCloud). Use this template to help you go through the key components to consider when setting up an AICOE (AI Center of Excellence). You can use it to conduct strategic planning, resource planning, and develop a well-defined roadmap.

SUMMARY

This chapter looked closely at the significance, formation, and the ongoing operation of the AI COE. It discussed how it is one of the strategic pillars for becoming AI-first, including some of the intricacies involved in setting it up and its evolution from a strategic focus to an operational one. Through a hands-on exercise, the chapter offered insights on how to implement an AI COE, including a step-by-step guide to overcome the challenges that you are likely to face.

The path to becoming an AI-first company has been laid. It's going to take leadership commitment, strategic planning, and an unwavering focus on execution. It's your turn to take action.

REVIEW QUESTIONS

These review questions are included at the end of each chapter to help you test your understanding of the information. You'll find the answers in the following section.

1. Conducting a company's AI maturity assessment during the Align phase helps
   A. To identify gaps in the company's vision and goals
   B. To assess the company's AI adoption across various dimensions
   C. To create a proof of concept during the Launch phase
   D. To optimize the company's AI efforts by expanding the adoption of AI
2. Identify the dimension in the AI maturity framework that is not discussed in this chapter.
   A. Strategy and planning
   B. Governance

    C.   Finance and accounting

    D.   People and change management

3.   A company is just beginning to hear about AI and trying to figure out how AI can help them. Which stage of maturity are they in?

    A.   Pilot

    B.   Operationalizing

    C.   Optimizing

    D.   Discovery

4.   What identifies the Optimizing stage?

    A.   Improving AI operations and technology

    B.   Maximizing business impact

    C.   Deploying multiple AI solutions

    D.   Developing an ethics framework

5.   What identifies the Transforming stage?

    A.   Improving AI operations and technology

    B.   Maximizing business impact

    C.   Deploying multiple AI solutions

    D.   Developing new products

6.   Which of the following is important when developing an AI strategy?

    A.   It should be communicated only to the C-suite.

    B.   It should not be flexible and should be followed strictly.

    C.   It should be aligned with the overall business strategy.

    D.   It is fine not to consider the competitive landscape.

7.   The focus of the core team implementing the AI pilot is

    A.   To establish the platform

    B.   To implement AI initiatives

    C.   To conduct a maturity model assessment

    D.   To establish a COE

8.   Why do you need a label in machine learning problem framing?

    A.   It helps to make predictions.

    B.   It helps to evaluate the model.

    C.   It identifies the type of machine learning problem.

    D.   It is a feature created during feature engineering.

9.   What is the primary focus of the machine learning problem framing phase in the machine learning lifecycle?

    A.   Data processing

    B.   Model definition

    C.   Defining the business goal

    D.   Identifying the type of machine learning problem

10.   Feature engineering is used

    A.   To evaluate the model's features

    B.   To collect and preprocess features

C. To create new data and transform existing data

D. To identify the business data

11. The primary responsibility of a machine learning engineer is

A. Running models and drawing insights

B. Ensuring the data pipeline is appropriately implemented

C. Designing the overall AI strategy

D. Deploying models into production

12. The primary role of a business analyst is

A. Collecting, cleaning, and analyzing data

B. Developing and validating assumptions and hypotheses

C. Bridging the gap between business and technical team

D. Developing the project plan

13. What should be the primary focus of the AI COE team?

A. To implement AI technologies consistently across the enterprise

B. To develop AI models that perform responsibly

C. To generate revenue for the company

D. To manage customer relationships

14. What is an AI operating model?

A. A formal structure or framework to implement AI in a scaled manner

B. A model to develop AI solutions for operations

C. A way to align AI operations with business goals

D. A model to operate AI solutions without compliance

15. An AI transformation plan is

A. A plan for implementing individual AI initiatives

B. A plan to increase the maturity levels of the organization

C. A plan to develop AI technologies

D. A plan to outsource AI development

ANSWER KEY

1.	B	6.	C	11.	D
2.	C	7.	A	12.	C
3.	D	8.	A	13.	A
4.	C	9.	D	14.	A
5.	D	10.	D	15.	B

23

Building Your AI Operating Model and Transformation Plan

If you don't know where you're going, any road will get you there.

—Lewis Carroll

You are now standing at an important juncture—architecting the framework that decides how your company will embed AI into its processes and sketch the master blueprint for your AI transformation. This chapter builds on the work done in the previous chapter, where you focused on establishing an AI COE.

Your emphasis now shifts to understanding and implementing an AI operating model that resonates with your organizational ethos to deliver both value and continuous innovation (see Figure 23.1). It is not just about technology or even strategy but is more about taking a customer-centric lens and navigating the intricacies of AI-driven innovation. You will focus on building cross-functional teams, instilling a culture of continuous improvement and innovation, and aligning with core strategic values.

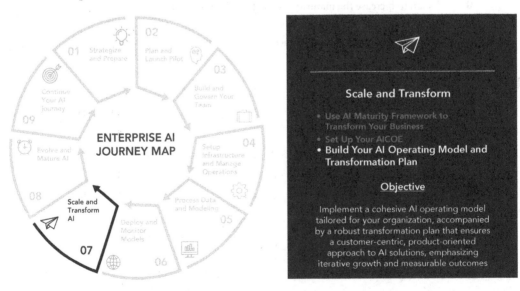

FIGURE 23.1: SCALE AND TRANSFORM: Build your AI operating model and transformation plan

It doesn't end there. You will be crafting a transformation plan tailor-made for you, which will act as a catalyst for transformation to come. You will chart out the long-term vision, objectives, and timelines. A hands-on exercise will help you to draft such a plan.

UNDERSTANDING THE AI OPERATING MODEL

The AI operating model is the second important pillar you need to scale your AI adoption. When you are trying to implement AI at the enterprise level, it is essential to have a formal structure or framework to implement AI in a scaled manner. You will find that the success of your AI initiative depends upon your organizational culture and the existing delivery structures, such as strategic management, program management, portfolio planning, program governance, and so on. You need a critical mass of people in the organization who can productionize and operationalize your AI platform in an AI-centric manner. Typically, organizations add layers of AI technology and project-based management on top of the existing operating models, but they will soon realize that they need a different operating model that is compatible with AI to leverage some of its benefits that go beyond simple business process automation to exploit newer, innovative opportunities as well.

The Purpose of the AI Operating Model

When trying to productionize your POC at an enterprise level, it is effective to keep an eye on establishing a steady-state operating model so you can scale your AI solution deployment to multiple use cases using a repeatable, iterative, and robust development and deployment process. An AI operating model provides a structured approach to take the AI project from ideation to deployment, along with ensuring alignment with business goals, complying with legal regulations, and facilitating collaboration between different teams and stakeholders.

As shown in Figure 23.2, an AI operating model includes the AI strategy; the processes to build, test, and deploy AI solutions; the different roles and responsibilities involved in the initiative; the tools and resources used; and the success metrics to determine success.

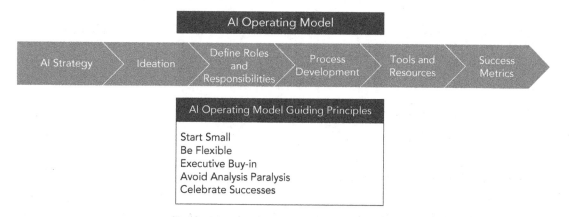

FIGURE 23.2: Components of an AI operating model

By ensuring that these aspects are taken care of, an operating model helps to increase the probability of success of AI initiatives.

> **TIP** *To sustain long-term growth and innovation for your business, position AI as not just a tool but as a force for business transformation through an AI operating model that instills AI-first thinking.*

When Do You Implement an AI Operating Model?

There is no specific time when an AI operating model needs to be developed. However, it is often helpful to define one when an AI initiative is getting started or when the organization has been informally implementing AI and the time has come for them to define a formal framework to increase the probability of success. For example, this could be after the launch, and when they're trying to scale the adoption of AI across multiple use cases, it might be an excellent time to develop the operating model. Another reason they may need an operating model is that they have a clear AI strategy, platform, and resources, but then there is a need to manage AI projects more effectively and measure the success of the projects.

> **TIP** *Some tips for developing a successful operating model are having executive buy-in, starting small, avoiding analysis paralysis, being flexible to incorporate changes as the technology is fast-moving, and ensuring that you celebrate successes, however small or big they may be.*

IMPLEMENTING YOUR AI OPERATING MODEL

Figure 23.3 shows the transformational steps used to build an AI operating model.

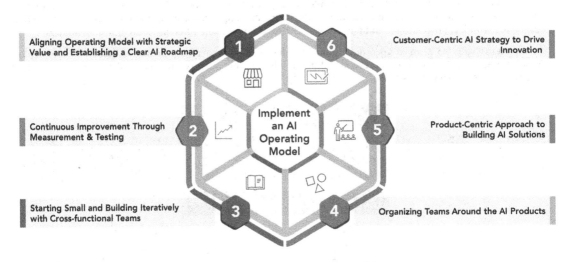

FIGURE 23.3: Six transformational ways to build an AI operating model

Customer-centric AI Strategy to Drive Innovation

This involves looking at your customer's pain points and using data to identify solutions to satisfy your customer's needs. As you can see in Figure 23.4, you must look at the current capabilities across the six dimensions discussed in the earlier chapter and assess them against your current AI operating model. You use that information to prioritize business outcomes and drive innovation without compromising security to come up with new solutions. Remember that this is an iterative, cyclical process where you identify your customer pain points, assess your current capabilities and gaps, prioritize your business outcomes, and then drive business innovation by implementing AI solutions continuously.

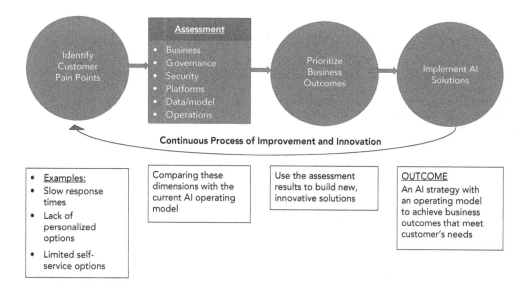

FIGURE 23.4: Customer-centric AI strategy to drive innovation

---

Case Study Example

For example, suppose a customer complains about slow response times, lack of personalized options, or limited self-service options. In that case, you start by assessing gaps in various dimensions such as business, governance, security, platforms, data/model, and operations, assess your current operating model, and devise a plan considering your business strategy. You may realize a talent gap, or the processes must align with your AI strategy. As a result, you may decide to implement a chatbot and come up with a plan along with an operating model to address the customer's concern.

By identifying any blocks to meeting the customers' needs and addressing them, your company can adopt AI successfully across the organization. The outcome is an AI strategy with an operating model that enables achieving business outcomes while meeting the customer's needs.

> **TIP** *Creating a map of the customer journey and tying them to the AI solutions to provide a seamless, connected customer experience is a good practice.*

Using a Product-centric Approach to Building AI Solutions

Building AI solutions from a product-centric approach implies moving away from a system and technology perspective into looking at the world as a set of products.

From an AI perspective, say you are building a chatbot. You can divide the AI solution into products such as natural language understanding, user interface, model for personalized recommendations, database migration, and data lake building, as shown in Figure 23.5.

BREAKING DOWN MONOLITHIC APPLICATIONS INTO PRODUCTS

Amazon broke down its monolithic Java e-commerce application into a collection of individual products such as the home page, the search page, the products page, the account pages, the shopping cart, personalized recommendations, and so on. Behind each one of these products was a team that was entirely focused on enabling that functionality from end to end, starting from the requirements gathering all the way to deploying the solution and making sure it performed well.

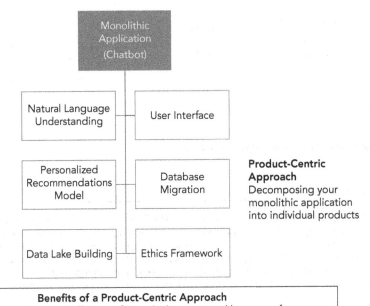

Product-Centric Approach
Decomposing your monolithic application into individual products

Benefits of a Product-Centric Approach
Increased focus, improved efficiency, faster deployment, and better performance

FIGURE 23.5: A product-centric approach to building AI solutions

TIP *Have a dedicated product team for each product or functionality with end-to-end ownership from ideation to deployment to continuous improvement.*

Organizing Teams Around the AI Products

Once the products have been identified, the next logical step is to define teams around this product model so that accountability and ownership can be established around that product (see Figure 23.6).

Establishing this clear ownership makes it possible to meet the customer's needs. While the business stakeholders within the COE are responsible for ensuring that the product requirements are aligned with the customers' business needs in line with the business strategy, platform stakeholders are responsible for deploying the products as reusable code and re-deployable platform components for their customers as required. Automation and self-service capabilities are essential aspects of this productization as they help increase high availability and reliability of the systems and security as well. These teams play a vital role in working together to build the required functionality and ensuring its success by working with the business and the technical stakeholders.

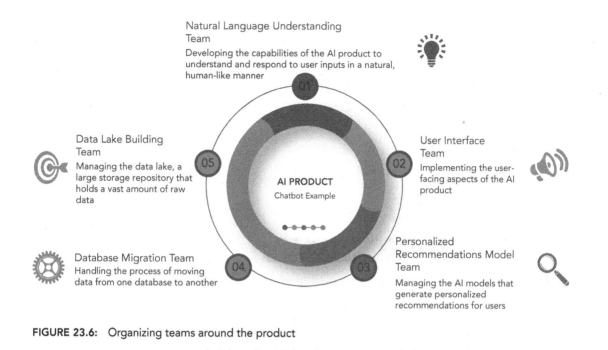

FIGURE 23.6: Organizing teams around the product

Use Case Example

In the case of the chatbot example, you would need to organize teams around the natural language understanding, user interface, recommendation model, database migration, and data lake. These teams would be responsible for setting up their product strategy, vision, and requirements to ensure they perform well in production.

Starting Small and Building Iteratively with Cross-Functional Teams

Another vital aspect you need to consider when establishing an AI operating model is to start small and build iteratively to support AI adoption. The first product team must be an AI pilot team, which should be cross-functional and focus on addressing concerns of viability, desirability, feasibility, and operability. As shown in Figure 23.7, as adoption grows, the AI pilot team should scale and specialize into multiple product teams, such as the AI business office (ABO) and AI platform engineering (APE).

Key roles in the AI pilot team include the product owner, AI architects, data scientists, machine learning engineers, and cloud engineers, with additional roles such as financial analyst, organizational change management specialist, and scrum master potentially added. Initially the pilot team focuses on the viability, desirability, feasibility, and operability of the PoCs, but as the AI adoption grows, you will be able to reap benefits such as increased specialization and greater impact to the organization.

TIP *Celebrating small wins will not only keep your team motivated but will also reinforce the value of an iterative approach.*

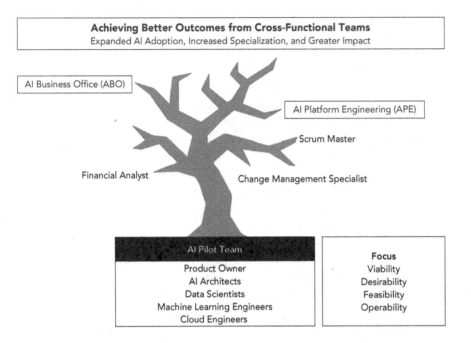

FIGURE 23.7: Start small and build iteratively with cross-functional teams

Continuous Improvement Through Measurement and Testing

Another critical aspect to consider when defining an operating model is ensuring that the product teams incorporate measurement and testing as part of building their solutions (see Figure 23.8). For example, when deploying a chatbot, they need to come up with metrics to measure the success of the chatbot in production as well as incorporate testing scenarios across different products to ensure resiliency is built into the product. As part of this need to build resiliency, the product owner is also responsible for identifying the other products on which this product depends so that they can consider all the dependencies and factor them into the project plan. By identifying the dependencies and incorporating them into the testing plan, it becomes possible for the product teams to test the other dependent services, proactively plan for self-recovery options, and increase the high availability of the products.

Use Case Example

Say your company has a product team responsible for a product recommendation engine that displays upsell/cross-sell products on your e-commerce website. Your product recommendation engine team could establish measures such as the recommendation engine's uptime, response time, and error rate to ensure they are delivering what is expected to meet the customer's needs.

The team may also need to measure other services their product depends on, such as a database or an authentication service. This would allow them to quickly identify any issues with these services that could impact their own product's performance or availability.

To ensure the continuous availability of their recommendation engine, the team could set up a testing environment that simulates the failure of dependent services and ensures their application can still function properly and recover itself in such scenarios. This would help the team identify and fix any issues early on before it impacts customers.

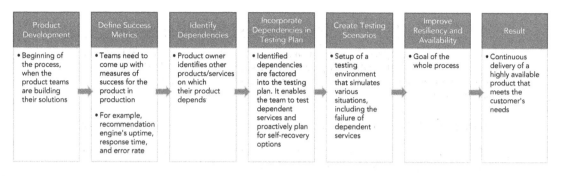

FIGURE 23.8: AI product testing and measurement framework

Aligning Operating Model with Strategic Value and Establishing a Clear Roadmap for AI

Finally, when establishing the operating model, you need to ensure that it is aligned with your business objectives and built in a manner to deliver upon the AI roadmap. You should be able to deliver iteratively, with minimal risks and a focus on quicker time to value (see Figure 23.9).

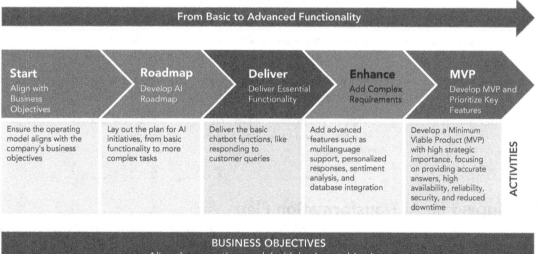

FIGURE 23.9: Aligning operating model with strategic value and establishing a clear AI roadmap

For example, suppose your team is building a chatbot. In that case, you may decide to deliver the essential functionality first, such as responding to customers' basic queries, and then add more complex requirements, such as multilanguage support, personalization of the responses, sentiment analysis, and integration with customer databases.

Moreover, suppose the chatbot is of high strategic importance to the organization. In that case, you may focus on building an MVP that aims to provide more accurate answers, which would mean your operating model delivery approach prioritizes high availability, reliability, security, and reduced downtime so as not to impact customer satisfaction negatively.

HANDS-ON EXERCISE: IMPLEMENTING AN AI OPERATING MODEL

Goal: The goal of this exercise is to give you and your team a practical sense of how to go about implementing some of the best practices suggested in this chapter. This exercise can be done in a training setting, in a workshop, or even as part of a real-world project planning process.

TASK NAME	TASK DESCRIPTION	TASK OWNER (ROLE)
Identify customer needs	Identify customer pain points and gather requirements for AI solutions.	Business analyst
Capability assessment	Assess current capabilities and gaps against the desired AI operating model.	AI strategist
Develop AI strategy	Develop a customer-centric AI strategy to drive innovation.	AI strategy team
Break down applications	Break down monolithic applications into AI products.	Technical architect
Team organization	Organize teams around the AI products.	Project manager
Iterative building	Start building iteratively with cross-functional pilot teams.	AI pilot team
Continuous improvement	Implement continuous improvement through measurement and testing.	Product owner, QA team
Align with strategic value	Align the AI operating model with strategic value and establish a clear AI roadmap.	Executive sponsor, AI strategist

Developing an AI Transformation Plan

The AI transformation plan is a strategic plan focusing on taking the organization forward in adopting AI at the enterprise level.

Unlike an AI portfolio, an AI transformation plan goes beyond individual AI initiatives and instead looks at the organization as a whole and contains a clear roadmap to increase the maturity levels of the organization in various areas such as culture, processes, and infrastructure. It takes into consideration that for AI to succeed and to be sustained in the long term, it needs to be integrated into the other parts of the organization, and therefore its focus is around enabling that integration.

The next section outlines some of the components of an AI transformation plan captured in Figure 23.10.

Vision

The Vision component contains an AI transformation initiative's overarching vision, goals, and objectives and explains how this vision helps the organization achieve its business goals.

AI Transformation Plan – From Vision to KPI Evaluation

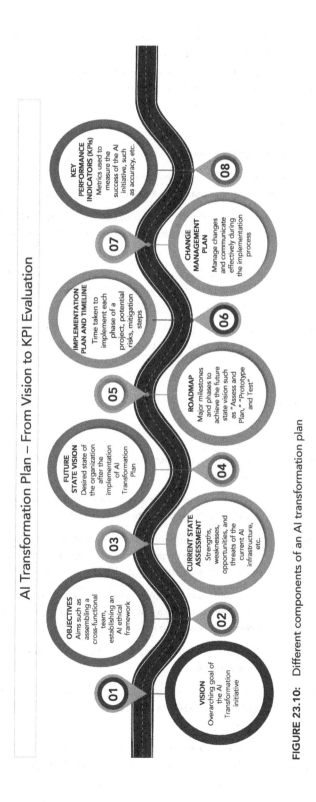

FIGURE 23.10: Different components of an AI transformation plan

The vision outlines how the transformation initiative will impact the organization's operations and the outcomes it aims to achieve through this transformation initiative.

For example, the vision could be "to become a data-driven organization focused on improving productivity and efficiency, making better decisions, and identifying new business opportunities through the adoption of AI technology."

These are other examples of vision:

VISION	VISION STATEMENT
Thrilling customer experiences	To provide thrilling customer experiences by providing personalized and proactive solutions by adopting AI technology
Enhanced services and operations	To leverage AI technologies to provide better, more personalized services to our customers while also enhancing our own operational efficiency and risk management capabilities
Personalized user experience	To utilize artificial intelligence to enhance and personalize the user experience by analyzing user data and behavior to recommend personalized content, improve the streaming quality, and automate our operations
AI in content creation and production	To use AI in content creation and production to optimize our offerings and create more engaging content for our audience

Objectives

Some of the objectives could be as follows:

OBJECTIVES	
AI readiness assessment	To assess and document the AI readiness capabilities and gaps across the organization
Comprehensive AI strategy	To develop a comprehensive strategy that includes top-level use cases for AI that align with the overall business strategy
Assemble AI expert team	To assemble a cross-functional team of AI experts, such as data scientists, machine learning engineers, data engineers, industry experts, and establish a center of excellence to assist with implementing and adopting AI
Ethical AI framework	To establish and implement an AI ethical framework that ensures the responsible and ethical use of AI in accordance with social, ethical, and regulatory considerations
Data management and infrastructure plan	To ensure data management and infrastructure plan is in place to develop and deploy AI at scale
AI deployment plan	To have a plan in place to develop and deploy AI at scale to meet business goals, deliver business value, and improve productivity, efficiency, and customer experience
Monitoring and deployment infrastructure	To have a monitoring and deployment infrastructure in place that ensures that the AI solutions operate satisfactorily post deployment

Current-State Assessment

The plan should contain the documentation of all the findings during the current-state assessment of the AI infrastructure process, people, and business domains. It should clearly list these strengths, weaknesses, opportunities, and threats for the organization that it will face during its AI adoption journey. The plan should be well geared to address the gaps discovered between the current-state assessment and the future vision laid out for the organization.

Future-State Vision

The future-state vision of the company should be well documented, as well as the benefits you hope to receive when you achieve that vision. It would depend on the use cases you identified in the Envision phase.

Roadmap

This is the most crucial part of the AI transformation plan because it documents all the significant milestones to achieve the future state vision during this AI transformation journey. It should contain all the major phases or milestones along with the individual projects, dates, and deliverables for each of those phases or milestones that help address the gaps identified.

The following table shows a sample roadmap with descriptions of the major milestones:

MILESTONES	DESCRIPTION
Assess and plan	Includes business objectives, AI opportunities, use cases, impact and feasibility analysis, data quality, availability and security assessment, technical infrastructure and resources, and the project plan and funding.
Prototype and test	Shortlist one to two use cases and build MVP, test MVP in a controlled environment, gather feedback, refine it, and test again iteratively. Finally, develop a plan to scale the solution and finalize the technical infrastructure.
Pilot and refine	Release pilot in the real world, collect data, and refine the solution based on feedback. Define a change management plan for stakeholders.
Roll out and continually improve	Roll out to a broader user base, monitor impact and effectiveness, continuously refine, and define new use cases based on experience.

Implementation Plan and Timeline

Develop an implementation plan and timeline that documents the time taken to implement each initiative phase of a project. Document the dependencies, risks, and mitigation steps for each of those initiatives and phases. Refer to the AI portfolio section for more information on this.

Change Management and Communication Plan

Document a clear change management plan that addresses assembling the team, aligning the leadership, and envisioning the future. This will set the foundation that will help you implement the AI transformation plan in a sustained, long-term manner. Refer to the change management section for more information on this.

Key Performance Indicators

The key performance indicators (KPIs) that determine the success of the AI transformation journey should be documented here. The baseline and the target KPIs should be documented here, and the measurement framework should also be established for periodic reporting.

You can use several metrics to measure the success of an AI transmission initiative. The following table shows various KPIs used to measure the success of an AI transformation initiative:

KPIS	DESCRIPTION
Accuracy of models	Measures the percentage of accurate predictions made by the AI models.
Efficiency of models	Measures the speed at which the predictions are made.
ROI	Measures the return on investment, calculated as the profits generated by the AI initiative divided by the investment made.
Customer satisfaction	Measures customer satisfaction, typically based on surveys, feedback forms, and customer reviews.
Employee satisfaction	Measures employee satisfaction, typically based on surveys and feedback forms.
Time to market	Measures the time it takes to deploy a model in production. The faster, the more competitive the organization can be.
Data quality	Measures the quality of the data. The better the data quality, the better the performance of the models.
Cost reduction	Measures the cost savings from the AI effort, calculated by comparing costs before and after the initiative.

WORKBOOK TEMPLATE: *AI OPERATING MODEL AND TRANSFORMATION PLAN*

Download the "AI Operating Model and Transformation Plan" template from the download section of the book. (www.wiley.com/go/EnterpriseAIintheCloud) Use this template to help you develop an AI Operating Model and Transformation Plan. You can use it effectively to scale AI capabilities while minimizing risks and maximizing ROI.

SUMMARY

This chapter took a deep dive into how to craft an AI operating model that fits businesses of all sizes. It unlocked some of the keys for achieving seamless AI integration, such as starting small, scaling with agility, building cross-functional teams around a product, and fostering a culture of innovation.

While the AI COE team will be responsible for developing and executing the AI transformation plan, the AI operating model will provide the framework and the best practices to foster AI adoption at your enterprise. The transformation plan includes vision and objectives, current-state assessment, future-state vision, roadmap, implementation plan, timeline, change management, and communication plan.

Regardless of whether you are beginning your AI journey or looking to mature your AI adoption, the lessons hereto are pivotal in integrating AI into your business and staying ahead of the innovation curve.

In the next chapter, we will discuss implementing generative AI.

REVIEW QUESTIONS

These review questions are included at the end of each chapter to help you test your understanding of the information. You'll find the answers in the following section.

1. What is an AI operating model?
   A. A formal structure or framework to implement AI in a scaled manner
   B. A model to develop AI solutions for operations
   C. A way to align AI operations with business goals
   D. A model to operate AI solutions without compliance

2. An AI transformation plan is
   A. A plan for implementing individual AI initiatives
   B. A plan to increase the maturity levels of the organization
   C. A plan to develop AI technologies
   D. A plan to outsource AI development

3. What are the three pillars to scale and become AI-first, as described in the chapter?
   A. AI operating model, AI transformation plan, customer-centric strategy
   B. AI center of excellence, AI operating model, AI transformation plan
   C. AI adoption at scale, AI innovation, AI roadmap
   D. AI center of excellence, AI innovation curve, AI operating model

4. Which of the following is NOT part of the AI transformation plan discussed in the chapter?
   A. Vision and objectives
   B. Future-state vision
   C. Timeline
   D. Marketing strategies

5. According to the chapter, what is vital for achieving seamless AI integration?
   A. Building cross-functional teams around a product and fostering a culture of innovation
   B. Focusing only on large corporations and excluding small businesses
   C. Ignoring the need for strategic alignment with business goals
   D. Starting with a complex plan that covers it all

ANSWER KEY

1.	A	3.	B	5.	A
2.	B	4.	D		

PART IX
Evolving and Maturing AI

This is where you peek into the crystal ball. I delve into the exciting world of Generative AI, discuss where the AI space is headed, and provide guidance on how to continue your AI journey.

24

Implementing Generative AI Use Cases with ChatGPT for the Enterprise

The best way to predict the future is to invent it.

—*Alan Kay*

Welcome to the exciting world of generative AI and ChatGPT, in particular, which has been creating news recently because of its ability to create realistic data by mimicking existing training datasets. It is like an artist who learned the style of Picasso or van Gogh and created similar pieces of art that mimic their art but are entirely new creations.

With every step in your enterprise AI journey, your understanding of AI and the ability to integrate AI within your company has been increasing. It's now an excellent time to explore the cutting-edge world of generative AI and its implementation opportunities. See Figure 24.1.

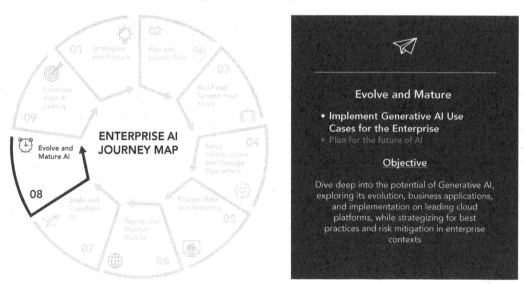

FIGURE 24.1: EVOLVE AND MATURE: Generative AI and ChatGPT use cases for your enterprise

This chapter gives you a tour of the exciting world of generative AI, starting from the innovative GANs to the intricate diffusion models. It guides you through the technological marvels that have revolutionized industries, from drug design to chip design.

With the strategy framework, risk mitigation plans, and other tools presented in this and other chapters in this book, you can make generative AI applications such as ChatGPT an enterprise reality. This is where innovation truly comes to life!

THE RISE AND REACH OF GENERATIVE AI

Even though generative AI has been creating a lot of news lately, it has not always been at the forefront of technology until now. The story of generative AI is one of resilience and continuous innovation, starting all the way from small statistical models to deep learning to large language models. And all of this within the last decade or so.

But what has changed recently has been the realization that AI can be used not only to generate novel content such as music, audio, and video, but in serious applications across industries such as drug discovery, chip design, buildings, and so on. The impact of generative AI on the economy is vast. McKinsey has already identified close to 63 generative AI use cases across 16 business functions that generate close to $2.6 to $4.4 trillion in economic benefits annually across industries.

Some of the applications of generative AI have been nothing short of astounding. Take, for example, DeepArt or DeepDream, which create lifelike, realistic artwork mimicking the style of van Gogh or Monet photos. What is really happening behind the scenes is that a generative model has been trained based on the paintings of these masters.

Or take the example of OpenAI's MuseNet, which can create 4-minute compositions by using 10 musical instruments and by combining new styles of music composed of a blend of country and Mozart and Beatles.

In the field of healthcare, Insilico Medicine is an example of a company that can find new drug candidates in a few weeks, which would typically take years.

Generative AI is a fascinating field and a subset of deep learning, as shown in Figure 24.2.

> **NOTE** *Generative AI is predicted to impact almost every business, function, product, service, and business relationship. Adopt it responsibly, ethically, and with robust testing.*

The Powerful Evolution of Generative AI

Generative AI is a type of AI that uses techniques to generate new, realistic artifacts based on its learning from existing artifacts. And these artifacts can range from audio/visual to programming and data assets, natural language, and designs, as shown in Table 24.1.

What is essential to understand is that the artifacts produced by generative AI can span beyond just content, and therein lies the power of generative AI.

When you have a tool that can generate not just content but also software code, music, videos, 2D/3D, art, product designs, game worlds, process flows, drugs, building designs, and so on, you realize this is not just hype but serious business with powerful implications for business, personal lives, and society.

TABLE 24.1: Artifacts That Can Be Created by Generative AI

TEXT	CODE	IMAGES	AUDIO/VIDEO	DESIGNS	2D/3D/DESIGNS	NLP	DATA ASSETS
Marketing (content)	Code generation	Image generation	Voice synthesis	Product designs	2D/3D models/scenes	Questions/answers	Training data (events, POS, behavior)
Sales (email)	Code documentation	Consumer/social	Music	Materials	2D/3D faces, bodies	Summaries/roundups	Text and Synthetic data
Support (chat/email)	Text to SQL	Media/advertising	Video editing/generation	Gaming worlds	RPA	Stories/narratives	Context data (e.g., Market conditions)
General writing	Web app builders	Design		Process Flows		Documents	
Note taking		Drawings/Photographs		Schematics (Drug Discovery, Building Designs)		Job listings	
Biology and chemistry		Art					
		Visual characters					

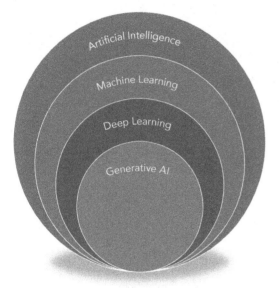

Artificial Intelligence
Tools and systems that simulate human intelligence to optimize business processes and decision-making

Machine Learning
Data-driven software algorithms that allow companies to predict outcomes and adapt autonomously to situations

Deep Learning
Advanced ML techniques that use neural networks to analyze massive amounts of data to identify patterns

Generative AI
Enterprise solutions that autonomously generate new content, designs, or products based on learned business data patterns

FIGURE 24.2: Generative AI is a subset of deep learning

Here is the Gartner definition of Generative AI:

> Generative AI enables computers to generate brand-new completely original variations of content (including images, video, music, speech, and text). It can improve or alter existing content, and it can create new data elements and novel models of real-world objects, such as buildings, parts, drugs, and materials.
>
> —*Gartner*

At this point, you already know what artificial intelligence, machine learning, and deep learning mean. If you are unsure, refer to Chapter 16, where I discuss this in greater detail.

In this section, you learn how generative AI evolved over a period of time to where it is now.

Deep Learning Processes Complex Patterns Through ANNs

Recall that deep learning is a type of machine learning that uses artificial neural networks (ANNs) that enable it to process more complex patterns than machine learning can. Artificial neural networks are inspired by the human brain and consists of many interconnected nodes, or neurons, as shown in Figure 24.3.

Semi-supervised Learning Uses Labeled and Unlabeled Data

These neurons are arranged in many layers that allow them to process more complex patterns. And these neural networks can process both labeled and unlabeled data. This idea of training a model using labeled and unlabeled data is known as *semi-supervised learning*. This concept allows the neural network to learn using a small sample of labeled data and a large amount of unlabeled data. While the labeled data helps the network learn the basic tasks, the unlabeled data helps the network generalize to new examples.

> **TIP** *Use deep learning techniques only when traditional machine learning techniques are not sufficient.*

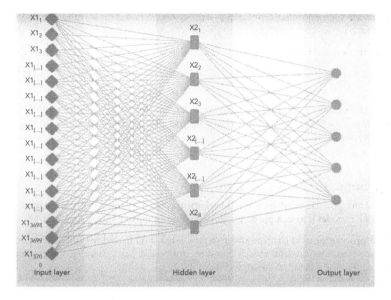

Input layer   Hidden layer   Output layer

FIGURE 24.3: Structure of artificial neural networks

Generative vs. Discriminative Models in Machine Learning

This is where generative AI comes in. It's a form of deep learning that also uses neural networks and can process labeled and unlabeled data using supervised, unsupervised, and semi-supervised learning techniques. As shown in Table 24.2, there are two types of models: generative and discriminative models.

The discriminative model is focused on predicting the label for new data points after being trained on labeled data points. Its focus is on understanding the relationships between the features and the labels.

TABLE 24.2: Discriminative vs. Generative Models

	DISCRIMINATIVE MODELS	GENERATIVE MODELS
Definition	A type of model that tries to learn the boundary between different classes	A type of mode that tries to model on how the data is generated
Purpose	Classify or predict data	Generates new data based on trained data
Training Data	Labeled data	Labeled and unlabeled data
Example Models	Convolutional neural networks (CNNs)	Generative adversarial networks (GANs), variational autoencoders (VAEs)
Training Approach	Tries to learn the decision boundary between classes	Tries to learn the distribution of the data itself
Applications	Text generation, image generation	Image classification, text classification, speech recognition
Model Complexity	Less intensive and complex	More compute-intensive and complex

On the other hand, generative models are focused on generating new data instances based on learning the probability distribution of the existing data.

In summary, generative models generate new data, while discriminative models try to distinguish between real and fake data.

> **NOTE** *It is not generative AI when the output is a number or a class, meaning it cannot be a probability or a classification. For it to be generative AI, the output needs to be in natural language, such as text, image, audio, or video.*

Foundation Models That Can Generate New Content

In the case of traditional machine learning, the classical supervised and unsupervised learning processes can take training code and labeled data to build a model that can predict a classification or cluster something.

On the other hand, the generative AI process takes in the training code, the labeled data, and the unlabeled data of all data types. It builds what is known as a foundation model that does not predict but instead generates new content in the form of text, images, audio, and video, as shown in Figure 24.4.

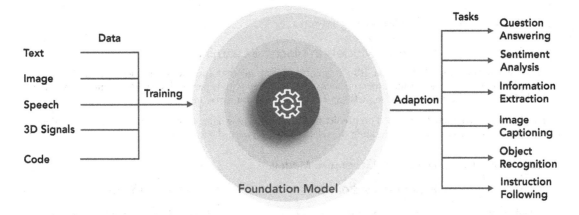

FIGURE 24.4: Inputs and outputs of a foundation model

Some examples of these foundation models are the Pathways Language Model (PALM) and the Language Model for Dialog Applications (LaMDA). These models have been trained on very large amounts of data from the Internet and have built foundation models that can now answer anything by asking a question, either via prompts or by asking verbally into the prompt.

> **TIP** *Training foundation models can be expensive, but they are impressive in performance, and hence it's important to put guardrails in place to ensure users are not impacted negatively.*

Large Language Models and Generative Image Models

You can have different types of generative models. Some would be large language models, and some would be generative image models. Table 24.3 shows the difference between generative language and generative image models.

TABLE 24.3: The Differences Between Generative Language and Generative Image Models

	GENERATIVE LANGUAGE MODEL	GENERATIVE IMAGE MODEL
Definition	A type of model that learns about patterns in language through training data	A type of model that produces new images through techniques like diffusion.
Purpose	Classify or predict data	Generate new data based on trained data
Training Data	Text data from sources like books and websites	Image data from datasets like ImageNet and CIFAR
Example Models	GPT-3 and GPT-4	Generative adversarial networks (GANs), variational autoencoders (VAEs)
Training Approach	Tries to learn the statistical properties of language and generates text accordingly	Tries to learn the statistical properties of image and generates image accordingly
Applications	Text generation, chatbots	Image generation, image-to-image translation
Model Complexity	Less intensive and complex	More compute-intensive and complex

Large language models are those that can understand, generate, and work with human language. The beauty of these models is that since they have been trained on such large amounts of text data, they understand various patterns, grammar, and even some real-world facts.

LLMs are considered large because they have a large number of parameters that have been learned through the training process. The more parameters the model has, the more it can learn and remember. For example, GPT-3 has 175 billion parameters, which is like saying they have a brain that can store about 175,000 copies of *War and Peace*. So, when you ask the GPT-3 model who won the soccer World Cup in 2020, having read this information in the past, it can immediately respond with the answer. And it gets even more interesting when you consider that GPT-4 has 100 trillion parameters, which by the same logic means storing 100 million copies of *War and Peace* in a brain.

LLMs are so huge that they demand a lot of compute power, which makes them out of reach for most enterprises to train their own language model. Instead, the trend is to fine-tune these models for specific uses cases or industries so that the LLM can operate efficiently and provide better performance for that particular use case content. For example, an LLM trained for healthcare will provide better accuracy for healthcare use cases.

Note that in addition to generative language models, you also have generative image models that can take an image as input and generate text, an image, or a video.

> **NOTE** *A large language model takes in text and generates text, an image, a video, or a decision.*

Enter ChatGPT: AI Conversational Chatbot

ChatGPT is a conversational chatbot application that uses an OpenAI service to create new content. The Chat-GPT OpenAI service serves the output from a large language model (LLM) that is trained on billions of words from multiple sources. The model has been fine-tuned by humans with their feedback by a technique known as *reinforced learning with human feedback* (RLHF).

Difference Between Foundation Models and Large Language Models

It should be noted that this is a fast-moving space, and I have attempted to capture the differences between foundation models and large language models for better understanding in Table 24.4. These are subtle differences, and the distinction between them may change as this technology and use cases evolve.

TABLE 24.4: Difference Between Foundation and Language Models

	LARGE LANGUAGE MODELS	FOUNDATION MODELS
Definition	A type of foundation model trained on large amounts of text data, consisting of billions of parameters.	A broader category of AI systems trained on datasets of any size and includes nontext data types and wider range of use cases and applications
Data Types Used for Training	Text data	Text, images, audio, video, and other sensory data
Size	Very large amounts of text data with billions of parameters	Any size
Primary Function	Specifically designed for language tasks such as generate text, translate text, question answering, and summarization	Designed to be adaptable for tasks beyond language tasks, which could include computer vision and robotics
Examples	GPT-3, Megatron-Turing NLG	BERT, RoBERTa, XLNet
Applications	Text generation, chatbots	Image generation, image-to-image translation
Intended Use	For NLP tasks	As a foundation for other AI systems

THE POWER OF GENERATIVE AI/ChatGPT FOR BUSINESS TRANSFORMATION AND INNOVATION

This section discusses the role that generative AI and ChatGPT can play in businesses, products, services, and relationships. Because of its ability to generate new and original content, generative AI can be a game-changer for many industries. This section explores a few possibilities. Generative AI can enhance efficiency, innovation, and personalization through a number of applications.

Business Transformation with Automated Content Generation

The ability to generate automated content on a regular basis, such as blogs, articles, and social media posts, is a huge advantage for businesses. It has enormous implications for content marketing applications, as shown in Figure 24.5.

Thought Leadership Through Improved Content Accuracy

Because gen AI trains on a large amount of data, it can look at patterns that a human eye cannot see and therefore can help produce high-quality content, enabling organizations and individuals to establish themselves as thought leaders in their space.

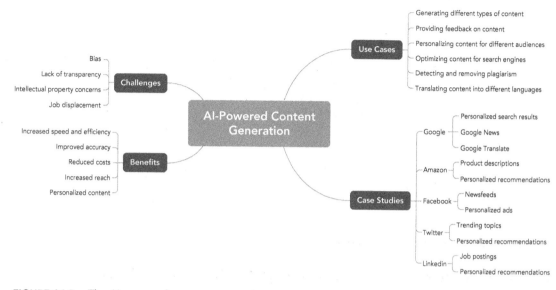

FIGURE 24.5: The AI-powered content generation use case

Innovation with New Business Ideas, Art, and Product Design

Regarding innovation, generative AI can create new business ideas, product designs, digital art and music, and chemical structures for potential new drugs.

By creating new and varied content that includes images, audio, videos, and text, companies can engage with their customers and keep them captivated with their offerings.

Another example of an innovative application of generative AI is *Pictionary*, which uses AI to guess what you are drawing. Behind the scenes, it uses millions of doodles from people worldwide to train itself.

In the case of product design, you have to generate many product design ideas, which would involve a lot of brainstorming, sketching, iterations, and, finally, shortlisting them. This would be a tedious, manual process and would consume a lot of time. On the other hand, say you are feeding hundreds of product designs from the past into a model, and the model returns new and innovative product designs that meet your product specifications and quality requirements. That is precisely what Autodesk's Dreamcatcher solution tries to do.

Autodesk Dreamcatcher is like having thousands of designers trying to create new innovative designs day by day, a round the clock.

Revolutionizing Experiences Through Personalized Emails and Product Recommendations

Concerning personalization, generative AI can help create different versions of personalized emails for different customers and recommend products based on past purchases. For example, using AI algorithms, Spotify recommends personalized playlists for millions of users based on their individual tastes every week. Another example is Fractal Analytics, which uses generative AI to create new landing pages and generate emails.

Innovative Product Features to Boost Customer Loyalty

Another area where generative AI can help you is in personalizing your products based on exactly what the users need. This can help companies be laser-focused on meeting their customers' user experience needs and drive customer engagement and loyalty.

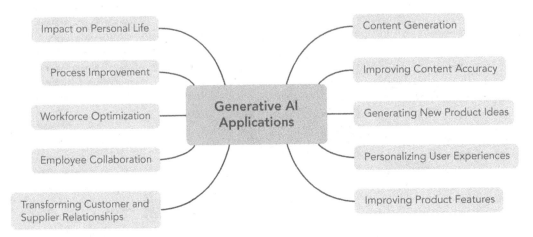

FIGURE 24.6: Generative AI applications

Transforming Customer Relationships Through Chatbots, Personalization

Generative AI has been instrumental in transforming customer relationships by analyzing customer behavior, preferences, and feedback to develop new product recommendations and responses and even create new products. This level of personalization can help engage with customers better and promote customer loyalty in the long term.

Another example is the application of generative AI to build a chatbot. Instead of having preprogrammed rules to answer the customer's question, you can have a generative AI chatbot similar to ChatGPT to answer a customer's questions in real time based on their style of language, preference, sentiment, and type of question.

Breaking Language Barriers, Better Supplier Relationships, and Global Trade

In the case of supplier relationships, using the natural language translation capabilities of gen AI, you can communicate with suppliers across multiple geographies and countries. This ability helps you create better partner relationships and promotes global trade.

Reimagining Workplace Efficiency with AI-Powered Assistants

Generative AI can also collaborate with internal employees to automate tasks and improve process efficiency and employee productivity. For example, GitHub's Copilot is an AI-powered assistant that can help developers to develop code faster. This opens up new opportunities because this concept of having a virtual assistant that can work with humans to improve employee productivity will be a game-changer when automating many of the business processes within the company.

Long-Term Workforce Transformation with AI as a Partner

Figure 24.7 shows how AI can be a valuable partner that enables long-term transformation in the workforce. The ability of the employee to work with AI will not only enhance their productivity. It will also enhance the ability to come up with new ideas with the help of the AI assistant, which can act as a creative partner. It now becomes possible to develop groundbreaking ideas and efficient execution strategies.

From Process Transformation to Life-Changing Applications

Generative AI has the potential to uncover hidden patterns and insights from large amounts of data that were not possible before because of the sheer size of the data. Armed with these new insights, gen AI can also propose changes to current workflows to eliminate process inefficiencies, remove bottlenecks, and automate tasks.

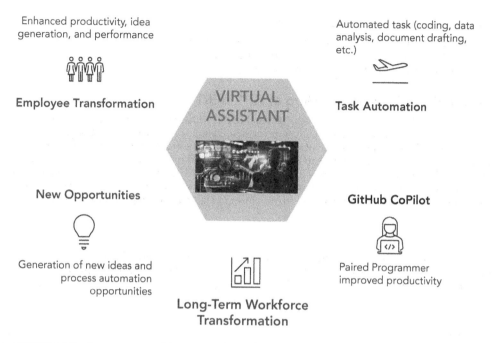

FIGURE 24.7: Long-term workforce transformation with AI as a partner
Source: Blue Planet Studio/ Adobe Stock

The uses of generative AI are not restricted to businesses alone but can also impact our personal lives. Take, for example, the Stanford University research, where they converted human brain signals into written text.

> **TIP** *Use generative AI not to replace creativity or other relationships but to augment your capabilities and open new possibilities to transform business and personal lives.*

The Fascinating World of Generative AI: From GANs to Diffusion Models

Now that you know what generative models do, you probably wonder how they work. Even though there are a number of generative models out there, three models stand out: generative adversarial networks (GANs), variational auto-encoders (VAEs), and transformer models. Despite their differences, they all follow the same principles: to learn the underlying patterns in the data and re-create data with similar data patterns.

GANs: Interplay of Generator and Discriminator Networks

The GANs model was invented by Ian Goodfellow and his team in 2014. It is based on the beautiful concept of two neural networks working against each other. One is called the Generator, which creates realistic data, such as images, based on the data it was trained upon. The other is the Discriminator neural network, which tries to critique the new image and find the difference between the real image and the generated version. This constant tussle between the two networks results in an incredibly realistic image.

> **TIP** *Use GANs to create realistic human faces and even photorealistic artwork out of sketches.*

VAEs: A Solution to GAN's Black-Box Problem

One of the drawbacks of GANs is that they operate like black boxes. We don't know how these models work. In such situations, VAEs can help because we can understand the hidden layers that drive the data. It is used in product recommendation engines and text generation use cases.

Transformers: The Behind-the-Scenes Hero of GPT, BERT

Transformers are the model behind models such as GPT-3 and BERT, which revolutionized text generation, summarization, translation, and more. Transformers were introduced in 2017 and have revolutionized the world of natural language processing because they simultaneously consider all the words in a sentence when trying to make a prediction. We already know that ChatGPT has taken the world by storm, as more than 100 million people registered for the tool in just a couple of weeks. When using ChatGPT, it feels almost like talking to a human, which is impressive. Another example of using a transformer model is when people use Gmail, where the autocomplete feature is based on a Transformer model. As shown in Figure 24.8, a transformer model contains an encoder and decoder.

> **NOTE** Transformers *have an encoder and a decoder, where the encoder encodes the input sequence and passes it to the decoder, which learns how to decode the representation for a relevant task.*

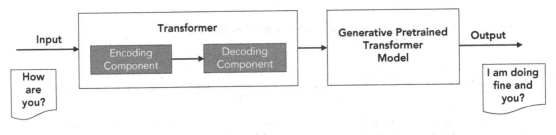

FIGURE 24.8: Components of a transformer model

Hallucinations: When Models Go Astray

Sometimes these models can generate outputs that are nonsensical or grammatically incorrect. This is known as hallucination and can happen when the model has not been trained adequately or on enough data or is trained on noisy data or has not been given enough context or constraints to work with.

From Text-to-Image to Text-to-Task Using Diffusion Models

While GANs and VAEs have held the limelight for the most part, diffusion models have also been making waves recently. Diffusion models take a unique approach to creating new data. They take the original image (the picture of a cat) and add noise to it to distort it slightly. They continue this process until it becomes unrecognizable. Then, it tries to recover the image by removing the noise with each step. In this process, it ends up creating a range of new cat images depending on the noise with which it started the recovery process.

> **NOTE** *Diffusion models can generate text-to-image, text-to-video, text-to-3D, and text-to-tasks.*

Text-to-3D can be used in video games, and text-to-task models can be used to carry out tasks such as question and answer, performing a search, or taking some action such as navigating a UI or updating a document. Table 24.5 captures the differences between GANs, VAEs, and diffusion models.

TABLE 24.5: Differences Between GANs, VAEs, and Diffusion Models

GENERATIVE MODEL	GANS	VAES	DIFFUSION MODELS
Working Principle	Two neural networks competing in a zero-sum game to generate new data that closely resembles the training dataset	A type of neural network that learns to encode and decode data by mapping it to a latent space	Adding noise to the original image and then removing the noise gradually to create a range of new images depending on the noise with which the recovery process started
Applications	• Image to image translation • Scenes and people • Realistic human faces • Artwork • Photorealistic photos of objects	• Image and video generation • Data compression • Anomaly detection	• Text-to-image • Text-to-video • Text-to-3D • Text-to-tasks
Examples	• StyleGAN • BigGAN	• Beta-VAE • VQ-VAE	• DALL-E • CLIP

DALL-E and CLIP are two diffusion-type models from OpenAI. DALL-E can generate images from text descriptions, while CLIP can understand both text and images and can relate them to each other. For example, you can ask DALL-E to create an orange in the form of an apple, and DALL-E will precisely do that to create a novel image that was never seen before.

Diffusion models are not without their challenges because they can be very computationally intensive and slower than GANs. Despite their challenges, diffusion models are fascinating and extend the limits of virtual reality and what's possible with Gen AI.

IMPLEMENTING GENERATIVE AI AND ChatGPT

Given its many risks, implementing generative AI and ChatGPT for your company is not a trivial task. Moreover, it is a constantly evolving space; you must keep close tabs on what's happening out there. Having said that, consider the different options you have when implementing generative AI or ChatGPT. Your options will span between buying off-the-shelf solutions and building them on your own. Figure 24.9 shows the different options laid out in front of you.

From Packaged Software to Pretraining Models

Consider these build versus buy options that are available when implementing generative AI:

➤ **Out-of-the-box options:** You already use the out-of-the-box option when you use ChatGPT for various natural language processing tasks such as summarizing, answering questions, translation, and so on.

The issue with that approach is that you need to figure out how your data is going to be leveraged by those companies.

➤ **Consuming APIs:** When you use APIs, cost is a critical factor because you are charged based on the tokens, you use both as a query to the API and the response you get back. It is therefore important to exercise controls over the amount of data input to the API as well as the amount of data generated from the API.

➤ **Prompt engineering:** The other option is prompt engineering, which has been gaining much attention lately. We are already seeing innovations in this space in the form of new models such as hugging space, GPT long chain, and so on.

➤ **Fine-tuning the LLMs:** The next best option that gives you even more control is fine-tuning the LLM model, which requires technical expertise from your company. The last option is very complex: pretraining a model, which is almost like starting from scratch; it's costly and therefore is ruled out for most companies.

➤ **Using a packaged software with embedded gen AI:** The easiest option is to use the packaged software where you don't need any technical team; anybody can use those. Examples of those are ChatGPT, Microsoft Bing, Google BARD, Adobe Firefly, and so on. In the future, we are going to see most of these large language models embedded in enterprise applications

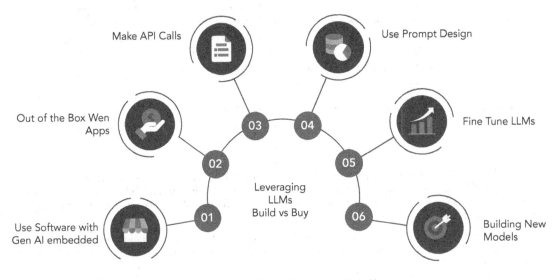

FIGURE 24.9: Build versus buy options when implementing generative AI

> **TIP** *Fine-tuning pretrained models can be a viable middle path between fully customized models and off-the-shelf products.*

Bridging the Gap Between External and Internal Knowledge

Implementing generative AI boils down to connecting the external knowledge gathered by these large language models with the knowledge that you have in your organization. As shown in Figure 24.10, some of these techniques are as follows:

➤ Prompt engineering

> ➤ Customized fine-tuning
> ➤ Retrieval augmented generation (RAG)

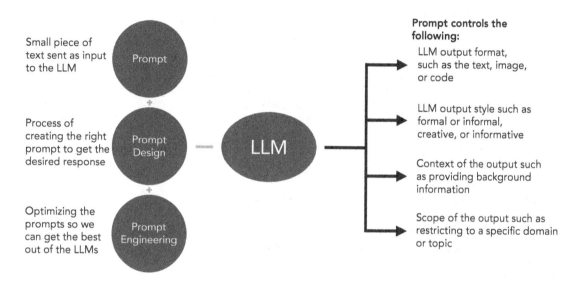

FIGURE 24.10: Using prompts to train LLMs

Enhancing LLM/ChatGPT Interactions with Prompts

A prompt is a small piece of text sent as input to a large language model and can be used to control the output in many ways.

Prompt design is a term used to describe the process of creating the prompt to elicit the desired response from the large language model. Think of prompt as not only a basic user request but also adding some background, instructions, and user context to the request so that the model can respond much more accurately.

Prompt engineering is the practice of optimizing prompts so that you get the best out of these large language models.

Improving Response Quality with Retrieval Augmented Generation

Retrieval augmented generation (RAG) is a powerful technique that combines the power of information retrieval and the NLP capabilities of a large language model, as shown in Figure 24.11.

For example, consider a chatbot in a banking scenario. You can use RAG to enhance the quality and relevance of your responses. Say a customer wants to know about the status of their transaction. You can break down the process into three steps.

1. **Retrieval:** During the retrieval process, the chatbot looks in the customer database and retrieves customer account information along with other relevant information related to the request from a large corpus of text.

2. **Augmentation:** The chatbot then combines the user request with the information it just retrieved from various sources and sends it to the large language model to compose a response.

3. **Generation:** The large language model uses the information in the user request, which contains real-world information to generate a creative, user-friendly, and relevant response to the customer.

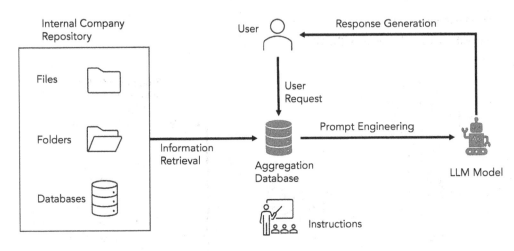

FIGURE 24.11: Retrieval augmented generation architecture

RAG has the following benefits:

➤ It improves the relevancy and accuracy of the information response as it's based on real-world data.

➤ It saves time and effort as it saves human effort to find relevant information from various sources related to the incoming request.

➤ Since you are using a single LLM, the response is always consistent.

The RAG approach has been used in various applications such as customer service, customer support, news writing, and even therapy.

RAG is also used in certain help desk use cases, where the language models can make their own API calls to other external systems, given their ability to create their own code. This allows them to create their own tools and then use that to respond to the user with suggestions.

> **TIP** *When integrating internal data with external data, pay attention to data privacy issues, access control security, and leverage domain experts to tailor models efficiently.*

BEST PRACTICES WHEN IMPLEMENTING GENERATIVE AI AND ChatGPT

This section discusses some best practices to follow when implementing Generative AI.

Ensuring Performance and Mitigating Risks Through Internal Pilots

First, it is essential to test your generative AI and ChatGPT use cases internally with your employees before releasing them to external customers. This will help you catch any issues with the model's performance, especially for things like hallucinations, which can cause severe damage to your reputation.

Communicating the Role of Generative AI in User Interactions

Second, it is imperative to be transparent with the users, whether they are employees, customers, or the public, and admit that when interacting with the application, they are working with a machine. This helps you build the necessary trust and avoid any misgivings in the future.

Ensuring Fairness and Bias Mitigation Through Continuous Testing and Guardrails

Third, set up the necessary guardrails to check for biases in the system and address them accordingly. Keep testing continuously to ensure they are working accurately.

Protecting Data Privacy and Security of Organizational Data

Ensure data privacy and security by talking to the model provider and confirming that the data input into the model will not be used outside the organization.

Building Trust Through Beta Testing

It is also vital to ensure that the applications are kept in beta mode for a sufficient amount of time and are released to the general public only once there is complete confidence in the accuracy of the models and the issues have been addressed.

> **TIP** *Be prepared to manage risks proactively: starting with a pilot, maintaining transparency with users, looking out for bias, handling data privacy issues, and planning for contingencies are vital.*

Strategy Considerations for Generative AI and ChatGPT

This section discusses the best practices to consider when implementing generative AI and ChatGPT, as shown in Figure 24.12.

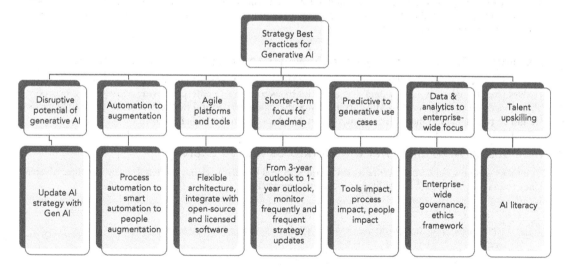

FIGURE 24.12: Strategy best practices for implementing Generative AI

Risk of Disruption

Generative AI and ChatGPT can disrupt the industry you are currently in. This could mean that you need to change your current AI strategy or complement it with generative AI and ChatGPT related strategy.

Shifting from Automation to Augmenting Humans with AI Assistants

From a vision perspective, this could mean you need to move from automating processes to smart automaton that uses AI to augmenting people with ChatGPT. So, the focus could move from displacing humans to having virtual assistants that act like managers or co-workers.

> **NOTE** *Virtual assistants can help employees make decisions at critical junctures, cope with stress during the day, mentor employees, and be impartial in their interactions with the employees.*

Agile Roadmapping to Embrace Continuous Strategy Refinement

From a roadmap perspective, you need to transition from a longer three-year outlook to having an annual roadmap, given the rapid change in technology. You need to review your strategy more frequently and refine it continuously.

Agile and Flexible Platforms for Future-Proof Infrastructure

Greater care needs to be exercised in the choice of platforms and tools given that you cannot change them easily, and the underlying infrastructure should be agile enough to accommodate new changes and integrate them easily with open source and licensed products.

Shifting from Prediction to Generation of New Artifacts

The use cases will change from predictive and automation type to generating new types of artifacts such as text, videos, images, audio, and code. As a result, the corresponding tools, processes, and skills will focus on generating new artifacts rather than predicting outcomes.

Expanding the Scope from Data and Analytics to Enterprise-wide Governance

Given the pervasive nature and impact of these generative AI solutions, you need to ensure that the AI strategy evolves from being just a narrow data and analytics focus to being an enterprise-wide strategy that incorporates governance aspects of generative AI/ChatGPT. Since this can have cultural implications, all responsible parties should be represented in these discussions, and an AI ethics committee may become more urgent.

Democratizing AI to Empower the Workforce with AI Literacy

The focus will now shift from having AI skills concentrated in a data science lab team or an AI center of excellence to making the employees AI literate across the enterprise.

> **TIP** *Anticipate disruption and bake it into your business strategy to create a competitive edge.*

Challenges of Generative AI and ChatGPT

This section discusses the challenges you need to overcome when adopting generative AI, as shown in Figure 24.13.

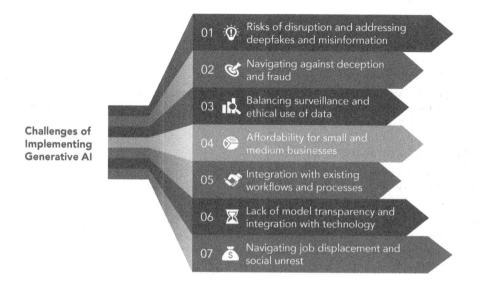

FIGURE 24.13: Challenges of implementing generative AI

Risk of Disruption

Large industry players run the risk of being disrupted by smaller players.

Addressing Deepfakes and Misinformation

The significant challenge of generative AI is the ability to create hyperreal audio, videos, and images that can deceive people. We have already seen a few incidents where people have been deceived, which has resulted in monetary fraud. Work with your cyber insurance providers to ensure you are covered for AI-related breaches.

Navigating Against Deception and Fraud

Another major issue of generative AI is that of bias. Because these models are being trained on biased data, they also generate biased results. You need to have policies or controls in place to detect when they happen and deal with them appropriately based on company policies and legal requirements.

Addressing the Potential for Incorrect Decisions due to Hallucinations

Depending entirely on the outcomes from the generative AI and ChatGPT models can be risky and lead to incorrect decisions, as sometimes these models can generate false information due to the hallucination effect discussed earlier.

Affordability for Small and Medium Businesses

Another primary concern is the need for high computing resources, which makes generative AI unreachable for small and medium-sized businesses.

Embracing Energy Efficiency and Renewable Solutions

There is also this concern about the vast environmental impact because of the large amounts of energy consumed to build and train these models. You must choose vendors that save energy consumption and use renewable energy more.

Integration with Existing Workflows and Processes

Another challenge is incorporating generative AI and ChatGPT use cases into existing workflows and processes.

Ethical Handling of Private Data

Generative AI uses a lot of private data to generate new synthetic data for training, especially in the case of healthcare. While the patient's information can be masked, getting the appropriate consent and being aware of privacy concerns is still essential.

Balancing Surveillance and Ethical Use of Data

Another privacy-related concern is that generative AI can be used to monitor people's activities and movements and even predict their future behavior, which can be a serious cause of concern.

Protecting Intellectual Property and Copyright Concerns

Users should be careful about inputting their personal or company information. They should assume that this information will become publicly available. Therefore, companies should implement controls to ensure their IP address is not compromised.

Lack of Model Transparency

How ChatGPT or generative AI models work is unpredictable, and even the companies behind them do not know how they work.

Integration with Technology

Integrating with existing technology and systems can be a challenge.

Navigating Job Displacement and Social Unrest

Generative AI and ChatGPT can do some of the jobs that humans can do, and this can potentially displace people from their jobs and cause social unrest. It is especially true for creators of content and code.

Safeguarding Humanity from Potential Harmful Models

It might sound like science fiction, but it is certainly possible for those seeking power over humanity to build power-seeking AI models whose goals are not aligned with humanity and could cause significant harm.

> **TIP** *Plan on investing in advanced deepfake detection techniques to mitigate the impact.*

Strategy for Managing and Mitigating Risks

Just as with any new technology, generative AI has its own challenges, and you need to implement some mitigation steps to address those risks, as shown in Figure 24.14.

HANDS-ON EXERCISE: MANAGING GENERATIVE AI RISKS

Goal: The goal of this exercise is to help those involved in implementing generative AI to manage and mitigate risks.

TASK DESCRIPTION	TASK OWNER	DELIVERABLES
Understand security and ethical risks: Document risks related to security, privacy, deep fakes, ethics, bias, etc., for safe generative AI implementation.	Security team, legal team, risk compliance team	Risk assessment document
Build AI risk awareness: Educate employees on the benefits and risks of generative AI, including data handling techniques.	HR team, training team	Training materials, employee acknowledgment forms
Define ethical guidelines: Establish policies for data privacy, ethics, fairness, transparency, and security.	Ethics committee, legal team	Ethical guidelines document, usage policies
Address bias and ensure cybersecurity: Implement tools and measures to detect/address bias and enhance cybersecurity.	IT team, security team	Bias mitigation report, cybersecurity protocols
Make energy-conscious choices: Select energy-saving infrastructure for model training.	Infrastructure team	Energy consumption report, selected infrastructure details
Continuous monitoring: Monitor the established controls and adapt as needed.	Monitoring team, compliance team	Continuous monitoring reports, adaptation strategies

FIGURE 24.14: Mitigating generative AI risks

GENERATIVE AI CLOUD PLATFORMS

When it comes to generative AI from a cloud perspective, you need to have a lot of compute power to train these large language models. By training these large language models with your own company data, you can use them to answer customer queries based on your company data. The major cloud providers provide the ability to train these models within your company's premises without losing control over the data and exposing it to the Internet by taking all security precautions and best practices. In addition to the cloud platform, you also need development platforms that can help you build generative AI applications on top of them.

Google's Generative AI Cloud Platform Tools

Google provides several generative AI cloud platform tools, namely, Gen AI Studio, Google AI platform, and TensorFlow.

Simplifying AI Model Development and Deployment with Generative AI Studio

Generative AI Studio is a good option for developers and users who want to develop generative AI models with less to no machine learning coding knowledge. It is a web-based platform with drag-and-drop features that users can use to build and deploy generative AI models. It makes exploring and customizing gen AI models, building, and deploying new models, and experimenting with different settings easier.

Generative AI Studio allows users to interact and train large foundation models from Google, such as PaLM 2, Imagen, Codey, and Chirp, to develop generative AI applications, including text, chat, text-to-image generation, and code completion.

> **NOTE** *When combined with the Model Garden provided in Google's Vertex AI platform, it can be a game-changer for software development agent generative AI applications.*

Figure 24.15 shows the foundation models available in the model garden. One promising application of generative AI using Google tools is Google's Magenta project, which is an application that can generate unique music in a particular genre or style based on the music shared by the user.

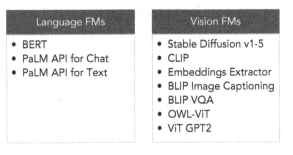

FIGURE 24.15: Foundation models in the model garden

No Code AI Development with Generative AI App Builder

Google's Generative AI App Builder allows you to create generative AI applications without coding. According to Google, it helps businesses and governments to build their own AI-powered chat interfaces and digital assistants. It connects conversational AI flows with out-of-the-box search experiences and foundation models and thus helps companies to build gen AI apps in minutes or hours.

Large-Scale Deployments Using the Google AI Platform

Google's AI platform is also an excellent tool to build, deploy, and scale generative AI models. Still, when compared to Generative AI Studio, it is more complex and needs some machine learning skills. However, it can be used for a larger-scale deployment and has more features.

Greater Control and Flexibility with TensorFlow

If you want greater flexibility and control over your generative AI machine learning process, TensorFlow will be your choice. It is an open-source software library developed by Google. Many state-of-the-art machine learning models, such as GANs, have been developed using TensorFlow.

Coding Made Easy with Google Bard and Colab Tool

You can use Bard to generate new code and convert it from one programming language to another. And if you use Google's free browser-based Jupyter Notebook, known as Colab, you can export the code from Bard directly into the Colab tool. Bard can help you debug the code, explain the code line by line, generate SQL queries to a database, and even create documentation and tutorials.

AWS Generative AI Cloud Platform Tools

This section discusses the AWS Generative AI Cloud Platform tools shown in Figure 24.16. It covers issues like what are the specific features and capabilities of AWS SageMaker, AWS CodeWhisperer, AWS Bedrock, and AWS Titan Models? How do these services work together to create generative AI applications? What are the specific benefits and use cases for AWS Trainium and AWS Inferentia2 instances in the context of generative AI applications?

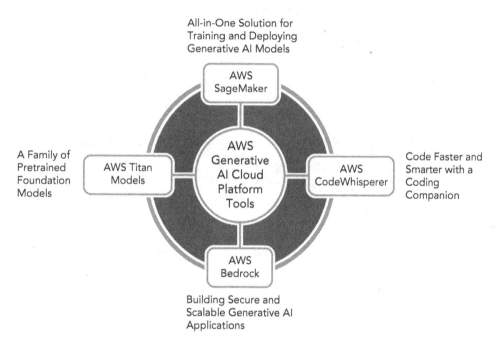

FIGURE 24.16: AWS Generative AI cloud platform tools

AWS SageMaker: All-in-One Solution for Training and Deploying Generative AI Models

SageMaker is another excellent tool to train and deploy generative AI models. It provides a comprehensive development environment to build, train, and deploy generative AI models. And it comes with its own debugger and other monitoring tools to manage bias, explainability, and so on.

Code Faster and Smarter with AWS CodeWhisperer

AWS CodeWhisperer is a coding companion that can increase the productivity of developers. Today's developers are challenged with repetitive coding, and constantly changing programming technologies prevent them from focusing on the creative side of programming. Imagine now as a developer, you can ask CodeWhisperer to provide the code to parse a CSV string of songs and return a list of songwriters, titles, ranking, and so on. Like magic, CodeWhisperer will return the entire function to you with all the code in the programming language of your choice. During a recent challenge, it was found that CodeWhisperer can help developers complete their coding 57 percent faster, and 27 percent were successful.

CodeWhisperer is available for Python, Java, JavaScript, TypeScript, C#, Go, Kotlin, Rust, PHP, and SQL. It can be accessed from IDEs such as VS Code, IntelliJ IDEA, AWS Cloud9, and many more via the AWS Toolkit IDE extensions. Having been trained on billions of lines of code, CodeWhisperer can identify security vulnerabilities such as Open Worldwide Application Security Project (OWASP) best practices and is an effective tool for handling open-source coding responsibly. Figure 24.17 shows the different steps involved when using AWS CodeWhisperer.

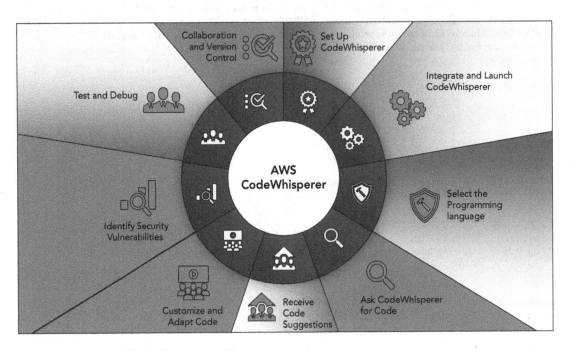

FIGURE 24.17:   AWS CodeWhisperer workflow

> **NOTE** *AWS CodeWhisperer is a game-changer because anyone with no coding experience or skills can now use it to create software code.*

Building Secure and Scalable Generative AI Applications with AWS Bedrock

Amazon Bedrock is a new service offered by Amazon for builders to access foundation modules and include them in their generative AI applications. For example, you can access FMs from AI21 Labs, Anthropic, Stability AI, and even Amazon FMs such as Titan via an API. Because this is a serverless service, you do not have to worry about the underlying infrastructure. All you need to do is choose the suitable model, customize it with your own data, then deploy it and incorporate it into your applications using familiar tools such as AWS SageMaker. Using AWS SageMaker implies that you can test different models using SageMaker Experiments and also use SageMaker Pipelines to scale your FMs.

> **TIP** *One of the most significant benefits of using AWS Bedrock is that you can create a private copy of the foundation module and then use your data within your own private VPC; therefore, your data security concerns are well addressed.*

Titan Models: Amazon's Generative LLM and Embedded LLM

In addition to AWS Bedrock, Amazon has come up with two large language models; one is a generative LLM, and the other is an embedded LLM. While the generative LLM can be used for tasks such as summarization, text generation, question and answering classification, and information extraction, the embedded LLM cannot generate new content but instead generates numerical representations known as *embeddings*. These embeddings can be used for use cases such as product recommendations and searches. By comparing these numerical embeddings, the model can provide more accurate, relevant, and contextual responses that are impossible with just word matching.

Another significant advantage of Titan models is that they can filter harmful content in the input data, the user input, and the output generated by the model. It makes it very usable in different use cases, such as customer service, finance, and education.

Using both Bedrock and Titan models, companies can customize these models for various use cases, such as answering customer queries using a chatbot, creating interactive course content for students, generating patient reports, and diagnosing diseases for patients, creating targeted ad copy and emails for customers, and detecting fraudulent transactions.

Optimizing Performance and Cost Using EC2 Trn1n and Inf2 Instances

Now say you were working with the foundation modules, and you're looking for a high-performing and cost-effective infrastructure. That's where Amazon EC2 Trn1n and Inf2 instances powered by AWS Trainium and AWS Inferentia2, respectively, will come into play. You can use Trainium instances to reduce the cost of training. In contrast, you can use Inferentia instances to reduce the cost of making predictions. As of this writing, AWS Trainium chips are built to distribute the training across multiple servers employing 800 Gbps of second-generation Elastic Fabric Adapter (EFA) networking. It allows you to scale up to 30,000 Trainium chips, which equals more than 6 exaflops of computing power, all within the same AWS Availability Zone. It is equal to an impressive petabit-scale networking capacity.

AWS Inferentia chips are optimized for models with hundreds of billions of parameters. As of this writing, each chip can deliver up to 190 tera floating operations per second (TFLOPS). On the other hand, AWS Trainium is a second-generation ML accelerator for deep learning training of 100B+ parameter models. Amazon Search and Runway use Trainium to train their models to generate text, translate languages and answer questions. They can reduce the time from months to weeks or even days while reducing the cost. Money Forward uses it to train its models to detect fraud. Figure 24.18 captures the features of AWS Inferentia and Trainium.

Azure Generative AI Cloud Platform Tools

This section reviews the generative AI cloud platform tools offered by Azure.

Transforming NLP Using the Microsoft Azure OpenAI Service

Microsoft Azure machine learning is another excellent tool for building and deploying generative AI models. It comes with its own prebuilt model registry. The Azure OpenAI service allows you to access a number of their models, such as ChatGPT, Codex, and Embedding models. You can access the NLP services these models offer using APIs, SDKs, and Azure OpenAI Studio.

AWS Inferentia2

AWS Trainium

- Deploying models with hundreds of billions of parameters
- Optimized for models with hundreds of billions of parameters
- Used by Helixon, Amazon Search, and Runway
- Reduced training time
- Used by Money Forward for fraud detection

- Training large language models (LLMs)
- Training mixture of experts (MoE) models
- Ability to distribute training across multiple servers
- 800 Gbps EFA networking
- Scaling up to 30,000 Trainium chips: equal to more than 6 exaflops of computing power
- Same AWS Availability Zone

FIGURE 24.18: Features of AWS Inferentia and Trainium

ChatGPT uses generative AI models to generate new content in response to users' natural language prompts. The OpenAI service allows you to leverage these services from ChatGPT and combine them with the security and scalability of the Azure cloud platform. Codex is an AI system developed by OpenAI to develop code from text.

The first step to building a generative AI solution with Azure OpenAI is to provision an OpenAI resource in your Azure subscription, as shown in Figure 24.19.

Create Azure OpenAI   ...

① Basics   ② Tags   ③ Review + submit

Enable new business solutions with OpenAI's language generation capabilities powered by GPT-3 models. These models have been pretrained with trillions of words and can easily adapt to your scenario with a few short examples provided at inference. Apply them to numerous scenarios, from summarization to content and code generation.

Learn more

Project Details

Subscription * ⓘ

Resource group * ⓘ

Create new

Instance Details

Region ⓘ   East US

Name * ⓘ   unique-name-openai

Pricing tier * ⓘ

FIGURE 24.19: Provisioning an OpenAI service in Azure

> **NOTE** *At this point, the OpenAI Azure service is available with limited access to ensure its ethical use. Certain models are available in certain regions only.*

Effortless Gen AI Development Using Azure OpenAI Studio

Azure OpenAI Studio provides access to building, managing, and deploying models. It's a cloud-based service that makes building gen AI applications using OpenAI's APIs easy. It is a preconfigured environment that comes with a GPU-powered compute instance, a Jupyter notebook, a collection of pretrained models, and access to OpenAI's API documentation.

To access OpenAI Studio, you need to create an account, launch the Studio instance, and then start building by importing a pretrained model or by training your own model using the Jupyter Notebook. Once done, you can deploy your application to Azure Cloud using the OpenAI API.

> **NOTE** *Azure OpenAI Studio is a great way to build your gen AI apps without worrying about the underlying infrastructure.*

Customizing Models in Azure OpenAI Service

When building apps with Azure OpenAI service, you need to choose a base model, and then you can customize it if required. These models are grouped by family and capability, as shown in Table 24.6.

TABLE 24.6: Base Models Grouped by Family and Capability in Azure

FAMILY	DESCRIPTION	BASE MODELS WITHIN THE FAMILY
GPT-4	Models that generate natural language and code. These models are currently in preview.	gpt-4, gpt-4-32k
GPT-3	Models that can understand and generate natural language.	text-davinci-003, text-curie-001, text-babbage-001, text-ada-001, gpt-35-turbo
Codex	Models that can understand and generate code, including translating natural language to code.	code-davinci-002, code-cushman-001

To make API calls to the model, you must deploy it. Note that you can deploy only one instance of the model. Once deployed, you can test it using the prompts. A prompt is the text input that is sent to the model's endpoint. Responses can come in the form of text, code, or other formats.

Prompts can be of various types, such as classifying content, generating new content, holding conversations, translating, summarizing content, picking up where you left off, and getting facts.

Azure OpenAI Studio Playgrounds for Model Testing

Playgrounds are useful interfaces that you can use to test your deployed models without developing a client application. Azure offers multiple playgrounds with different parameter-tuning options.

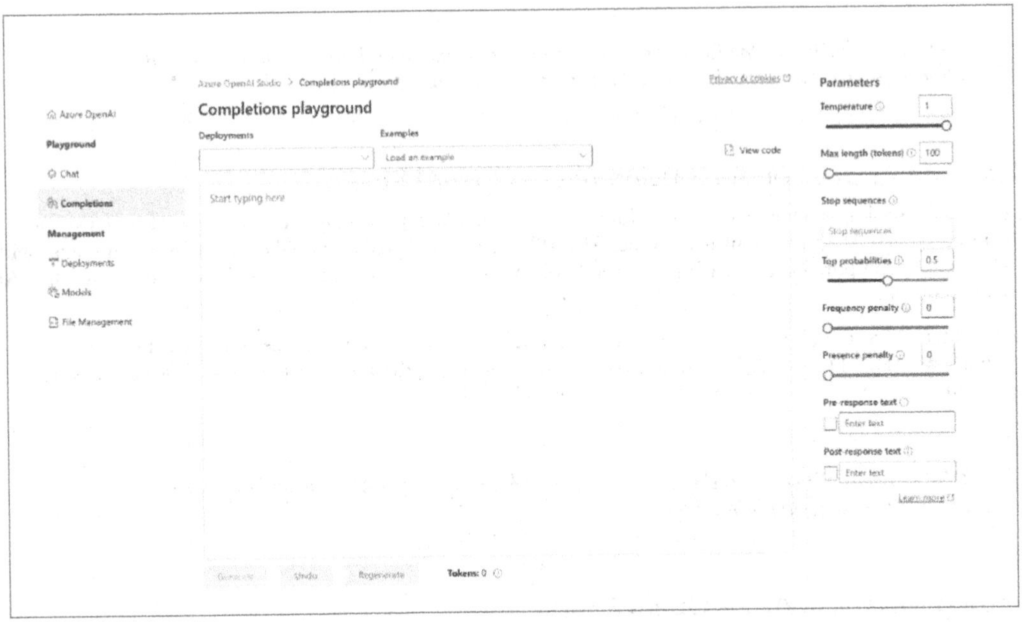

FIGURE 24.20: Azure OpenAI Studio playgrounds for model testing

Optimizing Model Behavior Using Playground Parameters

These playground parameters are used to change the performance of the models. Consider this list:

➤ **Temperature:** A lower value provides more predictable answers, while a higher value will result in more creative answers.

➤ **Max length (tokens):** A token is equal to roughly four characters in the English language. This sets the maximum number of tokens per model response.

➤ **Stop sequences:** These instruct the model to stop the response at a desired point, such as the end of a sentence or list.

Other parameters include top probabilities (top P), frequency penalty, presence penalty, pre-response text, and post-response text.

AI-Powered Code Assistance with GitHub Copilot

GitHub Copilot is like a pair programmer who can assist you in completing the code. It is trained based on an OpenAI Codex model and can provide coding suggestions and even write full functions. Using the tool can help improve the developer productivity by doing the following:

➤ Generating code for functions, classes, loops, and other programming tasks

➤ Filling in missing code

➤ Suggesting alternative code

➤ Translating code from one programming language to another

As shown in Figure 24.21, it can also troubleshoot bugs quickly by catching errors, enhance developer creativity by suggesting new ideas, reduce learning curves, and improve collaboration by increasing the readability and maintainability of the code.

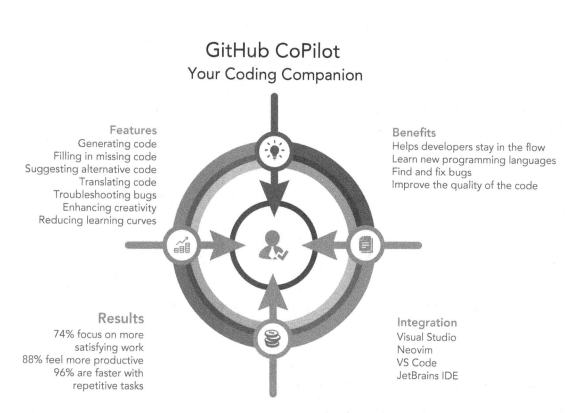

FIGURE 24.21: GitHub Copilot's features and benefits

To use GitHub Copilot, you just need to install the extension in your IDE, such as Visual Studio, Neovim, and JetBrains. Currently, you need to have an active GitHub Copilot subscription to use Copilot. While GitHub Copilot may differ in the details from AWS CodeWhisperer, it's similar in terms of its goals to improve developer productivity.

Additional Tools and Platforms

With the advent of generative AI, several tools and platforms have also come up to benefit businesses and individuals. This section discusses the ones shown in Figure 24.22.

OpenAI API Integrations

OpenAI has released many APIs for developers to access their models, such as GPT-3 and DALL-E. Take, for example, the Kuki.ai chatbot that leverages OpenAI APIs to provide an impressive conversational chatbot. Its ability to chat in almost 50 languages and handle so many conversational scenarios makes it a good candidate for customer service gaming, and so on.

Transforming Conversations with GPT-3, GPT-4, and ChatGPT

GPT-3 and GPT-4 are large language models created by OpenAI, and ChatGPT is a chatbot built on those models. These LLMs can generate text, translate languages, answer questions, and respond to you in a personalized manner depending upon your prompts.

> **NOTE** *The G in GPT stands for generative, P for pretrained, and T for transformer models.*

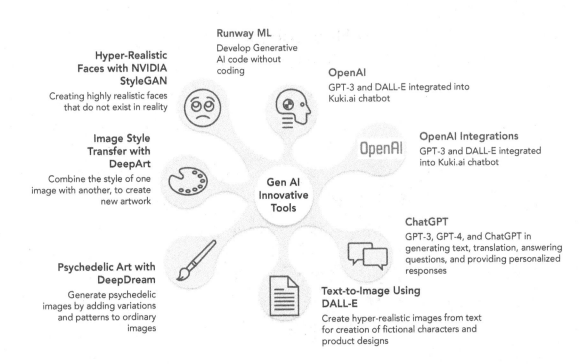

FIGURE 24.22: Additional gen AI tools and platforms

Text-to-Image Generation Using DALL-E 2

As discussed earlier, DALL-E2 is a generative AI model that can create images from text. It can create hyper realistic images that can be used to create fictional characters or even new product designs.

Unveiling Psychedelic Art with DeepDream

DeepDream is a generative AI tool created by Google that can create psychedelic images from ordinary images. It does this by learning the existing patterns in the image and creating strikingly new patterns and stunning images by adding variations.

Creativity Through Image Style Transfer with DeepArt

DeepArt is a generative AI tool created by Google that combines one image's style with another's content to create entirely new art.

Hyperrealistic Faces with NVIDIA StyleGAN

NVIDIA StyleGAN is a generative AI model that can create stunningly realistic faces that do not exist in the world.

Unleash Creativity with Runway ML

Runway ML helps users to develop generative AI code without coding. Whether it is creating a new artwork or designing a new font, Runway ML can provide you with generative AI models to build upon.

WORKBOOK TEMPLATE: *GENERATIVE AI USE CASE PLANNER*

Download the "Generative AI Use Case Planner" template from the download section of the book (www
.wiley.com/go/EnterpriseAIintheCloud). Use this template to plan for Generative AI use cases and
ensure you have factored in all aspects of planning for the generative AI use cases.

SUMMARY

In this chapter, you journeyed into the complex world of generative AI. You learned about the critical components
of deep learning, semi-supervised learning, generative versus discriminative models, diffusion models, foundation
models, and large language and large image models.

Ultimately, generative AI opens a new chapter of innovation and potential. It can revolutionize and disrupt businesses, augment human potential, and provide a new perspective for solving business problems. However, it is not
without risks, potential ethical concerns, and calls for an urgent need to protect data and user privacy and ensure
fairness and transparency in decision-making.

It is undoubtedly a new era for businesses and personal lives, and I look forward to seeing how this technology
evolves and transforms our lives.

REVIEW QUESTIONS

These review questions are included at the end of each chapter to help you test your understanding of the information. You'll find the answers in the following section.

1. What is the estimated economic benefit generated by generative AI use cases annually across industries
    according to McKinsey?
    A. $1.5 to $2.3 trillion
    B. $2.6 to $4.4 trillion
    C. $5.5 to $7.2 trillion
    D. $6.3 to $8.5 trillion

2. Discriminative models in machine learning are focused on
    A. Predicting the label for new data points
    B. Generating new data instances
    C. Understanding the relationships between the features and the labels
    D. Learning the probability distribution of the existing data

3. What is the main limitation of large language models (LLMs)?
    A. They can only understand text.
    B. They require a large amount of compute power.
    C. They can only generate text.
    D. They can work only with small amounts of data.

4. Variational autoencoders (VAEs) are beneficial because
    A. They can understand the hidden layers that drive the data.
    B. They are used in text generation use cases.
    C. They can operate like black boxes.
    D. Both A and B.

5. In terms of workforce transformation, AI can act as
   A. A competitor
   B. A partner
   C. A replacement
   D. None of the above

6. Which of the following is NOT an advantage of using retrieval augmented generation (RAG)?
   A. Improves the relevancy and accuracy of the information response
   B. Saves time and effort
   C. Inconsistent response
   D. None of the above

7. Which of the following is NOT a benefit of using Amazon EC2 Trn1n instances?
   A. Reduced training time
   B. Reduced training cost
   C. Increased model accuracy
   D. Increased model scalability

8. What is the unique feature of the DALL-E 2 generative AI model?
   A. It can create images from text.
   B. It can create new fonts.
   C. It can generate text, translate languages, and answer questions.
   D. It can create psychedelic images from ordinary images.

9. Which of the following is NOT a step in ensuring fairness and bias mitigation through continuous testing and guardrails?
   A. Using a variety of metrics to measure fairness
   B. Identifying and addressing any potential biases in the model
   C. Monitoring the model's performance over time
   D. Releasing the model to external customers

10. What is one potential outcome of the disruption caused by generative AI in the industry?
    A. A decrease in the use of automation
    B. An increase in the use of automation
    C. A need to adjust or complement the current AI strategy
    D. A need to abandon the current AI strategy

11. What privacy-related concern is associated with the use of generative AI?
    A. It cannot access private data.
    B. It can be used to monitor activities and predict future behavior.
    C. It protects all data with advanced encryption.
    D. It is incapable of handling private data.

ANSWER KEY

1.	B	5.	B	9.	D
2.	A	6.	C	10.	C
3.	B	7.	C	11.	B
4.	D	8.	A		

25

Planning for the Future of AI

The future belongs to those who believe in the beauty of their dreams.

—Eleanor Roosevelt

You have learned that AI is not a static field; instead, it continuously evolves rapidly, reshaping industries and personal lives. While generative AI resembles the latest pinnacle of current AI capabilities, it is equally vital to gaze into the future and discern the emerging trends.

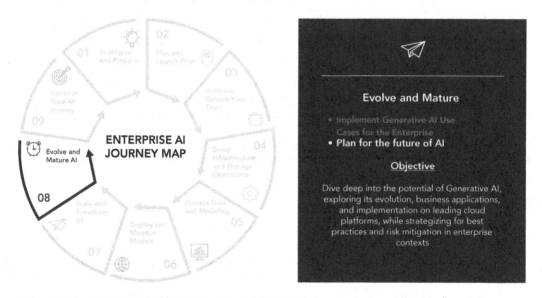

FIGURE 25.1: EVOLVE AND MATURE: Plan for the future of AI

In this chapter, you learn about the trends in the smart world powered by AR/VR, the captivating concept of the metaverse, and the intricacies of quantum machine learning. You also learn about the productivity revolution in industries, the impact of powerful technologies such as digital humans, and the growing popularity of AI at the edge.

This chapter also takes a quick look at the critical enablers poised to reshape AI's future, such as foundation models, knowledge graphs, hyper-automation, and the democratization of AI/ML.

This chapter provides you the opportunity to build a futuristic roadmap for continuous innovation and sustainable growth in the ever-evolving field of AI.

EMERGING AI TRENDS

We are living in an exciting world, and we haven't seen anything yet. The future of the world is smart. It is being shaped by several emerging technologies, such as AR and VR, the metaverse, and digital humans—all of which are covered in this chapter. The smart world is focused on improving the quality of its citizens. In addition, AI is transforming businesses to become more productive and efficient.

Behind this revolution are several emerging trends, such as AI in the edge, intelligent apps, compressed models, self-supervised learning, and generative AI. There are also several critical enablers, including ChatGPT, transformer models, foundation models, knowledge graphs, and the democratization of AI/ML, which are all accelerating this trend. This section looks at these trends.

Smart World

A **smart world** is about creating virtual replicas of the physical environment and the world we live in. It includes technologies such as virtual reality, augmented reality, the metaverse, and digital humans. The smart world is focused on improving citizens' quality of life. It can be done in many ways, such as the following:

➤ **Improving transportation:** Self-driving cars reduce traffic congestion and improve safety.

➤ **Managing energy:** AI can be used to optimize energy consumption and reduce the cost.

➤ **Improving healthcare:** AI can be used to cure diseases, find new drugs, and improve patient treatments.

➤ **Increasing security:** AI can be used to improve security, detect crime, and prevent terrorism.

➤ **Protecting the environment:** AI can be used to protect the environment through initiatives such as climate control, pollution control, tracking endangered species, and managing resources.

One of the key initiatives in the smart world category is Singapore's smart nation initiative, which includes developing a data exchange program where government agencies can share data and understand the customer's needs and problems better.

AR and VR Technology

AR and VR technology can be used to improve business operations and customer service and create new products. Here are some examples:

➤ **Retail:** Augmented reality can be used in the retail industry for customers to try on clothes, makeup, and other products. This can help customers make better product choices and increase customer satisfaction.

➤ **Education:** Virtual reality can be used for students to go on virtual field trips and experiment with difficult-to-access or hazardous products.

➤ **Healthcare:** In healthcare, VR can be used to reduce pain for patients, help them recuperate from surgery, and help them to walk after a stroke.

➤ **Manufacturing:** Employees can be trained under challenging terrains and environments and thus improve safety and reduce costs using virtual reality.

➤ **Marketing:** Both virtual reality and augmented reality can be used in marketing to create immersive experiences; for example, augmented reality can be used to insert products in the user's environment, while virtual reality can be used to create virtual experiences that customers can explore.

Metaverse

The metaverse can be thought of as a platform with which businesses can interact with their customers, employees, and partners.

Here are some examples of how it can be used:

➤ **Virtual meetings:** Meetings can be conducted virtually where participants can interact with each other and the environment.

➤ **Product demonstrations:** Businesses can demonstrate their products to their customers in a virtual world using AR and VR technology.

➤ **Virtual training:** Companies can provide immersive simulation environments where employees can train under challenging circumstances.

➤ **Remote work:** Employees can interact with each other through a platform that allows them to interact with other employees in a virtual environment.

AI models, natural language processing, and other AI/ML services can be used to enable these services.

Digital Humans and Digital Twins

Digital twins are virtual representations of physical objects, and digital humans are computer-generated representations of humans. They can be used in education, entertainment, and customer service. They are generated using AI machine learning and computer graphics technologies. From an enterprise perspective, digital humans can be used to give presentations to answer customer queries.

The benefit of having digital humans is that they are available 24/7, they always respond consistently to the customers, and they can be engaging. The disadvantage of using digital humans is that customers may think the interactions are fake, and they are often expensive to develop and challenging to scale, and maintenance is intensive.

HANDS-ON EXERCISE: STRATEGIC TECHNOLOGY IMPLEMENTATION

This exercise involves exploring the emerging AI technologies within a specific business or industry context, understanding the potential of these technologies, identifying potential use cases, and coming up with an initial high-level implementation plan.

You can ask your workshop participants to explore each of these areas and come up with deliverables such as presentations to explore real-world examples such as Singapore's Smart Nation initiative, AR in retail, VR in education, and digital humans in customer service, among others.

STEP	OBJECTIVE	DELIVERABLES	EXAMPLES
Form groups	To get into groups of three to four people	Groups formed.	Team 1, Team 2, Team 3
Understand smart world concepts	To grasp the smart world concept and its potential benefits	Write up or presentation on smart world concepts and benefits.	Singapore's Smart Nation initiative

continues

continued

STEP	OBJECTIVE	DELIVERABLES	EXAMPLES
Study AR and VR technologies	To learn the possibilities of AR and VR in various industries	Document or presentation detailing the applications of AR and VR.	Virtual reality in education, AR in retail
Explore the concept of the metaverse	To understand how metaverse can transform the way businesses interact	Concept note on the metaverse and its business applications.	Virtual meetings, product demonstrations in the metaverse
Learn about digital twins	To understand the concept and applications of digital twins	Write up or report on the application of digital twins.	Digital twins in manufacturing, healthcare, etc.
Understand the use of digital humans	To understand the concept of digital humans and their applications	A document or presentation detailing the use of digital humans in various fields.	Digital humans for customer service, entertainment, etc.
Analyze use cases	To identify use cases where these technologies could be impactful	Identify specific use cases for your chosen technology in your selected industry.	For example, using VR in education for immersive learning experiences or using digital humans in customer service to provide 24/7 assistance
Assess feasibility	To evaluate the feasibility of implementing these technologies in the chosen use cases	Consider the technical and organizational readiness, the availability of resources and potential challenges or risks associated with implementing your chosen technology for the identified use cases.	For example, skill sets, funding

STEP	OBJECTIVE	DELIVERABLES	EXAMPLES
Plan the implementation	To develop a preliminary plan for implementing the technology	Sketch out an initial implementation plan, including the necessary steps, resources, timeline, and expected outcomes. This can also include identifying necessary partnerships, training requirements, or changes in organizational structures or processes.	
Present the implementation plan	To share and discuss the plan	Speak about the salient points and explain and justify the plan.	

THE PRODUCTIVITY REVOLUTION

The productivity revolution refers to a set of technologies geared toward increasing an organization's productivity and potentially transforming it. It covers technologies such as AI/ML in the edge, intelligent applications, synthetic data, edge computer vision, self-supervised learning model compression, and generative AI.

All these technologies work together to enable this productivity revolution. The following sections discuss how.

AI in the Edge

AI in the edge involves deploying ML models in edge devices such as smartphone sensors rather than on the cloud. Deploying AI models in edge devices opens more possibilities, such as intelligent apps, compressed models, and self-supervised learning.

The benefits of AI on the edge are faster response times, lower bandwidth requirements, reduced cost, and higher security. An example of a challenge related to AI in the edge is that data security can be compromised when unauthorized individuals get access to those devices.

Intelligent Apps

Intelligent apps are software applications that use AI algorithms to provide intelligent and personalized services to users. They provide benefits such as personalized experiences, process automation, predictive analytics, and real-time decision-making. Intelligent apps include recommendation engines, chatbots, virtual agents, predictive maintenance applications, and fraud detection applications. These apps have the potential to revolutionize a companies' operations and customer service. See Figure 25.2.

> **TIP** *Be a part of the productivity revolution by leveraging technologies like AI/ML on the edge, intelligent apps, compressed models, self-supervised learning, and generative AI to increase productivity and transform your organization.*

FIGURE 25.2: Intelligent apps provide intelligent services to users.
Source: ImagineDesign / Adobe Stock

Compressed Models

Compressed models are about compressing the models in size and complexity without losing accuracy and performance. They open new possibilities concerning the deployment of the models on the edge. Model compression results in reduced storage, reduced bandwidth requirements, improved performance, lower cost, and improved security. However, it is not without drawbacks because, with the reduced size, it can lose accuracy, is also challenging to develop, and is available for only some models. As technology develops, some of these drawbacks may be eliminated, making this more effective.

Some examples of model compression techniques are defined here:

➤ **Pruning the weights:** Involves removing certain connections (weights) between the nodes of a neural network to reduce the size of the network.

➤ **Quantization:** Reduces the number of bits used to identify a weight. For example, using 8-bit integers instead of 32-bit floating-point numbers can reduce the model size and increase the speed of arithmetic operations.

➤ **Activations:** Refer to the outputs of the neural network. Reducing the size of the activations can also reduce the compute power required to train or use the model.

➤ **Knowledge distillation:** Involves using a smaller, simpler (student) model to replicate the behavior of a larger, complex (parent) model. By transferring the knowledge from the larger to the smaller model, you can deploy it on smaller devices with limited resources.

➤ **Low-rank factorization:** Involves approximating the weight matrices with the product of two lower ranked matrices to reduce the size of the model. This approach can result in loss of accuracy.

Self-Supervised Learning

Supervised learning is a type of machine learning where the model can be developed by training a large unlabeled dataset, and it develops its own features without supervision. Self-supervised learning provides benefits such as data efficiency, reduced bias, and improved performance. The advantage of self-supervised learning is that it can look at the existing data and try to come up with patterns and anomalies, which can then be used to make further predictions, classify new data, and make recommendations. In healthcare, it can look at a lot of imaging data and come up with patterns and anomalies that can then be used to treat new patients. Similarly, it can look at customer tickets and come up with patterns that relate customers with issue types and then use that information to automate responses to customers as well as to provide insights to the customer service reps to address those types of issues.

CRITICAL ENABLERS

This section looks at some of the critical enablers that are important for the development of AI and ML solutions in an enterprise that provides a company competitive edge (see Figure 25.3). They are critical enablers because they help to democratize the use of AI/ML, speed up the deployment of complex models, automate complex tasks, and increase efficiency, thus driving rapid productivity revolution in companies.

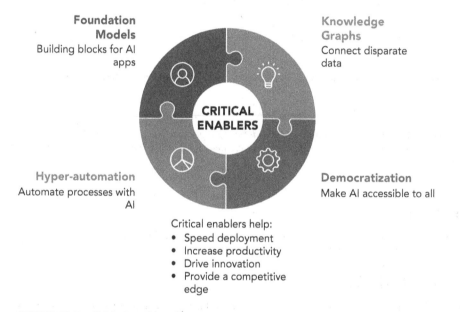

FIGURE 25.3: Critical enablers for enterprise AI

Foundation Models

You can think of foundational models as basic building blocks that form more complex AI solutions. These are large, pretrained deep learning models pretrained to create a particular type of content and can be adapted for other use cases. Foundational models, such as GPT 4 and Bard, can be pretrained models on large amounts of data and can be used for developing more complex models. They're primarily used for natural language processing, machine translation, and image recognition use cases. Once you have a foundation model, you can develop an application on top of it to leverage its content creation capabilities. For example, if you consider GPT model, you have other applications built on top of it such as Jasper and Copy.ai. This is one of the main reasons that we are going to see an explosion of a number of generative AI applications in the future.

Knowledge Graphs

Knowledge graphs are databases where entities and their relationships are stored so that models can quickly leverage them and be trained to make further predictions. This ability to represent data from various sources in graphs enables developers to use them in use cases such as product recommendations, and to resolve customer issues. Figure 25.4 shows a knowledge graph that displays a diverse set of entities and relationships to model real-world contexts and domains.

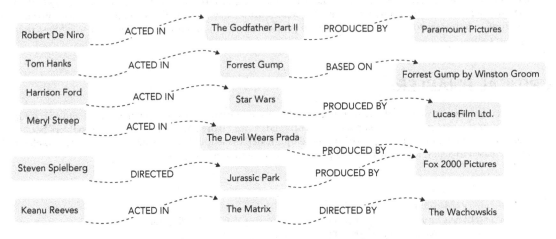

FIGURE 25.4:   Knowledge graph reflecting complex real-world data as meaningful relationships

> **TIP** *When developing AI and ML solutions, consider critical enablers such as foundational models, knowledge graphs, and hyper-automation to create a competitive edge for your enterprise.*

Hyper-Automation

Hyper-automation refers to the ability to automate business processes using machine learning, robot process automation, and natural language processing.

Democratization of AI/ML

The mobilization of AI/ML means making AI and ML services accessible to a broad group of users through user-friendly user interfaces, pretrained models and templates, and services that are hosted on the cloud.

Transformer Models

Transformer models are a class of neural networks useful for natural language processing. They are known for capturing long-range dependencies between different parts of a sentence and have been found to have exceptional performance in more effective conversations.

Keras and TensorFlow in the Cloud

These are popular machine learning libraries and frameworks used in the cloud. They use the AWS, Microsoft, and Google platforms.

Quantum Machine Learning

Quantum machine learning can revolutionize AI as it combines quantum computing with machine learning and enables the use of superposition and entanglement in calculations for faster computations and to solve complex problems previously unsolvable:

➤ **Superposition** refers to a principle where a quantum system can exist in multiple states simultaneously. Unlike classical bits, which can be only a 0 or 1, a qubit (quantum bit) can exist in both 0 and 1 states simultaneously with certain probabilities, which allows quantum computers to process a vast number of calculations simultaneously.

➤ **Entanglement** refers to a phenomenon where a group of particles can interact in such a way that the state of each particle depends on the state of the others, which allows for more interconnected and synchronized processing power.

HANDS-ON EXERCISE: EXPLORING CRITICAL ENABLERS FOR ENTERPRISE AI EXERCISE

This is a hands-on self-guided learning exercise where the participants conduct independent research to understand various emerging technologies and relate theoretical concepts to practical applications.

STEP	OBJECTIVE	INSTRUCTIONS	DELIVERABLES	EXAMPLES
1	To understand the role of foundation models	Research foundation models like GPT and BARD. Look into applications built on top of these foundation models.	A summary of the features, benefits, and real-world applications of foundation models	GPT-4 by OpenAI used to develop conversational agents like Jasper and Copy.ai
2	To understand the role of knowledge graphs	Learn about knowledge graphs, their creation, and their uses. Analyze how they can contribute to the understanding of context and connections.	A brief report on knowledge graphs with their uses in different industries	Google's Knowledge Graph used to enhance search engine results

continues

continued

STEP	OBJECTIVE	INSTRUCTIONS	DELIVERABLES	EXAMPLES
3	To understand the concept of hyper-automation	Research about hyper-automation, how it combines machine learning, robot process automation, and natural language processing to automate business processes.	A document describing hyper-automation and its potential business applications	Application of hyper-automation in a manufacturing setting to streamline production processes
4	To understand the concept of democratization of AI/ML	Explore how AI/ML technologies are becoming more accessible through user-friendly interfaces, pre-trained models, and cloud-based services.	A presentation on the democratization of AI/ML and its implications for businesses and individuals	Google's AutoML products that allow developers with limited machine learning expertise to train high-quality models
5	To learn about transformer models	Investigate Transformer models and their effectiveness in natural language processing tasks.	A report detailing the architecture and uses of transformer models	Transformer models used for machine translation tasks like Google's Neural Machine Translation (GNMT) system
6	To familiarize yourself with Keras and TensorFlow in the Cloud	Learn about these popular machine learning frameworks and their cloud implementations.	A tutorial or guide on using Keras and TensorFlow on AWS, Microsoft, and Google platforms	Building a neural network model using TensorFlow on Google Cloud

STEP	OBJECTIVE	INSTRUCTIONS	DELIVERABLES	EXAMPLES
7	To understand the concept of quantum machine learning	Study the principles of quantum machine learning and how it can revolutionize AI by combining quantum computing with machine learning.	A written essay or report on the principles of quantum machine learning and its potential impact on AI	Quantum machine learning algorithms implemented on quantum computers like IBM Q

EMERGING TRENDS IN DATA MANAGEMENT

There are a couple of exciting new trends that are happening related to AI modeling. Some are federated learning, AI at the edge, and quantum computing.

Federated Learning

Federated learning is a new approach that involves training the model across decentralized devices or servers that hold local data. This is helpful when you cannot move data to cloud servers due to security or latency concerns.

In the case study example about the retail business, this means you can train models using local store data while maintaining overall model consistency across the company.

AutoML

AutoML and the democratization of AI is another trend that is creating many citizen data scientists by creating intuitive and accessible models.

AutoML is a significant advancement that automates parts of the machine learning process. It not only makes model development faster and more accessible but also lowers the barrier to entry to implement AI.

> **NOTE** *Federated learning, AI at the edge, quantum computing, AutoML, and explainable AI are some exciting new trends in machine learning.*

Data Flywheels

A *data flywheel* describes a concept where, as more data is fed into the machine learning applications, more users start using the information, which creates more demand on the data, which in turn creates more insights that lead to new machine learning applications. This cycle continues and has come to be known as the data flywheel.

DataOps and Data Stewardship

The need to manage the data pipeline all the way from data creation to storage to consumption and deletion has come to the fore. This practice is known as DataOps. *Data stewardship* is an important role that ensures the quality, trust, governance, privacy, security, and ethics of the data assets.

Distributed Everything

Distributed everything involves connecting the data to the people and enabling no-code, low-code, self-service options to facilitate greater collaboration between people. These might be data scientists, machine learning engineers, business analysts, data engineers, and other stakeholders who want to facilitate data visualization and analysis.

WORKBOOK TEMPLATE: *FUTURE OF AI ROADMAP*

Download the "Future of AI Roadmap" template from the download section of the book (www.wiley.com/go/EnterpriseAIintheCloud). Use this template to capture key areas to focus on as part of planning your organization's journey with future AI innovations. You can use it effectively by constantly updating it frequently as the field of AI continues to evolve.

SUMMARY

You just traveled through the exciting world of AI, touching upon many innovations such as the metaverse, AR/VR, digital humans and twins, and similar technologies that are shaping the smart world. You also reviewed some of the productivity revolution technologies, such as AI on the edge, intelligent apps, self-supervised learning, and generative models like ChatGPT. Together, these technologies propel the advancements in the smart world in our personal lives and the productivity revolution in business.

This chapter also delved into the critical enablers that make these advancements possible, such as foundation models, knowledge graphs, ChatGPT, hyper-automation, transformer models, and leading tools like Keras and TensorFlow.

REVIEW QUESTIONS

These review questions are included at the end of each chapter to help you test your understanding of the information. You'll find the answers in the following section.

1. What is the metaverse?
   A. A platform for businesses to interact with their customers, suppliers, and employees
   B. A virtual world for remote work and virtual training
   C. A computer-generated version of the metaverse
   D. None of the above
2. What are compressed models?
   A. Models that are compressed in size and complexity without losing accuracy and performance
   B. Models that are uncompressed and have high complexity
   C. Models that have low accuracy and performance due to compression
   D. Models that have not been trained using machine learning
3. What is self-supervised learning?
   A. Models can be developed by training a large unlabeled dataset.
   B. Models are supervised by a human expert.
   C. Models that are trained on labeled data only.
   D. Models that are not used in industry.

4. What is generative AI?

   A. It can generate new types of data like the data it was trained on.

   B. It can perform only classification tasks.

   C. It can be deployed only on the cloud.

5. Choose one of the advantages of self-supervised learning.

   A. It requires a large dataset of labeled examples to be effective.

   B. It allows the model to develop its own features without supervision.

   C. It always outperforms supervised and unsupervised learning methods.

   D. It requires more human intervention compared to supervised learning.

6. What does a smart world focus on improving?

   A. Transportation only

   B. Healthcare only

   C. Citizens' quality of life

   D. Environment only

7. In the context of the metaverse, what can AI models and services enable?

   A. Product manufacturing

   B. Virtual meetings and interactions

   C. Paper documentation

   D. Physical transportation

8. Which technology refers to computer-generated representations of humans that can be used in customer service?

   A. Metaverse

   B. Digital humans

   C. Virtual reality

   D. Digital humans

9. What emerging trend involves creating virtual replicas of the physical environment and includes technologies like virtual reality and digital twins?

   A. Intelligent apps

   B. Self-supervised learning

   C. Smart world

   D. Compressed models

10. Which of the following benefits is NOT associated with AI on the edge?

    A. Faster response times

    B. Increased bandwidth requirements

    C. Reduced cost

    D. Higher security

11. What is a potential drawback of model compression?

    A. Improved security

    B. Reduced bandwidth requirements

    C. Loss of accuracy

    D. Reduced storage

12. What principle allows a quantum system to exist in multiple states simultaneously?
    A. Entanglement
    B. Superposition
    C. Quantization
    D. Activation

13. What tool can businesses use in the metaverse to interact with customers, employees, and partners?
    A. VR 360 goggles
    B. AI Fairness 360 toolkit
    C. Digital twinning
    D. Encryption techniques

14. What is a disadvantage of using digital humans in business interactions?
    A. They are available 24/7.
    B. Customers may think interactions are fake.
    C. They respond consistently to customers.
    D. They are engaging.

15. Which term refers to the concept where training the model occurs across decentralized devices or servers holding local data, especially when data cannot be moved to cloud servers due to security or latency concerns?
    A. Explainable AI
    B. Quantum computing
    C. Federated learning
    D. Edge computing

ANSWER KEY

1.	A	6.	C	11.	C
2.	A	7.	B	12.	B
3.	A	8.	D	13.	A
4.	A	9.	C	14.	B
5.	B	10.	B	15.	C

26

Continuing Your AI Journey

> The journey of a thousand miles begins with a single step.
>
> —*Lao Tzu*

Congratulations on making it this far! I'm impressed with what you've achieved, having deployed an AI/ML and potentially Gen AI solutions that have transformed your organization. This is a significant milestone and a testament to the hard work and dedication of everyone involved.

You gained insights from case studies, addressed challenges and initiated pilots, built your team, developed an infrastructure, processed data, and deployed and monitored models.

And you didn't stop there. As your expertise matured, you scaled your AI initiative using the AI maturity framework and AI center of excellence and then stepped up your game with generative AI use cases. Figure 26.1 shows this impressive journey.

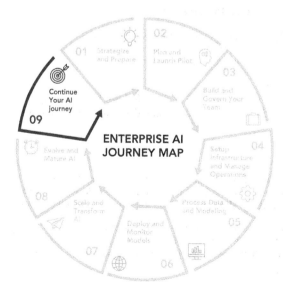

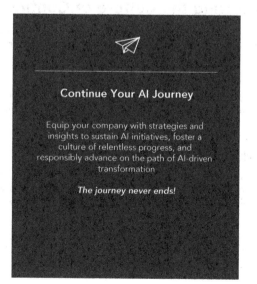

FIGURE 26.1: Continue your AI journey

But it is only the beginning of many more exciting things you and your company want to achieve. AI is an evolving field, and you must watch out for the latest opportunities and trends to capitalize upon.

Your current implementation would have also unlocked many more opportunities and opened up a new chapter in your digital journey. You must explore how to build upon your past success and lessons learned as you move on to the next phase in your AI adventure.

REFLECTING ON YOUR PROGRESS

It is important to take time to review what has been done so far.

Reviewing the Lessons Learned

As part of your previous AI/ML implementation, you have captured the lessons learned, including the successes, challenges, and opportunities to improve across different areas of your implementation. You should revisit the AI strategy, project management, governance, platform, operations, talent, and security areas and identify opportunities to work on in the next phase. For example, you may find that more training is required for your team or that you need to improve your data collection and preparation.

Exploring Opportunities for Improvement

Specifically, concerning your current implementation, you may want to explore the following:

➤ Adding new features to your solution

➤ Improving the accuracy of the solution

➤ Making your solution more user friendly

Embracing the Culture of Continuous Improvement

I know it is a cultural thing, but it is imperative. Every AI/ML implementation should be looked upon as an opportunity for continuous improvement. It is an opportunity to learn, iterate, and optimize.

Engage Your Business Stakeholders

Your business stakeholders are essential partners in this digital journey; this section discusses how to engage them. You should install a culture where you can encourage ideas from your stakeholders and promote innovation across your company.

Conduct Discovery Sessions

You will have to take your business owners with you because they are crucial in identifying those use cases for your implementation. They're very close to the business processes, and they are the ones who know what works well and what doesn't. Knowing that is important because that will help you to define your next scope of work.

Identify your stakeholders across different business units and functions in your company and set up a series of calls with them to explain the virtues of AI, including machine learning, deep learning, and generative AI. Explain clearly how AI/ML can help solve their business problems. Then solicit their pain points, concerns, and opportunities to improve their business processes and daily tasks.

Find Opportunities for Automation, Decision-Making, Customer Service

Your goal must be to continue to find new ways to improve your company's business processes. Here are some ways you can achieve that goal:

➤ Find tasks that you can automate with AI/ML

➤ Make better decisions with AI/ML

➤ Improve your customer service with a chatbot

Engage Technical Stakeholders in the Discussion

Ensure a partnership between the business and technical stakeholders in your organization. Your data scientists, business analysts, machine learning engineers, data engineers, and DevOps engineers should all be included in this discussion so that you can validate the feasibility of their ideas and then groom them properly to get them ready for execution when the time comes. Looking at the technical aspects of the implementation method, initial status is one of the critical factors to ensure the success of your machine learning implementation.

PLANNING FOR THE FUTURE: BUILDING A ROADMAP

You must look at your existing business processes and operations to scope your work properly.

Mapping Your AI/ML Opportunities

Review all your business processes by talking to your corresponding stakeholders and documenting all their pain points and opportunities to improve. Once you have documented them, look at the use cases that are possible through the use of AI technologies such as prediction, classification, clustering, forecasting, personalization, and generative AI. Try to map the AI/ML opportunities to the previously identified pain points and scope them into the body of work for the next phase.

Prioritizing Your AI/ML Opportunities

Once you have a comprehensive list of AI/ML opportunities and the corresponding business processes you will be working on, the next step is to work with your leadership to prioritize these opportunities for execution. To prioritize these proposals, you will factor in aspects such as feasibility, strategy alignment, business impact, availability of skill sets, resources, underlying platform, and data to build the models for this project.

Mobilizing Your Team for the Journey

Now that all the hard work has been done, the fun part of the journey is to mobilize your team for the actual implementation.

Promote Cross-Functional Collaboration

Talk to various stakeholders across business and technology and share ideas. Ensure you collect all the necessary implementation details from each of them and use that to drive the project implementation plan. Your team should consist of domain experts from the business, such as business analysts, data engineers, machine learning engineers, software engineers, data scientists, and even legal and risk management experts.

Develop a Project Implementation Plan

Leverage your experience from your previous project implementation and develop a new project plan. Ensure you capture all the activities, resources, and timelines accurately. You must ensure that you have clearly defined all the roles and responsibilities across different businesses and technology at every implementation stage. Talk to everybody and ensure that you have a commitment from them to execute the project.

Assess Your Current Skills and Build Your Team

This is probably one of the most critical parts of your activities because you will go in circles if you don't have a strong, capable team. The good news, though, is that you would have identified the gaps in the skill sets during the previous implementation, which should now help you address them as part of this planning phase. Capture all the gaps in a document and create an action plan to fill those gaps. Have a mix of action items such as sending people to the training, encouraging them to attend workshops and seminars, and encouraging them to take up certifications. Where necessary, talk to the recruiters to hire new talent either as permanent employees or as consultants for the duration of the project.

ENSURING RESPONSIBLE AI/ML IMPLEMENTATION

Ensure that you implement the best practices for your AI/ML implementation to ensure data privacy and security, ethics, etc.

Enabling Awareness Around AI Risks and Data Handling

It is important to educate your employees about the benefits of AI and the risks around it. Doing so will help you implement AI responsibly and ethically and manage secure data handling.

Implementing Data Security, Privacy, and Ethical Safeguards

You need to understand data privacy, security, and ethical risks well. You should implement effective security protocols such as access control, secure storage, and data encryption. Finally, ensure compliance with data privacy and security.

Defining Ethical Framework and Data Usage Policies

Ideally, you already have an ethical framework by now, and the data usage policy is well-defined. Take a second look at those policies and frameworks and try to refine them again based on the learnings and new regulations that may have popped up, given the fast-evolving nature of AI.

PREPARING FOR THE CHALLENGES AHEAD

The goal of this book is to help you navigate some challenges and adopt some best practices to avoid failures during the implementation. Unfortunately, there is only so much one can include in a book, and obviously, there is no substitute for real-life implementation experience because every company is unique. However, if you employ some of the best practices in this book, you will increase the probability of success by a long way. As we discussed during the first chapter, close to 80 percent of the implementations fail due to the complexity of an AI/ML effort. However, knowing the pitfalls and putting some measures in place would have gone a long way. Preparing for risks and eventualities is half the battle won, and that's the best we can do.

Encouraging Innovation, Collaboration, and High-Performing Teams

What is important is that you embrace a culture of innovation and continuous improvement, develop an atmosphere of openness and collaboration among your stakeholders across both the business and technology, and ensure that you have a high-performing team with all the skill gaps addressed.

Take note that this is a highly evolving space. You must always be on your toes, watching out for new developments and opportunities in AI. You need to ensure that your AI strategy is always current and take advantage of essential opportunities to stay ahead and avoid disruption. It will need strong leadership, and some tough decisions may need to be made. Be quick to celebrate successes and recognize individuals for their contributions.

Leveraging the Transformational Nature of AI

Leveraging AI/ML is a once-in-a-lifetime opportunity with a scale and impact many times larger than what we have seen thus far. AI is highly transformational in nature and can revolutionize your company's processes, drive innovation, and even transform your business models. Remember that with a strategic mindset, a committed team, and a culture of continuous improvement, you can achieve sustained success and leverage the full potential of this exciting technology.

My Personal Invite to Connect

Best of luck, and stay in touch with me at www.linkedin.com/in/rabijay1. You can also visit www.rabiml.com for my latest blogs and plans. I hope this is not the end but the beginning of our relationship on this AI journey. I hope to hear from you regarding your AI success and challenges, and remember that I will be around to celebrate your victories as well. Thank you!

INDEX

N